MARCUSE

MARCUSE

CRITICAL THEORY & THE PROMISE OF UTOPIA

Edited by
ROBERT PIPPIN
ANDREW FEENBERG
CHARLES P. WEBEL

MACMILLAN
EDUCATION

First published 1988

Published by
MACMILLAN EDUCATION LTD
Houndmills, Basingstoke, Hampshire RG21 2XS
and London
Companies and representatives
throughout the world

Printed in the United States of America

British Library Cataloguing in Publication Data
Pippin, Robert B.
Marcuse: critical theory and the promise of Utopia.
1. Marcuse, Herbert
I. Title II. Feenberg, Andrew III. Webel, Charles
191   B945.M2984
ISBN 0-333-44100-1
ISBN 0-333-44101-X Pbk

Contents

IV THE PSYCHOLOGICAL DIMENSION

V THE POLITICAL DIMENSION

VI THE TECHNOLOGICAL DIMENSION

ACKNOWLEDGMENTS

We are much indebted to the following institutions and persons: to the University of California, San Diego, for sponsoring a conference on Marcuse in March of 1980, where the chapters in Section I were first presented, and to the Academic Senate of UCSD for numerous word processing, translation, and editorial assistance grants; to Basil Blackwell, Publishers and the editors of *Praxis International* for permission to reprint the articles by Richard Bernstein and Jürgen Habermas; to Elsevier Science Publishers, Amsterdam, The Netherlands and the editors of *Theory and Society*, for permission to reprint the article by Martin Jay (vol. 11, no. 1, 1982); to Alfred Schmidt and Claus Offe for permission to translate and reprint their articles from *Antworten auf Marcuse* (Frankfurt am Main: Suhrkamp, 1968); to the editors of *Philosophical Forum* for permission to reprint the article by Robert Pippin (vol. xvi, no. 3, 1985); to the *Graduate Faculty Philosophy Journal* and to Frederick Olafson for permission to reprint the interview with Marcuse; to Pina Sylvers for her editorial and organizational assistance, and to Celia Shugart for her word-processing wizardry and her careful help in the preparation of the manuscript.

INTRODUCTION

Herbert Marcuse died on July 29, 1979, in Starnberg, West Germany ten days after his eighty-first birthday. He was commencing one of his frequent lecture/vacation tours when illness struck him in Frankfurt, after what became his last public appearance. Thus ended an extraordinary life of intense political activity, academic recognition, enormously influential teaching and writing, and amazing vitality.

Marcuse was born in 1898 in Berlin, the son of prosperous Jewish parents. After attending Gymnasium there and serving briefly in the military, he studied philosophy, literature, and economics at the universities of Berlin and Freiburg from 1919 to 1922. He received his doctorate with a dissertation on the German "Kunstlerroman" ("Artist Novel"), returned to Berlin, and tried his hand at publishing and bookselling. In 1929 he returned to Freiburg and the study of philosophy. There he worked with the two giants of early twentieth-century German philosophy, Edmund Husserl and Martin Heidegger. He started to publish, and in 1932 his *Habilitationsschrift, Hegel's Ontology and the Foundation of a Theory of Historicity*, appeared as his first book. This was a work which, under the marked influence of Heidegger, stressed heavily Hegel's less systematic and more historical strains, and which clearly and impressively evinced one of Marcuse's greatest talents - his synthetic, speculative imagination, his ability to bring together the insights of many thinkers and traditions in startlingly new ways.

After a favorable review of this book by Theodor Adorno, and on the recommendation of the Kurator of the University of Frankfurt, Marcuse was invited to join the Geneva office of the Institute of Social Research, the heterogeneous group of left-wing, non-Communist German intellectuals later referred to simply as "The Frankfurt School" or the proponents of "Critical Theory." Since it had already become painfully apparent that the advent of the Nazi regime would make the career prospects of a Marxist Jewish philosopher in Germany highly dubious, Marcuse's affiliation with the Institute, first in Geneva, then in Paris, and later in New York in July 1934, in effect signaled his emigration from his homeland as a political refugee. Together with Max Horkheimer, Leo Lowenthal, Friedrich Pollock, Adorno and others, Marcuse, during the years between 1934 and 1941, helped formulate the central ideas of "the critical theory of society," thereby revitalizing Marxism in particular and social theory in general. He also began to develop his own highly original interpretation, synthesis, and critique of phenomenology, Hegel, Marx, and Freudian psychoanalytic theory. The best known product of these years with the Institute is *Reason and Revolution: Hegel and the Rise of Social Theory*, which appeared in 1941 and attempted to rescue Hegel from the long-standing and well-entrenched interpretations that enshrined him as a philosophical and political conservative. Beneath the conservative shell of Hegel's more authoritarian pronouncements, Marcuse discovered a radical kernel - the dialectical theory of negativity - and spent the rest of his life making use of this approach in an attempt to analyze and criticize existing ideologies and social institutions.

From 1942 until 1950, Marcuse, who had become a naturalized American citizen, worked as a section head for the Office of Strategic Services. From 1951 to 1954 he did research and taught under the auspices of the Russian Institute of Columbia University and the Russian Research Center at Harvard, work which resulted in the book *Soviet Marxism*, published in 1958. In 1954 he joined the faculty at Brandeis University, where he taught until his retirement in 1965.

At about the time Marcuse was preparing to retire from Brandeis, the San Diego campus of the University of California was just beginning to offer courses. After he had given a typically impressive performance at a symposium on Marxism at U.C.S.D., Marcuse was quickly offered a three-year appointment to the philosophy faculty. The appointment was renewed with two more one-year contracts until he was retired, although reluctantly, as "Honorary Professor" in 1970.

During his years at U.C.S.D., Marcuse was one of the most important and influential figures at the university, constantly lecturing to packed audiences and directly involved in the anti-war movement and related New Left causes. When one of his doctoral students, Angela Davis, was dismissed from her teaching post at U.C.L.A. because of her membership in the Communist Party of America, Marcuse traveled around the state of California decrying this injustice. For his efforts, the Regents of the University of California voted henceforth to consider annually, on an individual basis, the reappointments of all professors who had attained the age of 70. Not uncoincidentally, the first candidate for such scrutiny was Herbert Marcuse, and even less surprisingly, while he was permitted to maintain his office and related faculty prerogatives, Marcuse was enjoined from continuing to teach undergraduates. Nonetheless, it was during the last decade of his life that he became internationally known as the "Father of the New Left." An entire generation of students and younger professors in Western Europe and the U.S. struggled through *One-Dimensional Man* (1964), rediscovered *Eros and Civilization* (1955), and sought to identify with the emancipatory agents of *An Essay on Liberation* (1969).

Finally, as the New Left splintered and weakened, and as the "working classes" continued to ignore the revolutionary role Marx had assigned them, Marcuse returned during his final years to the subject of his youth - aesthetics. In *Counter-Revolution and Revolt* (1972) and *The Aesthetic Dimension* (1978), the authentically radical historical subject was discovered no longer in the mode of production but in the free play of the imagination. Despite the fragmented and dispirited state of radical political activism in the 1970s, and his own invocation of "aesthetic form" as the representation of "true reality," when confronted by questions portending doom and co-optation, Marcuse remained concerned to reject vigorously the inclinations towards pessimism and despair implied by such queries. He often ended his lectures during this period with words of simple encouragement, with a phrase that might well serve as a fitting epitaph: *Weiter machen*! ("Continue!")

As the preceding sketch makes clear, any attempt to compile and organize a comprehensive, unified series of essays on the thought of Herbert Marcuse immediately encounters an obvious and difficult problem. The range of his interests throughout his long life was so wide that, at first glance, it seems to defeat any attempt at a view of the whole. Indeed, his intellectual and personal biography reads like some magisterial twentieth-century *Bildungsroman,* a novel about the growth and experiences of an individual from birth to old age that also reveals the historical forces at work in society in the same period. Marcuse's life, stretching as it did from the time of the Kaiser to the late 1970s, not only involved an encounter with such epochal events as World War I, the Russian Revolution, fascism, exile, World War II, the civil rights, anti-war, and student movements, Watergate, and the nuclear arms race, but his intellectual interests covered almost everything of importance in the Western European tradition of this period: the role of art in modernity; phenomenology, existentialism and the legacy of classical German philosophy; the crisis of Marxism and the vicissitudes of critical theory; the transformation of the capitalist mode of production and the intellectuals' disenchantment with the socialist project; Freud and the rise of psychoanalysis; the mixed blessings of technological progress; and the nature of the subject amidst a universe of one-dimensional things.

However, in the face of this gallimaufry of concerns, it is important not to lose sight of the unity Marcuse himself would have insisted upon, a unity necessary to keep in mind when understanding and assessing his work. Consider, for example, the following bold claim made in his famous 1937 article, "Philosophy and Critical Theory":

> The interest of philosophy, concern with man, had found its new form in the interest of critical social theory. There is no philosophy alongside and outside this theory.

This strong identification of his own project with that of the tradition of "critical theory" not only helps one to understand the context of Marcuse's work, but, especially, makes clear the dominant problem the Frankfurt School had to face after 1918, and particularly, after 1933:

> What, however, if the development outlined by that theory does not
> occur? What if the forces that were to bring about the
> transformation are suppressed and appear to be defeated?

The facts of history - the rise to power by the Nazis and the failure of the
proletariat to prevent it - make critical social theory "appear in a new light
which illuminates new aspects and elements of its object." Our interest in
this collection has been to exhibit the various ways in which Herbert
Marcuse came to understand this "new light," to try to illuminate the
project of critical theory by coming to grips with the dialectical
convergences between history and theory, as they were understood by
Marcuse.

Of course, to consider Marcuse primarily as a "critical theorist" does not
mean simply to concentrate exclusively on the more "abstract" or
"philosophical" elements of his work. For one thing, the enterprise of
critical theory itself begins by denying that there can be a radical
separation between philosophical issues and their historical, practical
context. Marcuse's work on what, in another's hands, would be the
abstract "issues" of art, history, repression, happiness, and liberation,
always reveals this historical consciousness, a clear connection between
why such issues are issues and problems in the first place, and the
historical, acting subjects who raise them at some period of history.
However, as the above quotations make clear, and as the very term critical
theory indicates, however this connection between theory and practice is
described, is not a reductionist relation, but a dialectical one. In what is
sometimes described as the "Hegelian" moment of the critical theory
enterprise, its proponents insisted on the importance and power of critical
thought *as thought* in practical liberation, and broke most clearly from
classical Marxism in their reformulation of this issue of the "negative"
power of intellectual activity and of socially relevant theory. Indeed, for
Horkheimer and Adorno in particular, the failure of traditional Marxist
critical theory to account for the "cunning of reason" in twentieth-century
history not only called for a broader, more adequate theory of social
change, class relations, ideology, and the like, that failure necessitated a
radical reconsideration of the *foundations* of critical theory, its original
account of human subjectivity, knowledge, desire, satisfaction, even of the
possibility of theory itself.

As the titles of the following chapters indicate, we have chosen to
concentrate on Marcuse's contribution to this reconstructive project. As
will also be clear, of course, discussions of such themes often extend far
into the details of Marcuse's theory and his social criticism. But,
particularly since this aspect of Marcuse has often been neglected in public
discussions of his work (especially academic discussions), we wanted to
collect essays broadly relevant to the themes of Marcuse as critical
theorist. Thus the attention to such themes as existential ontology,
historicity, metapsychology, totalization, aesthetics, Marxist theory,
negativity, ideology and technology, one-dimensionality, and subjectivity.
Obviously, we do not believe that this sums up all that ought to be said
about Marcuse, or that it should take some sort of precedence over the

historical and practical aspects of Marcuse's work and action.   Again, in Marcuse's terms, there cannot be such a separation of issues, but there certainly can be an independent discussion of Marcuse's contributions to the critical theory project, and that is what we have tried to begin to do.

The chapters that follow do not, though, and should not, share any unified or obvious interpretation of the critical theory of Herbert Marcuse. Nonetheless, we have tried to include chapters which, even if specifically focused on an individual theme, connect in some way with the larger issue of what "new light" needs to be shed on the foundations of critical theory in particular, and the infrastructure of Marxism and Western Philosophy in general.

What all this means is that the full picture of Marcuse that emerges from this collection is a complicated one, though, we think, not a chaotic one. We hope that, ultimately, what appear to be conflicting themes in Marcuse's theoretical work can be seen to belong together in ways more suggestive and determinate, even if incomplete, than his critics frequently allowed.   Indeed, it is a nice piece of dialectical irony that Marcuse should be often characterized by critics from the right as a wholly negative or destructive critic, merely tearing down the achievements of modern culture, technology, and economy, *and* by critics of the left as so full of positive promises of happiness as to be characterizable as "utopian," nonprogrammatic, even romantic. Throughout Marcuse's theoretical work, in any of the various contexts we have organized here, there are any number of attempts to work out how and why the critical and affirmative moments of social theory belong together, and how that unity should be understood. Some of the authors in this collection do not think that Marcuse succeeded in such a project, and some sharply criticize the nature of his attempt, but all, we hope, help to reveal Marcuse's fundamental intentions and accomplishments as a critical theorist.

We begin in Part I with three general accounts and assessments of Marcuse's whole project: Jürgen Habermas's compelling account of the ineliminably affirmative moment in Marcuse's critical theory, Richard Bernstein's argument about the importance and limitations of the crucial concept of "negativity" in all of Marcuse's work, and Martin Jay's analysis of the importance of the idea of "remembrance" in Marcuse's general theory of reification and repression.   In the remaining sections we include individual accounts of what we took to be the most important elements of Marcuse's multidimensional critical theory - his complicated early involvement with existential phenomenology, and the influence of that involvement on his later work, his life long fascination with the utopian and critical potential of the aesthetic dimension, his inventive appropriation of Freudian metapsychology, and the Marxist origins of his political and social theory, and the implications of that theory for what was perhaps his most controversial political claim (his "critique of pure tolerance"), and finally his assessment of technology, and the one-dimensional existence created, perhaps irretrievably, by a technological society.

Like the project of critical theory itself, this volume is incomplete, and necessarily so.   To claim to cover completely the work of such a protean thinker as Herbert Marcuse would be to misrepresent both this volume and the dialectical nature of the critical theorist himself. Like the man, Marcuse's critical theory is a multidimensional one. What we hope to offer is an overview of that multidimensionality, and thereby to carry the debates prompted by his work one step further.

PART I

□□□□□□□□□□

NEGATION
AND
AFFIRMATION

Herbert Marcuse always understood himself as contributing to the tradition of Marxist social theory and the Marxist revolutionary theory of history. However, like many members of the Institute and many other neo-Marxists, he believed that the historical situation of the first third of the twentieth century could not be adequately understood or confronted within the confines of traditional Marxist economic theory, and that a complete rethinking of the foundational issues of that tradition was called for. One extremely important problem that cut across most of the issues in this reconstruction of Marxism concerned the proper analysis of the capitalist phase of human history. Especially important was the foundational, methodological issue of how to understand historical *development* if scientific, economic models of prediction and an Hegelian, idealist teleology were abandoned. To some commentators, it seemed that the more well known, original members of the Institute, Horkheimer, Adorno, and Marcuse, never did successfully develop this "post-Marxist" understanding of the potential of actual human history, one that could explain theoretically and promise practically nonalienated labor, and nonoppressive social relations. Thus, for some, critical theory's reaction to the historical crisis of Marxism was to develop an exclusively and self-consciously *negative*, even potentially anarchistic, position, a rejection of bourgeois culture and only a rejection.

While this characterization may be partly true of, say, Adorno, it is not true of Marcuse, as all the essays in this Part demonstrate in a variety of ways. They all attempt a synoptic view of Marcuse's work, while treating a central topic that brings into focus Marcuse's various attempts to draw affirmative conclusions from his "negations" or "refusals." Jürgen Habermas emphasizes this affirmative, even "romantic" dimension in Marcuse, in clear contrast to Horkheimer and Adorno, even while he suggests the incompleteness of Marcuse's theoretical support for such a position. Richard Bernstein also stresses Marcuse's attempts to complete his intensely negative project with a revolutionary "promesse de bonnheur," even though Bernstein goes on to argue that Marcuse neglected a variety of theoretical, institutional and social issues in articulating that promise. And Martin Jay shows how this affirmative moment is present in Marcuse's attempt to redeem the historical past, to remember and preserve the subjectivity of human history and so the potential for the radical alteration of history by such subjects.

All three of these chapters were first presented at a conference held at the University of California, San Diego.

CHAPTER ONE

Psychic Thermidor and the Rebirth of Rebellious Subjectivity

Jürgen Habermas

I

We all remember what Herbert Marcuse kept denouncing as the evils of our age: the blind struggle for existence, relentless competition, wasteful productivity, deceitful repression, false virility, and cynical brutality. Whenever he felt that he should speak as teacher and philosopher he encouraged the negation of the performance principle, of possessive individualism, of alienation in labor - as well as in love relations. But the negation of suffering was for him only a start. No doubt, Herbert Marcuse claimed negation to be the very essence of thinking - as did Adorno and Horkheimer; but the driving force of criticism, of contradiction and contest carried him well beyond the limits of an accusation of unnecessary mischief. Marcuse moved further ahead. He did not hesitate to advocate, in an affirmative mood, the fulfillment of human needs, of the need for undeserved happiness, of the need for beauty, of the need for peace, calm and privacy. Although, certainly, Marcuse was not an affirmative thinker, he was nevertheless the most affirmative among those who praised negativity. With him negative thinking retained the dialectical trust in determinate negation, in the disclosure of positive alternatives. Marcuse did not, in contrast to Adorno, only encircle the ineffable; he made straight appeals to future alternatives. I am interested in this affirmative feature of Herbert Marcuse's negative thinking.

In this chapter, let me illustrate what I mean by "affirmative feature" with reference to a rather personal reminiscence. I have just re-read the two lectures which Marcuse gave when I first met him. For us it was a surprisingly new tone when we heard the following sentences:

3

The order of values of a non-repressive principle of progress can be determined on almost all levels in opposition to that of its repressive counterpart. Men's basic experience would be no longer that of life as a struggle for existence but rather that of the enjoyment of life. Alienated labor would be transformed into the free play of human faculties and forces. In consequence all contentless transcendence would come to a close, and freedom would no longer be an eternally failing project . . . . Time would not seem linear . . . , but cyclical, as the return contained in Nietzsche's idea of "the perpetuity of pleasure."[1]

This is not quoted from the Marcuse of 1967, who came to Berlin for intense discussions on violence and the expected end of utopia and who, at that time was hailed by the protesting students as their inspirational intellectual leader. Neither is that quote from the Marcuse of 1964, who came to the Max Weber centennial in Heidelberg, made his professional appearance as an important emigre-social theorist and immediately aroused excited discussions. I am speaking of the Marcuse of 1956, who came to Frankfurt for another centennial; the commemoration of the occasion of Freud's 100th birthday was the date of Marcuse's first academic return to Germany. I should mention that the international conference of *Freud in der Gegenwart*, where Marcuse lectured side by side with famous analysts such as Alexander, Balint, Erikson, and Spitz, was the first opportunity for young German academics to learn about the simple fact that Sigmund Freud was the founding father of a living scientific and intellectual tradition. In this context Marcuse opened his first lecture with sentences which, at a time when Freud and Marx were "dead dogs" and practically unknown at German universities, sounded strange and radical:

The psyche appears more and more immediately to be a piece of the social totality, so that individuation is almost synonymous with apathy and even with guilt, but also with the principle of negation, of possible revolution. Moreover, the totality of which the psyche is a part becomes to an increasing extent less "society" than "politics." That is, society has fallen prey to and becomes identified with domination.[2]

For us, the research assistants at the Institute of Horkheimer and Adorno, this was the moment when we first faced an embodiment and vivid expression of the political spirit of the old Frankfurt School. As a school it had been alive only during a few years of American exile. If there ever has been a Frankfurt School, it did not exist in Frankfurt, neither before nor after the Nazi period, but, during the 1930s, in New York. I was reminded of this fact, when Herbert, before his death in Starnberg, although already somewhat inhibited in his verbal fluency by a recent stroke, did not speak his mother tongue: the language of his last days was English. But let me return to our first encounter. What, in 1956, made a stunning impression was the outright style of Marcuse's thought and presentation.   You know better than I that Herbert Marcuse's spoken English never quite lost the mark of a Berlin accent, and his written English was never stripped completely of the clumsiness of the German grammar underneath.   But with his German it was the other way round. By the standards of the jargon of German philosophers Marcuse spoke a straight, affirmative language, easy to understand and without the rhetorical loopholes where the more shocking consequences of a dialectical argument might have found a hiding place.   Although rather a shy person, Marcuse was never afraid of being outspoken and for taking the responsibility for what he said, even for taking the risk of oversimplification, if there seemed to be no other way to address an important issue.   In the following years, when I became closer to Herbert Marcuse and learned more about the first generation of critical theorists, that affirmative feature which struck me from the very beginning became even more obvious.   Compared with Horkheimer, Lowenthal, and Adorno, with whom he had formed the inner circle, Marcuse represented a singular combination.

Since he first joined the Institute Marcuse has made the most "orthodox" contributions to Critical Theory.   This is true of his essays in the *Zeitschrift*, where Marcuse was chosen to write the article "Philosophy and Critical Theory," counterpart to Horkheimer's famous position paper on "Traditional and Critical Theory." But it is also true of his later writings, including the very last.   In *Reason and Revolution*, *One-Dimensional Man*, and *The Aesthetic Dimension*, Marcuse elaborated themes and arguments, and pursued lines of reasoning that were more or less shared by the whole group.   This orthodoxy is only one side, however, of Marcuse's work.   His work reflects, on the other side, quite distinct features that set it apart from the background tradition.   Marcuse received his philosophical training in Freiburg with Heidegger, and he never lost contact with Existential Phenomenology; Marcuse was, among his colleagues, the most professional in attitude; his major works, *Reason and Revolution*, *Soviet Marxism*, and *Eros and Civilization*, all are well placed in the context of related disciplines; they exemplify an almost conventional type of systematic academic presentation.

Marcuse's personal history followed, as compared to the biographies of those next to him, including Neumann and Kirchheimer, an almost opposite trend; he who started from a rather conservative theoretical position, became in the course of his life more and more radicalized. Moreover, he was the only one who assumed a direct political role; supported by his wife Inge, he deliberately took this role and played it at times with a considerable sense of the imponderables of political activism.

Take one example: When Marcuse was in Berlin in 1967 he was asked about his relation to the heroes of the Third World and, in his inimitable manner, gave the answer:

> I would not have mentioned Fanon and Guevara as much as a small
> item that I read in a report about North Vietnam and that had a
> tremendous effect on me, since I am an absolutely incurable and

sentimental romantic.   It was a very detailed report, which showed
. . . that in the parks in Hanoi the benches are made only big enough
for two and *only two* people to sit on, so that another person would
not even have the technical possibility of disturbing.[3]

Here, again, we encounter something very affirmative.   Imagine, for the
moment, that Adorno in a similar situation would have wanted to express
a similar intention!   He probably would have made a cautious appeal to a
poem of Eichendorff while anticipating what all of us today, after the
Vietnamese invasion into Cambodia, do think: that the facts will reveal as
an incurable romantic one who tries to affirmatively spell out utopia in
terms of particular examples, as Herbert did. What I have called the
affirmative feature is documented by a type of self-confessed romanticism
which is lacking in Adorno and Horkheimer, and even in Benjamin.
     The question that I would like to pursue is whether this peculiar feature
should just count as a trait of Herbert Marcuse's personality or whether it
is due to a theoretical position that separates him from his close friends.
Since there is a good deal of manifest agreement among the members of
the inner circle, we tend to think that the affirmative feature of Marcuse's
negative thinking indicates a difference rather in style and character than
in theory. How otherwise could we explain the fact that the author of the
deeply pessimistic *One-Dimensional Man* - a book which ends with the
quote from Benjamin, that it is only for the sake of those without hope,
that hope is given to us - that this man, less than one year later, inspired
the student movement with his hope?   I think there is another
explanation.   In Marcuse's version of critical theory we find a twist on an
argument which well can explain why Marcuse was different.   In order to
identify this twist I will briefly outline the main stages of the thought of
Herbert Marcuse.

II

     I will start with the transition from Heidegger to Horkheimer, and then
indicate the classical position of critical theory in the mid-thirties, with a
subsequent shift marked by Horkheimer and Adorno's *Dialectic of
Enlightenment*. From this perspective we will see the route which Marcuse
took as his way out of the dilemma posed by the alleged totalization of
instrumental reason.   He discovered this way with *Eros and Civilization*,
the book that appeared in 1955 and the substance of which was contained
in the two Freud lectures given at Frankfurt one year later.
     Marcuse's book *Hegels Ontologie und die Grundlegung einer Theorie des
Geshichlichkeit*, published in 1932, was planned as Habilitationsschrift.
The aspired Habilitation did not work out - Heidegger was soon to become
one of the Nazi-Rectors of the first hour.   That Hegel book was written
by one of the brightest students of Heidegger; it is the document of an
attempt to interpret dialectical thinking from a peculiar Heideggerian
point of view. Hegel is here presented as another ontologist who
conceived being as the essence of becoming - *Sein als Bewegtheit*.
Heidegger had a lasting impact on Herbert Marcuse - as much in terms of

personal loyalty, bridging the political abyss, as in terms of certain philosophical motivations. For Marcuse, Heidegger remained the one of *Being and Time*, moreover that Heidegger whose analysis of *Dasein* was received as a radicalized transcendental approach. Of course, after the period of *Being and Time*, both Heidegger and Marcuse moved in opposite directions. While Heidegger made *Dasein*, the abstract structures of the human world, dependent on some metahistorical fate, of an even more abstract *Sein* or fateful being, Marcuse, on the other hand, tried to link the ontological structures of the life world to the ontic, that is, to the contingent and concrete processes of society and history; he looked out for the dedifferentiation of the ontological difference. It was no accident that Marcuse, in this transitional period, did not move away from Heidegger by way of a critique of Heidegger. For the preparation of this lecture, Leo Lowenthal lent me his copy of *Hegels Ontologie*, and in this old copy I found a yellowed cut-out from the feuilleton of the *Vossische Zeitung* with a long and intense review of the three volumes of Karl Jaspers' *Philosophie*, written by somebody with the initials H.M., dated December 14, 1933. It is in this context of a criticism of Jaspers that we find a passage that indicates, still guarded by clauses, Marcuse's detachment from Heidegger. Here, Marcuse insists that the formal properties of historicity conceal rather than disclose the substance of history. He raises the question, "Whether it is not the case, that particular and contingent situations can destroy the authenticity of human existence, can abolish freedom or transform it into sheer illusion." Any talk about historicity, he continues, "must remain abstract and uncommitted until the analysis focuses on the concrete, 'material' situation" (*Vassiche Zeitung* NR. 339, 14 Dec. 1933).

The term "material" is printed in quotes, thereby inconspicuously referring to an earlier article of the same author on the recently discovered Paris Manuscripts, not by Karl Jaspers but by Karl Marx. This article shows how the young Marcuse appropriated the young Marx from the viewpoint of existential phenomenology, taking the very notions of *Praxis* and *Lebenswelt* as guidelines for the liberation from alienated labor. Marcuse was the first Heideggerian Marxist, anticipating Jean Paul Sartre's, Karl Kosik's, Enzo Paci's and the Yugoslav Praxis philosophers' later Phenomenological Marxism.

In the meantime, Marcuse had joined the Frankfurt Institute on its way to the United States. In his famous essay on "Philosophy and Critical Theory," published in 1937, Marcuse presents himself at the center of the Frankfurt School's theory. The vacant place of *Dasein* and *Geschichtlichkeit*, of the abstract structures of the human world, is now filled with a historically situated reason: "Reason is the fundamental category of philosophical thought, the only one by means of which it has bound itself to human destiny."[4] The abstract and ahistorical concept of reason which is at the heart of idealistic philosophy lends itself to all forms of ideology, but the bourgeois ideals, of cognitive and moral universalism on the one hand, of expressive subjectivism on the other, carry also a utopian content which transcends the limits of false consciousness. For Critical Theory those ideals "are exclusively potentialities of the concrete social situation. They become relevant only as economic and political questions and as such bear on human relations in the productive process, the distribution of the product of social labor, and men's active participation in the economic and political administration of the whole."[5] The demand for reason simply means, resonating indeed to an ancient truth, a demand for "the creation of a social organization in which individuals can collectively regulate their lives in accordance with their needs."[6]

At the time he wrote this, Marcuse was already aware of, and explicitly referring to, the fact that, with fascism and, moreover, with Stalinism, history had taken a course quite contrary to the predictions of Marxist theory. He therefore stressed the constructive as against the descriptive and explanatory role of theory, admitting that Critical Theory "must concern itself to a hitherto unknown extent with the past."[7] But Marcuse did not yet question the revolutionary dynamic of the productive forces developing in the womb of capitalism. The stifling of the proletariat, its lack of revolutionary consciousness, is still explained in the old vein: "Fettering the productive forces and keeping down the standard of life is characteristic of even the economically most developed countries."[8]

In the following years Marcuse elaborated the classical position of Critical Theory in careful studies on Hegel and the rise of social theory. At the same time, Horkheimer and Adorno, who had moved to Santa Monica, had already taken a somewhat different line. With *Dialectic of Enlightenment* (1944) they definitely lost their trust in the revolutionary dynamic of the productive forces, and in the practical impact of negative thinking. Both the productive forces and critical thought were seen in the perspective of merging with their opposite, with the forces of domination. As they develop they become aggressive, more and more subordinated to the imperatives of an instrumental reason which is no longer instrumental for the satisfaction of human needs, but gaining the autonomy of an end in itself. The totality of instrumental reason finds its expression in totalitarian society. I will not go into the subtleties of this gloomy exposition which Marcuse soon adopted. In the foreword to an English translation of his old essays, published three decades ago in the *Zeitschrift*, Marcuse declared the break in his thinking: "That . . . this was written before Auschwitz deeply separates it from the present. What was correct in it has since become, perhaps not false, but a thing of the past: . . . remembrance of something that at some point had lost its reality and had to be taken up again . . . . The end of a historical period and the horror of the one to come were announced in the simultaneity of the civil war in Spain and the trials in Moscow."[9]

Marcuse described this new period as a totalization of instrumental reason, that is, in the light of his own analysis in *One-Dimensional Man*: "Productivity and prosperity in league with a technology in the service of monopolistic politics seem to immunize advancing industrial society in its established structure." He then asks the central question: "Is this concept of immunity still dialectical?"

Adorno answered this question with a qualified "No"; he explained this

reaction in terms of his "Negative Dialectics." Marcuse, on the contrary, still stuck to an affirmative answer. According to Marcuse, the earlier theory, with its concept of a free and rational society, has made only one mistake - it did not promise too much but rather too little.

The reasons why Herbert Marcuse could both accept Horkheimer's and Adorno's analysis of the eclipse of reason and yet remain faithful to the political intention of early Critical Theory, are laid out in *Eros and Civilization* which, among Marcuse's books, is the most Marcusian.

Let me first state the question at issue. Marcuse agreed with Horkheimer and Adorno in their assumption that with the expansion of capitalism the project of instrumental reason would shape the entire universe of discourse and action, intellectual and material culture: "In the medium of technology, culture, politics, and the economy merge into an omnipresent system which swallows up or repulses all alternatives." On the other hand, Marcuse still maintained that the same project does undermine the stability of a domination which fuses technology with practical rationality, since "The progressive reduction of physical labor power in the production process . . . suggests possible liberation from alienated labor." If these objective possibilities are at all suggestive, we must, however, rely on a subjectivity which is still sensitive to a utopian horizon. This is the question then - how could Marcuse believe in the rebirth of rebellious subjectivity, if he accepted the first of the two arguments, in fact the core-argument of *Dialectic of Enlightenment*, that with each conquest over external nature the internal nature of those who gain ever new triumphs is more deeply enslaved?

It is at this point that Marcuse shows reservations based on his distinctive reading of Freud's theory of instincts. To put the argument in a nutshell: even if the individual, the sole bearer of reason, is more and more swallowed up by a totalitarian society, and even if this shrinkage of the ego is without any limits, we still may hope for the rebirth of rebellious subjectivity from a nature which is older than, and arises from below the level of, individuation and rationality. Marcuse has a chiliastic trust in a revitalizing dynamic of instincts which works through history, finally breaks with history and leaves it behind as what then will appear as prehistory. Let us recall how he interprets Freud's theory of patricide:

> This dynamic of domination, which begins with the institution of despotism, leads to revolution and ends after the first attempt at liberation with the reestablishment of the father in internalized and generalized, i.e., rational form, repeats itself . . . during the entire history of culture and civilization, although in diluted form. It does so as the rebellion of all sons against all fathers in puberty . . . and . . . in the ever recurring dynamic of revolutions in the past . . . . Insurrection succeeds and certain forces attempt to drive the revolution to its extreme point, from which the transition to new, not only quantitatively but qualitatively different conditions could perhaps proceed. At this point the revolution is usually vanquished and domination is internalized, reestablished, and continued at a higher level . . . We can raise the question whether alongside the

socio-historical Thermidor . . . here is not also a *psychic* Thermidor. Are revolutions perhaps not only vanquished, reversed, and unmade from the outside, is there perhaps in individuals themselves already a dynamic at work that *internally* negates possible liberation and gratification and that supports external forces of denial?

At a first glance, this consideration is nothing but a translation, of what the dialectic of instrumental reason means, into Freudian language. On a careful reading, the difference however comes to the fore - the difference is in the move to keep separate the internal or instinctual from the external or social forces of domination. If the psychic as compared with the sociohistoric Thermidor gains a dynamic of its own, it is no longer social theory alone, but the theory of instincts which also provides the key. The question, whether the psychic Thermidor must be repeated again and again, gains an almost existentialist dignity, since the answer to this question no longer depends on whether or not late capitalism, as an economic and a political system, can contain its inner conflicts.

From the metahistory of instincts Marcuse defends two related propositions. (1) There is no final opposition between Eros and Thanatos; in spite of their antagonism both are conservative in nature, both strive for pacification, and both are unproductive and similarly directed against a relentless struggle for existence. (2) As soon as the progress of civilization, which is based on the repressive modification of the instincts, increases, the existence of a surplus product not leading to individual gratification provokes a reaction from both Eros and Thanatos. Once instinctual repression loses its function for necessary self-preservation, the two conservative powers behind the scenes of civilization form a coalition and demand the recalling of energies from alienated labor.

III

This theory has the weakness that it cannot consistently account for its own possibility. If rebellious subjectivity had to owe its rebirth to something that is beyond - a too deeply corrupted - reason, it is hard to explain why some of us should at all be in a position to recognize this fact and to give reasons in defense of it. In this respect, Adorno was the more consistent thinker. However implausible the argument may seem, it had the function to preserve in Herbert Marcuse one of his most admirable features - not to give in to defeatism. But there is more to the search for an "instinctive" base of socialism. This effort is, after all, the result of a true philosophical intention. Marcuse did not want to fall back into existentialism, he did not want just to appeal to the vital needs of freedom or merely to evoke the pathos of emancipation. He felt the obligation to give theoretical explanations and thereby to ground action in reason.

Moreover, Marcuse was one of the few philosophers who were severely and chronically rebuked for the seriousness of their philosophical attitude. In summer 1967, at the Free University, Marcuse was exposed to a situation where he knew that any single word could have irrevocable

consequences. He was invited to talk about the use of violence, and he had just declared the unity of moral, sexual, and political rebellion, when he found himself confronted with questions about the doubtful nature of moral justifications. Some of the questions indicated a then widespread inclination, on the side of the students, to free political activism from the painful hesitations of moral-practical reasoning. One student complained about difficulties he had experienced in discussions with a worker: "What does this worker care about the terror in Vietnam? Humanitarian arguments wouldn't do, since humanity itself gave rise to terror." The student apparently referred, although in an elliptic and misleading form, to the core of the analysis of the eclipse of reason. But Marcuse was not irritated at all. "As to your suspicion about humanitarian arguments . . . we must finally relearn what we forgot during the fascist period, or what you, who were not even born . . . have not fully become conscious of: that humanitarian and moral arguments are not merely deceitful ideology. Rather, they can and must become central social forces." Another student countered this straight answer with a moral skepticism which in my country often reveals the strong influence of Carl Schmidt even on the left: "On the right of resistance: in your essay on tolerance you put this right in quotation marks, but now you have interpreted it as an ancient principle. What is this right based on? Is it a romantic relic of natural law, or is it a self-posited right and, if so, how can the opposition invoke a right which it must first generate?" In this moment, Marcuse decided to be inconsistent rather than irresponsible. He swept aside his own doubts on a corrupted practical reason which supposedly had been absorbed into a totality of instrumental reason. His answer was clear, without the slightest ambiguity:

> [A]ppealing to the right of resistance is an appeal to a higher law, which has universal validity, that is, which goes beyond the self-defined right and privilege of a particular group. And there really is a close connection between the right of resistance and natural law. Now you will say that such a universal higher law simply does not exist. I believe that it does exist. Today we no longer call it Natural Law . . . . If we appeal to humanity's right to peace, to the right to abolish exploitation and oppression, we are not talking about self-defined, special, group interests, but rather and, in fact interests demonstrable as universal rights.

Before his eightieth birthday, and in preparation for an interview on that occasion, Marcuse and I had a long discussion on how we could and should explain the normative base of Critical Theory. Last summer, seeing him for the first time since that discussion, Herbert was under intensive care in a hospital in Frankfurt, with all types of controlling apparatuses on his left and on his right. None of us knew that this was the beginning of the end. On this occasion, indeed our last philosophical encounter, Herbert made the connection with our controversy two years ago, telling me: "Look, I know wherein our most basic value judgments are rooted - in compassion, in our sense for the suffering of others."

NOTES

1. Marcuse, *Five Lectures*, p. 40.
2. *Ibid.*, p. 1.
3. *Ibid.*, p. 82.
4. Marcuse, *Negations*, p. 135.
5. *Ibid.*, pp. 142-3.
6. *Ibid.*, pp. 141-2.
7. *Ibid.*, p. 158.
8. *Ibid.*
9. Marcuse, *Negations*, p. xv.

CHAPTER TWO

Negativity: Theme and Variations

Richard J. Bernstein

Negativity is the deepest, most persistent, and most pervasive theme in Marcuse's work. It is a leitmotif that is in the background of almost everything that he wrote. It connects his varied interests in Hegel, Marx, Freud, and the radical critique of contemporary culture. My aim is to sound the depths of this theme, to explore some of its primary variations, and to show how it is the key for understanding the power - what Marcuse himself might have called the "explosive quality" - of his critique. I also want to show that the theme of negativity is not only the source of Marcuse's strength as a thinker, but harbors what I take to be crucial weaknesses in his "project." The spirit of my own analysis is to do what Marcuse so effectively did with other thinkers - to engage in an immanent critique.[1] The first task of such a critique demands that we grasp adequately what is being criticized.

The logical place to begin is with Marcuse's interpretation of negativity in Hegel. For it is Hegel - even more than Marx and Freud - who most profoundly shaped Marcuse's thinking. Or to be more precise, it is Marcuse's distinctive emphatic interpretation of Hegel that provides the essential clue for understanding what he means by negativity. We can trace this back to Marcuse's earliest writing on Hegel, but it is vividly and forcefully articulated in his first full-length book in English, *Reason and Revolution: Hegel and the Rise of Modern Social Theory*. There is scarcely a page of his Hegel interpretation that does not explicitly or implicitly refer to negativity. On the opening page of the preface - in his typical dialectical manner - Marcuse tells us that Hegel's system "could well be called a *negative philosophy*, the name given to it by its contemporary opponents.   To counteract its destructive tendencies, there arose, in the decade following Hegel's death, a positive philosophy which undertook to subordinate reason to the authority of established fact."[2]   For Marcuse, the battle between negativity and positivity is the most consequential and decisive battle in the contemporary world. It is not only a battle that takes place between competing philosophical or intellectual orientations.   We are threatened with the triumph of positivity which infects every aspect of culture and social reality, a positivity that reflects a basic impotence in the face of what is given, what appears as existing historical social fact. Everything Marcuse *said* and *did* was motivated by the basic desire to expose and combat the invidious consequences of positivity.

Hegel's philosophy is indeed what the subsequent reaction termed it, a negative philosophy.   It is originally motivated by the conviction that the given facts that appear to common sense as the positive index of truth are in reality the negation of   truth, so that truth can only be established in their destruction.   The driving force of the dialectical method lies in this critical conviction. Dialectic in its entirety is linked to the conception that all forms of being are permeated by an essential negativity, and that this negativity determines their content and movement.   The dialectic represents the counter-thrust to any form of positivism.[3]

For Marcuse, as for Hegel, it is crucial to distinguish sharply "abstract negativity," which results in emptiness, nothingness, in "mere" denial, from "determinate negation," by which the truth is revealed.   Marcuse stresses the theme that shines forth in the following passage from the Preface to the *Phenomenology*.

The life of Spirit is not the life that shrinks from death and keeps itself untouched by devastation, but rather the life that endures it and maintains itself in it.   It wins its truth only when, in utter dismemberment, it finds itself.   It is this power, not as something positive, which closes its eyes to the negative, as when we say of something that it is nothing or it is false, and then, having done with it, turn away and pass on to something else; on the contrary, Spirit is this power only by looking the negative in the face, and tarrying with it.   This tarrying with the negative is the magical power that converts it into being.[4]

I want to stress, as Marcuse does, the two-dimensionality of this concept of negativity.   There is negativity, opposition, critical judgment in the tension between the demands of Reason (*Vernunft*) and the positivity of an untrue, distorted, existing social reality.   "The realization of reason is not a fact but a task."[5]   For Marcuse, this first dimension of negativity has been the dominant characteristic of the tradition of philosophic thought which has opposed and implicitly condemned "the given facts that appear to common sense as the positive index of truth."   This aspect of negativity is embodied in the role that the concepts of "essence" and "universality" have played in philosophy from Plato through Hegel. In this respect, Hegel *is* the culmination of, and embodies the "truth" of, the history of philosophy - just as Hegel claimed for his system. But Hegel's distinctive genius is to be found in the move that he made from thought to being. Negativity does not simply exemplify itself in the way in which philosophy and critical thinking have opposed the positivity of existing fact, but Hegel saw that the power of negativity lies at the heart of being in all its forms. It is being itself, and *a fortiori* social reality itself, that contains negativity - contains its own opposition, and the seeds for its own ineluctable destruction and transformation. *"All things are contradictory in themselves."*[6] Herein lies the primary significance of Hegel's joining of Reason and History. With extraordinary perspicacity and persistence, Marcuse shows how this two-dimensional quality of negativity is revealed in every aspect of Hegel's philosophy.

> Even in the abstract formulations of the *Logic* we can see the concrete critical impulses that underlie this conception. Hegel's dialectic is permeated with the profound conviction that all immediate forms of existence - in nature and history - are "bad," because they do not permit things to be what they can be. True existence begins only when the immediate state is recognized as negative, when beings become "subjects" and strive to adapt their outward state of their potentialities.[7]

The actualization of these potentialities demands the destruction, the negation, of everything that inhibits them from their full realization. It is only by negation that Reason and Freedom can be realized.

But for all Hegel's insight into the power of negativity and the way in which it is *immanent* in being in all its forms, it is negativity that ultimately defeats Hegel himself. The consequences of Hegel's dialectic lead to the realization that "the inherent potentialities of men and things cannot unfold in a society except through the death of the social order in which they are first gleaned."[8] It is not that Marx simply refuted and negated Hegel, but for Marcuse it is more accurate and revealing to claim that it is "History and social reality themselves that 'negate' philosophy."[9] This is what Marx discovered. "In Hegel's system all categories terminate in the existing order, while in Marx's they refer to the negation of this order."[10] This is a transition to an "essentially different order of truth." We can locate here the movement from philosophy to Critical Theory which has the practical intent of fostering the destruction of a repressive, alienating and dominating social reality in order to further the struggle and realization for genuine freedom and happiness.

Consequently it is the "working out" of negativity that leads us from philosophy to Critical Theory. Critical Theory is like philosophy insofar as "it opposes making reality into a criterion in the manner of complacent positivism. But unlike philosophy, it always derives its goals only from the present tendencies of the social process. Therefore it has no fear of the utopia that the new order is denounced as being. When truth cannot be realized within the established social order, it always appears to the latter as mere utopia."[11]   Critical Theory claims to comprehend present existing social reality.   This theory can grasp the negativity that is implicit in social reality: it can focus on those very tendencies that can negate the existing order and have the power to bring about the full realization of human potentialities - potentialities which when realized culminate in the triumph of Reason, Freedom, and Happiness.

In 1937, Marcuse raised the basic question that confronts Critical Theory.

> What, however, if the development outlined by the theory does not occur?   What if the forces that were to bring about the transformation are suppressed and appear to be defeated? Little as the theory's truth is thereby contradicted, it nevertheless appears then in a new light which illuminates new aspects and elements of it object . . . . This situation compels theory anew to a sharper emphasis on its concern with the potentialities of man and with the individual's freedom, happiness and rights contained in all its analyses.[12]

This passage takes on greater poignancy when we remind ourselves of the context in which it was written.   It appeared at a time when fascism was gaining in ominous power, and when the Frankfurt thinkers were in exile in New York writing in German to an unknown audience. Furthermore, consider the significance of this passage against the background of the Marxist legacy.   For Marx, as Marcuse himself had argued, the power of negativity was embodied in the proletariat, the potentially revolutionary class that can destroy the existing social order and bring about its radical transformation.   But increasingly, Marcuse, like the other Frankfurt thinkers, was not only becoming skeptical about the *real* possibility of a proletarian revolution, but also about the adequacy of the framework of the critique of political economy for coming to grips with the negativity and the "*real*" potentialities of the contemporary world. But if one rejects, or is skeptical about, the Marxist conception of the role of the proletariat, and yet holds on to the conviction that the fundamental task of Critical Theory is to discover the form of negativity that can effect a radical transformation, then the hard question becomes: where does one discover this movement and negativity?   Critical Theory makes sense in a concrete situation where the "forces that were to bring about the transformation are suppressed and appear to be defeated." But it makes no sense if there is an absence of negative forces at work, and no evidence of hidden tendencies that can effect a revolution.   From the mid-thirties on, Marcuse's primary project became one of answering the very question he raised, of probing and searching for the power of negativity that lies hidden in existing social reality.   It is precisely this project that enables us to understand Marcuse's attraction to and dialectical use of Freud in *Eros and Civilization*.

Before passing on to the extraordinary use that Marcuse makes of Freud, I want to pick up on another variation of the theme of negativity, which is implicit in what I have already said, and sheds light on a significant aspect of Marcuse's style of thinking. Given Marcuse's understanding of negativity, we can appreciate why he was so hostile to the "sociology of knowledge," and suspicious of what he took to be positivistic reductions of the concept of ideology, which even proved seductive for many who thought they were following Marx. In 1937, reviewing some of the discussions that had appeared in the *Zeitschrift für Sozialforschung*, Marcuse wrote:

> Several fundamental concepts of philosophy have been discussed in this journal: truth and verification, rationalism and irrationalism, the role of logic, metaphysics and positivism, and the concept of essence. These were not merely analyzed sociologically, in order to correlate philosophical dogmas with social loci. Nor were philosophical constructs "resolved" into social facts. To the extent that philosophy is more than ideology, every such attempt must come to nought. When critical theory comes to terms with philosophy, it is interested in the truth content of philosophical concepts and problems. It presupposes that they really contain truth. The enterprise of the sociology of knowledge, to the contrary, is occupied only with the untruths, not the truths of previous philosophy.[13]

Marcuse not only said this, it is precisely what he *did* throughout his work. His interpretations of the philosophical tradition are self-consciously one-sided and frequently brilliant. He practiced a type of depth hermeneutics of negativity in which he sought to uncover the hidden truth implicit in these thinkers and their concepts - a hidden truth that almost always focused on their negativity. This is the way in which he interpreted Aristotle (who next to Hegel was Marcuse's favored philosopher), Plato, the Hedonists (including the Cyrenaics and Epicureans), Kant, and Schiller. This is also why he was relentless in his criticism of all forms of empiricism and positivism, and why he turned upon phenomenology itself, especially Husserl - for he claimed that the consequence of Husserl's thought was to "empty the concept of essence of its negative power."[14] Just as Marx began with a critique of religion and philosophy which sought to discover the latent truth implicit in them as well as the ways in which they mystify reality, so too this was what Marcuse sought to do with philosophy. Marcuse also argued that when philosophy came to an end (as it did with Hegel), one could no longer turn to philosophy to discover the expression of negativity and truth. For our time, phantasy and art become the forms in which the repressed dreams of freedom and happiness are expressed - albeit in a distorted form. It was Marcuse's search for the deepest and most powerful forms of negativity that led him to and shaped his interpretation of Freud - an interpretation in which Marcuse sought dialectically to use Freud against himself.

Eros and Civilization is Marcuse's most perverse, wild, phantasmal and surrealistic book. (I am not using these adjectives in a pejorative, but in a *descriptive* sense.) It is the book in which Marcuse probes the theme of negativity to its very extremity. It is strangely Hegelian and anti-Hegelian, Marxist and anti-Marxist, Nietzschean and anti-Nietzschean, and these oppositions are held together in an explosive tension. With an almost perverse, tabooed delight, Marcuse seizes upon those very aspects of Freud's thought which many thinkers, including the neo-Freudians, take to be the most dubious, unfounded, and speculative hypotheses: the late theory of instincts - the struggle between Eros and the death instinct; and Freud's reconstruction of the prehistory of mankind from the primal horde through patricide to civilization. Why? Because it is precisely in these apparently outrageous speculations - when properly deciphered - that the deepest level of "truth" latent in Freud is to be discovered. The drama that unfolds in Marcuse's analysis is anti-Hegelian in the sense that the development of civilization is not seen as the development of the stages or forms of consciousness, each embodying the truth of the preceding stages, and each contributing to the progressive realization of Reason and Freedom. And yet the mythic story that Marcuse presents *is* Hegelian insofar as in a world of increasing totalitarianism, alienation, repression and domination, the "return of the repressed" and the liberation of Eros *demand* the destruction and negation of the *"performance principle*: the prevailing historical form of the reality principle."15 The drama is structured as a grand, cataclysmic dialectic of negativity. It is anti-Marxist in the sense that there is scarcely any concern with the critique of political economy, the role of the proletariat, the conflict of classes, or the dialectical, historical development of modes and relations of production. And yet, Marcuse accepts and presses the Marxist thesis that it is precisely the development of capitalism - and more generally, advanced industrial societies - that creates the material conditions for a total and radical transformation of society.

Reason as it appears in *Eros and Civilization* is *not* primarily the Hegelian *Vernunft*, but rather the "logos of domination" which deeply fears, suppresses and represses the ineradicable instinctual demand for gratification and happiness.

> Civilization has to defend itself against the specter of a world which could be free. If society cannot use its growing productivity for reducing repression (because such usage would upset the hierarchy of the *status quo*), productivity must be turned *against* the individuals; it becomes itself an instrument of universal control. Totalitarianism spreads over the late industrial civilization wherever the interests of domination prevail upon productivity, arresting and diverting its potentialities.16

As Marcuse probes the hidden message of Freud, and dialectically transforms Freud, he begins to sound more and more like Nietzsche (and yet also anti-Nietzsche):

> Nietzsche speaks in the name of a reality principle fundamentally antagonistic to that of Western Civilization. The traditional form of

reason is rejected on the basis of being-an-end-in-itself - as joy (*Lust*) and enjoyment.[17]

The vision that Marcuse projects is one in which our deepest subterranean memories keep alive the dream of liberation, where "the *recherche du temps perdu* becomes the vehicle of future liberation,"[18] and where "the consummation of being is, not the ascending curve, but the closing of the circle: the *re-turn* from alienation."[19] The image of the closed circle which can be found at the beginning and the end of philosophy is no longer Aristotle's *nous theos* or Hegel's absolute idea, but the eternal return of the finite:

> Nietzsche envisages the eternal return of the finite exactly as it is - in its full concreteness and finiteness. This is the total affirmation of the life instincts, repelling all escape and negation. The eternal return is the will and vision of an *erotic* attitude toward being for which necessity and fulfillment coincide.[20]

The message and the rhetoric of *Eros and Civilization* are deeply disturbing. Marcuse's language is cataclysmic and apocalyptic - the language of "explosion," "total destruction," and "shattering" of the hardened, deadening, repressive crust of existing social reality. But it is also a revealing book because as Marcuse pursues negativity into the hidden recesses of our unconscious, he touches on those themes which are the most central ones of his own distinctive vision - the aesthetic, phantasy, play, imagination, and art.

I think we fundamentally misunderstand and distort Marcuse's vision if we think that he was merely concerned with the aesthetic as one dimension of human life or one aspect of culture. On the contrary, his vision is essentially and *intrinsically* an aesthetic one. Aesthetic categories permeate every aspect of Marcuse's thinking. The centrality of the aesthetic was already evident in Marcuse's early brilliant and ecstatic review of Marx's 1844 *Economic and Philosophical Manuscripts*. Marcuse was one of the first to declare that the publication of the *Manuscripts* "must become a crucial event in the history of Marxist studies."[21] In *Eros and Civilization* there is an almost playful use of the Heideggerian technique of philosophical etymology where Marcuse seeks to demonstrate "the inner connection between pleasure, sensuousness, beauty, truth, art, and freedom - a connection revealed in the philosophical history of the term *aesthetic*."[22]

Phantasy "plays a most decisive function in the total mental structure: it links the deepest layers of the unconscious with the highest products of consciousness (art), the dream with the reality; it preserves the archetypes of the genus, the perpetual but repressed ideas of the collective and individual memory, the tabooed images of freedom."[23] Sometimes Marcuse writes - and I believe that this is one of his core beliefs - that in our time not only is philosophy dead, but that Critical Theory itself is no longer adequate for keeping alive the "tabooed images of freedom." The Great Refusal, "the protest against unnecessary repression, the struggle for the ultimate form of freedom,"[24] can *only* find proper expression in phantasy and art - surrealistic and irrealistic art which inverts what we normally take to be reality. It is only phantasy - whose "logic" works beneath the control and domination of consciousness - that is uncompromising in its demands. This emphasis on phantasy and its expression in art even shows up in Marcuse's analysis and condemnation of "Soviet Marxism." It might seem strange that some of Marcuse's most incisive remarks about the role of art in society should appear in *Soviet Marxism*. But it is not at all strange when we grasp what Marcuse takes to be the essential "political force" of art:

> But art as a political force is art only in so far as it preserves the images of liberation; in a society which is in its totality the negation of these images, art can preserve them only by total refusal, that is, by not succumbing to the standards of the unfree reality, either in style, or in form, or in substance. The more totalitarian these standards become, the more reality controls all language and all communication, the more irrealistic and surrealistic will art tend to be, the more it will be driven from the concrete to the abstract, from harmony to dissonance, from content to form. Art is thus the refusal of everything that has been made part and parcel of reality . . . . The Soviet state by administrative decree prohibits the transcendence of art; it thus eliminates even the ideological reflex of freedom in an unfree society. Soviet realistic art, complying with the decree, becomes an instrument of social control in the last still nonconformist dimension of human existence.[25]

The dialectic of negativity - the theme that Marcuse shared with Adorno - reaches its extremity and deepest human level in phantasy and art - "the last still non-conformist dimension of human existence." *Eros and Civilization* ends with a vision of the possible union of instinct and reason where a *liberated* Eros even triumphs over death - Thanatos. But this is not Marcuse's last word.

One-Dimensional Man is Marcuse's most ambiguous book. But its ambiguity is rooted in the concrete social situation that Marcuse is addressing. Marcuse himself indicates this ambiguity when he tells us:

> *One-Dimensional Man* will vacillate throughout between two contradictory hypotheses: (1) that advanced industrial society is capable of containing qualitative change for the foreseeable future; (2) that the forces and tendencies exist which may break this containment and explode the society.[26]

But even this formulation does not accurately represent what Marcuse explores. For the first hypothesis that he lists still speaks of a society that "is capable of *containing* qualitative change." This presupposes that the power of negativity is still operative - still implicit in what we are, and still demands realization. Yet the spectre that haunts Marcuse's analysis is one where in advanced industrial societies human nature - even our instinctual nature - is being so drastically transformed that there is nothing left to be "contained" - that the power of negativity itself is being undermined and eliminated. Marcuse's inferno is one in which human beings are being so thoroughly desubliminated that there isn't even the possibility of the "instinctual revolt against the established reality principle," a nightmarish world in which "the last still nonconformist dimension of human existence" is being systematically eliminated, a world where even radical critics of society like Marcuse end up with their picture on the covers of slick magazines that titillate a society that "loves" its critics and renders them completely harmless. It is the world in which - to use Philip Reiff's term - there is the triumph of the therapeutic - where we treat ourselves and others treat us as ministering "cures" and "false" gratifications to "false" needs. This is a world that is *beyond* total alienation, repression, and domination. When there is nothing left to be repressed, the concept of repression itself loses all sense. It is perhaps evidence of "the cunning of Reason" (*die List der Vernunft*) that Marcuse's most pessimistic analysis of the fate of Western society, which raises the possibility that we may be living in a world where Critical Theory itself loses its meaning, was read by many as the great liberating tract of the sixties. But the reason for this is not difficult to discern when we consider the second more muted hypothesis that Marcuse explores - the hypothesis "that the forces and tendencies exist which may break the containment and explode the society." Marcuse still holds out for the possibility of that improbable configuration of tendencies and forces which will bring about a total revolution. We have not yet quite reached "the end of man," the end of the instinctual demand for liberation and happiness. No longer can we share Marx's confidence about the emergence of a class - the proletariat - which becomes the agent of revolution. But there is still a chance for "qualitative change." The full ambiguity of Marcuse's position - one which reflects the ambiguity of our situation - emerges sharply in the concluding sentences of *One-Dimensional Man*.

> But the chance is that, in this period, the historical extremes may meet again: the most advanced consciousness of humanity, and its most exploited force. It is nothing but a chance. The critical theory of society possesses no concepts which could bridge the gap between the present and the future; holding no promise and showing no success, it remains negative. Thus it wants to remain loyal to those who, without hope, have given and give their life to the Great Refusal. At the beginning of the fascist era, Walter Benjamin wrote: *Nur um der Hoffnungslosen willen ist uns die Hoffnung gegeben*. It is only for the sake of those without hope that hope is given to us.[27]

Marcuse's writings after *One-Dimensional Man* fluctuate between his two contradictory hypotheses: between the rhetoric of believing that we are on the verge of seeing the revolution come to life and the warning that we are left with only the (impotent?) Great Refusal.

But he never gave up hope; he never submitted to the despair of thinking that the power of negativity could not assert itself. He searched - in what sometimes seems like a desperate manner - for the signs of those social movements and tendencies that were progressive and liberating. He was open to new possibilities and enthusiastically supported them in speech and deed. He never accepted the lament over the death of the New Left, and he claimed that the women's movement may yet turn out to be the most radical movement of our times. To the end he encouraged and personified the demand for happiness and liberation. In all his activities he was "life affirming."

I have been primarily focusing on Marcuse as a negative thinker, as one of the most persistent radical critics of our time, but what was so beautiful about Marcuse (and I am using "beautiful" in a way in which he would have used it) is that there was a deep harmony between Marcuse as a thinker and Marcuse as a man. Those who knew him even slightly were deeply affected by his charm, his humor, his playfulness, his sheer zest and delight in living, his own capacity for the pleasure of being alive. It is this quality that evoked such profound resonances among those who were inspired by him, and so much hostility and *resentment* among those who envied him.

There is a temptation on an occasion such as this one where we have come together to honor Marcuse to eulogize him. But it is not my intention to give a eulogy, and I think that he would be impatient and disdainful of such academic rituals. Rather I have tried to present the strongest and most sympathetic case for Marcuse because I want to carry the spirit of negativity one step further and sharply criticize him. I want to explore the gaps and omissions in his powerful vision.

Every strong thinker has his or her insight and blindness. In critically assessing a thinker it is sometimes more revealing to focus upon what he or she ignores, doesn't explore, and doesn't say. So with Marcuse there are crucial problems for his own project that never quite come into the foreground - they are like a penumbra, hovering in partial obscurity. These are the themes and problems related to the nature of community, communication, intersubjectivity, and the nature of practical rationality in which individuals are oriented to working together to achieve a rational consensus concerning the norms that are to govern their lives. It would be a slander to suggest that Marcuse was unaware of these themes. There is plenty of evidence that he envisioned new ways in which individuals might communicate with each other and with nature, and which would overcome repression and domination. But there is little evidence that he ever subjected these themes to careful, systematic analysis. They certainly do not play the dominating role that the triad of Reason, Freedom, and Happiness plays in his critical thinking. Yet I want to suggest that without a proper analysis of these concepts, there is the real danger that Marcuse's triad remains abstract and "false," it lacks "determinate negation."

Consider the concept of Reason and the central role that it plays in Marcuse's thought. It certainly makes sense in interpreting Hegel to emphasize in the strongest possible way the contrast between abstract

Verstand and concrete *Vernunft* - and to stress the dynamic quality of Reason that works through history and demands realization - a realization that entails Freedom. Marcuse is extraordinarily incisive about the shrinkage and distortion of "Reason" in advanced industrial societies - and the ways in which reason becomes "the Logos of domination." We can appreciate his forceful critique of Weber's concept of *zweckrationalitat* and be sympathetic when he declares, "It is difficult to see reason at all in the ever more solid 'shell of bondage' which is being constructed. Or is there perhaps already in Max Weber's concept of reason the irony that understands but disavows? Does he by any chance mean to say: And this you call 'reason'?"[28] But we cannot leave matters here if our intention is to explore the possibility of developing concepts that are adequate for a critique of our contemporary situation. We cannot avoid the deep question that has been posed in theory and practice: Is there an alternative to "bourgeois reason"? Is there an alternative to the narrow economic sense of reason where we think of reason as simply the effective or efficient means to pregiven ends? I do not believe it is intellectually viable simply to invoke some variant of Hegelian *Vernunft* without a serious attempt to explicate this concept and to justify a more adequate and comprehensive understanding of rationality. Otherwise we are confronted with the danger that Hegel himself saw so well where "One bare assurance is worth just as much as another."[29] Without engaging in such a project, then, the very basis of a critical theory of society is threatened.

Nor do I think it is satisfactory to project an ideal of a "new *rationality of gratification* in which reason and happiness converge,"[30] where reason and instinct can unite, where the sensuous becomes rational and the rational becomes sensuous. What concretely does this mean? If we are to take seriously (or even playfully) the suggestion that the qualitative difference between "socialist society as a free society and the existing society" is to be found in the "aesthetic-erotic dimension"[31] then we must not only comprehend what we are talking about, but ask ourselves what type of social institutions in a "post-industrial" world can embody such a "rationality of gratification." We are confronted here not only with the danger of vacuity, but the more ominous danger where the demand for absolute liberation and freedom turns into its opposite - absolute terror.

This is not the place to sketch out what I mean by a comprehensive understanding of rationality that gives a prominent place to the type of practical rationality that can be institutionalized in a free society. But at least let me indicate that such a concept of rationality is not only intrinsically dialogical and communicative but places upon us the *practical* demand to work toward that form of democratic socialism in which the material conditions exist whereby individuals can confront each other as equals and jointly participate in open communication. It is my own conviction that we find the seeds for such a dialogical conception of practical rationality in the best work of the pragmatic thinkers - including Pierce, Dewey, and Mead[32] - a theme that has been taken up and extended in new ways by Apel and Habermas.

One of the great blind spots of Marcuse - and indeed of the older

Frankfurt thinkers - was the failure to see this and to misjudge the pragmatic movement as being only one more variant of the positivism that they abhorred and detested.

An analogous failure of "determinate negation" turns up in the meaning and role of the concept of potentiality - especially human potentiality. Marcuse is extraordinarily perceptive about the fundamental character of potentiality in Hegel, Marx, and even Freud. We cannot begin to grasp the distinctive power of Hegel and Marx unless we realize how they revitalized the concept of potentiality - a revitalization that represents a dialectical appropriation of the Greek, especially the Aristotelian, concept of potentiality which is so intimately related to *energia* and *dynamis*. Marcuse even tells us that "since ontology is the doctrine of the most general forms of being and as such reflects human insight into the most general structure of reality, there can be little wonder that the basic concepts of Aristotelian and Hegelian ontology were the same."[33] The deep motivation for Marcuse's relentless attack on all forms of positivism and empiricism is that they mutilate and abandon the concept of potentiality. If the real is mistakenly identified with the historically given, then we can no longer speak of a "true" human potentiality which has been suppressed and repressed by a "false" existing reality. We can no longer speak of the power of negativity that lies at the heart of all being and demands realization. The fate, indeed the very intelligibility, of Critical Theory depends on a viable concept of human potentiality. Marcuse emphasized this over and over again. But this very insight reveals a basic dilemma. For as Marcuse himself tells us, we can no longer accept the ontology and metaphysics of Aristotle and Hegel. And yet their concepts of potentiality are intimately bound up with their ontology and metaphysics. So the acute problem becomes, how are we to "reconstruct" the concept of potentiality? How are we to appropriate the vitally important idea that there is a "true" human potentiality which is being defeated by an "untrue" repressive reality without illicitly smuggling in a ontology and metaphysics that are no longer viable? How are we to negate the abstract concept of human potentiality and give it "determinate negation"? How are we to meet the challenge that relying on the concept of "true human potentiality" has become an intellectual crutch that lacks justification or warrant? This is not a rarified philosophical or intellectual problem when we remind ourselves that however much we condemn totalitarianism and facism as "untrue" and "evil," they are *also* realizations of human potentialities.

The type of failure or inadequacy that I have been pointing out in the appeal to the concepts of Reason and potentiality can also be seen in Marcuse's use of the concepts of Freedom and Happiness. I do not think that one finds in Marcuse the resources to make the subtle and crucial discriminations between *individual* and *public*, communal, freedom and happiness - the types of freedom and happiness that only come into existence and can be sustained through the sharing and interactions of individuals in their plurality. What always seems to be missing in Marcuse is not "Man" or "human potentialities," but *men* - or better, human beings in their plurality who only *achieve* their humanity in and through each other. I want to reiterate that Marcuse is certainly aware of what I am trying to stress. I think he was remarkably perceptive about the communal joy and happiness that is experienced when individuals join together and act together to oppose repression, domination, and exploitation. My criticism is that he failed to develop for us the concepts and theoretical orientation required to comprehend these phenomena.

It may seem outrageous, but I am tempted to suggest that Marcuse's deepest flaw was his failure to appreciate what is concretely involved in social and political life. After all, the emphasis on the primacy of the social dimension of human life is the primary legacy of Marx and Hegel. And yet, we never find in Marcuse a careful analysis of what precisely constitutes the sociality and intersubjectivity of human beings. For all Marcuse's emphasis on "social reality" and the negativity that lies at the core of "existing historical social reality" - expressions that are repeated over and over again in his work - he doesn't probe what is the meaning and "essence" of a "social being."

Hegel, at the beginning of the famous discussion of Lordship and Bondage, announces the theme of Recognition (*die Anerkennung*) - a theme that sets the task and indicates the telos of the rest of the *Phenomenology*. "Self-Consciousness exists in and for itself when, and by the fact that, it so exists for another; that is, it exists only in being acknowledged."[34] We know what the end of this journey requires for Hegel. For "Self-Consciousness" can only come to rest, can only complete its journey and thereby become what it truly is - infinite and free-when it is recognized by another "Self-Consciousness" that is itself infinite and free. The concrete realization of freedom can only be achieved in and through the freedom of the "others" that I confront. The realization of freedom makes no sense when it is thought of as an individual project which is not bound up with the freedom of "others" - "others" who no longer threaten and oppose me, but achieve and reflect the freedom that we mutually share. For Hegel, as for Marcuse, history thus far has been "the highway of despair," the history of domination and "false consciousness." This is the aspect of the Recognition theme that Marcuse continually emphasized. He agrees with Freud that there has been a "recurrent cycle" of "domination-rebellion-domination," where the "second domination is not simply a repetition of the first one; the cyclical movement is *progress* in domination."[35] If one reads history as Marcuse did, where we are reaching the dialectical extremity of this cycle, then it makes eminently good sense to focus on this aspect of the Recognition theme. But if we are to demystify this concept of Recognition, if we are to extract the "truth" implicit in this *Begriff*, and come to an understanding of what a society would be like in which the mutual achievement and recognition of freedom is to be realized, then we cannot avoid asking ourselves how is this freedom to be embodied in the social institutions. Society is not an abstraction; it consists of a complex interlocking set of social institutions and practices. We cannot responsibly avoid the hard questions of how institutions and practices in a socialist society are to embody Reason, Freedom and Happiness. If Critical Theory is to justify its claim to comprehend and encourage the real tendencies and potentialities that can effect such a revolution, then we must try to understand and engage in the forms of *praxis* that will bring us closer to the "qualitative difference" of a socialist free society.

The essential thrust of Marcuse's thinking and language is toward totality. He never waivered in his thinking that the dominant tendency of our time is towards totalitarianism. If this situation is to be confronted, then nothing less than a total revolution is required - a revolution that totally "negates," "destroys," shatters, explodes the performance principle- "the prevailing historical form of the *reality principle*." It is true, as I have emphasized, that Marcuse was always on the look out for and encouraged the signs of opposition - whether they were to be found on the streets of Haight Ashbury or the liberation movements in the Third World - that might yet combine into that configuration that could bring about such a revolution. But even here, what Marcuse was looking for was not piecemeal reform, but *total* revolution.

Although it was not his intention - indeed it was the *opposite* of what he believed and intended - I think that at times he was insensitive to the consequences of the rhetoric of the demand for total revolution: the growing sense of total impotence. Perhaps the greatest failing of the international New Left movement of the sixties was its naivete - how once it became clear that the phantasy and dream of a qualitatively different world in which the "rationality of gratification" triumphs was not to be immediately realized, many of those involved were all to ready to seek their gratification in other ways. This situation can certainly *not* be blamed on Marcuse. He fought despair, defeatism, and escapism to the end of his life. Nevertheless it is the dark side of the abstract demand for total destruction and total liberation.

I can well imagine a champion of Marcuse objecting to what I have been saying. Insofar as I criticize Marcuse for a failure of "determinate negation," insofar as I call for the need to try to develop a dialogic conception of rationality, insofar as I want to appeal to concepts such as communication, community and intersubjectivity in gaining a theoretical and practical perspective of what is going on in society - it is I who am being innocent and abstract. For I have failed to realize how all these concepts are in danger of being corrupted by "bourgeois reason," and have failed to appreciate the depth of the crisis we are experiencing. Today our plight is one where the whole heritage of philosophical and intellectual concepts in the West has been so thoroughly perverted and distorted, that one must resort to more drastic and radical means to keep the dream of freedom and happiness alive.

I certainly want to concede that all I have done is to make a few suggestions, and that if I take my own demand seriously, it requires "working out" and "working through" - my own project requires "determinate negation." But I would at least like to defend the idea that if there is any hope for Critical Theory, it cannot remain content with the "Great Refusal" and "negative dialectics." And I want to make such an *apologia* by appealing to what is latent in Marcuse himself. For there is a deep tension between what might be called the manifest of "official" theoretical orientation in Marcuse and what is latent and "unofficial."

The manifest position is one that tells the story of how everything in Western society has been relentlessly working toward the triumph of totalitarianism in all forms of culture and human life reaching down even to our unconscious instinctual phantasy dream world. It is this very logic of culmination that has created the material conditions and the possibility for a total revolution - even though such a revolution may never come to be and may remain only a dream.

But there is a latent, more muted thesis that keeps surfacing in Marcuse and which I think is closer to the "truth." For with the spread of domination and what frequently appears to be the inexhaustible "power" of the so-called Super Powers, there is also the counterthrust - the increasing awareness of impotence, impotence to deal with national and international crises. We are not simply living in a monolithic, interlocking technocratic society, but a society that keeps creating its own opposition, in which there is breakup: the spontaneous generation of movements of protest where suddenly individuals decide to take their fate into their own hands in the face of what appear to be overwhelming forces opposing them. Throughout the world the impotence of "power" is becoming sharper and more acute together with the creation of those tendencies, incipient movements, and public spaces within which individuals can collectively and communicatively act together to achieve mutually shared goals. It is this latent theme that I think represents Marcuse's true legacy. If we take this seriously, it requires those of us who have been inspired by Marcuse's own intellectual courage and joy to try again and again to comprehend what is going on in the prolonged crisis of our times and to engage in those forms of *praxis* that are still open to us. Not to make this attempt and to give in to defeatism would be to betray what is most vital in Marcuse's legacy - even when it requires us to negate and pass beyond Marcuse himself.

NOTES

1. See my earlier paper, "Herbert Marcuse: An Immanent Critique," *Social Theory and Practice* 1, no. 4, (Fall 1971).

2. Herbert Marcuse, *Reason and Revolution: Hegel and the Rise of Social Theory*. Second Edition (London, 1955), p. vii.

3. *Ibid.*, pp. 26-27.

4. Hegel's *Phenomenology of Spirit*, trans. A. V. Miller (Oxford, 1977), p. 19.

5. *Reason and Revolution*, p. 26.

6. *Ibid.*, p. 147.

7. *Ibid.*, p. 66.

8. *Ibid.,* p. 148.

9. *Ibid.*, p. 261.

10. *Ibid.*, p. 258.

11. Marcuse, "Philosophy and Critical Theory," in *Negations* (Boston, 1968), p. 143.

12. *Ibid.*, p. 142.

13. *Ibid.*, p. 148.

14. See "The Concept of Essence," in *Negations*, pp. 55ff.
15. Marcuse, *Eros and Civilization* (Boston, 1955), p. 35.
16. *Ibid.*, p. 93.
17. *Ibid.*, p. 121.
18. *Ibid.*, p. 19.
19. *Ibid.*, p. 118.
20. *Ibid.*, p. 122.
21. Marcuse, "The Foundations of Historical Materialism," in *Studies in Critical Philosophy* (London, 1972),   p. 3.
22. *Eros and Civilization*, p. 172.
23. *Ibid.*, p. 140.
24. *Ibid.*, p. 149.
25. Marcuse, *Soviet Marxism* (New York, 1958), p. 132.
26. Marcuse, *One-Dimensional Man* (Boston, 1964), p. xv.
27. *Ibid.*, p. 257.
28. Marcuse, "Industrialization and Capitalism in the Work of Max Weber," in *Negations*, pp. 225-26.
29. *Hegel's Phenomenology of Spirit*, p. 49.
30. *Eros and Civilization*, p. 224.
31. Marcuse, *Five Lectures* (Boston, 1970), p. 68.
32. See my discussion of Pierce and Dewey in *Praxis and Action*.
33. *Reason and Revolution*, p. 42.
34. *Hegel's Phenomenology of Spirit*, p. 111.
35. *Eros and Civilization*, p. 89.

CHAPTER THREE

Reflections on Marcuse's Theory of Remembrance

Martin Jay

In a book dedicated to the memory of Herbert Marcuse, it is perhaps particularly fitting to focus our attention on the special place held in Marcuse's thought by the concept of memory. Many of his earlier commentators have, in fact, already noted its importance.[1] One of the more astute of their number, Fredric Jameson, even went so far as to claim that the theoretical foundation of Marcuse's philosophy

> takes the form of a profound and almost platonic valorization of memory, anamnesis, in human existence. Indeed, it is not too much to say that Mnemosyne occupies something of the same emblematic and mythopoetic position in Marcuse's thinking that the deities of Eros and Thanatos hold in Freud's late metapsychology.[1]

But precisely what that position was and how it was defended has not yet been subjected to sustained critical analysis. The following remarks are thus intended as a first step in that direction.

From his earliest writings, beginning with *Hegels Ontologie* in 1931, until his very last, *The Aesthetic Dimension*, in 1977, Marcuse returned again and again to what he saw as the liberating power of remembrance. In almost all of his major works, most notably *Eros and Civilization*, *One-Dimensional Man*, and *Counterrevolution and Revolt*, he introduced a virtually identical defense of that power and expressed alarm at its current weakened status.   Matched among 20th-century Marxists perhaps only by Walter Benjamin,[3] Marcuse attempted to harness the energies of recollection for revolutionary purposes.

The sources of his persistent fascination with memory can be traced for analytical purposes to four separate stimuli: his early philosophical training, his adherence to critical Marxism, his special concern for aesthetics and his radical appropriation of psychology. Although often conflated in his discussions of anamnesia, these different sources contributed distinctive elements to his argument, elements which can be isolated and critically analyzed.   In so doing, the strengths and weaknesses of Marcuse's theory of remembrance can be more accurately assessed.

From its earliest beginnings, Western philosophy has been drawn to the issues raised by present knowledge of past events.[3]   From Plato's the *Meno* and the *Theaetetus* through Aristotle's *De Memoria et Reminiscentia*, Augustine's *Confessions*, Hume's *Treatise* on Human Nature, Bergson's *Matter and Memory* and on up to Russell's *Analysis on Mind* and Ryle's *The Concept of Mind*, the greatest philosophers of the Western tradition have wrestled with the epistemological puzzles presented by memory. Contemporary philosophers such as E. J. Furlong, W. von Leyden, Brian Smith and Norman Malcolm continue to devote long and learned studies to the same, still unresolved issues.[4]   Marcuse, however, seems to have paid little attention to this body of what might be called mainstream speculation about memory.   Aside from an occasional vague reference to the "ancient theory of knowledge as *recollection*,"[6] he ignored the arguments of these thinkers.   Instead, as might be expected, he relied far more on the less technical treatments of the problem in the German idealist and phenomenological traditions.

Although no firm evidence appears in his writings, it is likely that the latter first impressed upon him the importance of remembrance.   In particular, his philosophical apprenticeship under Martin Heidegger in the late 1920s should probably be accounted decisive in this regard.   For in Heidegger's *Being and Time* of 1927, a work whose influence on his early development Marcuse has freely acknowledged, memory played a central role.   To characterize the wayward course of Western philosophy since the pre-Socratics, Heidegger introduced the notion of *Seinsvergessenheit*, the forgetting of Being.[7] This forgetting, he contended, was so pervasive that language itself had lost the capacity to treat Being as a meaningful reality.   His own philosophy, Heidegger claimed, was an effort to reverse this collective amnesia and restore consciousness of Being to its proper place.   Although Marcuse soon came to recognize the vacuous nature of Heidegger's notion of Being, he nonetheless retained his teacher's insistence that something extraordinarily important had been forgotten in the modern world.   Because remembrance was a window on this fundamental reality, it had ontological as well as epistemological implications.

What these implications were became clearer to Marcuse in his first prolonged study of Hegel, directed by Heidegger, which appeared as *Hegels Ontologie* in 1931.   In examining Hegel's *Logic* with its central category of negativity, Marcuse argued

> This "not," this negativity which Being is, is itself never present in
> the sphere of immediacy, is itself not and is never *present*. This
> "not" is always precisely the *other* of immediacy and the other of
> presence, that which is never as *present* precisely *never* is and what,
> however, constitutes its *Being*. This "not," this negativity is the
> immediate present always already past at every moment. The
> Being of present being resides therefore always already in a past, but
> in a, to a certain degree, "intemporal" past (*Logic*, II, 3), in a past
> which still always is present and *out* of which precisely Being *is*. A
> being is at each moment what it is in its immediate present through
> memory . . . . With the phenomenon of memory, Hegel opens the
> new dimension of Being which constitutes Being as authentic
> having-beeness (*Gewesenheit*): the dimension of essence.[8]

Memory, *Erinnerung*, in other words, permits access to an essential,
"negative" level of reality, that "intemporal past" preserved on a second
ontological plane more basic than that of "positive" and immediate
appearance. The German language itself, so Hegel had noted, captured
this relationship: "In the verb *Sein* (to be) language has conserved
essence (*Wesen*) in the past participle of the verb, '*gewesen*.'"[9]

As Alison Pogrebin Brown has perceptively noted,[10] Marcuse's later
stress on two-dimensionality was foreshadowed here in his discussion of
the temporal aspect of Hegel's doctrine of essence. But whereas in *Hegels
Ontologie*, Marcuse identified essence entirely with the "intemporal past,"
in his later work, it was ambiguously related to the future as well. In his
1936 essay, "The Concept of Essence," written after his break with
Heidegger and his entrance into the Institute of Social Research, Marcuse
linked essence with the Aristotelian notion of potentiality. "All historical
struggles," he argued,

> for a better organization of the impoverished conditions of
> existence, as well as all of suffering mankind's religious and ethical
> ideal conceptions of a more just order of things, are preserved in the
> dialectical concept of the essence of man, where they have become
> elements of the dialectical practice linked to dialectical theory.
> There can also be experiences of potentialities that have never been
> realized . . . . In idealist philosophy the timeless past dominates the
> concept of essence. But when a theory associates itself with the
> progressive forces of history, the recollection of what can
> authentically be becomes a power that shapes the future.[11]

Yet, for Marcuse, the identification of essence with the past as well as the
future remained a powerful premise of his thought. Returning to Hegel
in *Eros and Civilization*, he enthusiastically endorsed his cyclical view of
time, remarking:

> The fact that remembrance here appears as the decisive existential

category for the highest form of Being indicates the inner trend of Hegel's philosophy. Hegel replaces the idea of progress by that of a cyclical development which moves, self-sufficient, in the reproduction and consummation of what *is*. This development presupposes the entire history of man (his subjective and objective world) and the comprehension of his history - the remembrance of his past. The past remains present; it is the very life of the spirit; what has been decides on what is. Freedom implies reconciliation-redemption of the past.[12]

And in *Counterrevolution and Revolt*, he contended, now with special reference to Goethe's view of science, "The Marxian vision recaptures the ancient theory of knowledge as *recollection*: 'science' as the *re*discovery of the true *Forms* of things, distorted and denied in the established reality, the perpetual *materialistic core of idealism*."[13]

What, of course, made it imperative for Marcuse to link essence with both the past and the future was this adherence to Marx. At first glance, Marcuse seems like an unlikely stimulant to the notion that recapturing the past, whether understood as the repository of essence or not, would be a revolutionary project. For all his stress on grasping reality historically, Marx himself appears to have had little use for memory as a radical tool. In the *Eighteenth Brumaire of Louis Bonaparte*, he mocked those earlier revolutions, such as the English and French, that had sought legitimacy by cloaking themselves in the mantles of their historical predecessors. "The social revolution of the nineteenth century," he argued,

cannot draw its poetry from the past, but only from the future. It cannot begin with itself before it has stripped off all superstition in regard to the past. Earlier revolutions required recollections of past world history in order to drug themselves concerning their own content. In order to arrive at its own content, the revolution of the nineteenth century must let the dead bury the dead.[14]

Although one might, as Christian Lenhardt has suggested,[15] read Marx's labor theory of value as a reminder to see the capital of the present as the coagulated labor power of previous generations, Marx himself never seems to have explicitly drawn the conclusion that remembering the workers of the past was a key stimulus to revolutionary consciousness. Instead, he contended, "the tradition of all the dead generations weighs like a nightmare on the brain of the living."[16]

It was not really until Georg Lukacs introduced the idea of reification in *History and Class Consciousness* that the emancipatory potential of memory was tapped by a Marxist thinker of note. Lukacs had, in fact, pointed to the power of remembrance in his pre-Marxist *The Theory of the Novel* while discussing time in Flaubert's *Sentimental Education*:

Only in the novel and in certain epic forms resembling the novel does memory occur as a creative force affecting the object and transforming it. The genuinely epic quality of such memory is t affirmative experience of the life process. The duality of interiorit and the outside world can be abolished for the subject if he (the subject) glimpses the organic unity of his whole life through the process by which his living present has grown from the stream of his past life dammed up within his memory.[17]

After Lukacs' conversion to Marxism in 1918, he no longer stressed the retrospective nature of totalization, as he had in *The Theory of the Novel*. A true totality would be achieved only when the proletariat, the universal class, dereified the objective structures of the social world and recognized them as their own creations. Totalization was thus a practical activity of the future, not a contemplative one directed towards the past. And yet, the concept of dereification implied a certain type of remembering, for what had to be recaptured were the human origins of a social world that had been mystified under capitalism as a kind of "second nature."

Marcuse recognized the link between memory and dereification, at least implicitly, in his 1932 essay "The Foundations of Historical Materialism," where he reviewed Marx's newly published Paris manuscripts. "Because it is dependent on the conditions pre-established by history," he argued,

the praxis of transcendence must, in order to be genuine transcendence, reveal these conditions and appropriate them. Insight into objectification as insight into the historical and social situation of man reveals the historical conditions of this situation and so achieves the *practical force and concrete form* through which it can become the lever of revolution. We can now also understand how far questions concerning the *origin* of estrangement and insight into the *origin* of private property must be an integrating element in a positive theory of revolution.[18]

The explicit linkage of dereification with remembrance came somewhat later in the work of Marcuse's colleagues at the Institute of Social Research. In an important letter of February 29, 1940, to Walter Benjamin, Adorno responded with considerable enthusiasm to the theory of forgetting propounded in Benjamin's essay "On Some Motifs in Baudelaire."[19] In that essay, Benjamin had introduced his now celebrated contrast between the integrated, meaningful experience he called "*Erfahrung*" and the atomizing, incoherent alternative he called "*Erlebnis*." Benjamin tied the former to Proust's idea of "involuntary memory," which he claimed was possible only when men were immersed in an ongoing, communal tradition. In the modern world, such a tradition was lacking; the only experience thus possible was the impoverished disorientation of *Erlebnis*.

In his letter to Benjamin, Adorno asked, "Wouldn't it be the task to connect the entire opposition between *Erlebnis* and *Erfahrung* to a dialectical theory of forgetting? One could also say: to a theory of reification. For every reification is a forgetting: objects become thinglike at the moment when they are seized without all their elements

neous, where something of them is forgotten."[20]
reason to assume Marcuse knew of this letter, in one
cluded in Horkheimer and Adorno's *Dialectic of*
d "Le Prix du Progres," the key phrase "all
ng" was reproduced.[21]   Significantly, it was linked
domination of nature, one of the Frankfurt School's
erns.   The lines preceding read: "perennial domination over
medical and non-medical techniques, are made possible only by the
process of oblivion.   The loss of memory is a transcendental condition for
science."[22]

In Marcuse's later work, the same linkages between forgetting,
reification and the domination of nature appear. The passage quoted
above from *Counterrevolution and Revolt*, with its veiled reference to
Goethe's theory of science as the recovery of primary forms, follows
directly a discussion of the redemption of nature as a "subject-object" with
intrinsic value in its own right.   The implication is that forgetting the
suffering of men is akin to forgetting the pain caused nature by its human
domination; remembrance somehow permits us to see the connections and
honor the subjective side of both nature and man.

"All reification is a forgetting" also served another function in
Marcuse's theory of remembrance, as a reminder of the negative potential
in art.   The final paragraph of *The Aesthetic Dimension* begins by quoting
the phrase from *The Dialectic of Enlightenment* and continues: "Art
fights reification by making the petrified world speak, sing, perhaps dance.
Forgetting past suffering and past joy alleviates life under a repressive
reality principle.   In contrast, remembrance spurs the drive for the
conquest of suffering and the permanence of joy."[23]

The third source of Marcuse's celebration of memory was, in fact, the
role it played in his vision of aesthetics.   For much Western art, as for
Western philosophy, memory has proven an object of singular fascination.
To the Greeks, Mnemosyne was the mother by Zeus of the nine Muses.
The more recent figure of Proust, to whom Marcuse himself referred
approvingly,[24] comes immediately to mind in this regard, but he was by no
means alone in associating art with remembrance.   The English
romantics, for example, were intensely interested in the links between
memory, personal identity and imagination.[25]   Wordsworth, in particular,
sought ways to recapture and render intelligible his personal past in such
works as *The Prelude*. Coleridge defined "the primary imagination" as "a
repetition in the finite mind of the eternal act of creation."[26] Later
Victorian writers, such as Dickens in *David Copperfield* and Ruskin in *The
Seven Lamps of Architecture*, attempted to light what Ruskin called "the
lamp of memory" in order to escape the dreary present and renew contact
with a more beautiful past.[27]

Although Marcuse never directly acknowledged the influence of the
Romantic tradition, he was clearly in its debt, as the following passage
from *Counterrevolution and Revolt* demonstrates:

> On a primary level, art is recollection: it appeals to a
> preconceptual experience and understanding which reemerge in and

against the context of the social functioning of experience and understanding - against instrumentalist reasoning and sensibility.[28]

No less Romantic was his privileging of music among all the arts as the most essential repository of recollected truth:

> These extreme qualities, the supreme points of art, seem to be the prerogative of music . . . and within music, of melody. Here the melody - dominant, *cantabile*, is the basic unit of recollection: recurring through all variations, remaining when it is cut off and no longer carries the composition, it sustains the supreme point: in and against the richness and complexity of the work. It is the voice, beauty, calm of another world here on earth . . . .[29]

In *The Aesthetic Dimension*, Marcuse introduced memory into the very heart of artistic form itself:

> The medium of sensibility also constitutes the paradoxical relation of art to time - paradoxical because what is experienced through the medium of sensibility is present, while art cannot show the present without showing it as past. What has become form in the work of art has happened: it is recalled, re-presented. The mimesis translates reality into memory.[30]

In short, for Marcuse the promise of future happiness embodied in art was dialectically related to its retention of past instances of joy and fulfillment.

In combatting the "affirmative character of culture"[31] as a realm of transcendent values, Marcuse was insistent on the sensuous, material, even erotic nature of artistic pleasure. His linkage of art and Eros was abetted by his radical appropriation of psychology into his version of Critical Theory, an appropriation that also strengthened his interest in the liberating power of remembrance. Psychology thus joined philosophy, critical Marxism and aesthetics as an especially potent source of his theory of memory. In *Hegels Ontologie*, he had warned against reducing memory to a psychological category,[32] but after his entrance into the Institute of Social Research, where psychology was a subject of considerable interest, he grew increasingly open to the psychological dimension of anamnesia. The psychology of memory to which Marcuse was drawn was not, to be sure, that of the experimentalists, such as Hermann Ebbinghaus,[33] whose scientific data on the functioning of memory he chose to ignore. It was instead the psychoanalysis of Freud that provided him with a psychological theory of memory to complement those he had derived from philosophy, Marxism and aesthetics. Beginning with his 1898 paper, "On the Psychic Mechanism of Forgetfulness"[34] and elaborating in later works such as *The Psychopathology of Everyday Life*, Freud had argued that the loss of memory was due to the repression of traumatic experience or unpleasant thoughts that had engendered pain or anxiety in the past, most of which were sexual or aggressive in nature. One of the fundamental objectives of psychotherapy was thus the anamnestic recovery of forgotten and repressed experiences, thoughts, desires or impulses. Once remembered, they could be dealt with in a conscious and responsible fashion, rather than being allowed to fester as the source of unconsciously generated neurotic symptoms.

Marcuse adopted Freud's linkage of forgetting and repression, but drew on an essay on childhood amnesia by his former Institute colleague, Ernst Schachtel,[35] to give it a subtle twist. Instead of emphasizing the forgetting of painful or traumatic episodes in the past, he stressed instead the repression of pleasurable activities that society could not willingly tolerate. The source of forgetting was thus not so much the intrapsychic needs of repression as the external demands of a repressive society. Citing Nietzsche's link in the *Genealogy of Morals*[36] between the training of memory and the origins of morality, Marcuse condemned:

> the one-sidedness of memory-training in civilization: the faculty was chiefly directed toward remembering duties rather than pleasures; memory was linked with bad conscience, guilt and sin. Unhappiness and the threat of punishment, not happiness and the promise of freedom, linger in memory.[37]

What should be remembered by man instead, Marcuse contended, are those promises and potentialities "which had once been fulfilled in his dim past."[38] There was a time, he claimed, in the "archaic" prehistory of the species before socially induced surplus repression, a time controlled largely by the pleasure principle, which remembrance should labor to rescue. As he put it in his later essay, "Freedom and Freud's Theory of Instincts,"

> Originally, the organism in its totality and in all its activities and relationships is a potential field for sexuality, dominated by the pleasure principle.

(The notion of "origin" as Freud uses it has simultaneously structural-functional - and temporal, ontogenetic, and phylogenetic significance. The "original" structure of the instincts was the one which dominated in the prehistory of the species. It is transformed during the course of history but continues to be effective as a substratum, preconscious and unconscious, in the history of the individual and the species - most obviously in early childhood. The idea that mankind, in general and in its individuals, is still dominated by "archaic" powers is one of Freud's most profound insights.[39])

Although in this essay[40] Marcuse acknowledged that freedom from certain of these archaic powers, most notably those associated with the death instinct, would be itself a liberation, the burden of his argument was that remembering others was a precondition for the achievement of a utopian future.

With the psychological component introduced in *Eros and Civilization*, Marcuse's theory of remembrance was essentially complete. It provided him a potent weapon in his attempt to find an Archimedean point for a Critical Theory no longer able to rely on the *praxis* of a revolutionary proletariat as its ground. For, insofar as recollecting a different past prevents men from eternalizing the *status quo*, memory subverts one-dimensional consciousness and opens up the possibility of an alternative future. Moreover, it does so in a way that avoids the traditional bourgeois and social democratic ideology of history as evolutionary progress. As Benjamin had often pointed out,[41] the belief in a smooth, unilinear flow of time helps preserve the tendencies for domination existent in the present. In *Eros and Civilization*, Marcuse approvingly quoted Benjamin's observation that clocks were shot at during the July Revolution as evidence of the link between stopping ongoing temporality and achieving revolutionary change.[42] And in *One-Dimensional Man*, he cited Adorno's similar insight that "the spectre of man without memory . . . is more than an aspect of decline - it is necessarily linked with the principle of progress in bourgeois society."[43] By negating the past as mere preparation for the future and seeing that future as an extrapolation of tendencies in the present, the ideology of progress justified the suffering of past generations as necessary. It also made impossible that recapturing of past moments of happiness and fulfillment which memory preserved as beacons for the future. In fact, so Marcuse argued, the very notion of progress with its never-ending dissatisfaction with the present and impatient yearning for an improved tomorrow was one of the earmarks of a repressive society. In a true utopia, "time would not seem linear, as a perpetual line or rising curve, but cyclical, as the return in Nietzsche's idea of the 'perpetuity of pleasure.'"[44] Memory, by restoring the forgotten past, was thus a model of the utopian temporality of the future. In other words, it was not merely the content of what is remembered that constitutes the liberating power of memory, but also the very fact of memory's ability to reverse the flow of time that makes it a utopian faculty. If there is to be a true human totality in the future, anamnestic totalization in the present is one of its prefigurations.

The claims Marcuse made for the liberating power of remembrance were thus obviously very large ones. What now in conclusion can be said about their validity? Any answer to this question must begin with a consideration of precisely what Marcuse thought should be remembered. For it is clear than emancipatory remembrance was far more than that indiscriminate preservation of everything in the past condemned by Nietzsche in his "Use and Abuse of History" and Benjamin in his "Edward Fuchs: Collector and Historian." If memory has been trained by civilization to preserve duties and guilt, it must be re-trained to recover something else.

Marcuse's notion of that alternative contained, however, a certain ambiguity. At times, the Marxist in him protested against the ontologization of the content of memory; the dialectical concept of essence, we have seen him argue in his 1939 essay, contains only the historical struggles and ethical and religious ideals of past generations. In *Counterrevolution and Revolt*, he protested in a similar vein: that recollection "is not remembrance of a Golden Past (which never existed), of childhood innocence, primitive man, et cetera."[45]   In contrast, what must be remembered are the actual historical experiences and desires of our ancestors, not some imagined prehistorical era of perfect bliss. Indeed, as Benjamin once noted,[46] revolutionary motivation may well stem more from outrage over the indignities suffered by our fathers than hope for the comfort of our children.

But despite the historical intentions of these passages, at other times in his work, Marcuse fell back on what must be called an ontological theory of anamnesis.   Although he abandoned Heidegger's notion of a Being that had to be recollected and he criticized Hegel's idea of essence as an "intemporal past," in his appropriation of psychoanalysis, he retained their ontological biases.   Freud's archaic heritage meant that an individual's promises and potentialities "had once been fulfilled in his dim past,"[47] or as he put it elsewhere, the sensous form of beauty preserved "the memory of happiness that once was."[48]   Jameson captures this aspect of Marcuse's theory of remembrance when he writes:

> It is because we have known, at the beginning of life, a plenitude of psychic gratification, because we have known a time before all repression, a time in which, as in Schiller's nature, the elaborate specializations of later, more sophisticated consciousness had not yet taken place, a time that precedes the very separation of subject from its object, that memory, even the obscured and unconscious memory of that prehistoric paradise in the individual psyche, can fulfill its profound therapeutic, epistemological, and even political role . . . . The primary energy of revolutionary activity derives from this memory of prehistoric happiness which the individual can regain only through its externalization, through its reestablishment for society as a whole.[49]

Although on the surface, this type of remembrance seems to be historical in the sense that it recaptures a reality that allegedly existed in the past, a closer look at Marcuse's use of the archaic heritage shows it to be something else.   For when confronted with the anthropological evidence that Freud's theories cannot be corroborated, he retreated into the explanation that "We use Freud's anthropological speculation only in this sense: for its *symbolic* value.   The archiac events that the hypothesis stipulates may forever be beyond the realm of anthropological verification: the alleged consequences of these events are historical facts . . . ."[50]   What this admission implies, as he put it in *An Essay on Liberation*, is "not regression to a previous stage of civilization, but return to an imaginary *temps perdu* in the real life of mankind."[51]

But if the plenitude "remembered" is only symbolic and the *temps perdu* merely "imaginary," can one really talk of memory in the same way one does when recalling the actual defeats and struggles of our historical predecessors?   How, in fact, can we distinguish a true memory from what Brian Smith calls a "mnemic hallucination,"[52] if the reality remembered never actually occurred.   What Marcuse was obviously doing here was introducing a myth of original wholeness, of perfect presence, of the "remembering"[53] of what had been dismembered, whose roots, if in memory at all, were in remembered desire rather than remembered fulfillment. Very much in the spirit of his problematic call for a "biological foundation for socialism,"[54] Marcuse's exhortation to remember an "imaginary *temps perdu*" allowed him to smuggle an *a priori* philosophical anthropology into Critical Theory.

His symbolic adoption of Freud's archaic heritage also allowed him to side-step another troubling aspect of his theory of remembrance: its undefended identification of individual and collective memory. "Individual psychology," he wrote in *Eros and Civilization*, "is thus *in itself* group psychology in so far as the individual itself still is in archaic identity with the species. This archaic heritage bridges the 'gap between individual and mass psychology.'"[55] But precisely how far the individual was in fact in archaic identity with the species Marcuse did not say. For all Marcuse's contempt for Jung, a certain affinity can perhaps be discerned here. Assuming too quickly that individual and collective memory were virtually the same, he never conducted those experiments in personal recollection so painstakingly attempted by Benjamin. Marcuse's own *Berliner Kindheit um neunzzehnten Jahrhundert* remained unwritten. Nor did he rigorously investigate the differences between personal memory of an actual event or thought in a person's life and the collective historical memory of events antedating all living persons. Because the latter is preserved in the archival records and the often opaque processes of collective behavior and belief rather than in the living memories of present people, the hermeneutic process of recovery is different in each case. The dialectic of restitution between the present and past is more than mere remembrance of things past. As Benjamin understood,[57] there is both a destructive and constructive move necessary to explode a previous epoch out of the continuum of history and make it active in the present. At times, when, for example, he linked memory to imagination as a synthetic epistemological faculty "reassembling the bits and fragments which can be found in the distorted humanity and distorted nature," Marcuse seemed to sense this. But he never adequately developed the dynamics of mnemonic *praxis*.

One final difficulty in Marcuse's appropriation of anamnesis for revolutionary purposes was the problem of accounting for the new in history. Although Marcuse was firm in insisting that remembrance did not simply mean retrogression - a mistake for which Jung was chastened in *Eros and Civilization*[58] - he did not entirely escape the reproach that recollection is too close to repetition. The inadequacies of anamnestic totalization were perhaps nowhere as clearly perceived as in the work of Ernst Bloch, who preferred another Greek term, *anagnorisis*, or recognition. In an interview given at the 1968 Korcula summer school, which Marcuse also attended, Bloch spelled out his reasons:

The doctrine of *anamnesis* claims that we have knowledge only because we formerly knew. But then there could be no fundamentally new knowledge, no future knowledge. The soul merely meets in reality now what it always already knew as idea.

That is a circle within a circle and just as inaccurate as the other
theory (*anagnorisis*) is revealing: that the new is never completely
new for us because we bring something with us to measure by it . . . .
Anamnesis provides the reassuring evidence of complete similarity;
anagnorisis, however, is linked with reality by only a thin thread; it is
therefore alarming. *Anamnesis* has an element of attenuation
about it, it makes everything a gigantic *deja vu*, as if everything had
already been, *nil novi subanamnesi*.   But *anagnorisis* is a shock.[50]

Based on Bloch's idiosyncratic ontology of the "not-yet," *anagnorisis*
meant that one could recognize figural traces of the future in the past, but
the past itself contained no archaic heritage of plenitude.

Whether or not Bloch's alternative seems superior to Marcuse's
depends on one's confidence in his highly speculative philosophy of hope,
which cannot be evaluated here.   His criticism of anamnesis, however,
makes an important point, which is clarified still further if we turn to Paul
Ricoeur's well-known dichotomy, which he applied to hermeneutics as a
whole,[60] between mnemonics as a recollection of meaning and mnemonics
as an exercise of suspicion.   Ricoeur placed Freud, Nietzsche and Marx as
the great exemplars of the interpretative art of suspicious demystification.
The recollectors of meaning were mainly men of religion, for the opposite
of suspicion was faith, faith in a primal word that could be recovered.   In
Bloch's terms, *anamnesis* is a doctrine that derives from the belief in an
original meaning that can be recollected, whereas *anagnorisis*, while
holding out hope for a plenitude in the future, is suspicious of claims that
it existed in the past.

If one were to survey the Frankfurt School as a whole, one would
conclude that its attitude towards these alternatives was mixed.   In
Benjamin's search for an *Ursprache*, a perfect language in which words and
things are one, there is an elegiac impulse for recollected meaning.   But in
his stress on the constructive and destructive aspects of memory properly
applied there was an awareness that simple recollection does not suffice.
Similarly, in Adorno's warning against a philosophy of origins, his
stubborn insistence on a negative dialectic of non-identity, and his
acceptance of the inevitability of some reification, the mnemonics of
suspicion were paramount.   When Horkheimer speculated on religion
and concluded that no matter how utopian the future might be, the pain of
past generations could never be redeemed through remembrance,[61] he too
questioned the possibility of recovering a primal wholeness. Especially
when in his more Schopenhauerian moods, he despaired of mankind ever
fully awakening from the "nightmare" weighing on the brain of the living
which Marx had seen as the legacy of the past.

Marcuse seems to have been attracted to both types of mnemonics.
The philosophical legacy he inherited from Heidegger and Hegel led him
to argue that something essential had been forgotten, whose content he
thought he saw in Freud's archaic heritage.   But his tenure at the
Institute of Social Research, where the critique of ideology was a far more
frequent practice than the postulating of utopian alternatives, seems to
have tempered his search for recollected meaning with a suspicion that it

might never be found. At the very end of the main argument of *Eros and Civilization*, his most utopian book, he borrowed Horkheimer's argument against memory as redemption:

> But even the ultimate advent of freedom cannot redeem those who died in pain. It is the remembrance of them, and the accumulated guilt of mankind against its victims, that darken the prospect of a civilization without repression.[62]

Remembrance must, in other words, always retain its demystifying critical impulse, bearing sober witness to the sufferings of the past, even as it offers up images of utopian fulfillment as models for the future.

For those of us who remember Herbert Marcuse with affection and respect, it is also valuable, I would argue in conclusion, to apply both kinds of mnemonics to his intellectual heritage. For a true elegy to a master of Critical Theory would mean furthering the spirit of critique that he so brilliantly embodied rather than merely recollecting his arguments as objects of respectful contemplation.

NOTES

1. See for example, Fredric Jameson, *Marxism and Form: Twentieth-Century Theories of Literature*, pp. 112ff.; Trent Shroyer, *The Critique of Domination: The Origins and Development of Critical Theory*, pp. 208ff.; John O'Neill, "Critique and Remembrance," in *On Critical Theory*, ed. John O'Neill; and the forthcoming study by Alison Pogrebin Brown, *Marcuse: the Path of his Thought*. For a very suggestive discussion of the role of memory in the Frankfurt School as a whole, which curiously ignores Marcuse's contribution in favor of Horkheimer's and Benjamin's, see Christian Lenhardt, "Anamnestic Solidarity: The Proletariat and its *Manes*," *Telos* 25 (Fall 1975). See also Russell Jacoby, *Social Amnesia; A Critique of Conformist Psychology from Adler to Laing* for an attempt to apply the Frankfurt School's theory of remembrance to the history of psychology in this century.

2. Jameson, *op. cit.*, p. 112.

3. Benjamin's theory of memory has been widely discussed in the context of his philosophy of history. See, for example, Peter Bulthaup, ed., *Materialien zu Benjamins Thesen "Über den Begriff der Geschichte"*; Jeanne M. Gagnebin, *Zur Geschichtsphilosophie Walter Benjamins. Die Unabgeschlossenheit des Sinnes*; there are also suggestive treatments of Benjamin's theory of memory in Jameson, *Marxism and Form*; Jürgen Habermas, "Consciousness-Raising or Redemptive Criticism - The Contemporaneity of Walter Benjamin," *New German Critique* 17 (Spring 1979); and Irving Wohlfahrt, "Walter Benjamin's Image of Interpretation," *New German Critique* 17 (Spring 1979). Another figure whose meditations on memory warrant mention is Siegfried Kracauer, a close friend of Adorno's and Benjamin's. See my discussion in "The Extraterritorial Life of Siegfried Kracauer," *Salmagundi* 31-32 (Fall 1975 -

Winter 1976).

4. For a brief survey of Western philosophy up to Bergson that deals with this issue, see Michael Wyschograd, "Memory in the History of Philosophy," in *Phenomenology of Memory*, ed. Erwin W. Strauss and Richard M. Griffith. For a brilliant discussion of artificial inducements to memory or mnemotechnics, from the classical period to Leibniz, see Frances A. Yates, *The Art of Memory*. On twentieth century analytic philosophy and memory, see W. von Leiden, *Remembering: A Philosophical Problem*, which deals with Russell and Ryle.

5. E. J. Furlong, *A Study in Memory*; von Leyden, *Remembering*; Brian Smith, *Memory*; and Norman Malcolm, *Memory and Mind*.

6. Herbert Marcuse, *Counterrevolution and Revolt* (Boston, 1972), p. 69.

7. Martin Heidegger, *Being and Time*, trans. John Macquarrie and Edward Robinson, *passim*.

8. Marcuse, *Hegels Ontologie* (Leipzig, 1932), p. 76. I am indebted to Alison Pogrebin Brown's manuscript for bringing this passage to my attention.

9. *Ibid.*, p. 78.

10. Brown, p. 153.

11. Marcuse, "The Concept of Essence," in *Negations* (Boston, 1968), pp. 75-76.

12. Marcuse, *Eros and Civilization* (Boston, 1955), p. 106.

13. Marcuse, *Counterrevolution and Revolt*, p. 69.

14. *Karl Marx: Selected Writings*, ed. David McLellan, p. 302.

15. Lenhardt, p. 149.

16. *Karl Marx: Selected Writings*, p. 300.

17. Georg Lukacs, *The Theory of the Novel*, trans. Anna Bostock, p. 127. It should be noted here that Lukacs' epic theory of memory with its assumption that the past could be recovered as a meaningful narrative leading up to the present was implicitly attacked by Benjamin in his "Eduard Fuchs: Collector and Historian," *New German Critique* 5 (Spring 1975), where he writes: "The historical materialist must abandon the epic element in history. For him history becomes the object of a construct (*Konstruktion*) which is not located in empty time but is constituted in a specific epoch, in a specific life, in a specific work. The historical materialist explodes the epoch out of its reified 'historical continuity,' and thereby lifts life out of this epoch and the work out of the life work," p. 29. Marcuse's attitude towards memory seems to have vacillated between these two alternatives.

18. Marcuse, "The Foundations of Historical Materialism," in *Studies in Critical Philosophy* (Boston, 1972), p. 35.

19. Benjamin's essay is translated in *Illuminations*, ed. Hannah Arendt, trans. Harry Zohn; Adorno's letter is reprinted in Theodor W. Adorno, *Über Walter Benjamin*.

20. *Ibid.*, p. 159.

21. Horkheimer and Adorno, *Dialektik der Aufklarung*, p. 274; the English translation by John Cumming unfortunately renders "*Verdinglichung*" as "objectification," which destroys the meaning of the

aphorism. It should be emphasized that the Frankfurt School did not believe that reification was *only* a forgetting, which could be undone by memory alone. Clearly, dereification, to the extent that it was possible, was a practical task.

22. *Ibid.*

23. Marcuse, *The Aesthetic Dimension: Toward a Critique of Marxist Aesthetics* (Boston, 1978), p. 73.

24. Marcuse, *Eros and Civilization*, p. 213.

25. For discussions of these links, see M. H. Abrams, *Natural Supernaturalism*, pp. 80-83; and Robert Langbaum, *The Mysteries of Identity: A Theme in Modern Literature*, chap. 1.

26. Coleridge, *Biographia Literaria*, ed. J. Shawcross, p. 202.

27. For a discussion of the role of memory in Ruskin and Dickens, see Carl Dawson, *Victorian Noon; English Literature in 1850*, pp. 123ff.

28. Marcuse, *Counterrevolution and Revolt*, p. 99.

29. *Ibid.*, p. 100.

30. Marcuse, *The Aesthetic Dimension*, p. 67.

31. Marcuse, "Affirmative Character of Culture," in *Negations*. The phrase was Horkheimer's invention.

32. Marcuse, *Hegels Ontologie*, p. 77.

33. Ebbinghaus, *Über das Gedachtnis*. Ebbinghaus was the pioneer of the experimental psychology of memory.

34. *The Standard Edition of the Complete Psychological Works of Sigmund Freud*, trans. James Strachey and Anna Freud, vol. 3.

35. Schachtel, "Memory and Childhood Amnesia," in *A Study of Interpersonal Relations*, ed. Patrick Mullahy, and in Schachtel, *Metamorphosis: On the Development of Affect, Perception, Attention and Memory*. Marcuse singled out for special praise Schachtel's discussion of the "conventionalization" of memory by society. He might also have mentioned Schachtel's linkage of memory with artistic creation and his depiction of childhood as dominated by the pleasure principle and "polymorphous perversity." Marcuse went beyond Schachtel in linking childhood amnesia with the repression of the species "childhood," which Freud had discussed in his speculations about "archaic heritage." Marcuse felt both were forgotten for social reasons, and argued, as Schachtel did not, that a different social order would allow the repressed to return in a healthy way.

36. Nietzsche, *The Genealogy of Morals*, trans. Walter Kaufmann, part 2, pp. 1-3; Marcuse did not, however, acknowledge Nietzsche's defense of a certain kind of forgetfulness in *Genealogy* as a mark of the noble man "beyond good and evil." For discussion of the positive role of forgetting in Nietzsche, see Alphonso Lingis, "The Will to Power," Eric Blondel, "Nietzsche: Life as a Metaphor," and Pierre Klossowsky, "Nietzsche's Experience of the Eternal Return," all in *The New Nietzsche; Contemporary Styles of Interpretation*, ed. with intro., David B. Allison.

37. Marcuse, *Eros and Civilization*, p. 212.

38. *Ibid.*, p. 18.

39. Marcuse, *Five Lectures* (Boston, 1970), p. 8.

40. *Ibid.*, p. 29.

41.   Benjamin, "Eduard Fuchs: Collector and Historian," and "Theses on the Philosophy of History," in *Illuminations*.

42.   Marcuse, *Eros and Civilization*, p. 213.

43.   Marcuse, *One-Dimensional Man* (Boston, 1964), p. 99.

44.   Marcuse, "Progress and Freud's Theory of Instincts," in *Five Lectures*, p. 41.

45.   Marcuse, *Counterrevolution and Revolt*, p. 70.

46.   Benjamin, "Theses on the Philosophy of History," p. 262.

47.   Marcuse, *Eros and Civilization*, p. 18.

48.   Marcuse, *The Aesthetic Dimension*, p. 68.

49.   Jameson, p. 113.

50.   Marcuse, *Eros and Civilization*, p. 54-55.

51.   Marcuse, *An Essay on Liberation* (Boston, 1969), p. 90.

52.   Brian Smith, p. 19.

53.   In a translator's footnote in *Negations*, p. 277, Jeremy J. Shapiro points out: "'*Sich erinnern*,' the word for 'to remember' or 'to recollect,' literally means 'to go into oneself.'   That is, in remembering, one is re-membered or re-collected by returning to oneself from a state of externality, dispersion, or alienation."

54.   Marcuse, *An Essay on Liberation*, chap. 1.

55.   Marcuse, *Eros and Civilization*, p. 51.

56.   Benjamin, "Eduard Fuchs: Collector and Historian"; see fn. 17.

57.   Marcuse, *Counterrevolution and Revolt*, p. 70.

58.   Marcuse, *Eros and Civilization*, pp. 134-35.

59.   Michael Landmann, "Talking With Ernst Bloch: Korcula, 1968," *Telos* 25 (Fall 1975), p. 178.

60.   Paul Ricoeur, *Freud and Philosophy; An Essay on Interpretation*, trans. Danis Savage, pp. 28ff.

61.   Max Horkheimer, "Thoughts on Religion," in *Critical Theory; Selected Essays*, trans. Matthew J. O'Connel and others, p. 130.

62.   Marcuse, *Eros and Civilization*, p. 216.   It might be noted that this stress on remembering the suffering of past generations is absent in Habermas' revision of Critical Theory.   For a critique of Habermas on this issue, see O'Neill, p. 4.

PART II

□□□□□□□□□□

PHILOSOPHICAL ORIGINS

As Marcuse explains in the interview that concludes this Part, it was Martin Heidegger's 1927 classic, *Being and Time*, that drew him back into the academic world, to Heidegger's seminars at Freiburg in the late twenties. Many of his early publications evince the very great influence of Heidegger's version of phenomenology on Marcuse's approach to a variety of social and political issues. Prior to Sartre and Merleau-Ponty and prior to the rise of phenomenological Marxism, Marcuse realized that the methodology of Heideggerean phenomenology might provide a unique way of illuminating and interpreting a number of important areas ignored or insufficiently explored by other critical theorists. While pre-Heideggerean "life philosophies" had also insisted that the "meaning" of such human activities as labor, or the family, or power, required interpretive attention to the "lived world" of the particpants, Heidegger's approach seemed to promise a systematic, yet concrete, philosophy of human life, indeed an analysis of human existence in the light of the meaning of Being itself. And Marcuse was clearly deeply impressed by such an attempt.

However, since Marcuse explicitly rejected Heidegger's approach, and after that rejection was never to write again on Heideggerean themes, including this material in our assessment of Marcuse's work is somewhat controversial. As Alfred Schmidt's essay reveals, there were from the beginning deep theoretical problems in the attempted synthesis of Heidegger's ontology and Marcuse's early Marxist revolutionary concerns. And, as Marcuse himself makes clear, there was also the disaster of Heidegger's political activity in the thirties, which Marcuse ties directly to the philosophy of *Being and Time*. But even with this rejection, Marcuse never abandoned the original promise of a "concrete" philosophy of existence, particularly of historical existence. Robert Pippin's essay argues that with his 1932 work on Hegel, Marcuse continued to work within the Heideggerean project, but with more emphasis now on the problem of "historicity," and that this aspect of Marcuse's Heideggerean period is a continuous one, evident in his more well known, post-war works. Indeed, understanding this continuity also helps illuminate Marcuse's commitment to the dependence of critical theory itself on its concrete historical conditions, a major difference between critical theory and traditional philosophy, and one not always as visible in the foundationalist project of much recent critical theory.

CHAPTER FOUR

Existential Ontology
And Historical Materialism
In The Work Of Herbert Marcuse

Alfred Schmidt

Translated by Anne-Marie and Andrew Feenberg

Now that Herbert Marcuse's work can be surveyed as a whole, the first question that confronts his intellectual biographer is that of the relationship in his turbulent development between Marxist materialism and themes drawn from Heidegger and his French followers. Formalistic studies of the outcome are insufficient; it is important to examine the most instructive stages of the highly conflicting relation between existentialist thought and Marxism in Marcuse's work. This relation also determines his later writings - albeit implicitly - and enters in particular into his interpretation of Freudian psychoanalysis.

Existentialist-ontological and Marxist tendencies confront one another in Marcuse's philosophy on the terrain of the *theory of history*. The present chapter proposes to examine the earliest phase in the development of Marcuse's largely unexplored concept of history. It should be clear at the outset that we will be engaged neither in traditional scholarly inquiry into Heideggerian or other "influences" on Marcuse; nor is the interest in Marcuse's books an academic end in itself, as can be seen from the student revolts.

47

The theme of history is particularly urgent for contemporary consciousness, since almost all social institutions aim to suppress the properly historical dimension in the thoughts and actions of man and to mobilize man against history's better and still unrealized possibilities. Science and philosophy were undoubtedly justified in rejecting the nineteenth century's antiquated, abstractly relativistic historicism, condemned already in Nietzsche's polemic *On the Advantages and Disadvantages of History for Life.* Yet today these disciplines must bear responsibility for completely eradicating historical reality from consciousness.[1]

The problem of the concrete-utopian horizon of existing conditions can be resolved only partially on purely theoretical grounds. Marcuse is one of the few thinkers today who seriously considers this problem. Like Sartre and Merleau-Ponty, he too advances from Husserl and Heidegger to material history. On the one hand, long before these French authors, he made a little-noticed attempt to link phenomenological and Marxist thought. On the other hand, the French Existentialists, especially after World War II, provided him with certain correctives for a historical materialism that had been distorted by evolutionism. These are the most important points that must be examined in a study of his earliest work.

In several studies written during the years 1928-1933, Marcuse appropriates Marx's theory under the horizon of Heidegger's *Being and Time.* Let us mention in particular the "Beiträge zu einer Phänomenologie des Historischen Materialismus,"[2] the essays "Über konkrete Philosophie,"[3] and "Neue Quellen zur Grundlegung des Historischen Materialismus,"[4] an interpretation of the *Paris Manuscripts* of 1844, as well as the treatise "Über die philosophischen Grundlagen des wirtschaftswissenschaftlichen Arbeitsbegriffe."[5] Marcuse's inaugural dissertation, *Hegels Ontologie und die Grundlegung einer Theorie der Geschichtlichkeit,*[6] also belongs in this context. While this last work does not in fact concern Marx, but rather is an attempt to discover the "basic characteristics of historicity,"[7] in it Marcuse writes in the same spirit as in the works on Marx mentioned above.

Let us first turn to the two essays which offer the formulations most relevant to our theme. The "Beiträge" are chiefly concerned to define the "mode of givenness" of historical materialism, very much in the style of Husserl. This mode of givenness consists primarily in the "theory of social action, the historical act," that is to say "the proletarian revolution."[8] Marcuse certainly does not deny that historical materialism involves independent conceptual work, i.e. a critique of bourgeois society. But he gives it less weight than it is given today, in which Marxian interpretation, after an anthropological phase, turns again to the critique of political economy, to the problems of objective *"Formbestimmtheit"* as they structure the work of the mature Marx. Marcuse considers the Marxian theory as a "science" only to the extent that revolutionary action "requires insight into its historical necessity, i.e. the truth of its being."[9] Of course this standpoint owes as much to the seething activism and decisionism of the twenties as to the weariness inspired by the superficial naturalistic interpretations of Marxism devised by Second International authors such as Kautsky, for whom Marx is a purely scientific thinker.

Formal-logical criteria such as consistency, absence of contradiction, and validity have no authority for revolutionary theory. The critic must therefore proceed in a rigorously immanent fashion and ask whether the theory succeeds in deriving the necessity of historical action from a "full comprehension of the phenomenon of historicity." This includes "the being, the structure, and the movement of events."[10]

One of the most significant consequences of *Being and Time* for recent bourgeois philosophy is the underestimation of history which, insofar as it is understood in terms of a specific content, is devalued along with all of being under the pretense of radicalizing historical consciousness. The "vulgar" interpretion of history to which, according to Heidegger, even Hegel's philosophy still subscribes, sticks to what is finished and past, to objective processes, to correlations of experience and consequence, to the domain of "spiritual" life as it exists apart from nature "in time," ultimately to the continuity of events as they are handed down from the past.[11] This interpretation has as little to do with "real historicity" as traditional historical research into sources. Nor does it unfailingly require it.

For Heidegger, the fact that the problem of "historicism" arose at all is "the clearest sign that history endeavors to alienate *Dasein* from its own historicity."[12] To be sure, both "vulgar" and professional historical thought acknowledge that man is the subject of historical movement. However, this does not satisfy Heidegger. Indeed, he does not bother to offer even a superficial critique of the essential object of materialist theory, the "ontical fact that man represents a more or less important 'atom' in the movement of world history and remains the plaything of circumstances and events."[13] What becomes clear to Heidegger is not the negativity of a society which, as he correctly states, suffers its own historical process as an impenetrable fate, but simply the inadequacy of non-ontological thought.

The thesis that man is a historically existing being implies for Heidegger the question of the "ontological conditions" on the basis of which "historicity" really belongs to the "subjectivity of the 'historical' subject," that is, to "*Dasein*."[14] As is well known, *Being and Time* tries to answer this question with a thorough analysis of "temporality," and it is here that Heidegger's enterprise proves itself to be a form of transcendental philosophy. As "*the ontological meaning of care*," characterized as "*Being-totality of Dasein*,"[15] temporality is the "condition of the possibility of historicity"[16] and this latter is in turn the condition for the possibility of empirical history. As a "temporal mode of being of *Dasein* itself, independently of whether or how *Dasein* exists as an entity (*Seiendes*)'in time,'"[17] historicity precedes "what is called history (world historical events).[18]

Löwith strongly emphasizes that, despite Heidegger's claim to the contrary, his reduction of history to historicity is miles away from concrete historical thought. No doubt he addresses the problem Dilthey posed of how to get beyond pure historicism, but he falls below Dilthey's sense of history (with its Hegelian inspiration), and masters that problem only insofar as he "radicalizes it and thereby eliminates it."[19]

Dilthey's famous *Aufbau der geschichtlichen Welt in den Geisteswissenschaften* employs his usual inadequate categories to achieve "knowledge of the universal framework of history,"[20] focusing particularly on "the structure of the historical formation"[21] that determines the individuals. He still wants to understand history from the enlightenment "point of view of humanity as a whole," in terms of which a continuous memory of the progress of mankind is formed through the very relativity of the individual stages.[22] In Heidegger, by contrast, the sociohistorical sphere is dismissed as "inauthentic" and opposed to "authentic historicity." In the latter, the real historical process reappears as "*Dasein's* event-structure," thrown together from the most paltry determinations, and privatized and irrationalized in a Kierkegaardian manner. The ineradicable domain of the ontic, dematerialized by philosophical procedures, opposes the ontological sphere.

Heidegger's "existential analytic" is reduced to what Dilthey, critically anticipating his successor, calls "an empty metaphysics of history."[23] This metaphysics imagines that its thought has become more "original" and that it has acquired a more concrete medium because it abstracts in such a refined manner from the collective essence of history ("objective spirit"). (Of course the latter must not be hypostasized either.) Dilthey also rejects Heidegger's thesis that one must start from the proposition that the purpose of each individual is in himself, that the "value of life" is only realized in the "individual being." The talk of "*Mitwelt*" and "*generation*," which influenced Marcuse, cannot hide this. Historicity is characteristic of "personal finite *Dasein*."[24] Its hidden ground, according to *Being and Time*, is "authentic being toward death, that is, the finitude of temporality"[25] which extends between birth and death.

Elsewhere in this same section Heidegger discusses once again the thesis of "resolute existence," unhindered by the anonymous "they," writing that "only the anticipation of death eliminates every contingent and 'provisional' possibility. Only being free for death gives Dasein its goal absolutely and strikes existence in its finitude."[26] This "ontological finitude" (Kojeve) is a detheologized repetition of Kierkegaard's definition of the "individual." It is unnecessary to point out that as such it is completely inappropriate to illuminate structures of human history underlying the historical process independent of all particular content. That we cannot avoid death is, at the level of abstraction chosen by Heidegger, rather a biological than a historical fact.

It was impossible to do without this necessarily sketchy exposition of Heidegger's relation to Dilthey's historicism and the contradiction between history and historicity in *Being and Time* because Marcuse's reception and transformation of fundamental ontology is only understandable against this background. His "*Beiträge zu einer Phänomenologie des Historischen Materialismus*" proceeds methodologically from the concept of the "fundamental situation," a concept that is tinged with individualism. This situation is one in which a man becomes conscious of his unique position with respect to his environment and the tasks arising from it.[27] It is expressed in Marx in a body of research that is not psychologically but objectively motivated. The literary expression of this research furnishes the material with which Marcuse defines not only the Marxian, but also the "Marxist fundamental situation."[28] This primordial unity provides the basis for the concrete development of Marx and Engels in their different periods.

In what does the "Marxist fundamental situation" consist? According to Marcuse, in "the historical possibility of the radical act, which will liberate a necessary new reality as the realization of the whole person. Its bearer is the consciously historical person, and his field of action is history, which is discovered as the basic category of human existence."[29] Already this quote shows that Marcuse considers Marxism primarily as a *positive philosophy* addressed to Heidegger's "fundamental question": "What is authentic existence and how is authentic existence possible at all?"[30] Significantly, Marcuse's interpretation ties in with Lukacs' decidedly eschatalogical theory of the proletariat as the subject-object of history, elaborated in *History and Class Consciousness*. Remarkably, it anticipates Sartre's "anthropology of revolution" and Merleau-Ponty's "philosophy of history from a practical standpoint" (Habermas)[31] although these concepts came into being only after World War II by means of an appropriation of the *Paris Manuscripts* in the light of a Kojevian Heideggerean exegesis of Hegel's *Phenomenology of Mind*.

Since Marcuse's discussion of Marxism draws primarily upon early works like *Critique of Hegel's Philosophy of Right, The Holy Family*, the "Theses on Feuerbach," and *The German Ideology*, it succeeds at times in skimming over the chasms that separate Heidegger's intentions from those of Marx and Engels. The texts written before 1845 lend themselves all the more to a specific philosophical interpretation as they are still imprisoned by Hegelian and Feuerbachian terminology and are accordingly "abstract." Nevertheless, under the old linguistic cover signs quite often appear of a newer, anti- or metaphilosophical content which Marcuse does not properly heed.

At the same time, he does not slavishly repeat the positions of *Being and Time*. Later we will discuss his quite cogent objections to Heidegger. Let us just mention here that Marcuse uses the term "historicity" (*Geschichtlichkeit*) indiscriminately to mean either "real history," or, in an uncharged sense, the "historical character" of a thing. This usage softens the crudity of more than a few Marx interpretations. On the whole, however, his predominant thesis holds that the historicity of *Dasein* is founded primarily by actual history.

This is particularly true of the concept of the "revolutionary situation," which, as is well known, for the later Marx also plays a considerable role as a moment in the historical process. According to Lenin, a revolutionary situation arises when, in a crisis of the whole nation, "there is a convergence of the degree of economical development (the objective conditions) and the degree of class consciousness and level of organization of the large masses of the proletariat (the subjective conditions which are indissolubly linked to the objective conditions)."[32]   It is clear that no a priori judgment can be made concerning the occurrence of this coincidence of factors; it is the outcome of an ever changing dynamic.

Marcuse inclines, on the contrary, towards founding the revolutionary situation in the "unity of the fundamental situation," which, he asserts, can now be interpreted appropriately since it is laid out "in the mode of being of human existence as historical."[33]   This point of view is consistent with Marcuse's idea that the act of revolution itself appears as the necessary form not of the historical movement but rather of an ontological "process" (*Bewegtheit*).[34]   To be sure, Marcuse occasionally uses the expression "capitalist society"; with Marx and Engels he speaks of "the transformation of (relations of) personal domination into objective ones."[35]   But, despite the insistence on historical concreteness, it is difficult to escape the realization that the social categories have been robbed here of their specific content.   While the political sincerity of his commitment is not in question, the fact is that his categories sink to the level of mere accessories of a reality that is "existentially" conceived.

Thus, the "reality of an inhuman existence,"[36] indicted by Marx and Engels in *The Holy Family*, is not manifested for Marcuse *in* the economic and ideological forms of the society in question, but stands *behind* these forms as inauthentic "activity," against which the "reality of human existence" must be summoned.   Marcuse does not want to characterize this "reality" as a reconciled condition, but as the "existential determination" of the "radical act."[37]   As in Fichte, whom Marcuse explicitly cites, objective relations are transformed into the material of duty; the domain of interrelated moments contained in the concept of "human praxis," so forcefully discussed in the "Theses on Feuerbach," shrinks down to an impoverished concept of the "Act."   The Act would be an "essential mode of action of human existence," with this latter as its goal.   Naturally, an act is radical if it changes not only "circumstances," but also "human existence in its being,"[38] and if, more precisely, it is characterized by a "concrete necessity" intrinsic to both the "actor" and the "environment."[39]   Marcuse does not investigate more closely the subjective and objective conditions of the proletarian revolution, just as he avoids going into substantive questions raised by Marxian social theory. If the "radical act" is synonymous with "historicity" and real becoming is derived from it, then dialectics is similarly derivative; the *immanent*, self-producing historical unity of the general and the particular is ontologically torn asunder.   The conditions of concrete action must first be constituted on the basis of what Marcuse calls the "foundations of existence."   As transforming praxis, dialectics atrophies into the application of an empty universal, lying beyond all historical change[40] and yet still "fatefully" present within it.   It is worthwhile lingering on Marcuse's theory of the "radical act" because it is an example of the very sort of "*action directe*" that is hotly debated again today.   It could provide a real content for Heidegger's interpretation of the historicity of *Dasein*, his discourse on "authentic   existence"   and   "anticipatory   resoluteness,"[41]   despite Heidegger's own view that nothing concrete can be made of them:

The resolute taking over of one's factical "there" signifies at the same time, that the situation is one which has been resolved upon. In the existential analysis we cannot, in principle, discuss what *Dasein factically* resolves in any particular case . . . . Nevertheless, we must ask whence, *in general, Dasein* can draw those possibilities upon which it factically projects itself . . . . Those possibilities of existence which have been factically disclosed are not to be gathered from death. And this is still less the case when one's anticipation of this possibility does not signify that one is speculating about it, but signifies precisely that one is coming back to one's factical "there".[42]

However, when the philosophically formulated affirmation of the possibility of historical action is expressed with such pathos and suggestiveness, then it can easily become its own content and lend itself to the justification of a sinister praxis. It is only a short step from expressionistic action for action's sake to the "*volkisch*" awakening of "heroic realism" in Baeumler and Krieck. As the year 1933 demonstrated, only minor modifications were required to adapt the ontology of *Being and Time* to the new situation. Adorned with the attribute "German," Heidegger's *Dasein* was all too hastily concretized.

From the outset, authoritarian ideology's call to action has always contained a pseudoactivist conformism, traces of which can also be found in the defiant reaffirmation by the Left. One thinks of Sartre's work, *Materialism and Revolution*, written in 1949. This essay contains an undoubtedly well-founded defense against Stalinist objectivism's hostility to the subject, in the course of which Sartre completely rejects the idea of social objectivity as a "myth" and blames materialism for not being a philosophy - as if that were not its distinguishing characteristic. As in Marcuse's "Beiträge," Sartre tries to understand the behavior of the revolutionary independently of the concrete historical contents of the Marxian critique of political economy and considers the concepts of "situation" and "being-in-the-world" sufficient in themselves for the purposes of a "philosophy of revolution" which considers socialism as "*the* human project" and claims to be the general philosophy of man.[43] In the anarchist phase of Sartre's existentialism, the historically bounded "transformation of the world" proposed in the Marxian *Theses* is ontologically merged with the "*acte gratuit*" in which every existing immediacy is freely transcended. When myths of oppressed classes becomes unusable, then they can be replaced by more suitable ones; Sartre recommends the myth of permanent revolution.

Marcuse's theory of the revolutionary act, to which we now return, attempts to clarify the problem of the concrete circumstances under which such an act is possible so as to analyze "the structure of historicity in general and the conditions of historical existence."[44] He sticks primarily to the *German Ideology*, which at first sight seems to justify his stance. There the authors speak of the "world-historical existence of the individuals" as "immediately connected to history."[45] However, this concept of existence, which Marcuse emphasizes so strongly, cannot be understood ontologically. It is derived from Feuerbach's sensualism and realism and forms the mediating link between the old mechanistic and the new dialectical materialism.

In opposition to the superficial idealism of the Young Hegelians, the *German Ideology* stresses that "human reality," far from being adequately explained by the categories of "self-consciousness," is enclosed in sociohistorical conditions. It is these conditions that are defining for determinations such as "being," "material praxis," "collective action," "production of life" which play the part of "the real basis that philosophers have presented as the 'substance' and 'being' of man."[46]   This is a non-positivist renunciation of speculation, and there is really no point in describing it as "existential." On the contrary. It is all too easy to be taken in by the terminological similarities and to translate the realities uncovered by historical materialism into a hazy and solemn ontological discourse that is supposedly more radical.

Marcuse falls into this error when he takes Heidegger's analytic of *Dasein* as the measure of the economic categories. In fact, according to Marx, these categories are neither purely "social-scientific" nor speculative concepts, but "forms of being, conditions of existence"[47] of a definite society. Marcuse seeks to discover whether the categories can fully account for the "basic phenomenon of historicity," to which he grants the highest concreteness. But Marx is from the start the more concrete thinker: he develops and criticizes the actual content that constitutes the living existence of human beings in the here and now, while *Being and Time* imparts to the reader the meager information that existence is "the substance . . . of man"[48] "being itself, to which *Dasein* is related in this or that fashion and to which it always somehow relates."[49]

Heidegger expresses these views already in the work in which he introduces the "question of being." There he talks primarily about the state of human affairs[50] despite his own proviso that he is not practicing anthropology or psychology, let alone sociology. For Marcuse too, the danger exists that the reader will confuse the relative truth of the isolated phenomenological analyses with the truth of that which they are intended to support: Heidegger's ontology.

Be that as it may, in *Being and Time* this ontology is still bound to the metaphysics that it rejects. The conventional tension between *existentia* and *essentia* stands behind the difference between daily (factical) and "authentic historical existence,"[51] which Marcuse too attempts to establish. The Hegelians, Marx and Engels, are similarly indebted. No matter how much they ridicule the hypostatized concept of "human being" (in the very passages Marcuse quotes from the *German Ideology*), they consider it insufficient to reject the concept as ideology, or to reduce it to immediate existence, and to affirm the - ever possible - "authenticity" of the latter. If one may employ such undialectical alternatives and speak in modern terms, then it might be said that they proceed in an "essentialist" rather than an "existentialist" manner. Not only do they sharply criticize Feuerbach's naive identification of the individuals' "determinate circumstances of existence" with their "being";[52] in their later work they also introduce the objective dialectic of being and appearance into those "circumstances of existence" which, by then, they characterize as politico-economic.

Let us turn to that aspect of Heideggerian phenomenology which is decisive for Marcuse, "historicity as the basic determination of *Dasein*."[53] In *Being and Time* he sees a "turning point in the history . . . of bourgeois philosophy," the point where, "disintegrating from within, it opens the way for a new 'concrete' science"[54] which consciously puts itself in the service of historical praxis.   Indeed, when Heidegger contrasts both the bourgeois concept of freedom and bourgeois determinism with "freedom as the possibility of choosing necessity," he sets up "history as the sole authority."[55]   For Marcuse, this is the most important aspect of his thought.   Clearly, the fact that Marcuse departs from what was then Heidegger's contemplative stance, giving the immediate present of his time a definite proletarian-revolutionary accent, does not overthrow Heidegger's thesis that ontical history is based in ontological historicity, but it does shake its undialectical rigidity.   We return now to Marcuse's idea of a "dialectical phenomenology."

When, in the *German Ideology*, Marx and Engels first describe the most general conditions of "all human existence, as of all history,"[56] the purpose is purely polemical and not, as Marcuse assumes, to advance fundamental philosophy.   It does not occur to historiographical materialism to derive the different life situations of *men* from an a priori concept of *man*.   From the standpoint of that materialism, it would make little difference whether such a *homo philosophicus* was explained by Cartesian self-consciousness, by a biological species being, or by the no less abstract "care-structure of *Dasein*."   Materialism's task is rather to explain from those general conditions why, especially in modern times, abstract discourse on man has acquired such significance in the most varied cultural domains.

"People have history," says Marx, "because they must produce their lives, and this in a determinate way.   This constraint is imposed by their physical organization, just as is their consciousness."[57]   This state of affairs, which is material in the narrower sense, determines man's active relation to the natural factors he encounters.   These factors change historically, so that what might be called "prehistorically" given "presuppositions" enter more and more into the continuity of history and become highly mediated.

Marx and Engels do talk about three "moments" or "relations" which "have coexisted from the very beginning of history, since the first man, and still today have an impact on history":[58] economic production, the generation of new needs, and the family.   However, even these moments do not constitute immutable ontological structures, since they only exist in the manifold forms they have taken in history.   Of course, one can inventory "the most general results . . . which can be abstracted from the historical development of men" but, as Marx and Engels add immediately, "in themselves, divorced from real history, these have no value whatsoever."[59]   The point is thus to deny such abstractions an ontological privilege over history.   Their higher degree of abstraction does not lend them special value.

Marcuse's essay "Über konkrete Philosophie" shows the consequences of attempting to devise a "methodical attack on the social sciences"[60] using Heidegger's "ontological *historicity of Dasein*" (which, as has just been shown, is incompatible with economic materialism). It is obvious that such an attack is needed to advance the knowledge of what constitutes the real interests and needs of men. One must also agree with Marcuse when he emphazises that ongoing historical reality is neither "an accidental facticity" nor "an autonomous world of things,"[61] and that such dead abstractions as contingency and necessity must be resituated in the "totality of human existence."[62] However, when this is accomplished within an ontological framework, it is not clear that a greater degree of concreteness is achieved.

What is accomplished when "social orders, social structures, political organizations" are no longer interpreted as ontical facts, but from the vantage point of "the becoming of *Dasein*?"[63] Or when "concrete philosophy" tries to reduce the conditions it analyzes to a "unified human existence"?[64] Does thought really come closer to the "concrete fullness" of immediately given *Dasein* when, "keeping the ontological structure of the world and *Dasein* in view," it "deconstructs" this latter "as a product of its own historicity."[65] Are the social and political needs of the present phase of the capitalist system dialectically understood when they are reduced to the widely discussed phenomenon of "existential crisis"?[66] It is no accident that with such an approach Marcuse arrives at formulations which, in the context, while not quite reducing theoretical knowledge to nothingness, nevertheless severely limit it. "Human being," as he defines it, "does not exist through knowledge, but as a result of fateful events in the determinate situation of the with-world and the environment."[67]

Marcuse already has a clear view of the methodological deficiencies of the various branches of the social sciences huddled together in the dominant university system: they stop at "mere analysis"[68] and evade the question of the historical purpose of knowledge. However, he does not achieve the insight that a real critique of reified consciousness can only consist in uncovering its real bases, i.e. the "reification" of human relations which occurs in commodity production. The corrective for superficial empiricism is not an equally empty ontology, but a dialectical method which effectively questions social conditions that appear as "'things' in terms of their structure, their relations and the laws of their development."[69] The point is to refuse to accept these "things" as such but instead to liberate the "mediations," the *real history* behind the capitalist immediacy.

As pointed out above, Marcuse's definition of the unity of theory and praxis suffers from his failure to come to grips theoretically with the problem of social objectivity, and to understand concretely the antagonism of the forces and relations of production. When he speaks of action, the obscure concept of "fate" or "destiny" crops up, and the "historical necessity" realized in the revolutionary act has no connection to an analysis of economic reality; instead, Marcuse sees that necessity as "a determination of historical *Dasein's* very being, always already given with its thrownness."[70]

Let us now examine the points where Marcuse turns away from Heidegger and tries to transcend his ontology in a "dialectical phenomenology." On the one hand, Marcuse does indeed identify serious insufficiencies in the phenomenological stance; but, on the other hand, he is too deeply influenced by phenomenology to be able to carry through his critical analysis. Marcuse asks whether Heidegger, since he fails to address the critical question of the *hic et nunc*, can do justice to his own attempt to center philosophizing on the concrete man in his concrete historical situation. Heidegger's ontology explains historicity "as the mode of being of *Dasein* itself, in which its full determination is grounded."[71] But then ontology should not remain completely silent about the nature of "authentic existence" today. When posed about "*Dasein* in general," this question and its answer remain free of both content and obligation. Although authentic existing is only possible as the "disavowal of that which in the contemporary works itself out as past,"[72] this does not entail for Marcuse a reference to the "resoluteness" of "solitary *Dasein*"; the point is rather to reconstruct "all the spheres of the public domain."[73]

In 1928, Marcuse could not yet know how close was the end of Heidegger's political abstention, which he deplored; nor could he know that it was directed solely against the "vulgar future" of a socialist transformation, but that Heidegger was perfectly ready to abandon this *parti pris* for a nationalist ideology which, like *Being and Time's* idea of the "moment," neither surrenders to the past nor aims at progress; which, in other words, forcibly maintains the status quo with the heroic attitude of doing something qualitatively new.

Marcuse's second sustantive objection to *Being and Time* also concerns the question of the concreteness of "*Dasein*." Heidegger does not characterize the world in its naturalness as something in itself, but as a "meaning-relation" grounded in a "*Dasein* that cares for it."[74] It can be asked how, on these terms, *Dasein* is to be more clearly understood. It cannot be defined as purely individual; for every epoch is characterized by a unity of experience, modified though it may be by the individuals. It is this unity which makes for intersubjectivity, not only logically and epistemologically, but in the practice of life.

Marcuse now enquires - and this is genuine Marxist thinking - where the boundaries of this "collectively" experienced world actually lie. These boundaries have certainly become historical and are subject to further historical change. If at the outset we disregard the world of the natural sciences, which is the same for everyone, then what Marcuse, following Dilthey, calls the "historical world" appears as daily "environment."[75] This latter is far from being a seamless unity. Not only is it fragmented into various cultural spheres, but even within these separate spheres there are unmediatizable "worlds of meaning," specific forms of psychosocial appropriation of objects. Marcuse is thinking of groups such as bourgeois, small farmers and proletarians under capitalism, while Heidegger's "*Dasein*" is neutral in terms of class (and sex as well).

Heidegger has not even noticed, much less examined[76] the problems that arise in this context, such as the "material constitution of historicity,"[77] its "material existence,"[78] indeed even the problem of "the material existence of history."[79] Marx did pay attention to the latter, which he defines as "the natural and economic basis"[80] of the current social formation. Although these concrete conditions have become historical, in their empirical immediacy they form that "facticity which can never be spiritualized" to which Dilthey refers; they are the concrete conditions of a given social situation and not the *condition humaine* as such. At this point, Marcuse forgets everything he had earlier stated about a Marxist "ontology of history." Now he articulates the most profoundly historical dimension of Marxist theory with all desirable clarity. Marxism is historical "in a twofold sense: first, because its object is a historical one and is treated as historical, and second, because it itself intervenes in the historical movement of a concrete historical situation."[81]

This is a valid remark which raises the question of the method that would do justice to the historical development of events. For the first time in his study, Marcuse deals here with the domain of problems treated by materialist dialectics, which grasps "every developed form in the stream of movement"[82] and thus revivifies processes that have rigidified into abstract things. He refers to the famous discussion on trade unionism of 1921, in which Lenin countered the formal and eclectic "definitions" of Trotsky and Bukharin with an excursus on dialectical logic:

> [D]ialectical logic requires that we go further. To really know a subject, one must understand and study all its aspects, all its relations and "mediations" . . . . Secondly, dialectical logic requires that one consider the subject . . . in its "self-movement," as Hegel says, in its becoming. Third, the complete "definition" of an object must include human praxis as a whole, both as the criterion of truth and as the practical determinant of the relation between the object and human needs. Fourth, dialectical logic teaches that "there is no abstract truth, that the truth is always concrete."[83]

We have quoted Lenin's argument at this length, because it circumscribes the precise concept of dialectics which Marcuse's phenomenological method must confront as soon as it attempts to follow Marx in considering human practice as the concrete mediation of the "material situation" of the object. Marcuse realizes that phenomenology cannot confine itself to merely "showing the historicity of its object": contrary to Heidegger, it must bring into the analysis "the concrete historical situation and its material conditions."[84] It must become a "method of action."[85]

Marcuse's attempt to give the phenomenological process historical content encounters a great difficulty: on the one hand, he is clearly aware that a serious account of the "material conditions" of the individuals' life processes must burst out of the ontological framework of "historicity" in which they are supposed to be founded. On the other hand - and here Marcuse remains bound to the Husserlian-Heideggerian position - these "material conditions" can be included only insofar as they serve the purpose of "revealing" a "basic structure of *Dasein*."[86] The formula, "material conditions of historicity," already contains the inner contradiction which remains unsettled: Marcuse would like to have his cake and eat it too. He is fully aware that the economic movement in its historical facticity (tendency) can only be derived from a concrete analysis of the situation and that therefore a "phenomenology of the basic structure of *Dasein* is unattainable."[87] However, historical materialism, which tries to understand that movement, must also include the "field of basic knowledge of the structure of historicity."[88] For, according to Marcuse the question of the truth of historical materialism can only be meaningfully addressed to that field.

Marcuse is striving for a synthesis of dialectical and phenomenological method, a dialectical phenomenology understood as a "method of thorough and radical concreteness." On the one hand, Heidegger's analysis of *Dasein* can only be completed by becoming a "phenomenology of concrete *Dasein* and of the concrete act that is required historically." On the other hand, the dialectical method must become phenomenological, that is, it must "appropriate concreteness as the complete understanding of its object, and do so also from a distinct angle which alone can make the object its own." It cannot be content with designating the historical locus of the reality it investigates, but it must also ask whether "its own meaning is not inherent in this reality as something which, while certainly not ahistorical, yet endures within all historicity." According to Marcuse, unless this far-reaching question is posed, the "decision to perform the historical act" is also impossible in the final analysis, at least insofar as it is to arise from adequate knowledge.[89]

The mutual correction of phenomenology and materialist dialectics that Marcuse has in mind, in which the one is ontologized and the other materialized, does not yield what he expects from it. This is because, at this stage of his development, he regards the materialist critique of speculative idealism as trivial or at least does not find it cogent. A point that has been decisive for the Soviet Marxist tradition escapes him too, namely, the extent to which the ontologized revolutionary dialectic suffers a sort of Hegelian dilution in being made into the essence of "most general forms of movement" (Marx). Conversely, a "materialized" phenomenology turns into a succession of partial empirical descriptions. If the concepts of phenomenology on the one hand and of historical materialism on the other are rigorously applied, then their "combination"[90] can only appear, as Heidegger would say, as their mutual "destruction."

Let us briefly consider what Marcuse's "Phänomenologie des Historischen Materialismus" looks like on the basis of the premises discussed above. Three interrelated problematics appear particularly important here because they still play a major role in contemporary discussions of Marxism: the relation between nature and history - a relation which is itself historical, the relation between the economy and ideology, and finally the question of the historical constituents of both the experiential and objective unity of social structures.

1. Soviet Marxist orthodoxy puts forward once again the later Engels' thesis according to which nature, in the reduced form investigated as "matter" by the mathematical natural sciences, obeys the "dialectical laws of development and movement." Thus on closer examination these laws represent the highest principles of being rather than specific scientific findings. Like Lukacs in *History and Class Consciousness*, Marcuse undoubtedly deserves credit for having pointed out so early the lack of a solid foundation for this naive ontological thesis. To be sure, there is a "dialectical natural science" for Marcuse, but it is not modern physics, as Engels maintains. Rather, it is "the history of nature in its relation to *Dasein*," that is, to the social structure. The established natural sciences can therefore disregard the historical and social mediations of their objects, while the history of nature in the strict sense remains external: "Nature *has* a history, but it *is* not history."[91]

2. Marcuse deals with the Marxian materialist theory of ideology in an utterly academic fashion, no doubt to avoid vulgarization, but with the result that he misses the essentially "strategic" character (Adorno) of the concept of ideology. Marcuse returns to Heidegger in an attempt to substitute a Marxist function for the latter's analyses of "worldhood" and "everydayness" so as not to leave these concepts in their elitist phenomenological purity. "*Dasein* is thrown being-in-the-world, and as such it is determined by its world, not only in the mode of a fall into the 'they', itself a dimension of *Dasein*, but also by the concrete historical environment and times of its birth." This is the "material condition" of the historical process, the "ultimate determination of *Dasein*, not only factically but also structurally."[92]

According to the phenomenological interpretation, "practical caring being" is *Dasein*'s primary mode of behavior. To it belong social relations and the functional appropriation of natural material. Thus for Marcuse it follows that: "Concrete historical *Dasein* is . . . to be understood from the way that it has provided for itself in its world and according to its world. *Dasein*'s primary care however concerns itself, its production and reproduction."[93]

Following this arduous path Marcuse finally reaches the question of the priority Marx assigns to the relations of production over cultural phenomena. This conception implies neither a "priority of worth"[94] nor an "ontical-temporal" priority.[95] The latter view would also contradict the belief of the theory's founders that the different forms of consciousness do not have independent histories, but change with the living actuality of man. Or, as Marcuse expresses himself phenomenologically and with reference to Karl Liebknecht's book *Studien über die Bewegungsgesetze der gesellschaftlichen Entwicklung*[94] "*Dasein* as being-in-the-world is always already both 'material' and 'spiritual,' 'economic' and 'ideological,' so that the ideological domains are co-reproduced already in the historical movement . . . . But there is a foundational relationship in terms of which the . . . ideal objects come to be based on the material. And it is indeed *ontological* ; . . . thus, it is not in terms of their value, their meaning . . . but in their existence, their (historical) occurrence . . . ."[97]

These are formulations which could support our thesis that, far from concretizing Heidegger's ontology, the dialectic is sacrificed to it. Once we disregard the completely empty terms "material" and "ideal objects," with which Marcuse himself is not completely at ease, and instead employ Marxist concepts to treat the relation of infra- and superstructure as an ontological "foundation," then it becomes clear that Marcuse's thesis not only leaves the question of possible correspondences, interactions and contradictions between these spheres unclarified, but above all, it chokes off the critical, self-transcending impulse of historical materialism. The situation is not improved when the genesis and validity of the forms of consciousness are rigidly separated from one another. Of course Marcuse is right when he says that information about the material preconditions of these forms is not relevant to the question of their truth or meaning. But this idea too becomes misleading if one fails to incorporate into the analysis the origins of spiritual products which have become objectively problematic.

In Marx ideology is a socially necessary appearance, but it is neutralized in Marcuse to become an object of phenomenological investigation, i.e. "the entire domain of ideal objects that can be produced in the concrete totality of a concrete historical existence."[98] In connection with this highly formal definition of ideology, Marcuse stresses that the statements of the materialist conception of history concern not individual *Dasein*, but society as a "concrete historical unit."[99] "*Dasein*'s historical unit," the subject of movement, is society and not the individual. But from this Marcuse concludes that "it is a wholly unjustified transgression of the phenomenological proofs of historicity" to attempt, "in the case of the *individual person*, to explain ideology on the basis of materiality."[100] It is unnecessary to insist on the irrelevance of these considerations to the concrete dialectic of the general and the individual, since they militate against the fact that society, especially bourgeois society, is mediated by the actions of the individuals, just as, vice versa, it conditions the latter. The category of the "individual person" is itself an ideology requiring explanation.

The situation is similar in the case of Marcuse's separation of the "immanent" and the "historical meaning (locus)"[101] of an ideology. Contrary to Marcuse's belief, these are not separated at all in Marx. Only the historical meaning is accessible to the dialectical method, while the immanent meaning, "as self-enclosed, independent unity,"[102] can be understood only phenomenologically. If anywhere, it is in this methodological dualism that the impossibility of a "dialectical phenomenology" becomes apparent.

3. The epistemological or epistemologically relevant implications of *Being and Time* spring from very different sources, which can in no way be reduced to a common denominator. Alongside the Husserlian elements there are elements from Kant's anthropologically oriented transcendental philosophy, the Nietzschian perspective, all of *Lebensphilosophie*, Uexkull's theory of the environment, and finally pragmatism. At the time Heidegger's theory appeared, Marxism's self-reflection, with its critique of epistemology, was still at its inception (even today it is not yet flourishing).

Thus Heidegger's analyses, which are close to praxis and realistically oriented, could impress a young author like Marcuse just as they have a whole series of recent East European philosophers; especially impressive is the thought (that goes back to Hegel) according to which the execution of a practical action is in itself cognitive and not the simple "application" of ready-made theories which come from the outside.[103]

Following Heidegger, Marcuse claims that the "primary historicity of *Dasein*" consists in the fact that "*Dasein* as thrown creates its form of existence from what has been, modifies it according to its own wish and thus again becomes present as fateful past for coming *Dasein*."[104]   This process also draws external nature into itself beyond the domain of work: nature not only represents the physical world of matter but exists also "as meaning-world in which *Dasein* is rooted."[105]   However, the much discussed "reality of the external world" is not so much overcome as confirmed by this approach.

Ontologically, the proximate encounter of historical *Dasein* (the real social human being) with objectively given things is not contemplative but practical, given the assumption that practice is always also a knowing. Those things thereby appear as "significances": they are "in a relationship that has become historical and has been historically transmitted."   To be sure, this "world of meaning" can be analyzed in an   abstract theoretical fashion, but things that have been reduced to quantitative determinations, pure forms and structures, are never what they are as components of human daily life.

Marcuse affirms this interpretation and defends it against the objection that it is an idealistic philosophy of immanence.   Nevertheless he critizises its lack of concreteness: "It is not *Dasein* in general that is always rooted in its world, nor is it worldhood in general that is always related to *Dasein*. Rather, a concrete *Dasein* always stands in a   concrete world and a concrete world relates to a concrete *Dasein* . . . . *Dasein* . . . is at any given time concrete *Dasein* in a determined historical situation (spatio-temporal position) and as such . . . it is determined by concrete, visible actuality.   It is not a unified world of meaning linked to a unified existence; *Dasein*'s ontological connection with the world is not a free floating abstraction, but is constituted in   concrete historical events."[106]

Here Marcuse comes closer to the Hegelian-Marxist dialectic of immediacy and mediation, and thus to the concept of society.   This latter is characterized in such a way that "individual existence" only becomes historically active in it and with it.   Moreover, it creates a concrete totality "in which and for which the worlds of meaning are constituted, which gives a direction to the overall state of affairs of the daily environment."[107]   As a mode of production and reproduction of life, it is the irreducible "fundament of every historical unity."[108]   From this concept of human-social praxis, which constitutes object and experience, Marcuse further derives the concept of revolutionary praxis (much like the Marxian "Theses on Feuerbach").

Marcuse's early theory of history, the incoherent, complex and contradictory character of which has been tentatively explained here, is not only an indispensable source for the understanding of his later works up until *One-Dimensional Man*, but also for the proper interpretation of a whole series of new Marxist positions in recent times. The ever present limitation of this theory lies in its attempt to understand Marxism "philosophically," i.e. as the analysis of a situation which not only possesses an immediate historical meaning, but also an "intrinsic meaning lasting through all historicity."[109] However, Marxian materialism is critical of philosophy because for it the world admits of only as much meaning as people have succeeded in realizing in their social institutions. Marxism scorns to explain the negative continuum of history from the starting point of a coherent, permanent human nature or an ontological foundation that discovers the particular in itself.

To the extent that every variety of "Heideggerian Marxism" hangs on to the idea of philosophical self-foundation, it fails in terms of a moment that is decisive for Marx. To be sure, it appeals constantly to social praxis, but subordinates it, as Habermas has argued, to a "meaning," which "in the end is deduced from 'consciousness in general,'"[110] from a transcendentally derived structure which nevertheless must be that of "the sociohistorical situation itself." Objectively, this means: "alienated work, from which the transcendence of alienation (as 'meaning') is derived, does not precede all history as the general structure of consciousness or the historicity of man, but is an aspect of this determinate historical situation . . . ,"[111] which still must be mastered.

NOTES

1. Cf., for the ideologically far-reaching "weariness of history" of the second half of our century, Kurt Sontheimer, "Der Antihistorismus des gegenwartigen Zeitalters," *Neue Rundschau*, no. 75, vol. 4, pp. 611-31. Sontheimer points out the extent to which history as an academic discipline, not to mention philosopy of history, is being displaced by the polished research techniques of contemporary social science. For a critique of structuralism as a trend which is consciously hostile to history, see also my essay "Über Geschichte und Geschichtsbeschreibung in der materialistischen Dialectic," in *Folgen einer Theorie: Essays über das 'Kapital' von Karl Marx* , especially pp. 105-107. In his work, *Karl Löwiths stoischer Ruckzug vom historischen Bewusstsein*, Jürgen Habermas employs a highly instructive case to show that even the attempt to abandon historicizing and practice-oriented thought in favor of a cosmological worldview such as the early Greek one, cannot escape the sphere of historical and social mediations. Cf. *Theorie und Praxis* (Neuwied/Berlin, 1963), pp. 352-370. Reinhard Lauth's transcendentally oriented work (in Fichte's sense) *Die absolute Ungeschichtlichkeit der Wahrheit*, rejects all historical philosophizing in a particularly blatant way. The fact that Lauth opposes Heidegger himself as a "knowledge relativist" is indeed characteristic: the present situation can no longer tolerate history, not even in the arid form of the concept of "historicity" derived from it.

2. In *Philosophische Hefte*, ed. by Maximilian Beck, no.1 (Berlin, July 1928), pp. 45-68.

3. Published in 1929, reprinted in Herbert Marcuse, *Philosophie und Revolution*, vol. 1, (Berlin, 1967), pp. 143-189.

4. Published in 1932, reprinted in *Ibid.*, pp. 41-136.

5. The treatise dating from 1933 is contained in Herbert Marcuse, *Kultur und Gesellschaft 2*, (Frankfurt am Main, 1965), pp. 7-47.

6. (Frankfurt am Main, 1932).

7. *Ibid.*, p. 1.

8. "Beiträge zu einer Phänomenologie des Historischen Materialismus," in *Ibid.*, p. 45. Here Marcuse repeats verbatim the "definition" of the Marxian concept of history given by Lukacs in his little book *Lenin*.

9. *Ibid.*

10. *Ibid.*

11. Cf. *Sein und Zeit*, 9th edition, (Tübingen, 1960), pp. 378ff.

12. *Ibid.*, p. 396.

13. *Ibid.*, p. 382. The translation is taken from *Being and Time*, trans., Macquarrie and Robinson, p. 433. Hereafter, the page number of English translations from this edition follow the German reference in parentheses. The translation has occasionally been modified slightly.

14. *Ibid.* (*Being and Time*, p. 434.)

15. *Ibid.*, p. 323.

16. *Ibid.*, p. 19. (*Being and Time*, p. 41.)

17. *Ibid.*

18. *Ibid.*; cf. also p. 376. (*Being and Time*, p. 41.)

19. Karl Löwith, *Heidegger, Denker in dürftiger Zeit*, 2d. ed., (Gottingen, 1960), p. 46.

20. Wilhelm Dilthey, *Gesammelte Schriften*, vol. 7, 3d. ed., pp. 252-291.

21. *Ibid.*, p. 254.

22. *Ibid.*, p. 256.

23. *Ibid.*, p. 284.

24. Löwith, *Heidegger*. We can disregard the fact that Heidegger's later works themselves go back, under the title of "Seinsgeschicks," to the concept of historicity that is still mediated by man.

25. *Being and Time*, p. 386.

26. *Ibid.*, p. 384.

27. Cf. "Beiträge," p. 46.

28. *Ibid.*

29. *Ibid.*, p. 47.

30. *Ibid.*, p. 55.

31. Cf. *Theorie und Praxis*, pp. 299-306. This development of a "Heideggerizing" Marx interpretation finds an echo in the attempt (which is also influenced by the later Husserl) of a series of Eastern-European philosophers to replace ossified dialectical materialism with an anthropocentric "Philosophy of Praxis"; this is evident in a serious form in the *Dialektik des Konkreten*, a book by the Czech philosopher Kosik. However, it is even more apparent in the group of authors (perhaps Petrovic and Grlic) around the Jugoslav magazine *Praxis*, who are throwing overboard essential Marxist positions under the pretext of

destalinisation.

32. Lenin, "Zwei Taktiken der Sozialdemokratie in der demokratischen Revolution," in *Ausgewahlte Werke in zwei Bänden*, vol. l, (Berlin, 1955), p. 430.

33. Marcuse, "Beiträge," p. 46.

34. *Ibid.*, p. 68.

35. *Die deutsche Ideologie*, (Berlin, 1953), p. 74.

36. *Ibid.*, p. 137.

37. "Beiträge," p. 47.

38. Cf. *Ibid.*

39. *Ibid.*, p. 48.

40. Cf. *Ibid.*, p. 58.

41. *Sein und Zeit*, p. 382.

42. *Ibid.*, p. 382ff. (*Being and Time*, p. 434.)

43. Sartre, *Materialismus und Revolution*, cf. p. 105.

44. "Beiträge," p. 49.

45. *Die deutsche Ideologie*, p. 33.

46. *Ibid.*, p. 35.

47. Marx, *Zur Kritik der politischen Ökonomie*, Introduction, (Berlin 1951), p. 263.

48. *Sein und Zeit*, p. 117.

49. *Ibid.*, p. 12.

50. This situation and the strict phenomenological methods of *Sein und Zeit* make it understandable, as do the circumstances of the time, why critical intellectuals of bourgeois origin like Marcuse believed that a thorough examination of Heidegger would contribute to their own political self-understanding. Forty years later, an attempt to bring together early Marxian motifs with the later Heidegger(!) can only lead to pseudolyrical fluffed-up obscurantism; it dominates for instance Kostas Axelos' book, *Einfuhrung in ein kunftiges Denken: Über Marx und Heidegger*, (Tübingen, 1966). Its sole merit consists in bringing together Heidegger's rare remarks about Marx.

51. "Beiträge," p. 67.

52. *Die deutsche Ideologie*, p. 39ff., cf. also p. 600.

53. "Beiträge," p. 45.

54, *Ibid.*, p. 54.

55. *Ibid.*, p. 52.

56. *Die deutsche Ideologie*, p. 24.

57. *Ibid.*, p. 27, footnote.

58. *Ibid.*, p. 26.

59. *Ibid.*

60. Marcuse, *Über konkrete Philosophie*, p. 155.

61. *Ibid.*

62. "Beiträge," p. 58.

63. *Über konkrete Philosophie*.

64. *Ibid.*, p. 160.

65. *Ibid.*, p. 171ff.

66. *Ibid.*, p. 164; cf. also p. 162 and p. 170.

67. *Ibid.*, p. 174.

68. *Ibid.*, p. 172. In the essay "Über die philosophischen Grundlagen des wirtschaftswissenschaftlichen Arbeitsbegriffs," he rightly criticizes its scientistic narrowness - but here too he starts out from positions characteristic of a (praxis-) ontology.

69. *Ibid.*, p. 156.

70. "Beiträge," p. 67.

71. *Ibid.*, p. 55.

72. *Sein und Zeit*, p. 386. (*Being and Time*, p. 438.)

73. "Beiträge," p. 56.

74. *Ibid.*

75. *Ibid.*

76. Marcuse acknowledges that Dilthey has gone further on this central question, and he quotes the following passages from the *Aufbau der geschichtlichen Welt in den Geisteswissenschaften* (p. 287ff.): "Epochs are different from each other in their structure." The latter "contains a connection of related ideas, which reign in different domains. . . .But it must be recognized that the background to these ideas is a power which cannot be conquered by this higher world. And this is everywhere the case. The facticity of race, of space, of the relations of forces builds everywhere an unspiritualizable basis. It is Hegel's dream to believe that the epoch represents a step in the development of reason." Remarkably, Marcuse mentions that Dilthey in his analyses, always comes up against "this indissoluble material existence of history" (*Ibid.*), "in spite of his clear recognition that historicity has its own proper structure." If anywhere, it is here that it becomes clear what Dilthey's view has to do with Heidegger's "Geschichtlichkeit des Daseins": it is the *ontologized* form of Dilthey's transcendental conditions of the "understanding" of history, but no less idealistic for that matter.

77. "Beiträge," p. 56.

78. *Ibid.*, p. 57.

79. *Ibid.*, p. 56.

80. *Ibid.*, p. 57.

81. *Ibid.*

82. Marx, *Das Kapital*, vol. l, (Berlin, 1955), postface to the second edition, p. 18.

83. Lenin, "Noch einmal über die Gewerkschaften, die gegenwartige Lage und die Fehler der Genossen Trotzki und Bucharin," in *Zwei Arbeiten zur Gewerkschaftsfrage*, p. 64.

84. "Beiträge," p. 59.

85. *Ibid.*

86. *Ibid.*

87. *Ibid.*, p. 66.

88. *Ibid.*, p. 60; cf. also p. 61, where the terms "structure of historicity in general" and "laws of movement of history" are discussed at one level.

89. *Ibid.*, p. 59. Marcuse anticipates Merleau-Ponty's and Sartre's experiment with Marxism after the second World War with this idea also of a "dialectical phenomenology." In what is the most significant immanent-dialectical analysis of Husserlian phenomenology as epistemology, Adorno has demonstrated the irreconciliability of the

"phenomenological antinomies," while keeping a steady eye also on Heidegger; implicit therein is also the impossibility of uniting phenomenology and dialectics, if both methods are to retain their strict meaning. Cf. *Zur Metakritik der Erkenntnistheorie*.

90. "Beiträge," p. 59.
91. *Ibid.*, p. 60; cf. also p. 62 and 64.
92. *Ibid.*, p. 62.
93. *Ibid.*
94. *Ibid.*
95. *Ibid.*, p. 63.
96. (München, 1922).
97. "Beiträge," p. 63.
98. *Ibid.*
99. *Ibid.*
100. *Ibid.*
101. *Ibid.*
102. *Ibid.*, p. 64.
103. *Sein und Zeit*, cf. p. 69ff.
104. "Beiträge," p. 61ff.
105. *Ibid.*, p. 62.
106. *Ibid.*
107. *Ibid.*, p. 64.
108. *Ibid.*, p. 65.
109. *Ibid.*, p. 59.
110. *Theorie und Praxis*, p. 311.
111. *Ibid.* In the 1847 article, "Die Kommunisten und Herr Heinzen" in the *Deutschen-Brusseler-Zeitung* the young Engels emphatically rejected the notion that communism proceeded from a philosophical a priori. He says: "Mr. Heinzen imagines that communism is a certain doctrine, which proceeds on the basis of a specific core principle and draws further conclusions from it. Mr. Heinzen is very wrong. Communism is not a doctrine, but a *movement*; it does not start with principles, but with *facts*. Communists do not have as their postulate this or that philosophy, but all of previous history and especially its actual contemporary results in the civilized countries . . . . Communism, in as far as it is theoretical, is the theoretical expression of the position of the proletariat . . . and the theoretical summary of the conditions of the liberation of the proletariat." In Marx/Engels, *Werke*, vol. 4, (Berlin, 1964), p. 321ff.

CHAPTER FIVE

Marcuse On Hegel And Historicity

Robert B. Pippin

I

Herbert Marcuse's early (1932) study of Hegel, *Hegels Ontologie und die Grundlegung einer Theorie der Geschichtlichkeit*,[1] has been largely ignored in most important twentieth century discussions of Hegel, historicity, and the cluster of problems that have come to be known as the Critical Theory enterprise.

In many respects this neglect is, *prima facie*, understandable. First, as a work of Hegel scholarship alone, the book can appear grossly anachronistic. Hegel may have had a "system" or a "science" or a "Logic," but he certainly did not think of his project as an "ontology" in any standard sense, and while he did (very infrequently) use the term historicity (*Geschichtlichkeit*), that term acquired a distinct philosophical significance only in Dilthey and, especially, Heidegger,[2] and does not seem an appropriate interpretive term for Hegel. Secondly, all those issues that have led so many twentieth century neo-Marxists to Hegel do not appear in *Hegels Ontologie*, suggesting that the work may indeed be a piece of dispensable, "pre-Critical" juvenalia.[3] There is no direct treatment of the problem of subjectivity, of consciousness and its ideological distortions, of Hegel's rich philosophical discussion of alienation, of that Hegelian notion of "satisfaction" that includes but transcends labor, nor of his attempts to interpret human activity and its "conditions" in a genuinely dialectical rather than reductionist manner. Instead, we find discussions of "*Bewegtheit*" (translatable, if at all, as "motility"), "life," "*Geschehen*" ("happening" or "event"), and such chapter headings as "The transformation of knowing motility into the motility of absolute knowing"; all heady stuff, suggesting the hand of Marcuse's great teacher and master neologist, Heidegger.

Of course, on the other hand, it would be foolish to attend only to this apparent anachronism and prominent Heideggerean cast, and on that basis alone to reject the work as neither a significant comment on Hegel, nor as a contribution to Critical Theory. After all, it was this book that, thanks to Adorno, helped get Marcuse into the *Institut*,[4] and that historical connection alone might lead one to question more carefully its thematic appropriation of Hegel and possible "Critical" status. More substantively, I think it can indeed be shown that the largest issue in the book (an "ontological" theory of "historicity") is in fact not only a legitimate aspect of Hegel, but quite important in any full understanding and assessment of Marcuse's later work. Further, although a much more ambitious and complicated claim, I think that one can also begin to see that many aspects of what Marcuse here suggests must be faced in a foundational theory of historicity (e.g., as opposed to such approaches as historical determinism, *Weltanschauung* relativisms, or teleological or developmental idealisms) must in general be faced and dealt with if the foundations of Critical Theory itself can be defended. (Moreover, these aspects have not, I believe, been correctly identified in the best attempts hitherto to understand Marcuse's Heidegerrean period.[5])

To be sure, it should be admitted that many elements of Marcuse's interpretation and its relation to his later work and Critical Theory are incomplete, and are presented in a form that is often merely suggestive, quite elliptical at points, occasionally highly speculative and even sometimes simply dogmatic. But still, I want to claim, or at least begin to claim, that there are lines of approach pointed to here that can rival in insight and subtlety some of the equally elusive and important conversations with Hegel and Heidegger that characterize so much of Adorno's theoretical work, and that can be seen to extend all the way into the contemporary version of the continuing debate between the Critical and hermeneutical, post-Heideggerean approaches to history.[6] Marcuse's attempt may not (and I think it does not) finally succeed, but it is well worth some more attention.

II

The overriding purpose of *Hegels Ontologie* is interpretive. Marcuse wants to show Hegel's foundational role in the development of a theory taken up and expanded by Dilthey and Heidegger: the theory of historicity (*Geschichtlichkeit*). At the conclusion of the book, he states that goal clearly:

Herewith we believe that we have made clear the connections in which Hegel discovered and developed the theory of historicity, at least clearly enough to be able to recognize these connections as the presuppositions under which the philosophic theory of historicity stands today. The above interpretation should justify the initially asserted essential proposition that the question of the ontological status (*Seinscharaktaren*) of historicity demands an encounter with Hegelian ontology.[7]

This passage reveals clearly what Marcuse thinks this theory of historicity is; it is an "ontology," and that characterization immediately raises a number of problems. We need to know how Marcuse is using the notion of ontology, especially since, somewhat in contrast to other members of the *Institut*, he continued to use the notion freely (referring in 1978, for example, to the "ontological foundations" of Marx).[8]

Prior to the modern period, the basic (though not exclusive) issue in ontology was the investigation of "being *qua* being." This inquiry was to be distinguished from an analysis of what it is to be this or that being, and was to complete the philosophic ascent to the highest generality in principle, that presuppositionless *arche* always already presupposed in the understanding of any being. In a less prominent, but often equally important aspect of the ontological tradition, such an inquiry into "being itself" was often also supposed to function as an answer to the question of the "ground" of the beings, the culmination of the search not only for the highest generality, but for the most fundamental origin or source, an ultimate justificatory principle. (This aspect, although visible in Plato, is, of course, most prominent in the theological tradition, where the problem of Being often meant the problem of the "highest Being.")

The history of this tradition is obviously too rich and complicated to summarize briefly. Suffice it to say here that, already greatly qualified by Aristotle, it was, virtually, completely ended by Descartes' "epistemological turn," and, especially, by Kant, and it is not the notion of ontology appealed to by Marcuse. The very possibility of identifying "being itself" does not, for him, survive the Kantian critique of the dogmatic tradition and of intellectual intuition, and the corresponding Kantian and post-Kantian theories of subjectivity and constitution.[9]

Yet, obviously, Marcuse has not abandoned the notion in favor of a theory of knowledge, or subjectivity, of production, or of "the Concept" as the highest principle.[10] Just as obviously, even though there is no independent discussion of the meaning of ontology in *Hegels Ontologie*, Marcuse makes clear everywhere that he is relying on Heidegger's quite non-traditional version of ontology.[11] In the opening paragraph, in explaining the ontological dimensions of the problem of history, he writes

Historicity is the name of what it is that determines history as "history" and distinguishes it (say from "nature" and "economy"). Historicity designates the meaning (*Sinn*) of what we intend when we say of something: it is historical - historicity designates the meaning of this "is": the meaning of the being of the historical (*den Seinsinn des Geschichtlichen*).[12]

It is this reference to *Sinn* and *Seinsinn* that gives away the Heideggerean orientation of the work. In fact, this orientation is so deeply embedded in the book's approach that it is hard to extract clearly, and is much more visible in the explicitly methodological essays written in this same period, especially "Beiträge zu einer Phänomenologie des Historischen Materialismus"[13] and "Über konkrete Philosophie."[14] But in the details of *Hegels Ontologie*, the Heideggerean presuppositions come to the fore and can be stated as follows.

First, Marcuse follows Heidegger's phenomenological orientation in assuming that the problem of being cannot be posed simply as "What is there?" Rather, as the above passage begins to make clear, the problem of Being, or of any being, is the problem of the "meaning" of being, where this also assumes that the question must be posed within the "horizon" of that being for whom Being can be an issue, can have a meaning. Ultimately, in Heidegger, this way of asking the question of Being (as the question of *"Dasein's"* or the human relation to Being) leads to an "existential analytic" of *Dasein* as the primary ontological problematic. In *Hegels Ontologie*, a similar orientation leads Marcuse to pose the problem of Being in terms of the concept of *"Leben"* in Hegel, a notion that Marcuse, interpreting rather freely, treats very much like Heideggerean *Existenz*. Secondly, Marcuse assumes, with Heidegger, a difference between "ontological" and "ontic" issues, and that any relation to any individual being *(Seinde)* always already presupposes an "orientation" to Being *(Sein)*, an orientation that is the fundamental component of the "world" within which any one being "is what it is." In *Hegels Ontologie*, this dimension of Heidegger's ontology leads Marcuse to concentrate the first part of his book on Hegel's *Logic*, where, he argues, Hegel's "fundamental" ontological orientation is presented and defended.

All of this, of course, is still quite introductory and abstract. At this point, one can only say that Marcuse's use of the notion of ontology follows Heidegger's claim that a prior investigation of "the meaning of Being" is necessarily presupposed in any inquiry into specific human dealings with the world; that the problem of Being itself "is an issue" or "has meaning" only (or "primordially") with reference to this world (as an issue for *"Dasein"*) and that this "fundamental ontology" cannot be resolved by an appeal to "facts," "natures," "entities," or any *Seinde*, since Being is that by virtue of which any such "ontic" dimension can be understood as what it is. However, to understand Marcuse's approach more clearly than these Heideggereanisms allow, we need more details of his claim that in Hegel there is a "theory of Being" that *is* a theory of historicity, finally, the historicity of human "life." This characterization of human existence is *the* decisive presupposition in any subsequent understanding of the things human.

Here, though, the waters get even more tenebrous, since Marcuse's terminology remains wholly within the Hegelian and Heideggerean context he has chosen for his explanation. The clearest problem with this terminology is the importation of the notion of historicity into Hegel. In its broadest sense, the notion of historicity just means that the historical past has a continuing effect on the present (is, as Heidegger claims, "stretched along into" the present) and that that effect cannot be treated as a causal effect. That is, historicity cannot be understood as a "scientific" theory about the relation between events, and certainly not a causal theory, because the historicity thesis is that there *are* not "separate" events "in" history affecting each other. One of the events *is* what it is only in relation to its past.

As we have seen, the official definition of the term historicity in *Hegels Ontologie* is simply "that which constitutes and delimits history as history ... it is the mode of being of 'the historical'."[15] Now in this book, such a theme for investigation leads to some very wide ranging ontological discussions as Marcuse interprets Hegel as holding that all Being is an occurrence, or event, a *Geschehen*. And, of course, all this is quite general. No one would deny that at least human beings have histories, and that it might be important to understand past facts in trying to understand the present. But the thesis of historicity is more radical than such platitudes suggest. This radicality is clear in a later passage, where Marcuse, discussing the notion of finitude in Hegel's *Logic*, says approvingly:

> From here on, Hegel has broken through to a totally new dimension: the universal historicity of beings. He has thereby laid the way to the first essential interpretation of historicity. The occurring (*Geschehen*) of finite beings is no development to a somehow predetermined or undetermined goal; in general no occurring from ... towards, but an occurrence purely in itself. It is immanent to being. *Finite beings do not have histories, they are histories*[16] (my emphasis).

Thus, something within the human "world" cannot *be*, say, "late monopoly capitalism" except as a thoroughly historical phenomenon; its very being involves it in some historical story without which it would not be what it is. Now of course, even when distinguishing mere history from historicity, the radical nature of the claim is still not yet out. What we have said might be true simply by virtue of the temporal characteristics of the description used, and not as a component of what the thing is. In the same way, we might argue, calling someone an adult involves a necessarily temporal reference, but nothing earthshaking seems to result philosophically. What is ontologically significant is the denial that alternate descriptions of monopoly capitalism - this set of productive and consuming relations, etc. - could tell us *what* this form of life is. One tries to demonstrate this claim in much the same way Heidegger tried to show the "priority" of much of his existential analytic in *Being and Time*, by showing that these alternate descriptions either do not describe what the phenomenon *is*, or if they do, do so by presupposing in various ways the historicity dimensions. Marcuse does not attempt such a demonstration in detail here but there are several examples of what he has in mind in other work of this period. Perhaps the clearest is his explanation of what we understand when we understand that something *is* a "factory" in his 1931 "Zum Problem der Dialektik."[17] Indeed, it is worth noting at this point that while in *Hegels Ontologie*, Marcuse's discussion of this ontological claim is quite far-reaching, and sometimes seems to involve quite a general claim about all "Being," there is no decisive departure from the claim he had made earlier in this article that

> only human existence and all the objects, formed, created and animated by *Dasein* in its existence, are historical according to their being.[18]

However, again, the full scope of Marcuse's claim cannot be appreciated properly if one stays this close to his own formulations. As only a few passages make directly clear, what Marcuse is claiming is that Hegel himself did not fully understand the radicality of his own thesis about historicity (on p. 5, Marcuse says that this thesis is presented "implicitly"). Marcuse professes to discover in the *Science of Logic* a commitment to a claim that Being (the meaning of Being in human existence) is *necessarily* historical, that any such determinate meaning is always only a moment in a continuous process of self-transformation, even self-negation. This then would mean, as the passage quoted earlier suggests, that Hegel misunderstands his own theory if he understands change, development, negation and the like in terms of some ultimate *completion*, whereby history itself is overcome.[19] To claim that the historicity thesis in Hegel is *ontological* is to deny *just this claim*; it is to assert that existence is not simply "temporarily" or contingently "historical," self-transformative, or dissatisfied, as a result of a temporary human finitude. Thus, as well, the terminological liberties taken by Marcuse. He insists on historicity (the *permanent* character of human "historicizing") rather than history, and even on the inelegant *Bewegtheit*, rather than *Bewegung*, for the same reasons.

We have not yet seen *why* this continuous "historizing of history" (*Vergeschichtlichung der Geschichte* to borrow Schmidt's phrase[20]) occurs, and why it occurs in the ways Marcuse thinks it does. But it is already possible to see the potential importance of this approach for the Critical Theory enterprise. After all, the one great problem in Hegel for the members of the *Institut* was his "identity theory," the (apparently) ineliminable affirmative moment in his theory wherein he claims that history is intelligible only as the continuing, progressively more successful attempt to reconcile subject and object in Absolute Knowledge. What Marcuse is claiming is not just that Hegel has misidentified the *terms* of this identity (with, say, too idealistic a view of "subject," rather than class, or social subject), or its time (it has not "yet" occurred), both familiar Marxist criticisms. He is claiming to find *in* Hegel the resources to show that such reconciliation cannot occur; that existence in its very "being" is unreconcilable, or historical.

We shall see shortly how many aspects of this claim, once it is more fully presented, might be of relevance for Marcuse's later work. We ought to admit here though that all this is indeed a heterodox view of Hegel,[21] one to which both interpretive and philosophic objections can be raised. But it is important now also to note briefly that it is not simply anachronistic, that it develops a genuinely Hegelian tendency, even if in a radical direction. Indeed, one could say that what Marcuse is calling the ontological dimension is clearly present in Hegel's famous insistence (often neglected in post-Hegelian thought) that not only must "substance become subject" but "subject must become substance," an insistence that the domain of human subjectivity not remain "ideal," a separate "finite" domain, whether epistemologically (as in Kant) or practically (as in Fichte), but that it finally understands itself as "infinite," the "whole" or Being itself. In this context one can also see Marcuse's interpretive radicality. He is claiming that the core of Hegel's enterprise is misconceived if we attend to this substantiality apart from, or simply as a result of, its "becoming." That "core," according to Marcuse, is the becoming itself, not its origin or result.

III

Admittedly, we still face in these characterizations the problem of terminological obscurity, and it would be a major task in and of itself to clarify the situation sufficiently to assess just how Hegelian Marcuse's approach is. But, again, I would hope that enough of his position is clear so that one can see further aspects of its potential importance. Not only, as noted, does this approach radically de-emphasize the "affirmative" or "positive" tendencies in Hegel (on, presumably, Hegelian premises), it begins to lay a foundation for many elements of Marcuse's (and others') full Critical Theory, and his (and their) appropriation of Marx. To claim, for example (as Horkheimer and Marcuse did)[22] that what distinguishes "traditional" from "critical" theory is the latter's constant attention to and incorporation of its own "historical conditions" can now be seen *not* to be a claim either of "historical relativism" or "determinism." It is not the former since Marcuse's ontological thesis about historicity denies that there *could be* a past historical epoch "closed" to us, intelligible only within its own (perhaps irretrievable) historical assumptions. Any "past" *exists* only in the way it is stretched along into the present; only with the "historizing" activity and remembrance of historical subjects. It denies as well that there could be something like a present epoch "in" which subjects, as separable elements, are determined and act. All such *Weltanschauungen* philosophies, ironically, detach subjects from the very history made so important, rendering them instead victims of the very historical point of view *they* create and sustain.[23] It is not the latter ("determinism") because there can be no "law of development" that can *itself* be detached from the historical totality it is meant to explain; it too is as much historical *explicandum* as *explicans*. Thus one can also see that a *full* defense of a frequently heard refrain of anti-scientistic Marxism - that it is *only* in bourgeois society that the means of production dominate and even determine relations of production and culture, that they do not do so "eternally"[24] - may have to depend on something like the thesis Marcuse is defending here. That is, to defend such a claim fully, one would want, presumably, not just to leave the door open for another, perhaps more inclusive, socioeconomic or naturalistic model of explanation; one would want to deny the possibility of such ahistorical attempts. Moreover, the orientation visible in this book also begins to make clearer why Marcuse insisted so strongly on attending to the specific "utopian" possibilities created in the present, and why he proceeded in so unsystematic (or "specifically historical") a way. Finally, it also, by rejecting any ahistorical, external, and so extra-"human" "ground" of history, by insisting on the historicity of all the elements in history, helps account for the unmistakable moral appeal of Marcuse's work. His work always assumes possible *subjects* of history, an assumption that depends on many of the elements of the explanation of "the historical" developed here. But it is also true that enough of Marcuse's position is visible to indicate the great potential problems it faces. A consideration of one such, often heard problem, best presented by Alfred Schmidt, can help turn us to the other major components of Marcuse's theory.

The Schmidt objection (presented in "Existential-Ontologie und Historischer Materialismus bei Herbert Marcuse"[25]) stems from his concentration on only those essays written before *Hegels Ontologie*, where Heidegger and phenomenology play a much more prominent role than Hegel. Basically, Schmidt adopts Karl Lowith's objection to Heidegger,[26] and applies it to Marcuse, that Heidegger has regressed beneath even the level of Dilthey's understanding of history and has produced only an "empty metaphysics of history."[27] No talk of a revolutionary *"Grundsituation"* or "authentic decision" (common to Marcuse's early essays) can disguise the lack of concreteness, and indeed the theoretical incapacity to incorporate any consideration of concrete material conditions into a *critique* of a historical situation. Marx's all important discoveries in the *German Ideology*, Schmidt argues in detail, cannot be incorporated into *Daseinformen* or *Existenzbedingungen* without losing their critical force; there is finally no way to connect Marxism with phenomenology, even existential phenomenology. His basic, pointed question: "Are the historical-political needs of a contemporary level of the capitalist system dialectically understood if they are reduced to a foreground phenomenon for a crisis of *Existenz*?"[28] The historicity thesis, when pursued with an eye to possible historical action, allows only a vacuous Heideggerean view of "authentic" decision, with all the infamous ambiguities about what counts as "authentic."

Such criticisms are familiar, of course, to readers of Adorno and, indeed, were often voiced by Marcuse himself in explaining his break with Heidegger.[29] And they are serious, damaging objections. The only question is, Are they relevant to what Marcuse is doing in *Hegels Ontologie*, and does that attempt help prepare a more successful way to preserve the historicity thesis while solving the "problem of content"? Answering such large questions is difficult and will require attention to more of the details of the work and Marcuse's later books. However, from what we have seen of the approach taken by Marcuse, it is already possible to suggest an initial difficulty with the way Schmidt poses his question, a difficulty that leads directly to the "critical" dimensions of Marcuse's theory.

Schmidt suggests, in one of those terrible compressed phrases possible only in philosophical German, that the problem in Marcuse's use of Heidegger is to find a way "to content-ualize historically" his approach (*geschichtlich zu verinhaltlichen*).[30] Yet this notion of "incorporating" a "content" seems to me to suggest a point of view that, from the perspective of *Hegels Ontologie*, leads to several problems of its own.   It suggests a historical subject (or social subject, or even class) that acts "on the basis" of an "analysis" of material conditions, as if these conditions (*Inhalt*) were somehow simply encountered by such a subject, armed with some theory of social development, or species-being or the like.   This in turn suggests that those conditions and that theory can be understood as in some way "detached" from, or at least independent of the *specific*, historical, active, self-interpretive social subject.   And, it is one thing to suggest that, prior to *Hegels Ontologie*, Marcuse had not found a way of understanding just how such "materiality" was *itself* to be understood as an aspect of the self-transforming and so "historizing" process of "*Leben*."   It is quite another to counterpose to Marcuse's approach an original dualism of "factual" content and historical agent.   In the latter case, the radicality of Marcuse's claim for historicity (its "ontological" status) has not been answered in any detail. An alternative way of looking at things has simply been proposed.   Moreover, there are plenty of indications in *Hegels Ontologie* that the former difficulty, admitted as such, is just what Marcuse is trying to solve, and it is to that attempt, to understand *Leben*, and its "essential" content, to which we need to turn.

IV

While Marcuse's procedure in *Hegels Ontologie* is more explanatory and speculative than analytic, he does try to defend the theoretical position he presents in so much detail.   Basically, that defense proceeds by beginning with the point of view of Kant's *Critique of Pure Reason*, and then by presenting and supporting various, interconnected components of Hegel's appropriation, and criticism, of Kant.   At the center of that defense is a position not only decisive for the whole theory of historicity, but what ought to be an answer to Schmidt. Clearly we need to know at some final or fundamental level why we should accept the above claims about the permanent historicity of human existence, on what foundations do all the dimensions and consequences of that thesis rest?   And it is within such a foundational account of the "origin" of historical activity that we should be able to find Marcuse's account of how we should understand any concrete historical negation, where we should get the resources to avoid relapsing into an abstract, "decisionistic" position.   We know already that the whole historicity thesis is radical enough to render problematic, in any search for this origin, an appeal to an extra- or prehistorical ground: "the" struggle for self-preservation, "the" production of the means of existence, "the" need to overcome alienation, or even, as in Kojeve's equally Heideggerean reading of Hegel, "the" struggle to the death for recognition.   Is there, though, anything *like* a counterpart to these positions in Marcuse's account, one that could direct our inquiry into actual history so that we could see the concrete origin of the "motility"

(*Bewegtheit*) Marcuse finds so decisive?

There are basically two connected attempts to answer this question, corresponding to the major claims of the book's two parts. In the first part, Marcuse tries to use the approach of the *Science of Logic* to explain why the vast manifold of human activity would not be intelligible except as a *constant* alteration of "self-externalization" (*Selbstentausserung*) and "self-internalization" (*Selbsterinnerung*), differentiation, alienation and production on the one hand, identification, reconciliation and recovery on the other. Within that explanation is a defense of the notion that clearly sets Marcuse apart from a purely Heideggerean approach - his acceptance of Hegel's doctrine of "essence" (*Wesen*). With that notion, he wants to be able to distinguish a merely subjective or contingent response to some developed historical whole, from an objective, or, as he begins to say more frequently, truly "free" appropriation of the past. In the second part of the work, where the focus is on the concept of *Leben*, he appropriates Hegel's account of the preliminaries and details of the structure of "actual" (*wirkliche*) human history. He then tries to show how those details themselves further establish and exhibit the unavoidable historical "being" of human life, all in a concrete way. I shall discuss each approach, briefly, in turn.

Clearly, one way to look at Schmidt's objection is to see that it stems from the lack, so far, of a developed explanation of what is to count as a *genuine* self-transformation in the history of human *being* (at an "ontological" level), as opposed to a mere incidental (or "ontic") alteration. We need to be able to identify a "stretching the past along into the present" that *is* "historical" - to distinguish, say, the French Revolution, Stoicism, empiricism, or the Beautiful Soul, from minor provincial elections, mental fatigue, a fad, or an eccentric moral theory. Without such an account, we can now say, the danger in Marcuse's approach is, paradoxically, the opposite of what Schmidt suggests. Instead of a subject "empty" of content, courageously creating its own, we'd have a kind of mad totalization of contingent, historical content. *Every* aspect of any subject, or any subject's self-understanding or decision would simply look like one momentary "shape of spirit" randomly succeeding another; a kind of instability in individuals, or societies or epochs that would make a "subject" unidentifiable as such, much less one capable of individually deciding anything. And this is a problem Marcuse explicitly recognizes. At one point, he himself calls it the *Leitfrage* of his interpretation: "how can this motility (*Bewegtheit*) which is simultaneously a motility collapsing into negativity, into always being-other, constitute and preserve any unity of being?"[31] And yet, earlier he himself had helped generate his problem by speaking favorably of the Jena *Logic*'s claim for "absolute unrest" (*absolute Unruhe*) and by continually highlighting and approving Hegel's remarks about "absolute" negativity.[32]

Further, we have already seen why this problem develops as it does. (Cf. the passage from p. 63 quoted above.) Marcuse unambiguously insists that "the motility of Spirit requires no instigation *and no goal*."[33] It is just the absence of this possible appeal to an "end" of history that makes preserving a genuinely dialectical, determinate theory of change

difficult and which threatens to push the position into the anarchistic one
sketched above (or even, one might say, a "Foucaultean" theory of radical
"alterity"). For, a dialectical analysis of a form of life, or practice or social
institution presupposes a rejection of any wholly "positive" account of that
phenomenon; it insists that that phenomenon is "what it is" only in
relation to "what it is not," what it has been and, determinately, could
be.[34]   Clearly then, how one establishes *its* "true possibilities" (and thus
its "two-dimensionality") is crucial in any dialectical enterprise.   And, in
its traditional versions, in both Hegelian and Marxist theory, such a
determination must appeal to the course of human history as a whole if
this essential/contingent delineation of possibility is to be made.   Such a
putative completion (wisdom, or classlessness, or happiness) is what
explains both the necessity of the transformations and negations (the
dissatisfying incompleteness of an "early" stage) and it is what allows one
to explain which alterations contribute to the "essential" dimensions of
that phenomenon's role in history.   Finally, we have also seen why
Marcuse's approach cannot allow such a projected end point.   Clearly if
historicity is an ontological characteristic of experience, if human being
just *is* this "motility," then the "end of history" looks not like completion,
but an inhuman stasis, or death; at least like an ideological distortion of
human being itself.   More specifically, there can be no ahistorical *basis* on
which to project this final historical goal.   Such a projection can always
only be an extension of individual capacities, social potentiality and the
achievements of a historically specific point of view. The only "human
nature" on which to base one's utopian speculations is human being as it
has come to be historically, and so any such speculation cannot serve as an
"absolute" criterion from which "essential" and "contingent" possibilities
can be distinguished.

Yet, contrary to the essays used by Schmidt, Marcuse does not allow
such Heideggerean statements of finitude to end or even wholly to
determine the discussion.   He has tried throughout to demonstrate that
while there is always a process of continuous "difference," dissolution,
"*Entzweiung*" and so ultimate self-negation in all human enterprises, there
is also a moment of unification, wholeness, internalization and
identification with the products of such activity.   In many different
contexts throughout *Hegels Ontologie*, he holds up this possible "self-
internalization" as a way of understanding what "essential" continuity in
historicity amounts to.   What is essential in the manifold possibilities of
any historical period is the extent to which subjects can and do understand
the "totality" of that period *as* their own historical doing, and thereby
actively *assume* the role of subject.   Practices, philosophies, and
institutions which help make self-conscious and render concretely possible
this "free" subjectivity are what can be said to be essential, or the "truly"
historical elements of human "*Bewegtheit*."[35]

Admittedly, this is still sketchy, and Marcuse remains throughout the
book at such a fairly abstract level, even though he refers continuously to
this role of concrete "unification" and specific "totalities" in history.
Recall again the premise of his claim:

> The mere actuality or positivity (*Ansichsein*) of beings never and nowhere constitutes the real being of those things (what it really is) and therewith never the ontological unity and truth of those beings.[36]

According to this view, it is only by such an understanding of the historical character of such totality, its origin in human agency and its concrete possibilities, that the "essence" of such appearances can be established, that what even here Marcuse calls the "two-dimensionality" of such forms of life is established. This "essence," then, here and in the 1936 essay, "The Concept of Essence," must be understood as a thoroughly historical category, and not as a kind of anachronistic Aristotelian notion.[37] Now what it means to consider this recollected essence of a totality as a historical notion depends for its full defense on Marcuse's insistence that the essence of some historical form of life *can* be understood as the interconnected *unity* of a whole series of historical appearances, that a culture's religion, mode of production, philosophy, law, etc., can be accounted for as a whole, each illuminating what the other is, by all being aspects of human agency, and that this whole, and not the fragmentary self-understanding of any part, *is* what this form of life essentially is. And this is obviously a large and controversial issue, to which I shall return later. The only point relevant here is that Marcuse's notion of the "essence" recovered in such recollection, the notion that separates him from Heidegger, must still be understood in terms of the claims about historicity he makes throughout this book. Thus he writes that the notion of essence must be understood "without appeal to what is traditional in philosophy with respect to essence,"[38] and that "The doctrine of essence as the present quality of 'having come to be' is the essential, systematic place where the discovery of the historicity of beings finds its essential preservation in the *Logic*."[39] It also is at least supposed to mean that such recollection can reveal "potentialities" for future transformations only concretely, only in terms of the totality of some form of life, and not in terms of some universal law of development. Or:

> Possibilities are indeed always already actual. Everything which I can become as this determinate person, is already there, not in the sense of a mystical determination, but in the concrete relation between me and the existing manifold of situations, out of which and only in terms of which I can become what is possible for me.[40]

Again, such claims at least indicate one way to understand what genuine or essential historicity amounts to, and so prevent Marcuse's position from collapsing into Schmidt's "empty metaphysics." Marcuse seems to have in mind something like a distinction between ontological manifestations of historicity and mere historical change that is based on a distinction between activities that at least in a partial way allow the recovery and preservation of human authorship for a historical totality, and those that are only the continuation of some naturalistic or mechanistic mystification and suppression of that historicity. In fact, it gradually becomes clear that this is just what he has in mind when, towards the end of the book, he describes his own unusual interpretation of "Absolute Knowledge":

> The hidden necessity of history is, from the viewpoint of Absolute Knowledge, the transparent freedom of spirit; spirit knows that nothing can occur *to* it in history, that it (spirit) remains in history only with itself (*bei sich selbst*) and so it *allows* itself to occur in history[41] [emphasis added].

Admittedly, it is still just barely possible to see through the metaphors and abstractions of such statements and determine what exactly is being said. But even at this airy level, it is important to face a number of potential problems. For one thing, Marcuse is trying to introduce this affirmative moment or criterion without committing what he has often cited as Hegel's error: viewing this self-conscious "realization of historicity" as the moment of wisdom, an "escape" from history itself. The development of "essential" human freedom is not completed in some moment wherein human freedom is *attained*, in perfect "identity" and so at the end of history. It is only the subject's recovery of history as its own, a realization that only begins (indeed, first makes possible) an attempt to create a form of life consistent with such freedom. However, even with this very statement, we can see that the feared Hegelian Absolute moment has not at all been excluded. The realization of historicity is not *itself* one among many of the continuous "historizings" of human spirit. Even at such a starkly abstract level, it is the "riddle of history" solved and which knows itself solved. It is at least *the* attainment of the possibility of human freedom, and it is an attainment that seems strictly inconsistent with the ontological claims made throughout for the unavoidably historical character of *all* human self-consciousness.[42]

Even more seriously, though, we still know very little about specific ways in which both this distortion and this liberation occur. There is a great deal of talk about "self-externalization" and "difference" and so on, but so far little about what *kind* of externalization or remembrance, in what contexts, with what consequences, etc. Moreover, as we have seen, Marcuse does not believe that the historicity thesis is established only by showing the "logical" necessity of alienation and identification in human praxis, the impossibility of understanding such praxis except in such terms. *Leben* itself can be seen concretely to be and to have to be "historical" in its very being. And that side of Marcuse's case needs a hearing too.

V

This is especially important because, in his discussion of historical *Leben*, Marcuse does seem to appeal to a kind of "existential need" that propels history, one that often sounds analogous to the ahistorical or anthropological candidates considered earlier. There is talk, for example, of a "lack" (*Mangel*)[43] in attempts at a genuine self-identification or self-relating (*sich verhalten*), a lack Marcuse, in his most Hegelian or "idealist" moments, simply refers to as an "obscurity" (*Dunkelheit*), an obscurity that requires only "clarification."[44]   Later he refers to the "insufficiency" (*Mangelhaftigkeit*) of existence, the absence (*Fehlen*) of "true completed unity and identity."[45]

To explain this existential "lack" Marcuse returns to some of Hegel's earliest theological writings, and tries to trace the elements of Hegel's continuing reflections on *Leben* that explain the nature of this lack.   In doing so, even while still stressing the abstract categories of "unity" and "difference" that function in these accounts, Marcuse himself begins to stress that these "formal" determinations of the concept of historicity are "insufficient,"[46] that the concept must be seen in its "true actuality" (*wahre Wirklichkeit*)[47] if it is to be fully defended.   In proceeding in this direction, he concentrates on Hegel's account in the *Phenomenology of Spirit* of the progressively more determinate elements of human, self-conscious rationality.   (That is, Marcuse concentrates on the structural analyses of Chapter Four and Five of the *Phenomenology*, not the exhibition of this historical activity in concrete Western history, in Chapter Six.   This difference, we shall soon see, evidences a fatal ambiguity in Marcuse's position.)   Most of this account stays close to an explication of the Hegelian categories of "immediate life," relation to other-being (*Anderssein*), negativity, self-consciousness, relation to an other self-consciousness, desire, and recognition.   But what is revealing about this explication is that Marcuse, consistent with his own position, tries to avoid the impression that somehow these "truths" about concrete human existence or "life" are themselves the "ground" or basis of his general ontology.   For example, when commenting on "desire" (*Begierde*) he characterizes it as "the original stance of the self over against being, a way of being, not a psychic act . . . "[48] and tries to show *not* that human desire explains or helps justify the "coming-to-itself in other-being" of life (*Zusichselbstkommen im Anderssein*), but, as the very terms of his explanation make clear, the situation is supposed to be the other way around, a strange result in a search for "true actuality."   (Or, the highly abstract "ontological" dimension fully retains its priority.)   In fact, he makes this unusual methodological claim himself, directly,[49] and continues to refer to it throughout his analysis of the supposedly concrete categories of deed, work, and "*Die Sache selbst.*"   Accordingly, and quite consistently, when he again reaches the point of showing how the structural characteristics of human "historizing" are to establish a *critical* or "genuinely" transformative, point of view, he again points only to the illumination of historicity itself, and he suggests that this illumination alone can resist the "reification" and distortion of human freedom that occurs when historicity is forgotten, or ideologically suppressed when a form of life is viewed in part or whole as natural or necessary.

Accordingly, while Marcuse struggles to preserve a dimension of affirmation, two-dimensionality, and thereby a positive concept of "freedom," his constant insistence here on the ontological nature of historicity continually creates problems for that impulse.   First, such affirmative impulses tend to re-establish the moment of Absolute, or unhistorical knowledge that his whole theory is meant to undermine. Second, we get no evidence (given Marcuse's exclusion from his interpretation of Chapter Six of the *Phenomenology*) about which institutions and practices would be consistent with his self-conscious historicity, and why. Now again, such a reticence is understandable, given his larger claims. The details of such an affirmative moment should "depend" on the concrete context. But it is still hard to see any general outline here for deciding such questions *in concreto*. Third, as a result of these problems, there are several indications that Marcuse feels himself pulled in a totally different direction, towards abandoning the radicality of his account of human finitude and history, and towards a potential moment of genuine transcendence, not just another moment in the continuous process of historicity.[50] Such dilemmas and such tendencies help formulate what I believe to be a decisive question for Marcuse's later work: Does he abandon the radical elements of the historicity theory (its ontological orientation) and if so does he provide a way of answering the objections to that abandonment he himself has provided? Or, does he retain it, and try to find a way of developing a more concrete and critical analysis that is consistent with it? Perhaps the best place to begin to look for an answer to such a question is his next major treatment of Hegel, *Reason and Revolution*.

VI

As we shall soon see, there appear to be in this work important alterations in Marcuse's understanding of Hegel and the Heideggerean version of historicity he had partially defended in *Hegels Ontologie*. In particular, Marcuse insists on the insufficiency and incompleteness of philosophy, argues for the priority of social theory, and focuses much more attention on the theme of materialism. Yet it is also clear that *Reason and Revolution* still preserves many of the decisive elements of the position defended nine years earlier. Most clearly, what Marcuse wants to preserve and defend in Hegel is the central place given in his system to "negativity," the "power" of thought and action to reject and transform any putative "positive" reality, and the impossibility of understanding any such reality except in relation to this possibility. Accordingly, in *Reason and Revolution*, he again rejects in Hegel all those aspects of his thought that tend to suppress or overcome this negating potential, and thereby its decisive consequence, *Bewegtheit*. In *Hegels Ontologie*, Marcuse had rejected Hegel's view of a final, transcendent, "absolute" moment in history as inconsistent with the ontological claims Marcuse believes he has discovered in Hegel. Likewise, in this work, he also rejects Hegel's final "rational synthesis," repeats his charge that the *Philosophy of Right* and the *Philosophy of History* are the most undialectical, least defensible parts of Hegel's system, and stresses again that "There is a stark truth in Hegel's strangely certain announcement that history has reached its end. But it announces the funeral of a class, not of history."[51]

Secondly, although completely unacknowledged now, there are several passages that continue to make use of an unmistakably Heideggerean orientation. In an early explanation of Hegel's enterprise, Marcuse evidences no hesitancy to interpret Hegelian ontology in terms of the

Heideggerean distinction between *Sein* and *Seindes*. (He says only that Hegel's position "implies" this distinction.)[52]   Moreover, when rejecting a "scientific" view of Marx's economic analysis, he reverts to earlier form again, construing the Marxist categories as "determining factors for human existence" and inserting in the text, again without elaboration and defense, those notions crucial to the Heideggerean period, "*Daseinsformen*" and "*Existenzbestimmungen*."[53]

But most important in this continuity is the emphasis on historicity or the "being of the historical" as the *foundational* premise in Hegel, Marx, and any genuinely dialectical theory. This foundational claim, and the resonances of his earlier views of its meaning are clear when he first states his understanding of Hegel's "idealism."

> If the being of things consists in their transformation, rather than in their state of existence, the manifold states they have, whatever their form and content may be, are but moments of a comprehensive process, and exist only within the totality of that process. Thus they are of an "ideal" nature and their philosophical interpretation must be idealism.[54]

Further indications of the dimensions and consequences of this claim are everywhere apparent throughout the work (especially in his interpretation of the *Science of Logic*). He stresses again here that ". . . the intrinsic connection, between the *Logic* and the other parts of the system, and above all the implications of the dialectical method, destroy the very idea of timelessness."[55] And that "mind is of its very essence affected by time, for it exists only in the temporal process of history."[56] In the second Preface to the book, he praises dialectical thought for analyzing "the world of facts in terms of its internal inadequacy" and goes on to explain how all facts "continually translate the past into the present" and that "dialectical analysis ultimately tends to become historical analysis."[57]   Moreover, there is also a continuing recognizable emphasis on the "totality" or whole of some historical form of life as a way of understanding the contradictions that develop within that whole.

> The world must not remain a complex of fixed disparates. The unity that underlies the antagonisms must be grasped and realized by reason, which has the task of reconciling the opposites and "sublating" them in a true unity. The fulfillment of reason's task would at the same time involve restoring the lost unity in the social relations of man.[58]

With this passage we are obviously returned to our earlier problem of understanding this "lost unity" more concretely, and here again, in *Reason and Revolution* many of the earlier answers and problems resurface. In the Preface, Marcuse had prepared the way for a familiar answer by claiming that "All facts embody the knower as well as the doer; they continuously translate the past into the present. The objects thus 'contain' subjectivity in their very structure."[59]   When he much later draws out the consequences of this position for understanding the "development" of history, he makes a claim we have heard before. In rejecting an organic view of historical development (from fixed "potentiality" to "actuality"), Marcuse stresses by contrast that "the highest form of development is reached only when self-consciousness exercises *mastery over the whole process*"[60] (emphasis added). This seems to repeat the claim of *Hegels Ontologie* that the *only* notion of development consistent with the historicity of existence is a development toward the realization of historicity itself and the self-conscious subjectivity of agents in that realization. This seems exactly what he means when he says, "It is the realization of freedom and happiness that necessitates the establishment of an order wherein associated individuals will determine the organization of their life."[61] Shortly after this passage he refuses to speculate further on the content of history after this realization, saying only "The rest is the task of man's liberating activity."[62]

This "respect," one might call it, for the historically specific character of such "liberating activity" (the impossibility of deducing it speculatively) even extends well into Marcuse's interpretation of Marx and the issue of "materialism," the issue that seems to suggest a break with parts of the earlier position. For Marcuse not only adopts a historical view of Marx's economic theory, he goes on to insist that "dialectic" itself, and the whole account of negativity on which it is based, is *not* a general theory, that, repeating the point made above, "Once mankind has become the conscious subject of its development, its history can no longer be outlined in forms that apply to the pre-historical phase."[63] And such a claim not only makes clear the continuity of Marcuse's understanding of historicity and its foundational role, it also makes clear that many of the problems raised by that position are still present in *Reason and Revolution*.

That is, even while Marcuse is now insisting, much more directly and centrally than he had done before, that historical activity cannot be conceived as *any* sort of development or self-transformation, that it essentially involves the struggle for human "happiness" and that that struggle must involve as its decisive components social organization and labor, he does not yet appear willing to project any very specific view of the content of that happiness. And, I hope it is becoming clear, the reason for this hesitancy continues to be a belief in the impossibility (I think it is still fair to say "ontological" impossibility) for projecting an ahistorical, universal, utopian "goal" to history. To be sure, he clearly does not himself consider even the brief indications he gives here of this happiness (subject's "mastering" the historical process) to be anything like a completion or end to history. He writes:

> [T]he struggle with the "realm of necessity" will continue with man's passage to the stage of his "actual history", and the negativity and the contradiction will not disappear. Nevertheless when society has become the free subject of this struggle, the latter will be waged in entirely different forms.[64]

Yet, as our earlier discussion indicated: (a) it *does* appear that this achievement is a decisive "end" to the "struggle" of history itself as history has come to be understood, and, accordingly, that it would seem more consistent with the thesis of historicity to regard that achievement not as human happiness *simpliciter*, but as only a specific "historical" shape of spirit; and (b) in the terms provided by Marcuse, it is hard to see why these new forms of "struggle," "negativity," and "contradiction" should be regarded as a decisive transformation of human history, rather than a mere alteration in its course. In sum, as before, Marcuse seems again pulled, for compelling reasons, in both directions, towards a reconstituted, non-idealist "Absolute," and towards preserving the radicality of his historicity thesis.

Yet, at this point, it would clearly be unfair to Marcuse to try to develop his position wholly within these theoretical terms. After all, he has provided us with what he considers to be examples of concrete historical analysis which demonstrate what the *present* reveals about the possibility of becoming "the free subject" of the historical struggle, and what, in the present context, *that*, specifically, means.

VII

Throughout it has been clear that the crucial element for Marcuse in the liberation of historical subjects has been the ability by those subjects to recover *all* the elements, the "totality," of a specific form of life, as what such elements essentially *are*: products or expressions *of* that subjectivity. Since our emphasis has been on Marcuse's use of Hegel, we have been concentrating on the philosophic and conceptual issues involved in that recovery. Clearly, though, as the very notion of totality itself makes clear, it would be a serious distortion of Marcuse's position to pretend that this "consciousness" of historicity alone was the only important element in the liberation of subjectivity. Specifically, within that totality, the *sensuous* elements of subjectivity are at least as, if not more, important in Marcuse's fuller account. At least, they assume that priority in the present age. For in this age, it is sensibility that has emerged as the most important, even decisive, dimension in the ability of social subjectivity to "realize" itself as the true subject of history. The transformation of desire, satisfaction, pleasure, happiness and the like into commodities, and the almost completely successful ability of contemporary institutions to suppress this alienation between subjects and their own sensual being is the context in which Marcuse's concrete extension of his theory of historicity can be most clearly seen.

And, obviously, no justice can be done to that analysis here. But it is possible to see, however briefly, how the problems developed above persist in different forms in these more well-known works, and thereby to summarize finally the foundational problem of historicity in Marcuse's enterprise.

In one obvious sense, the central thesis of *Eros and Civilization* supports much of what has been said here. One of the aspects of Freud's meta-psychology which so appealed to Marcuse was his historical explanation of the basic "dialectic" of civilization and repression. It was the general idea of repression and social stability as an historically *achieved* result which makes it impossible to consider that "reality" in its own terms, and which demands that it be assessed in terms of the historical price paid, in terms of the "return of the repressed."   Indeed Marcuse argued that Freud did not go far enough, did not see that his version of the reality principle was itself a historically contingent one, one that could be assessed differently from our point of view.   It thus emerges as a historically contingent "performance" principle.   Moreover, even more surprisingly, Marcuse follows the logic of such a historical perspective to an occasionally extreme end point, and far from smuggling in an *a priori* anthropology into critical theory (as readers of Marcuse sometimes charge), argued that even the *instincts* should be viewed as historical phenomena.   He writes that "the nature of the instincts is subject to change if the fundamental conditions that caused the instincts to acquire this nature have changed"[65]; that there can be a "non-repressive development of the libido under the conditions of mature civilization"[66]; and he excoriates the revisionists for neglecting to note that "in Freudian theory, impulses are modifiable, subject to the vicissitudes of history,"[67] and that the relativity of the performance principle would even affect "[Freud's] basic conception of the instinctual dynamic between Eros and Thanatos."[68]   But, however much such remarks indicate the consistency of Marcuse's position, they return us again to the difficulty of understanding the "affirmative" aspects of Marcuse's theory, given this emphasis on historicity.   In this book, that problem is particularly clear in the critique of revisionist Freudians.   At his most sarcastic and negative, Marcuse criticizes Fromm, Horney, Harry Stack Sullivan and the like for their conformist and adaptive ego-psychology, even though much of their revision of Freud would seem consistent with much of Marcuse's own version of historicity.   That is, in mediating the opposition between instinctual satisfaction and the reality principle, an opposition which seemed to Marcuse to make Freud so revolutionary, they could just be accepting the possibility of a historical transformation of instincts under some different reality principle or other. To oppose them, Marcuse writes in a strangely different way when he insists, "Psychoanalysis elucidates the universal in individual experience. To that extent, and only to that extent, can psychoanalysis break the reification in which human relations are petrified,"[69] and he goes on, when struggling to preserve the critical dimension in Freud, to admire Freud's biologism again.

Of course, the core of Marcuse's criticism of the revisionists can be preserved without Freudian biologism. The earlier quoted admission that the instincts themselves are historically mutable presupposes the necessity of profound social change in order for such historical alteration to occur. As a "phylogenetic" thesis, it is hardly a warrant for a more ego-oriented, adaptive, or what Marcuse called a Norman Vincent Peale ("accentuate the positive") therapy. On Marcuse's Hegelian assumptions, such historical transformation is possible only within the totality of social life, and not as an effect of will between therapist and patient.

However, an opponent might still object that if some of Marcuse's own theses are admitted, then there is *finally* no reason to think that some genuine "universal in individual experience" can be discovered and affirmed, that, for example, phantasy in a capitalistic society should represent a true "return" of *the* repressed. Rather, under a thorough and effective capitalism, such phantasy might just *become* "capitalistic phantasies" in the deepest sense.

To be sure, this is not a possibility which is lost on Marcuse. In fact, this kind of extension of the doctrine of historicity is precisely what lies behind the so-called "more pessimistic" stance noticeable in *One-Dimensional Man*. There Marcuse continues to claim unambiguously that "human needs are historical needs,"[70] admits that the questions of the truth or falsehood of "need" are "historical throughout and their objectivity is historical," and extends this notion of historicity "down to their [humans'] very instincts."[71] It is this unambiguous historical view of such "needs" which grounds the famous "contradictory hypothesis" of *One-Dimensional Man*:

(1) That advanced industrial society is capable of containing qualitative change for the foreseeable future; (2) that forces and tendencies exist which may break this containment and explode society.[72]

As is well known, when Marcuse comes to assess the second possibility at the end of the book, his outlook is not terribly hopeful. When he asks

how can the administered individuals - who have made their mutilation into their own liberties and satisfactions, liberate *themselves from themselves* as well as from their masters?[73]

he answers that "At the present stage of development of the advanced industrial societies the material as well as the cultural system denies this exigency."[74]

I would suggest, given all that we have seen so far, that this dilemma is not comprehensible as a contingent feature of advanced industrial society alone. Given Marcuse's continued reliance on some of his earliest claims about the fundamentality of the thesis of historicity, it should not be surprising that it would at some point be difficult for him to know what to say about those whose historical self-transformation results in an active rejection of any truly subjective role. If history itself cannot be conceived to have a necessary telos, nor an original "ground" or pre-historical "origin," there is certainly no reason why the course of actual history should *not* reach a point where it is transformed into a permanent stasis, where the affirmation of a social order is not so much the result of an ideological *suppression* of subjectivity, but the *final* transformation of subjectivity into *something else altogether*. In this context, it is easy to understand Marcuse's search for a pre- or extra-historical element or "class" to whom to re-assign the role of historical agent. (Not to mention Marcuse's final attempt to discover an "*autonomous*" aesthetic dimension. Not for nothing was the German title of his last work, *Die Permanenz der Kunst*.[75])

VIII

I have been arguing that Marcuse never wholly abandons the views concerning historicity apparent in his first Hegel book and that such a theme is essential to his own view of the possibility of negative or critical thinking. I have also been suggesting that it is hard to make out exactly how Marcuse thinks the critical appropriation of the past demanded by the consequences of the historicity thesis is to be explained. We seem to find only discarded alternatives for such an explanation; Hegel's theory of absolute knowledge, Heideggerean authenticity, orthodox Marxist notions of prediction and crude naturalism, Freudian biologism. There are even suggestions in *One-Dimensional Man* that no *practically* relevant criticism is even possible. In general, it would now seem as if this historicity thesis could become an aspect of a critical theory only in one of two possible ways.

One would be to attempt to extract from historical recollection characteristics which can be argued to be indispensably involved in any possible "free" continuation of the past. We could discover in such recollection, in other words, "conditions" for human interaction which if violated can be shown to have generated deep contradictions in the continuing attempts by societies to legitimize themselves in various historical contexts. We could show that these contradictions are only resolved by strategies of force, hypocrisy, propaganda, or, in general, repression, or by progressive attempts to actualize such historically discovered conditions more adequately. The "essence" discovered in such recollection would then initially be formal, and itself legitimated in great part by the historical *story* we give of the emergence, development, avoidance, and partial actualization of such conditions for human autonomy. (History would then be a story of the constant "return" of Kantian-like repressed conditions of autonomy.[76])

Of course, apart from hints at such an approach in his notion of the illumination of the historicity of existence, Marcuse did not develop any detailed "transcendental" account of such "conditions." From what has been sketched here, his response to such a move would be to claim that just as there is no *a priori* philosophic anthropology, there is no *a priori* "ideal" condition necessary for distinctively human agency in any historical epoch. Any such ideal is itself a historically achieved standard, and must be seen in terms of the historical whole in which it emerges. To argue otherwise, he would claim, is theoretically to violate many of the crucial claims of historicity, and practically to postulate a mere "ought" or *Sollen*, too indeterminately related to historical conditions for its meaning and possible actualization to be understood.

On the other hand, Marcuse seems to appeal to the earlier mentioned notion of historical *totality*, to essence as the actually *achieved* conception of autonomy, actuality and legitimacy, and that only within these actual conceptions can we discover the strains of inherent inconsistency or even contradiction involved in such a historically localized totality. Critical theory will then remain radically historical, focused on what present conditions, understood or remembered historically, reveal about potentiality for negation. There are no eternal standards, then, of either a formal or substantive variety. There are just localized analyses, like those offered in *One-Dimensional Man*, of what promises, for example, automation holds *within* the historical development and rationale of industrialization itself ("freedom from toil"), or what we might expect to be the outcome of rapid industrialization in the Third World.[77]

Such a view is historical in the original sense proposed by Marcuse in 1932. It ties critical analysis to the historical conditions of some determinate social community, but avoids historicism by arguing that the historical rootedness of participants in this community is a result of their own interpretation, "recollection" and integration of the past. They are the agents who, in various complex and often unself-conscious ways, "stretch the past along into the present" and they are the ones who could alter that community. To be sure, this can only be done in terms of concrete historical possibilities, and these can only be discovered "locally," by critical attention to the "essential" achievements of a community considered as a totality. But again, there are no programmatic "rules" or formal guidelines for such criticism. There are only the actual contradictions in any community's attempt to make life better for itself. Indeed, this famous "non-programmatic" aspect of Marcuse's thought could be said to represent most the continuing influence of Heidegger on his view of history, and the continuing, unresolved problems that influence caused.

Admittedly, both such alternatives face familiar problems. The formal approach, in past uses at least, often can only offer the most general and abstract standards of historical assessment - allowing us, for example, to condemn the formal inconsistency of state religion, slavery, or private tyranny, but wondering about historical institutions like private property, or forms of labor. The latter, more historical view, aside from its general ungroundedness, often seems incapable of doing more than pointing negatively at a society's internal contradictions, with little programmatic or pragmatic suggestions for transformation or correction.

As I indicated in summarizing the former view, I am not sure these alternatives are that necessarily opposed, but I would suggest that such are the alternatives that Marcuse's theory of historicity present us with. In that respect, it must be said that Marcuse's project remains philosophically unfinished, deeply committed both to the thesis of historicity and the necessity of criticism in the historical appropriation of the past, but with no final integration of these strands. I would add immediately, however, that, in considering the above alternative directions his position could take, it is no slight tribute to Marcuse that his thought returns us again to such fundamental alternatives in the German philosophical tradition, a tradition still struggling with the choices posed by two of its greatest thinkers, Kant and Hegel.

NOTES

1.   I use the second edition, Herbert Marcuse, *Hegels Ontologie und die Theorie der Geschichtlichkeit* (Frankfurt, 1968). (In this edition Marcuse had changed the title from *Hegels Ontologie und die Grundlegung einer Theorie der Geschichtlichkeit*.)

2.   For the relevant historical background on the development of the theory of historicity see *Briefwechsel zwischen Wilhelm Dilthey und dem Grafen Paul Yorck von Wartenburg*, 1877-1897.

3.   Such a suspicion is intensified, of course, by the fact that Marcuse, by the mid-thirties, had explicitly rejected phenomenology and Heidegger. I shall try to show, however, that the most important thematic results of this Heideggerean interpretation of Hegel persist as foundational elements of much of the later Marcuse.

4.   See Martin Jay, *The Dialectical Imagination*.

5.   Especially Alfred Schmidt's "Existential Ontologie und historischer Materialismus bei Herbert Marcuse," in *Antworten auf Marcuse*, pp. 17-48. (Translated in this volume.) Paul Piccone and Alexander Delfini in "Herbert Marcuse's Heideggerean Marxism," *Telos* 6 (Fall 1970), pp. 36-46, at least try to show the persistence of Heideggerean themes in Marcuse's later work, but their discussion of Heidegger is too brief (and too inaccurate) to be of much help, and they ignore completely the clearly Hegelian qualifications on Marcuse's Heideggereanism. There exists a study of Hegel's role in the development of the Frankfurt School, Friederich W. Schmidt's, "Hegel in der kritischen Theorie der 'Frankfurter Schule'", in *Aktualitat und Folgen der Philosophie Hegels*, pp. 21-61. However, Schmidt's interest is in contrasting the "radicalization" of Hegel's dialectic in Horkheimer and Adorno, with the "reduction" of dialectic in Habermas, and he omits any treatment of Marcuse.

6.   That is, the Gadamer-Habermas controversy.

7.   *Hegels Ontologie*, p. 363.

8.   "Theory and Politics: A Discussion with Herbert Marcuse, Jürgen Habermas, Heinz Lubascz, and Telman Spengler," *Telos* 38 (Winter 1978-79). There is other,   substantial evidence of this orientation in Marcuse. See "Philosophy and Critical Theory" in *Negations* (Harmondsworth, 1968), pp. 148-9, p. 152, and p. 158. See also "The Foundation of Historical Materialism" re-published in *Studies in Critical Philosophy* (Boston, 1973). See especially p. 17 (and the reference to *Hegels Ontologie*), p. 24, and pp. 29ff, after Marcuse's remark about the "discovery of the historical character of the human essence."

9.   There are of course other uses of "ontology" that may be of relevance to the post-Hegelian tradition. See Carol Gould, *Marx's Social Ontology*. From the point of view explored in this essay, though, the question that could be raised for Gould's approach and others like it is whether it can avoid the dilemmas of Marcuse's ontology of activity, constitution,   and   history,   without   relapsing   into   a   traditional "Naturontologie," of a pre-Kantian variety, with its familiar problems.

10.   In fact, Marcuse is explicitly rejecting any view of Hegel's *Logic* which sees it as a "methodology" or a Kantian "Kategorienlehre."

Whether, though, treating the work as an "ontology" can consistently answer the methodological questions that must be raised will have to be addressed in what follows.

11. The clearest expressions of the debt to Heidegger (aside from the sweeping statement of debt at the beginning) occur on pp. 36, 42, and 218. Of course, I am referring here, and throughout, to the Heidegger of *Sein und Zeit*, not the post-*Kehre* Heidegger who, apparently, rejected this "subjectivist" orientation.

12. *Hegels Ontologie*, p. 1.

13. In *Philosophische Hefte* 1 (July 1928), pp. 45-68.

14. In Herbert Marcuse, *Philosophie und Revolution*, Bd. 1 (Berlin, 1967), pp. 143-89.

15. *Hegels Ontologie*, p. 1.

16. *Ibid.*, p. 63.

17. Herbert Marcuse, "On the Problem of the Dialectic," trans. by Morton Schoolman and Duncan Smith, *Telos* 27 (Spring 1976), pp. 19-20.

18. *Ibid.*, p. 21. See also *Hegels Ontologie*, p. 200.

19. *Hegels Ontologie*, pp. 166, 168, 337.

20. From *History and Structure*. See my discussion below of Schmidt's approach in this book, note 42. The source for such expressions is Heidegger's account of the "temporalizing of temporality" in *Being and Time*.

21. A point Marcuse freely admits. See *Hegels Ontologie*, pp. 47 and p. 126. In general, I shall not be concerned here with the philological accuracy of Marcuse's treatment of Hegel. My interest here is what that interpretation says about Marcuse's position and so for the moment shall ignore what I regard as problematic aspects of Marcuse's treatment of the historical Hegel. For a brief indication of some of the philological problems Marcuse's views would face, see Michael Theunissen's discussion in *Die Verwirklichung der Vernunft: Zur Theorie-Praxis Diskussion im Anschluss an Hegel, Philosophie Rundschau*, Beiheft 6. See also notes 42 and 75.

22. Max Horkheimer, "Traditional and Critical Theory" in *Critical Theory*, and Herbert Marcuse, "Philosophy and Critical Theory."

23. The *loci classici* for distinguishing "historicity" from the "historicism" of the nineteenth century occur in Heidegger, *Being and Time*, section 76; and H. G. Gadamer, *Truth and Method*, p. 204. The more sophisticated historicists are figures such as Ranke, and later Rothaker, but the curious historicist blend of positivism and relativism is visible in F. S. Stahl, whom Marcuse vigorously attacks in *Reason and Revolution* (Boston, 1960), pp. 360ff. On the issue of Dilthey, see Michael Ermath's useful book, *Wilhelm Dilthey: The Critique of Historical Reason*.

24. As Marcuse argues in *Reason and Revolution*, p. 317. See also A. Schmidt, *History and Structure*.

25. See note 5.

26. A. Schmidt, "Existential Ontologie . . . ," p. 22.

27. *Ibid.*, p. 23.

28. *Ibid.*, p. 35.

29. See for example, the interview "Heidegger's Politics: Interview with

Herbert Marcuse by Frederick Olafson," *Graduate Faculty Philosophy Journal*, 6, no. 1 (Winter 1977), pp. 25-40.

30. A. Schmidt, "Existential Ontologie . . . ," p. 40.

31. *Hegels Ontologie*, p. 205.

32. *Ibid.*, pp. 68, 166, 321.

33. *Ibid.*, pp. 337-8.

34. Cf. *Reason and Revolution*, p. x.

35. Marcuse puts it this way in *Hegels Ontologie*, pp. 351, 354, 361.

36. *Ibid.*, p. 121.

37. Herbert Marcuse, "The Concept of Essence," transl. by Jeremy Shapiro in *Negations*, p. 70. This essay is crucial in understanding how Marcuse wants to appropriate the notion of historicity without the implications of abstractness and relativism he finds in Dilthey and Heidegger. See his remarks on "abstract historicity" on p. 78. However, as we shall see, what he tries to extract from a historical view of essence, and what actually results, are two different things.

38. *Hegels Ontologie*, p. 77.

39. *Ibid.*, p. 79.

40. *Ibid.*, p. 106.

41. *Ibid.*, p. 354.

42. Cf. Michael Theunissen, *Gesellschaft und Geschichte: Zur Kritik der Kritischen Theorie*, pp. 29, 31. Since I have mentioned Schmidt prominently, I will add that the problem cited here continues to be an important one in Schmidt's own work, especially the recently translated *History and Structure*. In that work, Schmidt is out to criticize "structuralist," "anti-humanist," "anti-historical" interpretations of Marx, such as Althusser's. He argues that Althusser has misconceived *Capital* as an independent scientific inquiry (*Forschung*), that it should instead be seen as a "presentation" (*Darstellung*) of the "conceptuality" *of* capitalist society itself, *its* (and only its) highest, most complete mode of self-understanding.) *Capital* represents Marx's "second" appropriation of Hegel, of the *Science of Logic*, Hegel's own "presentation" of a *historical* form of self-understanding. (Cf. especially pp. 16, 34, 38, 64, 105, and the remark on historicity and Critical Theory, p. 79.) But this approach raises the difficulty just presented even more radically than it appears in Marcuse. Such a claim itself clearly rests on a *theory* of historicity (a meta-level account of the *Logic* and *Capital* that cannot *itself* be "presented" as an *example* of some historical self-understanding). But if it *isn't*, one can predict difficulties in reconciling this "meta-logic" with the content of the claims made *for* historicity. Moreover, from what we have already seen in *Hegels Ontologie* it is clear that Marcuse, with his concern for "essence" "totality" and "Absolute Knowledge" is much more aware of this problem than is Gramsci, as his "humanist" position is presented by Schmidt. For an interpretation of Hegel that tries to avoid the "paradoxes of wisdom," see my "Hegel's Phenomenological Criticism," *Man and World* 8 (1975), pp. 296-314.

43. *Hegels Ontologie*, p. 123.

44. *Ibid.*

45. *Ibid.*, p. 253.

46. *Ibid.*, p. 208.

47. *Ibid.*, p. 212.

48. *Ibid.*, p. 276.

49. *Ibid.*, p. 283.

50. Even towards a much more traditional ontology, a "Naturontologie." See also note 75.

51. *Reason and Revolution*, p. 227.

52. *Ibid.*, p. 40.

53. *Ibid.*, p. 274.

54. *Ibid.*, p. 138.

55. *Ibid.*, p. 224.

56. *Ibid.*

57. *Ibid.*, p. x.

58. *Ibid.*, p. 45.

59. *Ibid.*, p. viii.

60. *Ibid.*, p. 238.

61. *Ibid.*, pp. 317-18.

62. *Ibid.*, p. 322.

63. *Ibid.*, p. 316.

64. *Ibid.*, pp. 316-7.

65. Herbert Marcuse, *Eros and Civilization* (Boston, 1966), p. 138.

66. *Ibid.*, p. 139.

67. *Ibid.*, p. 272.

68. *Ibid.*, p. 132.

69. *Ibid.*, p. 254.

70. *One-Dimensional Man* (Boston, 1964), p. 4.

71. *Ibid.*, p. 6.

72. *Ibid.*, p. xv.

73. *Ibid.*, pp. 250-51.

74. *Ibid.*, p. 252.

75. *The Aesthetic Dimension* (Boston, 1978), especially, pp. 6, 10, 72-73. Of course, it should also be admitted that what I have called the "other dimension" to Marcuse's work, particularly his reliance on the rather vague and unhistorical notions of "nature," "need," and "eros," are not incidental to his later (post *One-Dimensional Man*) work, and that they cause serious theoretical problems in his position. I would, though, claim that this dimension too stems from the way Marcuse, and others in the *Institut*, understood the Hegelian foundation of dialectic (or rather, I would claim, misunderstood it). For some suggestions about this aspect of Marcuse, and its Hegelian roots, see Theunissen, *Gesellschaft und Geschichte*.

76. This is a very crude and brief summary of some of the strategy recently used by Apel and Habermas. I should add that, at this point, such a Kantian turn in critical theory has yet to integrate fully a theory of history into its formal account of "ideal" speech-act situations. See, *inter alia*, Karl Otto Apel, "Sprachaktstheorie und transzendentale Sprachprogramatik - Zur Frage ethischer Normen," in *Sprachprogramatik und Philosophie*, and, for an attempt to integrate such a formal approach with historical considerations,· Jürgen Habermas, "Toward a

Reconstruction of Historical Materialism" in *Communication and the Evolution of Society*, pp. 130-77.

77.   Or, in *One-Dimensional Man*, ". . . a specific historical practice is measured against *its own* historical alternatives." p. x (emphasis mine).

CHAPTER SIX

Heidegger's Politics:
An Interview
With Herbert Marcuse

Frederick Olafson

Olafson Professor Marcuse, you are very widely known as a social philosopher and a Marxist; but I think there are relatively few who know that Martin Heidegger and his philosophy played a considerable role in your intellectual career. Perhaps we could begin by just laying out the basic facts about that contact with Heidegger and with his philosophy.

Marcuse Here are the basic facts - I read *Sein und Zeit* when it came out in 1927 and after having read it I decided to go back to Freiburg (where I had received my Ph.D. in 1922) in order to work with Heidegger. I stayed in Freiburg and worked with Heidegger until December 1932, when I left Germany a few days before Hitler's ascent to power, and that ended the personal relationship. I saw Heidegger again after the War, I think in 1946 - 47, in the Black Forest where he has his little house. We had a talk which was not exactly very friendly and very positive, there was an exchange of letters, and since that time there has not been any communication between us.

Olafson Would it be fair to say that during the time you were in Freiburg you accepted the principle theses of *Being and Time* and that you were, in some sense, at that time, a Heideggerian? Or were there major qualifications and reservations even then?

Marcuse I must say frankly that during this time, let's say from 1928 to 1932, there were relatively few reservations and relatively few criticisms on my part. I would rather say on *our* part, because Heidegger at that time was not a personal problem, not even philosophically, but a problem of a large part of the generation that studied in Germany after the first World War. We saw in Heidegger what we had first seen in Husserl, a new beginning, the first radical attempt to put philosophy on really concrete foundations - philosophy concerned with the human existence, the human condition, and not with merely abstract ideas and principles. That certainly I shared with a relatively large number of my generation, and needless to say, the disappointment with this philosophy eventually came - I think it began in the early thirties. But we re-examined Heidegger thoroughly only after his association with Nazism had become known.

Olafson What did you make at that stage of the social aspect of Heidegger's philosophy - its implications for political and social life and action? Were you yourself interested in those at that stage, did you perceive them in Heidegger's thought?

Marcuse I was very much interested in it during that stage, at the same time I wrote articles of Marxist analysis for the then theoretical organ of the German Socialists, *Die Gesellschaft*. So I certainly was interested, and I first, like all the others, believed there could be some combination between existentialism and Marxism, precisely because of their insistence on concrete analysis of the actual human existence, human beings and their world. But I soon realized that Heidegger's concreteness was to a great extent a phony, a false concreteness, and that in fact his philosophy was just as abstract and just as removed from reality, even avoiding reality, as the philosophies which at that time had dominated German universities, namely a rather dry brand of neo-Kantianism, neo-Hegelianism, neo-Idealism, but also positivism.

Olafson How did he respond to the hopes that you had for some kind of fruitful integration of his philosophy with, let us say, a Marxist social philosophy?

Marcuse He didn't respond. You know as far as I can say, it is today still open to question whether Heidegger ever really read Marx, whether Heidegger ever read Lukacs, as Lucien Goldman maintains. I tend not to believe it. He may have had a look at Marx after or during the Second World War, but I don't think that he in any way studied Marx.

Olafson There are some positive remarks about Marx in Heidegger's writing, indicating that he was not at all . . .

Marcuse That's interesting. I know of only one: the *Letter on Humanism*.

Olafson Yes.

Marcuse Where he says that Marx's view of history excels all other history. That is the only remark. I know the *Letter* was written under the French occupation after the World War, one didn't know yet how things would go, so I don't give much weight to this remark.

Olafson More generally, how do you view the importance of phenomenological and ontological analyses of the kind that Heidegger offered in *Being and Time*, their importance I mean, for purposes of social analysis. You've made it clear that Heidegger himself was not interested in developing them in that direction. Do you think that they might have had uses beyond those that he was interested in?

Marcuse In my first article ("Contribution to a Phenomenology of Historical Materialism," 1928), I myself tried to combine existentialism and Marxism. Sartre's *Being and Nothingness* is such an attempt on a much larger scale. But to the degree to which Sartre turned to Marxism, he surpassed his existentialist writings and finally dissociated himself from them. Even he did not succeed in reconciling Marx and Heidegger. As to Heidegger himself, he seems to use his existential analysis to get away from the social reality rather than into it.

Olafson You see these pretty much dropping out of the work of people who have perhaps begun with ontology and phenomenology, but have gone on to . . . .

Marcuse Yes.

Olafson To Marxism. You don't see a continuing role for that kind of . . .

Marcuse I don't think so. You see, I said at the beginning, I spoke about the false concreteness of Heidegger. If you look at his principle concepts, (I will use German terms because I am still not familiar with the English translation) *Dasein, das Man, Sein, Seiendes, Existenz*, they are "bad" abstracts in the sense that they are not conceptual vehicles to comprehend the real concreteness in the apparent one. They lead away. For example, *Dasein* is for Heidegger a sociologically and even biologically "neutral" category (sex differences don't exist!); the *Frage nach dem Sein* remains the ever unanswered but ever repeated question; the distinction between fear and anxiety tends to transform very real fear into pervasive and vague anxiety. Even his at first glance most concrete existential category, death, is recognized as the most inexorable brute fact only to be made into an insurpassable *possibility*. Heidegger's existentialism is indeed a transcendental idealism compared with which Husserl's last writings (and even his *Logical Investigations*) seem saturated with historical concreteness.

Olafson Does that leave social theorists then with materialism or behaviorism as some kind of working theory of human nature? I take it that both Heidegger and Sartre have been attempting to resist philosophies of that kind. Does the dropping out of phenomenological and ontological elements in social theory mean an acceptance, de facto, of behaviorism?

Marcuse No, it does not. It depends entirely on what is meant by ontology. If there is an ontology which, in spite of its stress on historicity, neglects history, throws out history and returns to static transcendental concepts, I would say this philosophy cannot provide a conceptual basis for social and political theory.

Olafson   Let me take you up on that reference to history.   This is one of the things that Heidegger interested himself in quite considerably and there are at least two chapters in *Being and Time* that deal with history. Here of course the treatment is in terms of what Heidegger called historicity, or historicality, which means that the theme is treated in terms of a certain structure of individual (primarily individual) human existence, that is to say the individual's relationship to his own past, the way he places himself in a tradition, the way he modifies that tradition at the same time as he takes it over.   Does that work seem to you to have a lasting value, to have an element of concreteness?

Marcuse   I would see in his concept of historicity the same false or fake concreteness because actually none of the concrete material and cultural, none of the concrete social and political conditions which make history, have any place in *Being and Time*.   History too is subjected to neutralization.   He makes it into an existential category which is rather immune against the specific material and mental conditions which make up the course of history.   There may be one exception: Heidegger's late concern (one might say: preoccupation) with technology and technics. The *Frage nach dem Sein* recedes before the *Frage nach der Technik*.   I admit that much of these writings I do not understand.   More than before, it sounds as if our world can only be comprehended in the German language (though a strange and torturous one).   I have the impression that Heidegger's concepts of technology and technics are the last in the long series of neutralizations: they are treated as "forces in-themselves," removed from the context of power relations in which they are constituted and which determine their use and their function.   They are reified, hypostatized as Fate.

Olafson   Might he not have used the notion of historicity as a structure of personal existence in a different way?   Isn't it important for a social theory to show how an individual situates himself in a certain society, in a certain tradition?   Isn't it important that there be a characterization of that situation that is not just given at the level of relatively impersonal forces and tendencies, but that shows how the individual ties into those forces and tendencies?

Marcuse   There most certainly is a need for such an analysis, but that is precisely where the concrete conditions of history come in.   How does the individual situate himself and see himself in capitalism - at a certain stage of capitalism, under socialism, as a member of this or that class, and so on? This entire dimension is absent.   To be sure, *Dasein* is constituted in historicity, but Heidegger focuses on individuals purged of the hidden and not so hidden injuries of their class, their work, their recreation, purged of the injuries they suffer from their society.   There is no trace of the daily rebellion, of the striving for liberation.   The *Man* (the Anonymous Anyone) is no substitute for the social reality.

Olafson: Heidegger sees individual human beings as concerned above all with the prospect of their individual death, and this supersedes all the kinds of concrete social considerations that you have mentioned. Do you think that that emphasis and that lack of interest in the concrete and the social comes out of his theological training or bent of mind?

Marcuse: It may well be that his very thorough theological training has something to do with it. In any case, it is very good that you bring up the tremendous importance the notion of death has in his philosophy, because I believe that is a very good starting point for at least briefly discussing the famous question of whether Heidegger's Nazism was already noticeable in his philosophy prior to 1933. Now, from personal experience I can tell you that neither in his lectures, nor in his seminars, nor personally, was there any hint of his sympathies for Nazism. In fact, politics were never discussed - and to the very end he spoke very highly of the two Jews to whom he dedicated his books, Edmund Husserl and Max Scheler. So his openly declared Nazism came as a complete surprise to us. From that point on, of course, we asked ourselves the question; did we overlook indications and anticipations in *Being and Time* and the related writings? And we made one interesting observation, *ex-post* (I want to stress that, *ex-post*, it is easy to make this observation): If you look at his view of the human existence, of being-in-the-world, you will find a highly repressive, highly oppressive interpretation. I have just today gone again through the table of contents of *Being and Time*, and had a look at the main categories in which he sees the essential characteristics of existence or *Dasein*. I can just read them to you and you will see what I mean: "idle talk, curiosity, ambiguity, falling and being-thrown-into, concern, being toward death, anxiety, dread, boredom" and so on. Now this gives a picture which plays well on the fears and frustrations of men and women in a repressive society - a joyless existence: overshadowed by death and anxiety; human material for the authoritarian personality. It is for example highly characteristic that love is absent from *Being and Time* - the only place where it appears is in a footnote in a theological context together with faith, sin and remorse. I see now in this philosophy, ex-post, a very powerful devaluation of life, a derogation of joy, of sensuousness, fulfillment. And we may have had the feeling of it at that time, but it became clear only after Heidegger's association to Nazism became known.

Olafson Do you think that Heidegger as a man was simply politically naive? Do you think he understood the implications of his collaboration with the Nazi Party as Rector of the University of Freiburg?

Marcuse Well, I can speak rather authoritatively because I discussed it with him after the war. In order to prepare my answer, let me first read the statement which he made, I quote literally: "Let not principles and ideas rule your being. Today, and in the future, only the *Fuhrer* himself is German reality and its law." These were Heidegger's own words in November 1933. This is a man who professed that he was the heir of the great tradition of Western philosophy of Kant, Hegel, and so on - all this is now discarded, norms, principles, ideas are obsolete when the *Fuhrer* lays down the law and defines reality - the German reality. I talked with him about that several times and he admitted it was an "error"; he misjudged Hitler and Nazism - to which I want to add two things, first, that is one of the errors a philosopher is not allowed to commit.   He certainly can and does commit many, many mistakes but this is not an error and this is not a mistake, this is actually the betrayal of philosophy as such, and of everything philosophy stands for.   Secondly, he admitted, as I said, it was a mistake - but there he left the matter.   He refused (and I think that somehow I find this rather sympathetic), he refused any attempt to deny it or to declare it an aberration, or I don't know what, because he did not want to be in the same category, as he said, with all those of his colleagues who suddenly didn't remember any more that they taught under the Nazis, that they ever supported the Nazis, and declared that actually they had always been non-Nazi.   Now, in the case of Heidegger, as far as I know, he gave up any open identification with Nazism I think in 1935 or 1936.   He was not Rector of the University any more.   In other words, from that time on he withdrew, but to me this in no way simply cancels the statement he made.   In my view, it is irrelevant when and why he withdrew his enthusiastic support of the Nazi regime - decisive and relevant is the brute fact that he made the statement just quoted, that he idolized Hitler, and that he exhorted his students to do the same.   If, "today and in the future," only the *Fuhrer* himself is "German reality and its law," then the only philosophy that remains is the philosophy of abdication, surrender.

Olafson   In his discussions with you did he give any indication of his reasons for withdrawing, or what he believed the "mistake" of Nazism to be?   I'm wondering in particular if it was motivated by anything that one would call a moral consideration, or . . .

Marcuse   In fact, I remember he never did.   No, he never did.   It certainly wasn't anti-Semitism.   That I remember.   But he never did, you are quite right.   I think I do understand now why he turned against the pre-Hitler democracy of the Weimar Republic - because life under the Weimar Republic certainly in no way conformed to his existential categories: the struggle between capitalism and socialism, waged almost daily on the streets, at the work place, with violence and with the intellect, the outburst of a radically rebellious literature and art - this entire world, "existential" throughout, lies outside his existentialism.

Olafson   There's one important concept in *Being and Time* which we haven't alluded to, and that is the concept of authenticity or *Eigenlichkeit*, a concept that has known a wide popularity, I guess, both before and after Heidegger, implying a certain false relationship to oneself, and thereby a certain false relationship to one's fellow men and I suppose to one's society.   Does this strike you as a concept, in Heidegger's development of it, that has any continuing utility?

Marcuse   It is an interesting concept.   Again, if I remember how he actually defines authenticity, the same categories come to my mind, which I would call rather oppressive and repressive categories.   What is authenticity? Mainly, if I remember correctly, and please correct me if I don't, the withdrawal from the entire world of the others, *Das Man*, I don't know what the English translation is . . . .

Olafson The anonymous anyone.

Marcuse Authenticity would then mean the return to oneself, to one's innermost freedom, and, out of this inwardness, to decide, to determine every phase, every situation, every moment of one's existence. And the very real obstacles to this autonomy? The content, the aim, the What of the decision? Here too, the methodical "neutralization": the social, empirical context of the decision and of its consequences is "bracketed." The main thing is to decide and to act according to your decision. Whether or not the decision is in itself, and in its goals morally and humanly positive or not, is of minor importance.

Olafson There is another side to the concept - I agree with what you have been saying about this side of it - but there's another side in which Heidegger treats inauthenticity as a kind of deep attempt that human beings make to present themselves to themselves in a form that suppresses or blocks out the element of decision, the element of responsibility for themselves, that incorporates them into some kind of larger, whether it be physical or social, entity, and thus relieves them of the necessity for decision. Now that bears (it seems to me, perhaps I am wrong) some analogy to things that you have had to say about tendencies in modern technological society.

Marcuse Yes, I certainly wouldn't deny that authenticity, in a less oppressive sense, is becoming increasingly difficult in the advanced society of today, but it seems to me that even in the positive sense, authenticity is overshadowed by death, by the entire interpretation of existence as being toward death, and the incorporation of death into every hour and every minute of your life. This again I see as a highly oppressive notion, which somehow serves well to justify the emphasis of facism and nazism on sacrifice, sacrifice *per se*, as an end-in-itself. I think there is a famous phrase by Ernst Junger, the Nazi writer, who speaks of the necessity of sacrifice "*am Rande des Nichts oder am Rande des Abgrunds*" - "on the edge of the abyss, or on the edge of nothingness." In other words a sacrifice that is good because it is a sacrifice, and because it is freely chosen, or allegedly freely chosen, by the individual. Heidegger's notion recalls the battle cry of the fascist Futurists: *Eviva la Muerte*.

Olafson You mentioned Sartre's name a while ago, and I'd like to turn now, if I may, to the relationship between Heidegger and Sartre. As you yourself have pointed out, I think, on occasion - Sartre's *Being and Nothingness* is very heavily dependent upon Heidegger's *Being and Time* as, of course, it is upon other works in the German tradition, like *The Phenomenology of Mind*. Heidegger, on the other hand, has from the standpoint of his latter thought, repudiated any suggestion of common ground between these two philosophies, or these two statements. And that, of course, has been contested by others. How do you see this problem of the relationship between Heidegger and Sartre, and the relationship of Heidegger to the whole wider phenomenon of existentialism in the post-war period?

Marcuse   Well, it is a large question and I can only answer a small part of it.   I believe there is a common ground between Sartre's early work and Heidegger, namely the existential analysis, but there the common ground ends.   I would do injustice to Sartre if I would prolong it beyond that point.   Even *L'Etre et le Neant* is already much more concrete than Heidegger ever was.   Erotic relationships, love, hatred, all this - the body, not simply as abstract phenomenological object but the body as it is sensuously experienced, plays a considerable role in Sartre - all this is miles away from Heidegger's own analysis, and, as Sartre developed his philosophy, he surpassed the elements that still linked him to existentialism and worked out a Marxist philosophy and analysis.

Olafson   Doesn't the *Critique of Dialectical Reason* still strike you as a very idiosyncratic version of Marxism still marked importantly by the earlier thought?

Marcuse   It is important, and again it contains elements of truth, but I don't know whether you can really incorporate them into his earlier work, and his later work I just haven't followed adequately, so I wouldn't know.

Olafson   The interesting question that arises of course in connection with that is what Heidegger's place would be in the history of Western philosophy so conceived, because it has seemed, as you were saying, to many that *Being and Time* was a final turn on the transcendental screw, as it were, and that he would stand then in the same tradition as the people that he seems to be criticizing so trenchantly.

Marcuse   In the specific context of the history of philosophy, this may be true.   In the larger political context, one may say that German Idealism comes to an end with the construction of the Nazi state.   To quote Carl Schmitt: "On January 30, 1933, Hegel died."

Olafson   And yet Heidegger's philosophy enjoyed enormous prestige in Germany in the post-war period.   I think that is beginning to slack off a bit . . .

Marcuse   True.

Olafson   . . . or has been for the last decade, and I suppose it was more the later philosophy than the philosophy of *Being and Time* that formed the basis for that renaissance of interest in Heidegger.   Do you have any impressions of his influence on German intellectual life in the post-war period?

Marcuse   I only know, as you said, that by now it has been reduced considerably.   There was a great interest in Heidegger for quite some time after the war, and I think you are right, it was mainly the late work and not the early work.

Olafson   Theodor Adorno, a former colleague of yours, has characterized that influence in highly critical terms.

Marcuse   Yes.

Olafson   As a glorification of the principle of heteronomy, which I take to mean essentially the principle of external authority of some kind.   If that is true then there is a kind of paradox in the fact that a philosophy of will and self-assertion, of authenticity, has turned around into an ideological basis for an essentially heteronomous and authoritarian social orientation.

Marcuse Yes, but as we discussed, I think the roots of this authoritarianism you can find (again *ex-post*) in *Being and Time*, and the heteronomy may not only be that of outside authorities and powers, but also, for example, the heteronomy exercised by death over life. I think that Adorno has this too in mind when he speaks of it.

Olafson Do you think that Hegel *is* dead, that classical German philosophy is effectively at an end? Can there be continuators, more successful, perhaps, than Heidegger?

Marcuse You mean the tradition of German Idealism?

Olafson I mean, is it still possible for living philosophies to be built on the great classical authors, Hegel and Kant, whether through revision, or however? Are these still living sources of philosophical inspiration?

Marcuse I would definitely say yes. And I would definitely say that one of the proofs is the continued existence and development of Marxist theory. Because Marx and Engels themselves never failed to emphasize to what extent they considered themselves as the heirs of German Idealism. It is, of course, a greatly modified idealism, but elements of it remain in social and political theory.

Olafson I think you've already characterized, in general terms, what permanent effect Heidegger's philosophy, his teaching, had upon your own thought, upon your own philosophical work. Is there anything that you want to add to that? On balance, does the encounter with Heidegger seem to you to have enriched your own philosophical thinking, or is it something that you essentially had to see through and overcome?

Marcuse I would say more. There was, as I said, the mere fact that at least a certain type and kind of thinking I learned from him, and at least the fact - which again today should be stressed in the age of structuralism - that after all the text has an authority of its own and even if you violate the text, you have to do justice to it. These are elements which I think continue to be valid to this very day.

Olafson The analysis of the situation of the individual human being, the conscious human being - is this susceptible, do you think, of continuing treatment?

Marcuse No. As far as I am concerned, the existential analysis *a la* Heidegger today, I don't think there is anything in it I could say yes to, except in a very different social and intellectual context.

Olafson Could you give us any indication of what the nature of that context might be?

Marcuse That is very difficult. It would open up a completely new topic. The entire dimension that has been neglected in Marxian theory, for example, how social institutions reproduce themselves in the individuals, and how the individuals, by virtue of their reproducing their own society act on it.   There is room for what may be called an existential analysis, but only within this framework.

Olafson   Well, thank you very much.

Marcuse   You're welcome.

PART III

□□□□□□□□□□

THE AESTHETIC DIMENSION

Herbert Marcuse's first and final major works were books that dealt chiefly with matters deemed "aesthetic." This is no accident. From his dissertation of the 1920s to *The Aesthetic Dimension* in the late seventies, Marcuse was vitally concerned with such questions as the relationships between artists and societies, the nature of such concepts as beauty, taste, and art, and the respective roles of the imagination and eros in transforming and emancipating the creative individual and humanity as a whole. In fact, while few of his pieces in the half-century that intervened between *Der deutsche Kunstlerroman* and *The Aesthetic Dimension* deal systematically with aesthetic matters, even fewer ignore completely what might be called the *Leitmotif* of Marcuse's entire work - the idea of emancipation. Ultimately, Marcuse sought to overcome contradictions in the historical realm, not in the postulate of a genuinely revolutionary subject, but in the ideal of artistic transcendence. The *"promesse de bonheur"* heralded by more conventional radical thinkers as the ultimate goal of revolutionary class struggles was for Marcuse finally to be glimpsed within the aesthetic, and not the political, dimension.

The utopian and idealist strains running through all of Marcuse's work are perhaps most self-evident in his discussions of art and society. While drawing substantially from the legacy of classical German Idealist aesthetics, particularly Schiller and Hegel, Marcuse sought also to historicize aesthetic categories such as art and taste in a manner alien to both Idealism and contemporary analytic aesthetics. He thus drew upon the historical materialist approaches of Marx and Engels, Lukacs, and Brecht, if somewhat more indirectly. Marcuse did not succeed in overcoming this tension between idealism and historical materialism, either in his approach to art or in his work as a whole. And Stephen Bronner does not try to explain away or ignore this problem, one basic to the epistemology of critical theory in general. Rather, Bronner's piece recognizes both the merits and limits of utopian thinking, Marcuse-style. Whatever the difficulties inherent in critical theory's approach to art, the dialectical vision that informs Marcuse's synoptic view of the emancipatory potential of artistic creativity is often absent from almost all discussions today regarded as "aesthetic."

CHAPTER SEVEN

Between Art And Utopia: Reconsidering The Aesthetic Theory Of Herbert Marcuse

Stephen Eric Bronner

When this chapter first appeared as an article over ten years ago (The first version of this essay was published under the title of "Art and Utopia: The Marcusean Perspective" in *Politics and Society* 3, no. 1, Winter, 1973, reprinted in Ira Katznelson et al., *The Politics and Society Reader*, David McKay, Inc.: New York, 1974), Herbert Marcuse's work was fundamentally underestimated by the academy despite his remarkable political impact on the student movement of the sixties. "Critical Theory" was new to America and traditionalists never really grasped how Marcuse's use of the dialectical method exploded the conformist sterility of mainstream social science for so much of the left-wing intelligentsia. Most establishmentarians dismissed Marcuse as a "guru," and few recognized the depth of the tradition which he appropriated, the extraordinary range of his work, or the extent of his philosophical influence upon thinkers as different as Norman O. Brown and Jürgen Habermas, as well as the circles that clustered around journals like *Telos* and *New German Critique*.

During those ten years, a beautiful edition of Marcuse's collected writings appeared in Germany,[1] while a number of important secondary sources were published in the United States.[2] But, if Herbert Marcuse's intellectual eminence now seems academically secure, the political impact of his thought has waned. And this is particularly true regarding his belief that a new aesthetic conception must play a central role in developing any sociopolitical alternative to the given order.

The collapse of a radical movement from below, coupled with the triumph of Reagan's conservatism, has thrown the left on the defensive. In conjunction with the economic decline from the boom years of the sixties, for right or wrong, speculative theory has given way to a defense of the most progressive aspects of the welfare state. Through this shift, Marcuse's philosophical concerns of the sixties have essentially vanished from the public discourse of the left. Semiotics, deconstruction, and various forms of post-structuralism have supplanted Marcuse's aesthetic theory and his attempt to bring words like beauty, softness, and sensuality into the political vocabulary.

The appearance of the present volume has provided the opportunity to revise my old essay. This is necessary both to address the mistakes and theoretical flaws in the original, and to deal with works which were unpublished at the time. But to avoid any mechanistic reformulation that would eradicate the original flavor, it is probably best that the basic structure remain intact. Thus, where the first part of the essay will elaborate Marcuse's own perspective, the second will involve a critique of his aesthetic theory.

As far as that critique is concerned, it is still the case that there are only three basic ways to criticize a philosophical conception. One involves externally attacking the central thesis while positing a different *a priori* assumption. Another lies in simply asserting that a given line of reasoning runs counter to empirical reality. If the first approach often leads to a total dismissal of the argument and what can be gained from it, the second necessarily accepts the sacrosanct status of the given and so inherently denies any attempt whatsoever at speculative thought.

There remains a third type of criticism, however, which may be termed *immanent critique*. This form of criticism is "dialectical" by its very nature since the internal logic of the original argument is confronted as its presuppositions are called into account. Even so, such an approach will neither simply dismiss the original argument entirely nor view the status quo as inviolable and finished. Instead, immanent critique will subvert and build upon the original theory in order to glean new insights. Such a mode of thought is central to the traditions that influenced Herbert Marcuse, and it was in this spirit that he pursued his own intellectual project. Especially under present circumstances, it is this critical spirit that deserves to be maintained.

Herbert Marcuse's first major work was his posthumously published dissertation, *Der deutsche Kunstlerroman* (The German Artist Novel). In retrospect, it provides a fine beginning for what would become Marcuse's life-long attempt to comprehend the contradictory relation between art and social life. Building on the early work of Georg Lukacs,[3] this study manifests both the influence of Hegel and a Neo-Kantianism which was popular in 1922. Even then, Marcuse argued that the self-perception of the artist along with his role must be understood in terms of the society in which he lives. Sharing the romanticized view of the past as well as the pessimism about the present which was dominant amongst the avant-garde, Marcuse claimed that in pre-modern times the artist needed no personal perspective which would contradict that of the given social order. Since social life was itself harmonious and non-alienated, the artist's aesthetic product would mirror that harmony and fullness.

But the situation changes in modernity, which is actually defined by the destruction of that prior harmony. As the division of labor is extended under capitalism, fragmentation and alienation necessarily result. Consequently, the artist is forced to redefine himself and his role. As a self-conscious subject, he will stand in opposition to a society which has instituted a fundamental rupture between art and life. Thus, if a new self-awareness arises on the part of the artist, that consciousness itself has its roots in a differentiated society which alienates the artist from his world. If the artist is therefore condemned to reproduce this separation and the fragmented character of social existence in his work, he will do so through an aesthetic form which actually projects into the future that very harmony which has been lost in the present.

When *Der deutsche Kunstlerroman* appeared, this transcendent and utopian unity which the bourgeois artist sought to secure in the aesthetic form retained a political complement in the German working class' attempts to actualize a "new community" through the socialist revolution. Obviously there is an idealist component to such an assessment. But, it makes little difference. Following the close of World War II, Marcuse concluded that traditional class contradictions had ideologically been "flattened out." Though "objectively" socioeconomic class contradictions continued to exist, Marcuse believed that the "subjective" consciousness of the need for radical change had been paralyzed by the affluence and technological progress of advanced industrial society.[4]

The emancipatory potential within art had therefore become divorced from that proletarian "agent" of history which originally was to institutionalize a qualitatively different mode of life and which now found itself integrated into the status quo. Art would thus be forced to stand in total opposition to the existing order. This modern opposition between art and reality, however, retains both a metapsychological and an anthropological dimension in Marcuse's thought.

Following Freud, for Marcuse, civilization is "first of all progress in work - that is, work for the procurement and augmentation of life."[5] This, however, demands a denial of "Eros" and the life instinct's desire for immediate gratification along with the "containment of the pleasure principle." In Marcuse's view, that occurs when humanity first confronts the "reality principle" which is fundamentally based on economic scarcity. But, peculiar to the capitalist state of development is the fact that this "reality principle" will become intrinsically identified with the "pleasure principle" so that "under its rule society is stratified according to the competitive economic performance of its members."[6] As a consequence, additional limits on gratification will be put into effect above and beyond that minimum level of repression which is indispensable for human interaction. Socialization will occur in particular ways and progress will become identified with the growth of the existing order rather than with the attempt to actualize the unactualized values of emancipation. This will ultimately create the basis for Marcuse's political support of environmentalism, ecology, as well as his opposition to the instrumental domination of nature and the equation of "progress" with "growth."[7]

These matters aside, however, the potential of Eros itself will become channelled through institutions like the patriarchal-monogamic family, the Church, the hierarchical division of labor, the mass media which subvert the existence of a truly private sphere, etc. Institutions such as these become the instruments through which "surplus repression" is extracted and maintained for the benefit of the given order.[8]

Derived from Marx's notion of "surplus value," "surplus repression" has its objective basis in the "false needs"[9] that are endemic to the production process of advanced industrial society. If "planned obsolescence" can be used as an example, the system will quantitatively create these needs which will then attempt to be satisfied even as new ones are produced. The effects of this production process will, however, also "reproduce" the repressive values and desires of the existing order within individuals themselves. Thus, where surplus repression can objectively be considered as quantitative in sociopolitical terms, its effects become qualitative in the subjective, psychological "infrastructure" of society's members. In turn, this makes the objective recognition of the existing situation dependent upon a subjective consciousness of freedom which the given attempts to deny. Social controls will shape a psychological condition that enforces guilt when the boundaries of the existing order attempt to be transgressed. Once again, Freud's metapsyschology provides the avenue for securing the anthropological basis of Marcuse's analysis, and Paul Robinson is correct in suggesting that Marcuse's treatment of the primal crime may be seen as an allegory which symbolizes the rise of capitalism.[11]

For Marcuse, human history does not begin with the revolt of the sons and brothers against the primal father. Instead, history begins with the original ascension of the father who, in monopolizing the mother(s), limits enjoyment to himself alone as he imposes labor on the sons. Exploitation and domination result from the unequal distribution of work and satisfaction.[12] This will ultimately drive the sons to revolt. But guilt will be experienced in that revolt. Consequently, following their victory, the sons will actually imitate the father and develop their own forms of repression as a punishment. Institutions such as religion will simultaneously assuage and perpetuate that guilt while retaining their own organizational and material interest in the continuation of repression even under conditions in which it might no longer be necessary.

This past remains shrouded in a mist. Too terrible to recall, its effects remain since "the essence of repression lies simply in the function of rejecting and keeping something out of consciousness."[13] As a consequence, humanity will lose control over its history since such repression will foster actions that are at once unconscious and non-directed. These acts will never retain a consciousness of any specific object or society to be transformed or created. Destruction, however, is a real possibility with regard to this non-directed libidinal energy.

Such destructive social activity is only fostered by the institutions of advanced industrial society and stands in direct opposition to a "sublimated" practice. Sublimation is based on a previously desexualized libido which is directed towards a specific object. In contrast to the acts which are spurred by repression, sublimation is necessarily creative since it will "still retain the main purpose of Eros - that of uniting and binding - insofar as it helps towards establishing the unity or tendency to unity which is particularly characteristic of the ego."[14]

When Marcuse applies these concepts to the condition of an artwork in advanced industrial society, a cyclical process is seen as going into effect. Where repression is brought to bear upon the individual through institutionalized controls, he will attempt to vent his libidinal energy through a sublimated practice that will result in a work of art. But, the very society which the artwork attempts to oppose will transform that *oeuvre* and "absorb" the erotic, libidinous content which provides the aesthetic object with its emancipatory "truth." As a consequence, repression will literally increase through society's subversion of sublimated activity.

Thus, Marcuse's real point involves the manner in which the ego's potential is undermined and major works are manipulated by advanced industrial society. Institutionally, this becomes manifest in the culture industry which can turn any work into a fad or a "spectacle." Thus Marcuse provides a metapsychological underpinning for a social and organizational mode of action which his follower, Shierry Weber, claims can lead to:

> The perversion of the aesthetic: whereas the aesthetic is a totality formed by sublimation of the instincts, the spectacle releases instinctual energies but does not bind them into forms. On the other hand, the spectacle as aesthetic and as consumption prevents the individual from experiencing action and process; he is an actor only as an object and a subject only as a spectator; he consumes rather than makes.[15]

The culture industry feeds on such spectacles and, in this vein, Shierry Weber will reflect Marcuse's concern that the repetition of the basic rhythm and the noise level of rock music will serve "to break down the ego to permit the diffuse release of sexual and aggressive energy, thus substituting annihilation and explosion - escape from the self - for discovery and integration."[16] A similar result can take place through commercial simplification of a work to the point where its critical and emancipatory qualities are liquidated. Thus, classics will be reduced to Monarch Notes and *Don Quixote* will become *Man of La Mancha*. In such instances, the existing "reality principle" will be strengthened by the libido which it has absorbed or diffused. This is what Marcuse terms "repressive desublimation," or the channelling of sublimated activity into socially acceptable - and ultimately repressive - forms.

A type of repression therefore arises which is "unnecessary" and so, in Hegelian terms, "irrational."[17] But, the very irrationality of this repression becomes obscured by the pervasive ideological power of advanced industrial society since "reason presupposes freedom, the power to act in accordance with knowledge of the truth, the power to shape reality in line with its potentialities."[18] This is what demands a qualitative break from the "vicious cycle of progress," and it is here that the basis for Marcuse's utopian conception emerges.

Given that the recognition of surplus repression occurs only to the extent that the prevailing criteria of freedom and progress are denied, if the dialectical method is to remain valid, it must "risk defining freedom in such a way that people become conscious of and recognize it as something that is nowhere already in existence."[19] Once freedom is defined in this way, even if it remains subjectively unrecognized, the potential for utopia will objectively be maintained as "the determinate socio-historical negation of what exists."[20] Insofar as art and the aesthetic form oppose this "flattened out," repressive reality, they alone will reassert the utopian possibility. And this must be the case since culture emerges through the free sublimation of Eros. Thus, art itself will manifest both the validity of the life-instinct along with "the truth of the human condition (which) is hidden, repressed - not by a conspiracy of some sort, but by the actual course of history."[21]

The aesthetic realm confronts the world of repression with "*la promesse de bonheur*" (Stendhal), along with the "inner truth" of civilization. If the repression of Eros and its longing for freedom is the principle upon which civilization is constructed, a "second history" of humanity emerges "in the negation of the principle that governs civilization . . . . [Art] is attained and sustained fulfillment, the transparent unity of subject and object; of the universal and the individual."[22]

Schiller once said that "freedom lies in the realm of dreams." And, in this sense, art contradicts the existing order with its "inner truth" as it manifests the freedom to shape reality in terms of the imagination. This is the basis for the transcendent character of art. Indeed, aesthetic creation necessarily involves a "rational transgression [which becomes] an essential quality of even the most affirmative art."[23]

Nevertheless, if there is an inherently transcendent quality which binds "affirmative" and "negative" art, the distinction remains important. Affirmative culture, which particularly marked the early phases of bourgeois development, was based on the belief in an inner sanctity and freedom. This inner realm was divorced from the external world of misery, ugliness, and want.[24] Thus Keats,[25] like most of the romantics, would look back to an idealized community (*Gemeinschaft*) as a response to the horrors of the industrial revolution and bourgeois society (*Gesellschaft*). The subjective experience of individuality would be retained, however, through what might be termed a flight of the heart. And this flight would be possible for everyone since it depends only on a spiritual communion with nature which is totally dissociated from the concrete conditions of society at large. Still, Marcuse recognizes that through this mechanistic dichotomy between the internal and the external, a "resolution can only be illusory. And the possibility of a solution rests precisely on the character of artistic beauty as illusion [*Schein*]."[26]

This illusion projects a transcendent utopia. But, believing that happiness can exist internally and independent of the actual external conditions which prevail, artworks of this type can abrogate their critical function in sociopolitical terms and perhaps even help perpetuate the given state of affairs. At the same time, however, the beauty which even affirmative culture evidences will necessarily stand as the "negation" of the commodity world and of the values and attitudes which are required by it. Perhaps this negation has no concrete referent, and relates only to the experience of an abstract subject. But, nevertheless, for Marcuse "the beautiful illusion" (*schöner Schein*) will help "render incorrect even one's own assertion that one is happy."[27]

Unfortunately, since this conception of affirmative culture presupposes the sacrosanct character of the inner realm, it will ignore the possibility that the social world can subvert the subjective experience. And, generally speaking, this is what Marcuse believes has occurred in advanced industrial society. What his colleagues in the "Frankfurt School," Max Horkheimer and Theodor Adorno, termed the "culture industry" will literally introject a "happy consciousness" into society's members.[28] This "happy consciousness" will make them complacent to the point where they will lose the desire for emancipatory change and so come to terms with the existing order and its evils. Thus, Marcuse's individual of the "happy consciousness" will be thrown "back upon himself, learn to bear, and in a certain sense, to love his isolation."[29]

At the bohemian margins of society, however, avant-garde movements arose in the beginnings of the twentieth century which sought to oppose this development. A "negative" culture of all-encompassing protest sharpened the critical faculty, emphasized the subject, and reasserted the utopian dream. In this sense, Andre Breton could call for the "Great Refusal" which, in Marcuse's terms, demands an attempt to increase the distance between social reality and the aesthetic sphere from the standpoint of revolt. Thus, Marcuse's support of experimental, modernist works which consciously attempt to estrange themselves from the given order.

Still, it is important to note how the technique of estrangement (*Verfremdungseffekt*) was employed by the artist who actually introduced it: Brecht. For, in a sense, Brecht's purposes were always at odds with Marcuse's aesthetic conception. That playwright neither wished to remove his work from the real, identify with the avant-garde, empty art of general social experience as such to deny its propagandistic effects, nor allow his public to forget that they were sitting in a theater. For Brecht, estrangement does not take place through asserting the subjective and indeterminate experience of the individual, but through the distance that allows for reflexivity regarding the sociopolitical world. Aside from Brecht's direct attack on Schiller and traditional idealism in *St. Joan of the Stockyards*, his aesthetic form seeks to emphasize a determinate, communicable, and socially relevant content. Even in early works like *Baal* or *In the Jungle of the Cities*, Brecht shows little sympathy for the "beautiful illusion" which supposedly harbors a utopian negation and it is precisely through eliminating *elements* of feeling - mawkishness, sentimentality, empathy (*Rührung*) - that he endeavors to make the audience intellectually understand its own estrangement.

This is all very different from the indeterminate character of the "Great Refusal" as presented both by the turn of the century avant-garde and by Marcuse himself.   From Marcuse's standpoint, it is sufficient that through a new experimental use of aesthetic forms "words, sounds, shapes, and colors [will be] insulated against their familiar ordinary use and functions; thus they [are] freed for a new dimension of existence."[30]

That attempt defines the avant-garde tradition to which Marcuse adhered, and which achieved a certain popularity with segments of the student movement.   That is the tradition of Expressionism, Surrealism, and "modernism" in general whose founding fathers include Baudelaire, Lautreamont, and Rimbaud.   But, even with regard to this experimental tradition, Marcuse retains his critical stance.   It is his contention that the necessary estrangement of art from society, which these artists sought to manifest, is now being impaired along with the transcendent quality of their aesthetic experiments. Indeed, the power of the "second history" of civilization is now being encompassed by the first and even "negative" art is no longer safe.

> [Art becomes] part of the technical equipment of the household and of the daily work world.   In this process, [artistic works] undergo a decisive transformation; they are losing the qualitative difference, namely the essential dissociation from the established reality principle which was the ground of their liberating function.   Now the images and ideas, by virtue of which art, literature, and philosophy once indicted and transcended the given reality are integrated into the society, and the power of the reality principle is greatly extended.[31]

In response to the early subjective forms of modernism, Gropius, Moholy-Nagy and the Bauhaus movement attempted to wed art to industry and technology.   Then, socialist realism made art the handmaiden of authoritarian political policies. But, today, it is possible to hear music performed and created by an electronic instrument which sits alone on the stage.   Television provides excerpts from Beethoven to Stravinsky while a voice tries to sell a product.   A Campbell's soup can becomes an *oeuvre*, while prints of the masters decorate the home.   The result is the transformation and integration of high art.[32]

Formerly, a work of art could at least be seen as a singularly human product.   Under present circumstances, the commodity form absorbs the emancipatory content and undermines the singularity of the work itself.   The aim of the work becomes irrelevant, the experience of a work becomes subverted, while computers begin to define what is commercially viable to the point where instrumental rationality becomes inextricably tied to the production of the work itself.   Thus, in line with Marcuse's thinking, Jacques Ellul can claim that "mechanization has penetrated into the subconscious of the artist"[33] and that the artistic imagination will become ever more subordinated to technique.   What is more, the capital necessary for television, movies, and radio will create a further substantive constraint that provides a vision of "artistic expression subordinated to a censorship of money or the state."[34]

This will have pronounced effects upon both the potential of the aesthetic form as well as the ability to comprehend it. The matter becomes particularly clear with regard to the role of the hero(ine). Traditionally, the hero transcended reality through his extraordinary accomplishments that demanded a confrontation with the given order. As with Oedipus or Odysseus, the traditional hero sought to negate the hypocrisy and pettiness of society, its misery and limits. The repressed longing for freedom, peace, and emancipatory change, the hope as well as the pathos of humanity become incarnate in the figure.

That presentation changes in the literature of the "Great Refusal." The hero is turned into the anti-hero: Michel, Gide's "immoralist," or Kafka's Joseph K. These anti-heroes either find themselves on the boundaries of society or as ordinary people who cannot come to terms with the conditions of their existence. The point is no longer what this individual actually does. Indeed, an early prototype of this character - like Goncharov's "Oblomov" - can appear as an indolent procrastinator who need not act at all while other figures suggest a different mode of life through their dreams, ruminations, etc. Nevertheless, the repression of the existing society can either be exposed through the portrayal of those conditions which create the individual's misery or through a description of those possibilities for happiness which are ignored.

But, for Marcuse, neither the hero nor the anti-hero retains his original emancipatory function in advanced industrial society. The technological achievements of that society itself have either dwarfed the earlier accomplishments or turned them into palpable fare. Thus, it was the United States that landed a man on the moon through a collective effort while the prefabricated melodrama of the culture industry has supplanted the authentic anguish of the traditional hero when faced with his choices. Where the ordinary human being is presented as a "happy consciousness" on sit-coms, anti-heroes "are no longer images of another way of life, but rather freaks or types of the same life, serving as an affirmation rather than a negation of the established order."[35]

The result is a "non-conformist conformity" (Adorno) whose conditions emerge from the affluence of advanced industrial society. In Marcuse's view, poverty and misery are no longer visible in daily life for the majority of the population. Through the creation, satisfaction, and re-creation of false needs, individuals will be content to enjoy their existence in accordance with those values which are propagated by the status quo. Satisfied, complacent, and introjected with the "happy consciousness," the individuals of advanced industrial society have become ideologically incapable of valuing even the possibility of a different enjoyment, peace, or a more embracing and sustained gratification.

As the positive potential incarnated within the hero and the critical negation manifested by the anti-hero are vitiated, the very conception of a life which is not subordinated to the "performance principle" is denied. Under such circumstances, contradictions will be assimilated if not resolved. Thus, the possibility of "negative thinking, which is the only viable source of artistic creation in Marcuse's view, will be diminished and the quality of thought and education itself will degenerate.

The negation which is inherent in the aesthetic *oeuvre* will thus itself be negated by advanced industrial society. As a consequence, works of art will

> suffer the fate of being absorbed by what they refute. As modern classics, the avant-garde and the beatniks share the function of entertaining without endangering the conscience of the men of good will. This absorption is justified by technical progress; the refusal is refuted by the alleviation of misery in the advanced industrial society. The liquidation of high culture [thus becomes] a by-product of the conquest of scarcity.[36]

Indeed, it is even possible to go further. New heroes will emerge, emptied of emancipatory content and turned into repressive instruments which assure the continuation of the status quo. The "beautiful illusion" of the aesthetic appears to become concrete, even as emancipation becomes more abstract and more difficult to perceive.

> The stars, the consorts of royalty, the kings and champion sportsmen have the function which demigods had in mythology; they are human to a superlative degree and therefore to be imitated; their behavior has a normative character. But as they are not of this world one can only imitate them in a small way, on one's own level, and not presume to match oneself with them in reality.[37]

"Happiness" exists, but it is truly experienced only by them: the demigods. Supplanting the traditional hero with the potential and transcendence which he once embodied, the demigod is also able to overpower that critical negation which the anti-hero once projected. Handsome, rich, stylish, and smiling, the demigod becomes the perfect expression of the "happy consciousness" no matter what the intent of the songs he sings or the characters which he portrays. No less a commodity than those shows and commercials in which he stars, the demigod is at once the ideal and the tool of contemporary society. Indeed, he appears as the ideal only because he is the tool. Thus, the demigod becomes the instrument by which hope is managed while hope itself becomes identified with an unimaginable cash value which the masses can never possibly secure.

Emancipation becomes fame, and fame is itself defined by the market. Vicarious participation in the lives of celebrities becomes identified with real gratification. And, as the deformed hope substitutes itself for real emancipation, the masses are taught to acquiesce and maintain their commitment to the status quo and its values. All this will necessarily have a pronounced impact on the subject's experience of an artwork and even undermine that "catharsis" which served as the foundation of classical aesthetic theory.

Now, Aristotle probably overestimated the experience purgation - or catharsis - on Athenian audiences. People attend the theater and a comedy was always played after t prevent the public from "walking out shaken." But, liberating emotional experience actually took place or r situation is different. Even should catharsis prove effective, under present circumstances it will simply foster the illusion that liberation is a private affair of the heart.

In the same way that advanced industrial society subverts the cathartic experience, it attempts to absorb the negative, critical potential of traditional forms. Art will therefore necessarily be forced to transvalue and alienate itself from an alienated society. To the same extent that art seeks to "reach the masses," the work's content will be turned against itself by the culture industry even when that work attempts to express a "revolutionary" message.[38] As a "radical" work becomes a popular commodity, the liberal and tolerant image of the status quo becomes ever more secure. Only through its estrangement from the given order will art remain able to preserve itself as the negation of that order. Only in this way can "la promesse de bonheur" be recaptured and saved from subversion by the institutional organs of a repressive cultural system.

Still, Marcuse does not simply succumb to the temptations of "anti-art": painting without line or color, music without score, destruction of language and form as such. In his view, anti-art breeds reification in spite of itself by reaching the point "where the oeuvre drops out of the dimension of alienation, of *formed* negation and contradiction, and turns into a sound game, a language game - harmless without commitment [while employing a] shock which no longer shocks . . . ."[39]

Insofar as anti-art denies the validity of "art," it will deny the utopian potential of the aesthetic form as well. In this sense, Marcuse's contempt for anti-art involves its attack on form as such. Thus, he can happily claim that "the passing of anti-art [will result in] the reemergence of form. And with it, we find a new expression of the inherently subversive qualities of the aesthetic dimension, especially beauty as the sensuous appearance of the idea of freedom."[40]

Embodied in the "style" of a work, the aesthetic form subjects "reality to another order, subjects it to the 'laws of beauty.'"[41] In defining this aesthetic form, Marcuse will therefore build on *The Critique of Judgment* when he claims that:

[The] aesthetic form in art has the aesthetic form in nature (*das Naturschone*) as its correlate, or rather desideratum. If the idea of beauty pertains to nature as well as to art, this is not merely an analogy, or a human idea imposed on nature - it is the insight that the aesthetic form, as a token of freedom is a mode (or moment?) of existence of the human as well as the natural universe, (and so retains) an objective quality.[42]

It is from within the Kantian tradition that Schiller's fundamental impact on Marcuse's aesthetic emerges. That objective quality within the aesthetic is fantasy, which at once becomes the vehicle for the estrangement as well as the recovery of humanity's "inner truth."[43] For Schiller, fantasy carries within itself the "play impulse" that serves to mediate between a "sensuous impulse," which is receptive and ethereally passive, and a "form impulse" which seeks to exert mastery over nature. The work of art will combine both as it projects that "purposeful purposelessness" (Kant) which constitutes a new experience of existence beyond that of the "performance principle."

Connected to nature, with fantasy as its content and "play" as its purpose, the aesthetic form will therefore constitute for itself an ideal object: humanity. But this is an emancipated humanity which has been aesthetically transformed into a "living shape." That potential for liberation within existence itself thus becomes the transcendent concept which covers "all aesthetic qualities of phenomena and - in a word - what we call *Beauty* in the widest sense of the term."[44] In this sense, quoting Schiller, Marcuse can suggest that the "play impulse" - with its "objective as beauty and its goal as freedom" - harbors an aesthetic sensibility which can only be realized in the utopian liberation of humanity.

From this utopian perspective, life will become the work of art and art will no longer stand outside life. Life itself will therefore change through the continuous experience of what Schiller originally saw as the essential quality of play: "lightness" (*Leichtheit*). Embodied in the form of art, this quality allows the transcendence of social reality and provides the audience with a hint of that utopian condition which stands beyond the oppression of the given order.

The aesthetic form will therefore project a "harmonious truth" of the imagination which, as it calls the misery of the existent into question, also enables art to retain its utopian function. Unfortunately, however, traditional art forms in advanced industrial society will now simply create an illusion (*Schein*) which "necessarily subjects the represented reality to aesthetic standards and thus deprives it of its terror."[45] Thus naturalism and realism in particular lose their critical function since their very attempts to decrease the distance between art and reality will increase the likelihood of their integration and repressive desublimation by the status quo. Indeed, for Marcuse art in advanced industrial society can only survive where "it cancels itself, where it saves its substance by denying its traditional form, thereby denying reconciliation."[46]

Nevertheless, Marcuse's utopian perspective does not simply posit a better world in the future which is emptied of the creative content of the past. Instead the critical transvaluation of the past, the unrealized hopes and dreams of humanity itself which have been embodied in art from the dawn of civilization, become the content for what is to emerge in the utopian future. In other words,

the truth value of the imagination relates not only to the past, but also to the future: the forms of freedom and happiness which it invokes claim to deliver the historical *reality*. In its refusal to accept as final the limitations imposed upon freedom and happiness by the reality principle, in its refusal to forget what can *be*, lies the critical function of phantasy.[47]

The relation between art and utopia therefore becc
Simultaneously, art will serve as the critical response to a re
even as it provides the "container" for the utopian conscio...
world. Indeed, the erotic and harmonious character of art's truth itself
becomes the justification of that utopia to be achieved.

But, that is not all. Following Schiller, Marcuse will take the position
that it is necessary to pass through the aesthetic in order to resolve the
sociopolitical contradictions of the existing order in an emancipatory
fashion. Thus, Marcuse's thought converges with the demands of a
student movement which at once recognized how capitalism is also a
cultural system and how a cultural alternative is fundamentally crucial to
any truly radical politics.

In this sense, Marcuse's theory points to a revolution more radical than
any of the revolutions of the past, and fantasy will play a crucial role since
it inherently seeks "to satisfy those wishes which reality does not satisfy."[48]
Like Breton, Marcuse seeks to negate the totality of repression while
projecting the possibilities of liberation through new modes of aesthetic
expression and comprehension. And so, the concept of reality itself must
be extended to include the subconscious, dreams, hallucinations, etc.
Politics can therefore no longer be identified with the mere concern over
power, policies, and the state. Instead, it must encompass an
emancipatory transformation of experience itself.

This is where the surrealist influence, as well as the political importance
of the aesthetic, emerges for Marcuse. Art in revolt, the artist as non-
conformist, the utopian desire to reconcile all contradictions including
that of the imaginary and the real, the experimental attempt to develop
new aesthetic forms, and the radical ideal of a "new man,"[49] are all central
tenets of both Marcuse's thought and surrealism. And, in the same way
that Breton looked to the Trotskyists as vehicles to actualize his vision, so
did Marcuse look to the student movement.

Such is the sense of Marcuse's famous claim that "the fight for Eros is a
political fight." But, if the potential within the aesthetic form cannot be
actualized until the given society is "exploded," this is not to say that art
will simply "disappear" in the new order. "At the optimum, we can
envisage a universe common to art and reality, but in this common
universe, art would retain its transcendence."[50]

Art can disappear only in a stage of civilization where people are unable
to distinguish between beauty and ugliness, good and evil. But, such a
stage would be nothing less than "barbarism at the height of
civilization."[51] Art will not simply disappear through praxis, and Marcuse
decries the idea that one should mechanistically draw the direct
consequences from an artwork and then go on to actualize them in
instrumental and reductive terms. Though the utopian truth of art itself
demands revolutionary praxis, art

cannot submit to the actual requirements of the revolution without
denying itself. But art can and will draw its inspirations and its very

form, from the then prevailing revolutionary movement - for revolution is in the substance of art.[52]

The critical and transcendent character of art remains as a continual self-criticism of the revolution in terms of the utopia to be achieved. At the same time, however, the erotic content of art will be set free through emancipatory practice and so guide the participants in combatting and destroying the institutions of surplus repression. Through a "junction of art and revolution in the aesthetic dimension,"[53] this newly freed Eros would manifest itself in the movement since the needs would arise for the destruction of these institutions as well as a new consciousness which could perceive their "irrationality."

Marcuse recognized that it would already require the existence of a "new man," who is simultaneously unable to tolerate existing social repression and so freed from its effects, to make such a revolution. But, this very contradiction actually pulled Marcuse closer to the student movement since it was those at the "margins" of society who took the revolutionary lead rather than the working class. In fact, the integration of the working class actually confirmed Marcuse's point that the preconditions of abundance had already been achieved. This could be seen as paving the way for new revolutionary subjects and creating the preconditions for an emancipated culture.

Of course, Marcuse realized that an equal distribution of social wealth - and not simply abundance - was a crucial prerequisite for his utopian conception. Only under such material conditions is it even possible to conceive of a "universe common to art and reality." But, under such conditions of equal material well being and radical aesthetic consciousness, social reality might change its shape.

> Techniques would then tend to become art, and art would tend to form reality: the opposition between imagination and reason, higher and lower faculties, poetic and scientific thought, would be invalidated. Emergence of a new Reality Principle: under which a new sensibility and a desublimated scientific intelligence would combine in the creation of an aesthetic ethos.[54]

Thus, even a new science with a new *logos* would become manifest. Technology would no longer be employed to produce products for the sake of products, and humanity would become the true master of the machine. The operationalist rationality under which contemporary society functions, along with the division between technology and art, would be overcome through a new "sensibility."

Through this "new sensibility," a new type of rationality would prevail in which art's "ability to project existence, to define yet unrealized possibilities would be envisaged as *validated by and functioning in the scientific transformation of the world.*"[55] Indeed, humanity would come to recognize nature as a subject in its own right and new modes of interaction would foster the "pacification of existence."

And as the erotic content of beauty along with the unactualized utopian projections of the past would be recaptured, humanity would become "playful" and "beautiful" in terms of Schiller's "living shape." Through this "new sensibility," humanity would no longer be ashamed of sensuousness or the atrocities which it committed in the past. The guilt of the primal crime would be expiated through the newly found and liberating potential of memory. Ultimately, time itself would be transformed. No longer conceived in unilinear terms, but rather as an internal circular process, an emancipatory "eternal recurrence" (Nietzsche) would truly enable humanity to fully recapture its repressed past. In this utopia, people would be "biologically" incapable of committing violence[56]; evil would be banished and Thanatos, the death instinct, would be conquered. Sexuality would turn into sensuality as the erogenous zones would begin to spread themselves over the whole body, abolishing genital sexuality in favor of a new "polymorphous perversity." Thus, quoting Baudelaire, Marcuse envisions a truly new world where "tout n'est qu'ordre et beauté; Luxe, calme, et volupté."

The popularity that surrounded Herbert Marcuse in the sixties was not merely due to his contention that a "one-dimensional" society had emerged. It was also due to the motivations which his thought inspired. Indeed, Marcuse crystallized a moral hope for a new order that confronted a period which proclaimed the "end of ideology." The times were right in that period of affluence for a revolutionary perspective which presupposed the ability of the status quo to at least partially fulfill those "false needs" that it generated. But, at the same time, Marcuse recognized something which the reformers and "pragmatists" still refuse to consider. The desire for a qualitative change never merely springs from empty stomachs, but also from the conscious ideological desire for a different and happier mode of life in the future.

Whatever the inadequacies of Marcuse's theory, his thought extends the boundaries of freedom and breaks its identification with the institutions of the status quo. Indeed, more than anyone else in America, Marcuse rescued the concept of utopia from its popular definition as a fixed state of happiness that retains so many values of the status quo or a "nowhere" in the sense of Thomas More and Samuel Butler. Indeed, he saw how the conditions of advanced industrial society penetrated into the very experience of individuals. But, as in Marx's *Paris Manuscripts*,[57] Marcuse never simply took experience for granted in trans-historical terms. Instead, it was correctly seen as historically mutable, and this very historicity of experience created the speculative basis for its emancipatory transformation.

Furthermore, Marcuse's concern with emancipation also provided the demand for extending the intellect through the need for a critical encounter with those repressed longings of humanity's cultural past.[58] These repressed hopes constitute what Ernst Bloch called the "underground history of the revolution." And it is this which provides an ever-expanding content to that utopian condition which Marcuse attempted to formulate.

Marcuse's thought sought to confront the fundamental values which advanced society takes for granted. Long before the bulk of American society realized the terrible consequences of Vietnam, Marcuse undermined the optimism that had been inherited from the fifties. The cultural system of capitalism received formulation along with its effects and, through Marcuse's work, it became clear that progress could no longer be identified with the status quo and the commodity world. That the effects of a new more modern oppression dared to be raised was remarkable in itself in the American context. And Marcuse recognized that these hopes must be pinned on an *unfinished* notion of freedom and happiness if a critical norm is to be maintained through which contemporary repression could be exposed in the positive terms of an emancipatory alternative.

Denying a transcendent, utopian perspective means chaining revolt to the immediate terms of a given order and, in this sense, the thrust of Marcuse's philosophical enterprise cannot simply be dismissed. Given the triumph of Reagan and a truly conservative climate, the assumptions of the pragmatists and reformers are not so strong that they simply can be accepted without question.

Thus, Marcuse's thought demands a speculative and immanent critique. And this critique must necessarily begin with those traditions which his theory attempted to synthesize. Consequently, in the Kantian vein, Marcuse attempted to identify an inherently transcendent aesthetic form with the critical and utopian character of art. And, in keeping with a radical Kantian perspective which still essentially remains unconcerned with the material elaboration of sociohistorical processes, Marcuse's emphasis upon art's need to divorce itself from the real makes sense.

Unfortunately, however, such a divorce can never constitute a "negation" in Hegelian terms. For Hegel always emphasized the distinction between a "negation" and an "opposition." An opposition, like that between "art" and "anti-art," is inherently abstract and sociohistorically "indeterminate" or undefined; the "opposition" will therefore be defined by what it opposes and so, lacking any positive definition of freedom on its own, will continue to exist on the same plane of repression as the very order which it seeks to explode. On the other hand, a "negation" of the given order will always be sociohistorically specific or "determinate." Thus, retaining a presentiment of the values of freedom which remain to be achieved, the "negation" of the given order must always remain somehow connected to the real. It is this which, for Hegel, enables art to supply "out of the real world what is lacking to the notion." That notion of freedom, however, inherently demands a reflexive and rational formulation. Yet, for Hegel, art can only provide an "intuitive" formal awareness of freedom and therefore needs to be "mediated" by the rational, sociopolitical truth which is embodied in philosophy.

The aesthetic form therefore cannot be conceived in isolated terms, and so it cannot simply be considered as the "container" of utopian truth as Marcuse contends. In order to extract the real potential that is hidden within art, critical aesthetic perception must be linked to a social theory that seeks rationally and reflexively to justify the "emancipatory" qualities of the values which underpin it. In other words, as against social theory or philosophy, it is useless to ask art to raise questions which will find their answer through the logic of the presentation precisely because the imagination need not adhere to any prescribed logic.

Seeking a "negation" of the status quo, while continuing to insist that the aesthetic form must remain transcendentally estranged from reality *a priori*, an internal contradiction appears in Marcuse's thought which stems from his attempt to combine a Hegelian purpose with a Kantian form. And this is not merely a pedantic point. That contradiction will provide the ground for the arbitrariness which creeps into Marcuse's method as well as the one-sided, trans-historical, and ultimately "abstract," characterization of art's utopian potential.

In this vein, the real "dialectical" relation between art and society will become suppressed in favor of that "erotic truth" which the aesthetic form supposedly contains *a priori*. Consequently, if the utopian potential in art demands a critical social theory to appropriate it in emancipatory terms, Marcuse's claims that the aesthetic form is utopian by definition and that art will necessarily represent an "erotic truth" become mere assertions.

Even if a work does arise *from the urgings of* the repressed life instinct, it is one thing to say that Eros provides a psychological moment in the creative process and quite another to identify Eros with the object created. Of course, in specific works like *Tristan and Isolde* that may be the case; in other works, like those of the Marquis de Sade, however, that need not be the case at all.

A utopian potential or "truth" cannot therefore simply be trans-historically and teleologically posited with "art" *a priori*. If it appears at all, that truth will only become manifest in particular artworks in varying degrees. In this sense, there is nothing to be gained from discussing the aesthetic form in an hypostatized manner. The actual qualitative differences between works demands the construction of derivative categories which stand in relation to those needs that the artwork exposes and to the sociopolitical values by which they can be addressed in emancipatory terms.

Abstract differentiations regarding "affirmative" and "negative" culture will add little to such a project. What can be "affirmative" in one context can become "negative" in another and vice versa. Indeed, whether a work becomes "affirmative" or "negative" depends neither exclusively upon the "culture" as such nor upon an autonomous treatment of the work in terms of an equally autonomous aesthetic form. Each work is embraced by a certain public within the community at large,[59] which provides the initial basis for its "transcendence" as well as its immediate "negative" or "affirmative" characterization. Through the interaction of the work with that public, and that particular public with the broader community, a work becomes defined within a sociohistorical context that it *may* be able to transcend.

Such transcendence, however, demands a critic within that context; otherwise there is no basis for any claim about the inherently utopian or "negative" qualities of art. Indeed, only to the extent that this context itself is called critically into question does the possibility of linking the evaluation of the particular work to a broader emancipatory vision become possible.

Thus, Marcuse's vision flounders not only on the rock of concreteness. It is also blind to the political dimension through which it can alone be appropriated, and this becomes markedly evident in his ideas on censorship. Aside from the fact that Marcuse never discusses the institutional dangers of censoring even reactionary ideas, he actually believes that art should be preserved from this type of political activity. Though Marcuse would censor certain ideas where "the pacification of existence, where freedom and happiness are at stake,"[60] and so oppose a relativistic tolerance which inherently gives as much value to one idea as another, he goes on to say that:

> [C]ensorship of art and literature is regressive under all circumstances. There are cases where an authentic oeuvre carries a regressive political message - Dostoevski is a case in point. But then the message is canceled by the oeuvre itself: the regressive political content is absorbed (*aufgehoben*) in the artistic form: in the work as literature.[61]

That the political message of the artwork is necessarily "canceled" is simply an assertion. But the assertion belies the supposed autonomy of the aesthetic form. *Perhaps* in the case of Dostoevski, the political message is absorbed within the aesthetic form of the work. But, as in the case of Ernst Junger's works, even formal masterpieces can have a pronounced political impact upon the consciousness and mores of a given society. Aesthetic mastery need not cancel a reactionary political content: the two can happily coexist.

In fact, it is impossible to make a general assertion that "the regressive political content is absorbed (*aufgehoben*) in the artistic form." This is certainly not the case with the vicious anti-semitism that becomes explicit in the works of Celine or Gustav Freytag, which clearly had real reactionary effects upon the prevailing cultural climate. Furthermore, the theoretical straitjacket of "autonomy" in which Marcuse places art essentially prevents an understanding of the entire genre of "non-fiction fiction" or journalistic fiction which is exemplified in some of Norman Mailer's work.

Again the categories are lacking, and so there is no way to determine whether works which carry an explicit political appeal should be regarded as politico-cultural tracts or as artistic *oeuvres*. If Marcuse mistakenly accepts the authoritarian logic of censorship in the philosophico-political realm there is neither a material, institutional, nor theoretical justification for denying its applicability to art. For if censorship is necessary to counter political and philosophic threats to the "pacification of existence," it becomes simply arbitrary to ignore the same threat when it is levelled from the artistic sphere.

In this manner, Marcuse's attempt to separate art from reality actually leads to the reified division between intellectual and aesthetic appreciation, as well as to support for an abstract estrangement of the subject from his world. This is of particular importance to the previous discussion of the hero, and the atypical characteristics which he assumes in modern literature. Obviously, Marcuse's concern is not with the "hero" per se, but rather with a subject who is facing extinction in advanced industrial society. Though Marcuse formally gave up his early interest in existentialism,[62] the logic leads back to Kierkegaard whose views were attacked in *Reason and Revolution*. For it was Kierkegaard who originally recognized that the traditional "tragic hero" projects a universal and communicable truth which is open to social manipulation, even if that truth calls the pettiness and misery of the existing order into question. Thus, Kierkegaard sees the need to supplant this hero with the "knight of faith" who affirms a trans-historical subjective truth and an existential situation in which

> the particular is higher than the universal - and yet in such a way, be it observed, that consequently the individual after having been in the universal now as the particular isolates himself as higher than the universal.[63]

Kierkegaard is willing to draw the consequences of the subject's alienation in a way which Marcuse is not. If the traditional hero makes his choices according to an ethical standard which allows the existing order to judge his actions, the "knight of faith" actually manifests that critical separation from the given order which Marcuse desires. Unfortunately, however, that separation will then become frozen into a trans-historical paradox from which any utopian reconcilation between individuals and their world becomes impossible. Employing the biblical example of Abraham, Kierkegaard makes his point forcefully.

> The ethical expression for what Abraham did, is that he would murder Isaac; the religious expression is, that he would sacrifice Isaac; but precisely in this contradiction consists the dread which can well make a man sleepless. And yet, Abraham is not what he is without this dread.[64]

The criteria by which an individual makes his choice, and the criteria which any order employs to evaluate it, will then become mutually exclusive. This is the basis of Kierkegaard's category of existential dread (*Angst*) as well as a host of other consequences. Thus, in contrast to Marcuse, Kierkegaard realizes that the paradoxical situation in which an individual finds himself will propel his subjectivity beyond any dialectic and so lead to the "suspension of the telos." At the same time, however, the unique experience of the subject is preserved precisely because it has been removed from the sociohistorical judgment of the given repressive order.

To be sure, Kierkegaard's thought is religious in character; the "knight of faith" gains his sense of self through a belief in God whose inspiration provides him with the power to act. But, once a world arises in which "God is dead" (Nietzsche), once the individual views himself as a secular entity, his power will become dissipated even as the dread remains. In such a situation, which actually becomes worse in advanced industrial society, the similarity with Marcuse's aesthetic position should not be ignored. An atomized entity, the subject, will attempt to express this experience in art which seeks to deny an advanced industrial society that is defined by its adherence to instrumental rationality.[65] But, through seeking to deny this rationality in the name of his experience, Jacques Ellul can note that major tendencies of modern art will therefore guide "us in the direction of madness; and indeed, for modern man there is no other way. Only the madness is inaccessible to the machine."[66]

Dwarfed, isolated, and alone, the subject "trembles" when thrown into the complex and enormous technological society which sophistically seeks to transform existential desires into wants that can be materially satisfied and "dread" into an illusory "happy consciousness."

Under such circumstances, it is only natural that an oppositional response should emphasize a subjectivism which turns its back upon the given order entirely. And yet, as Hegel already observed, fundamental problems will arise from this perspective.

> In that the subject desires to penetrate into the truth and has a craving for objectivity, but yet is unable to abandon its isolation and retirement into itself, and to strip itself free of this unsatisfied abstract inwardness, [this subjectivity] will manifest a seizure of sickly yearning.[67]

This is not merely a matter of "anti-art." There is a truth in Hegel's words which applies to many artists of modernity who attempt that very break from the real which Marcuse's aesthetic demands. A specific case in point is William Burroughs' *Naked Lunch*. This work describes a junkie's vision of reality with a bitter energy, extraordinary imagery, and a cynicism that culminates in Burroughs' notion of the "algebra of need." Through this concept, Burroughs seeks to show how society turns individuals into addicts and that it basically makes no difference whether this addiction takes the form of power, money, altruism, sex, or drugs. Differentiations are denied, social effects are ignored, and the result is Hegel's "night in which all cows are black."

Now, from the standpoint of the sociology of literature, it would be possible to claim that Burroughs' work contains a legitimate moment of critique which he then extrapolates and hypostatizes into a trans-historical and universal condition. But Marcuse's theory inherently militates against such an approach to aesthetics. Beginning from the standpoint of the aesthetic form and its inherently utopian character, there is no immanent manner by which that utopian potential can be extracted from a position which renders the concern with any emancipatory alternative useless. All that remains is an abstract and "indeterminate" indictment of reality as such which betrays any erotic potential in favor of an overriding negativism.[68]

Such an abstract indictment is not unique to Burroughs, but is, rather, a dominant theme in the literature of advanced industrial society. Samuel

Beckett provides an even more extreme example. From *Waiting for Godot* through *Endgame* and *Krapp's Last Tape*, he draws the audience back into their own particular selves to the final silence. Perhaps Marcuse is thinking of just this silence when he calls Beckett's work "the most uncompromising, most extreme indictment . . . which precisely because of its radicalism repels the political sphere . . . [As] there is no hope which can be translated into political terms, the aesthetic form excludes all accommodation and leaves literature as literature. And as literature, the work carries one single message: to make an end with things as they are."[69]

But, once again, the last claim is merely an assertion. If politics as such is denied, then an emancipatory politics and its values will be denied as well. What subjectively *may* be experienced as rebellion, can also appear as a purely stoic resignation to the repression of the given order. If Beckett's *Endgame* speaks to the particularity of each member of the audience in objectively incommunicable terms, questions of critique, rebellion, and emancipation are anything but the necessary consequences. Beckett's silence can just as easily deny social commitment, undermine the estrangement effect, explode a determinate negation, and even potentially destroy the potential for liberation which results from the interaction between the work and a "public." As such art estranges itself from society and its reality principle, it also alienates itself from the very possibility of a discourse to determine its emancipatory potential. Thus, the very silence which Beckett's works project might actually constrain the imagination and its potential.

Nevertheless, Marcuse's particular view remains adamant on the liberating power of the imagination, and so he holds that within the aesthetic form "the surrealist program must still be valid." In this sense, however, Marcuse appears to contradict his previous evaluation of Beckett insofar as - following the surrealists - "the dream must become a force of changing rather than dreaming the human condition: it must become a political force."[70]

Granted that in such a dream the images need not take on an objectively cognitive quality. But, it must take on some quality beyond the silence of inwardness. In Marcuse's view, Beckett's work is clearly distinguished from the pretentious "games" of an anti-art which has placed itself outside "the dimension of alienation." That may subjectively be the case, but it can also be argued that objective result is the same. Concrete negation gives way to abstract opposition and, insofar as the experience of the work itself becomes literally incommunicable, the artistic revolt - or lack of it - becomes a purely arbitrary matter which is closed to critical evaluation.

It is important to state that Marcuse was always highly critical of the anti-intellectualism which appeared in certain New Left trends. But, his aesthetic theory does not take into account the manner in which the door is opened to irrationalism and arbitrariness. If this theoretically results from the fact that there is no perceived mediation between the "dream" and its public, between the "aesthetic form" and social reality, that theoretical flaw becomes evident in the arbitrary responses to particular works. In "the night in which all cows are black," comprehension will be immediate, subjective, emotional, and potentially solipsistic. Marcuse would agree that it is simply impossible to determine reflexively the experience and potential of a white canvas, or a composition without score. He would also agree that, in Hegelian terms, immediate knowledge must always be mediated by self-conscious reflection with regard to a freedom that remains to be realized.

But Marcuse never provides either the mediations themselves nor the categories by which such mediations might be derived and comprehended. Lacking such categories, Marcuse's position actually undermines his legitimate attempt to free the aesthetic form from the repressive constraints of the given order. Thus, in attempting to make the aesthetic form "oppose" reality through a fundamental divorce, it is as if Marcuse forgets his own insight that the individual experience of that form will have been fundamentally affected by the advanced industrial society in which he lives. The subjective and abstract character of the form itself will thus become a logical consequence. As a result, the purely subjective and arbitrary nature of the aesthetic form can actually relativize and so undermine even that "promesse de bonheur" which it is said to contain.

This demands a transvaluation of the entire notion of the aesthetic form with an eye to its indirect relation to history and social reality. Ernst Fischer is therefore correct in claiming that form is where "transmitted experience is preserved and all achievement is kept safe . . . . Form is social experience solidified."[71] Indeed, this even needs to be taken a step further. It is precisely the social character of experience itself which, in the case of a concrete work of art, allows form to mediate between the artist and the content which he wishes to express.

What results is an "objectification," a work that stands separate from the artist who produced it and which *can* even deny his original intentions and prejudices. Along with social reality itself, those original intentions will be aesthetically transvalued. But, this does not mean that the work's relation to reality has simply disappeared.[72] In this aesthetic objectification, form and content can only be differentiated abstractly since one will necessarily affect the other. Thus, if form gives the content of a work its shape and makes that content communicable, the choice of the content to be expressed will also obviously have an effect upon the form that is chosen to express it.

In itself, however, all this has nothing to do with the values which the work expresses or which will be attached to it. Consequently, Marcuse's emphasis upon the "form" and the inherently radical character of modernist experimentation is mistaken. For there is nothing intrinsically progressive in the choice of one form or style over another. If experimental modernism can project radical utopian qualities in the works of an Ernst Toller, it can also produce the opposite in the works of a Nazi like Hanns Johst; if realism can produce a Thomas Mann, it can also produce a Robert Brasillach. Neither art nor the "aesthetic form" is therefore necessarily emancipatory. Indeed, the work of art will only assume an emancipatory value when its aesthetic comprehension is *indirectly* linked to a critical, sociopolitical theory of actual conditions that projects the values of emancipatory social transformation.

This in no way violates the idea of aesthetic transcendence. In fact, Marcuse himself merely presupposes the concept and he is never able to recognize that "art" is not transcendent; some *works* become transcendent and others do not, but this issue never emerges in his aesthetic theory. And the reason is that transcendence cannot merely be defined as an intrinsic quality of an autonomous aesthetic form. Instead, transcendence is a social act which demands a perception of its indirect connection *to that historical order which is transcended.*

Different works express different needs, different hopes, and different possibilities. But the potential of each emerges only when it is grasped by "its own audience of artlovers" (Marx). Whatever the form, the emancipatory or regressive character of a work *can* only become evident in a continuing interaction with a changing audience that seeks to discover and rediscover the critical and mutable value of the work itself.

That discovery demands a critic who will distill that liberating potential - or lack of it - from this aesthetically solidified set of social experiences. Perhaps one work will portray the repression of society while another will project the still unrealized emancipatory hopes of the future. But this is all moot unless there is already consciousness which *chooses* to recognize either.

The appropriation of an artwork's utopian potential cannot then be simply presupposed. Instead, it involves an act of criticism which will take place among critics and audiences of different persuasions that harbor different sociopolitical values. Arising within the context of the given society's "material level of culture" (Marx), the emancipatory appropriation of a work will therefore involve the radical critic in a continuous battle to elucidate, preserve, and potentially redefine, that "promesse de bonheur" which the work may harbor.[73] If that is the case, however, then the critical aesthetic endeavor must itself be mediated by an articulated political worldview whose critical and emancipatory values themselves can be justified in a free discourse.

But, if an emancipatory aesthetic demands some connection to a political worldview and is therefore necessarily linked to the real, it does not follow that art must then become the propagandistic servant of the existing order or even a party which subjectively seeks to change that order. Such was the case with "socialist realism" in the thirties. In this respect, Marcuse wrote one of the finest works on Soviet ideology, and he provides a superb analysis of how the transcendent character of art is undermined by this governmentally-sponsored genre.[74] Indeed, it is true that the forced "objectivity" of the socialist realist form will essentially abolish real subjectivity and that the oeuvre itself will be subjugated to the given political line of the Communist Party.[75]

Yet, a number of points should be made here. First of all, such a subjugation to dogma can take many forms and involve many political perspectives; Sartre raised virtually the same point with regard to Francois Mauriac, the Nobel Prize winner, whose art was deemed "inauthentic" since he constrained the freedom of his characters in the name of Catholic orthodoxy.[76] Secondly, it is always a mistake to equate the genre with those works that comprise it, especially when the categories for evaluating such works are lacking.   In the same way that various rock songs retain a quality beyond that of the genre as defined by AM radio, it is possible that a major work of socialist realism can actually break through the politically imposed constraints of the "style" and, through the "content" portrayed, provide an "objective" criticism that can contradict the artist's original political intentions; this might well be the case with Mikhail Sholokhov, another Nobel Prize winner, or Anna Seghers.   On the other hand, John Heartfield - an innovator in the use of photo-montage - could attempt to communicate a politically prescribed message for the covers of the German Communist Party's popular magazines through an avant-garde form which unintentionally contradicts the Third International's dogmatism.

Generally speaking, however, Marcuse's indictment of "socialist realism" is well grounded.   Indeed, the excesses of "socialist realism" have provided the aesthetic equivalent of what Brecht termed the "Stalin trauma" with regard to political art in general and the representational forms of naturalism and realism in particular for many radical critics.   But it is really time to recognize that formal experimentation will not *necessarily* have a more critical and emancipatory content than a representational emphasis upon content.   Indeed, the critical function of each is different,[77] and both actually stand in danger of losing their emancipatory character.   For Lukacs is basically correct in his assessment that:

> The more developed capitalist society is, the more developed are both its (aesthetic) poles: the increasingly abstract and empty stylization as well as the increasingly servile and photographic naturalism which clings to immediate surfaces.[78]

In this vein, as Marcuse recognizes, the particular form of sociopolitical organization will have a pronounced impact on the type of art that will be produced as well as upon the manner in which its critical qualities will become manifest. Thus, in Marcuse's view, it is precisely because the political and ideological contradictions of advanced industrial society have subjectively "flattened out" that art must fully estrange itself from an alienated reality. But, Marcuse agrees that objective contradictions remain, and there is no reason to ignore them as a source of artistic creation.

Looking back upon his early childhood when he first started to write, Sartre ironically highlights the experience which Marcuse sees as the condition of "one-dimensional" existence.

> I had armed myself to defend mankind against terrible dangers, and everyone assured me that it was quietly on its way to perfection. Grandfather had brought me up to respect bourgeois democracy: I would gladly have unsheathed my pen for it.   But with de Fallieres as President, the peasant voted: what more could I ask?   And what does a republican do if he has the luck to live in a republic? He twiddles his thumbs, or else he teaches Greek and describes the

monuments of Aurillac in his spare time. I was back where I had started from, and I thought I would stifle in that world without conflicts which left the writer unemployed.[79]

Sartre ultimately discovered some of those conflicts which had once seemed hidden. If objective contradictions continue to exist, then to dismiss them as material for art in favor of a formal aesthetic rejection of the real might actually link the aesthetic form itself to those values of the given order which securely separate art from life.

Even from the standpoint of the subject's integrity and uniqueness, the aesthetic examination of his experience need not involve a divorce from the reality in which he exists. A confrontation can take place in many ways, including an encounter with the "absurd" as Camus demonstrates so beautifully in *The Fall*. Existential anguish is a reality even if existentialism itself cannot explain its real sociohistorical production or content. Thus, even Trotsky could ask "if art will not help this new man to educate himself, to strengthen and refine himself, then what is it for? And how can it organize the inner life, if it does not penetrate it and reproduce it?"[80]

The preservation of subjectivity may involve more than a flight from the objective world that constrains it. Indeed, perhaps it is in the direct confrontation with his objective world that the subjective experience may aesthetically provide a potential impetus to the imagination. Perhaps the aesthetic transvaluation of experience can allow the purely subjective consciousness of oppression to expose the structure of those conditions in which the individual objectively lives, the need for changing them, and the values which would make such a transformation emancipatory in character.

But, if this is a real possibility the use of new and experimental forms of aesthetic creation also present a problem that cannot simply be ignored. Thus, Sartre can note:

[M]odern music is shattering forms, breaking away from conventions, carving its own road. But exactly to whom does it speak of liberation, freedom, will, of the creation of man by man - to a stale and genteel listener whose ears are blocked up by an idealist aesthetic. Music says "permanent revolution" and the bourgeoisie hears "evolution, progress." And even if among the young intellectuals, a few understand it, won't their present impotence make them see this liberation as a beautiful myth, instead of their own reality?[81]

The real point is not the anti-intellectual fetish of popularity which always ignores the objective and substantive constraints of the culture industry along with the socioeconomic context in which works become popular. Rather, it is Sartre's perception of how such an aesthetic position can actually build a sense of frustration that throws the subject ever further back upon himself - which is precisely what Marcuse claims is the condition of individuals in advanced industrial society that his transcendental aesthetic seeks to oppose.

The question is one of the context of support in which an artist works. Sometimes a work which sells a few thousand copies can have an impact far beyond its sales, while an extremely popular work can be quickly forgotten. But, in contrast to Marcuse and many of his early associates at the Institute for Social Research in Frankfurt, the fact that an artwork becomes a commodity does not necessarily exhaust its emancipatory or critical character, and the extent to which it becomes popular is not inversely related to its revolutionary quality; Sartre, Chaplin, Gunther Grass and a host of others can serve as examples. As an objectification, despite its existence within the commodity form, the work of art can still transcend its period and so provide new sources of revolutionary promise for future generations.

Even Marcuse's call for the self-conscious estrangement of art from society, retains an ideological dimension which he ignores. Brecht made this point in a different context in his debate with Lukacs over the "progressive" character of modernism *vis-a-vis* realism:

> Whether a work is realist or not cannot be seen merely from having a look whether it is similar or not to existing works that are called realist and [which] were realist in their own epoch. In each case one must compare the description of life, . . . with life itself. . . . A work is comprehensible not merely because it is written exactly like the other works before it. Something had to be done to make them comprehensible. So we, too, must do something to make new works comprehensible. It is not a question merely of what is popular, but of what can be made popular.[82]

Aside from the fact that estrangement or difficulty is not necessarily a virtue, what may be termed estrangement or difficulty varies between publics and historical periods. Thus, the modernist and experimental poetry of Bob Dylan - which should be totally estranged from the existing order according to Marcuse's own aesthetic criteria - has achieved an enormous popularity without any sacrifice of quality. The question of a work's estrangement from the existing order or its "comprehensibility" must therefore be discussed in terms of the over-riding sociocultural conditions which actually make a work "estranged" or "comprehensible." Thus, it becomes necessary to turn from the particular work and the abstract discussion of form to "the material level of culture" of a given society and its opponents.

In the given context, it was logical that Marx and Engels should have stressed the value of realism.[83] And it also makes sense that this tradition should have been supported by both the early Social Democratic as well as the later Communist movement. The sociopolitical purpose was clear; with a vibrant movement on the rise, the works of a Goethe or a Balzac would simultaneously build a commitment to the unrealized values of the revolutionary bourgeoisie and also portray the manner in which those ideals were denied by the very class which originally fostered them. Marx and Engels did not share Marcuse's assumption that it would be necessary to pass through the aesthetic dimension to transform the world politically in an emancipatory manner. Liberation would occur through the proletarian revolution and the development of a class consciousness which derived from the workers' realization of their concrete political and economic interests.

In Marcuse's view, advanced industrial society has ideologically reconciled class conflict through a cultural system and so undermined the working class as the revolutionary subject of history. It is for this reason that his analysis of the effects of the culture industry and its effects upon society at large are of such importance. If these effects actually reach into the infrastructure of the individual, the need to reassert utopian goals and begin to develop the actual content of revolutionary emancipation becomes ever more critical as Marcuse suggests.

Given the rise of a student movement which fundamentally equated cultural rebellion with political revolt in the era of the Vietnam War,[84] Marcuse's aesthetic concerns with a "new sensibility" and a "pacification of existence" assumed a directly political character as they expanded the perception of freedom and inspired motivations for revolt. But Marcuse never explained how the necessary estrangement of art from the society of the present could be transformed into the utopian intervention into the reality of the future. Obviously, it would be foolish to chastise Marcuse for failing to provide a strategy or a tactics *a priori*. But there is a question whether this is even epistemologically possible from Marcuse's perspective regarding the transcendental nature of the aesthetic form since the new order would "end the segregation of the aesthetic from the real."[85]

Nevertheless, there is a speculative beauty to Marcuse's utopian conception. The aesthetic moment would penetrate into the very *logos* of thought and so harmonize the requisites of reason with the desires of sensuality. Indeed, history would assume a new meaning in which the unrealized utopian demands of the past would become the content for future practice.[86] Thus, the understanding of reality itself would be transformed, since even time would be transvalued and the "tyranny of becoming over being" would be broken.[87] Marcuse's vision therefore confronts death itself. And there is a speculative daring in his emphatic claim that only by transvaluing the fear of death will reality truly manifest the "attained and sustained fulfillment" of the aesthetic form.

Building on Freud's metapsychology, Marcuse is therefore able to project "nirvana" as a speculative possibility in terms of a new subjective "infrastructure" which militates against all repression and fear. Still, there is a danger that emerges when Marcuse accepts the trans-historical perspective of Freud's metapsychology without any concrete referent. Thus, Marcuse never addresses the possibility that certain elements of the human experience may deserve to be repressed and that such a perspective can ignore the actual effects upon individuals that historical conditions engender.

That becomes evident in Marcuse's abstract attempt to reconcile "subject" and "object," the individual with his world, in a pacified existence. In the abstract, however, this can easily lead to what Geza

Roheim called the "dual unity" situation.[88]   As society becomes the. mother who will equally distribute her bounties to a universe of brothers, freed from the repression and guilt of their relation to the father, any truly private realm would become a threat to that very communality which has been achieved. Indeed, even the desire to create an individual personality would reimpose that guilt which stemmed from the primordial attempt to overthrow the father. Although Marcuse implicitly denies it,[89] his pacification of existence might therefore not lead to making the tension between subject and object "non-aggressive" and non-destructive," but to lowering ego boundaries which both Freud and Roheim view as "a characteristic feature of schizophrenia."[90]   Under such circumstances, a situation can arise which Freud termed a state of "psychological misery" (*psychologisches Elend*) in which the identification between members of a society is so close that there can be no ego reward for activity at all.[91]

That Marcuse ignores this possibility is due to his one-sided, abstract response to the reappropriation of the "emancipatory" past. Now, recapturing the liberating moments of "*les temps perdu*" is a crucial concern of any utopian vision in the post-Hegelian world.   And, like his colleagues in the enterprise of critical theory such as Ernst Bloch, Walter Benjamin, and Theodor Adorno, Marcuse is correct in rejecting Hegel's assumption that the emancipatory characteristics of a given period will necessarily be retained and superseded (*aufgehoben*) in the next phase of history.   But, as Marcuse himself recognized, if that is the case then Hegel would also be mistaken in his assumption that the antagonistic contradictions of one period would necessarily be reconciled in the next.

Unfortunately, however, Marcuse does not follow through on the implications.   For, given this situation, the emancipatory moments of the past cannot simply reveal themselves since they will necessarily remain intertwined with historically regressive elements.   Thus the need arises for developing the criteria through which the emancipatory moments of the past can be recognized as such and then employed to expand the content of liberation.   Without these criteria, the entire attempt to transvalue the past can easily lead to arbitrariness, eclecticism, and the retention of residual repressive features from the past.

In order to develop such criteria, some notion of "progress" must be maintained - Marcuse's abstract call for the transvaluation of time notwithstanding.   Indeed, the point is missed when the issue is framed in terms of whether "progress" should either be supported or denied. Instead, the real question involves how "progress" should be determined.[92]   And, in this regard, the matter of production cannot simply be ignored through an emphasis upon "abundance" as the prerequisite for a utopian condition.

Though Marx may have been a child of his time when considering the relation between progress and technological expansion, he was acquainted with Schiller's work and still refrained from embracing the "play impulse." Possibly he recognized that the concept would undermine his materialist method and his concern for "dialectical specificity" (Korsch); possibly he feared the over-emphasis upon "intuitive comprehension" (*Verstehen*) were the aesthetic to assume primacy in guiding society.[93]   More to the point, however, is the fundamental character of Marx's enterprise. Where Marcuse builds his utopia on the passive and idyllic vision of Orpheus or Narcissus,[94] Marx's project was essentially that of Prometheus or Faust. In a sense, Marx did not even desire the pastoral "pacification of existence." Instead, he called for a dynamic society in which the "cunning" of a pre-history would be conquered through individuals actively participating in a democratically controlled production process with new humanistic criteria that will derive from a new form of sociopolitical "association."

Marx therefore retains the notion of humanity as *homo faber*, along with a class perspective that Marcuse finds flawed. Thus, in *The Communist Manifesto*, the authors can claim that "in bourgeois society, living labor is but a means to increase accumulated labor. In communist society, accumulated labor is but a means to widen, to enrich, to promote the existence of the laborer."[95] Where Marx will demand the substitution of creative work for existing forms of debilitating labor, Marcuse wishes to merge labor with "play." Consequently, although Marcuse admittedly believes that labor cannot be abolished and sees the need for a "limited" mastery over nature, "in this utopian hypothesis labor would be so different from labor as we know it or normally conceive of it that the idea of the convergence of labor and play does not diverge too far from the possibilities."[96]

In this respect, Marcuse's attempt to supplant labor with play would also call for a new science and a new technology. For mastery is not quantitiative and creation itself necessarily implies both a certain technical proficiency as well as an *esprit sérieux* which is anything but "playful" in Marcuse's sense of the term. But, even if Habermas is wrong in suggesting that work and science retain an ontological character that cannot be transformed,[97] Marcuse's argument essentially dispenses with the question of production entirely and so provides no manner for his new order to either maintain or reproduce itself. Even more importantly, however, Marcuse never developed a substantive critique of the scientific method. Instead, he simply conflated the critique of "science" and "technology" with a critique of the uses to which they are put. Where such a formulation actually obscured the real issue, it also kept Marcuse's utopian vision hanging in the abstract with only a transcendent aesthetic to provide the alternative conception with its content.

And yet, at the time, it did not seem so abstract at all. The abstraction seemed to have a vehicle for its realization. But, the marriage of the abstract and the real was unhappy even during the honeymoon. Where Marcuse presupposed the need for a new system of production, the American movement was populist and Jeffersonian in spirit. The traditions were at odds from the beginning, but both sides sought to make the marriage work. Where Marcuse's aesthetic uncompromisingly opposed the status quo, the impetus for the movement itself seemed to derive from the "outcasts" of America society: students, minorities, intellectuals, women disgusted with the subservience that they had to endure. Aside from the fact that Marcuse placed an unbridled hope in the new feminism that was emerging, what he philosophically projected had a certain counterpart in those who took part in a "counter-culture" which appeared to prefigure an unrepressed mode of communal life, a rejection of the prevailing socioeconomic norms of success, racism, sexism, war, and inequality, as well as a real spirt of revolutionary emancipation.

It is true that Marcuse opposed the equation of sexual freedom with the "new sensibility" that his aesthetic envisioned, and that he was often at odds with the tactics as well as the tastes of the movement. But it is also true that, in contrast to many of his old Frankfurt School colleagues like Adorno and Horkheimer, he supported the movement sincerely. And yet, if *An Essay on Liberation* was dedicated to the struggles of the French students and workers of 1968, Marcuse's last work - *The Aesthetic Dimension* - reflected a very different period.[98]

This was probably Marcuse's weakest and most traditional work. At the time it was written, the movement was over. Advanced industrial society attempted to absorb the gains. The critical individual who resisted stood isolated and perhaps in more danger than before, while the spirit of the "new sensibility" had vanished. Probably as a consequence, Marcuse emphasized even more strongly the need for a total break of the aesthetic from the real.

"Political" art, and even Brecht, came under attack and the utopian project faded into the shadows of the discourse. Furthermore, the systemic analysis of actual conditions, and the attempt to define new motivations for action, gave way before an over-riding emphasis on transcendence *per se*. For this alone was to insure that the authentic experience of the subject would be preserved and that its "non-identity" (Adorno) with a repressive social reality would be maintained. Retaining a fundamental relation to his earlier works, while undermining the sociopolitical "promise of happiness" in favor of the subject's transcendent redemption through art, *The Aesthetic Dimension* is a work of defeat that portrays the impotence of art when confronted with the victory of the reaction. But this retreat may perhaps also be seen as a response to the power which Marcuse originally placed in art and which the aesthetic does not - and arguably should not - possess.

Shelley's claim notwithstanding, the artist is not "the unacknowledged legislator of the world" and art is not the "container" of liberation. "Art" varies in its qualities and its styles, and its diversity cannot simply be subsumed within an "aesthetic dimension." A critical aesthetic can expand the perception of what emancipation entails. But it cannot and need not specify the preconditions which would underpin that liberated condition. Nor is it incumbent upon aesthetics *necessarily* to provide an illusory reconciliation of real contradictions. Still, art can foster an understanding of what conditions need to be changed and, when indirectly linked to reality through a speculative social theory, aesthetics can provide a critique of what has been achieved in terms of what remains to be accomplished. Yet, the aesthetic realm neither incarnates utopia nor exhausts its potential even while asserting the recognition of freedom as an unfinished process.

And so, if Herbert Marcuse's thought provides a path-breaking step in the development of speculative theory and utopian thinking, its limit emerges precisely where the need for an equally utopian political response to the conformism, anti-intellectualism, and oppression of the "one-dimensional" order begins. Still, this is precisely what Herbert Marcuse's thought serves to foster. Indeed, it is a testament to the method which he employed that his own utopian concerns can be critically transvalued and infused with a different content and different values that project the need for a society where "the forms of life will become dynamically dramatic, (where) the average human type will rise to the heights of an Aristotle, a Goethe, or a Marx. And [where] above this ridge, new peaks will rise."[99]

NOTES

1. Herbert Marcuse, *Schriften* 1 (Frankfurt, 1978).
2. The most important are: Morton Schoolman, *The Imaginary Witness: The Critical Theory of Herbert Marcuse*; Barry Katz, *Herbert Marcuse and the Art of Liberation;* and the excellent volume by Douglas Kellner, *Herbert Marcuse and the Crisis of Marxism.*
9. Cf. Georg Lukacs, *Die Seele und die Formen* and *The Theory of the Novel.*
4. Marcuse, *An Essay on Liberation* (Boston, 1969), p. 54.
5. Marcuse, *Eros and Civilization: A Philosophical Inquiry into Freud* (New York, 1962), p.74.
6. *Ibid.*, p. 41.
7. Cf. Marcuse, "Protosocialism and Late Capitalism: Toward a Theoretical Synthesis Based on Bahro's Analysis," in *Rudolf Bahro: Critical Responses*, ed. Ulf Wolter.
8. *Eros and Civilization*, p. 34.
9. It should be noted in this context that Marcuse mechanistically draws a distinction between "true" and "false" needs without analytically justifying the rigid distinction. In contrast, Marx recognized that a more complex process is in operation; thus religion may be "the opium of the masses," but it is also the "sigh of the oppressed creature" in a heartless world. In short, for a utopian conception, the opium will be used as long as the conditions which make its use necessary continue to exist.
10. The "total organization of society under monopoly capital and the growing wealth created by this organization can neither undo nor arrest the dynamic of its growth: capitalism cannot satisfy the needs which it creates." Herbert Marcuse, *Counterrevolution and Revolt* (Boston, 1972).
11. Paul A. Robinson, *The Freudian Left*, p. 208.
12. Marcuse, "Progress and Freud's Theory of Instincts," in *Five Lectures* (Boston, 1969), p. 37.
13. Sigmund Freud, "Repression," in *General Psychological Theory,* ed. Philip Rieff, p. 105.
14. Sigmund Freud, *The Ego and the Id*, trans. Joan Riviere.
15. Shierry M. Weber, "Individuation as Praxis," in *Critical Interruptions*, ed. Paul Breines, p. 37.
16. *Ibid.*, p. 55.
17. For a clear explication of the dialectical relation between reason and necessity, as well as its implications, see Frederick Engels, *Ludwig*

Feuerbach and the End of Classical German Philosophy, in Karl Marx and Frederick Engels, *Selected Works* 3 volumes (Moscow, 1969), vol. 3.

18. Marcuse, *Reason and Revolution: Hegel and the Rise of Social Theory* (Boston, 1969), p. 9.

19. Marcuse, "The End of Utopia," in *Five Lectures,* pp. 68-9.

20. *Ibid.*

21. Marcuse, "The Affirmative Character of Culture," in *Negations*, trans. Jeremy J. Shapiro (Boston, 1969), p. 230.

22. *Eros and Civilization*, p. 105.

23. Marcuse, *One-Dimensional Man* (Boston, 1964), p. 63.

24. *Counterrevolution and Revolt*, pp. 92-3.

25. Perhaps this idea will gain a certain clarity with a stanza from Keats' "Ode to a Nightingale":

> Away! Away! for I will fly to thee,
> Not charioted by Bacchus and his pards,
> But on the viewless wings of Poesy,
> Though the dull brain perplexes and retards:
> Already with thee! tender is the night,
> And haply the Queen-Moon is on her throne,
> Cluster'd around by all her starry Fays;
> But here there is no light,
> Save what from heaven is with the breezes blown
> Through verdurous glooms and winding mossy ways.

26. *Negations*, p. 118.

27. *Ibid.*, p. 122.

28. Cf. Max Horkheimer and Theodor W. Adorno, *Dialectic of Enlightenment,* trans. John Cumming, pp. 120ff.

29. *Negations*, p. 122.

30. *Counterrevolution and Revolt*, p. 98.

31. Marcuse, "The Obsolescence of the Freudian Concept of Man," in *Five Lectures*, p. 58.

32. There is already a hint of this in Hegel's point that it has "become more or less obligatory for a cultivated man to possess some acquaintance with art, and the pretention to display oneself as a dilettante and connoisseur (is) pretty universal." Cf. G. W. F. Hegel, *On Art, Religion, and Philosophy*, ed. J. Glenn Gray, p. 38.

33. Jacques Ellul, *The Technological Society*, p. 129.

34. *Ibid.*, p. 128.

35. *One-Dimensional Man*, p. 59.

36. *Ibid.*, p. 70.

37. Reimut Reiche, *Sexuality and Class Struggle,* p. 71.

38. *Counterrevolution and Revolt*, p. 101.

39. Marcuse, "Art and Revolution," *Partisan Review* (Spring 1972), p. 178.

40. *Ibid.*, p. 179.

41. *Counterrevolution and Revolt*, p. 99.

42. *Ibid.*, p. 67.

43. In a way, this fits with Freud's view of fantasy as the only thought activity which is preserved from reality testing and which still remains subordinate to the pleasure principle. Cf. Sigmund Freud, "Two Principles in Mental Functioning," in *General Psychological Theory*.

44. Friedrich Schiller, *On the Aesthetic Education of Man*, p. 76.

45. *Eros and Civilization*, p. 131.

46. *Ibid.*, p. 132.

47. *Ibid.*, p. 135.

48. Sigmund Freud, "The Theme of the Three Caskets," in *Character and Culture*, p. 76.

49. Cf. Andre Breton, *What is Surrealism?*, pp. 50-73 and *passim*.

50. "Art and Revolution," p. 182.

51. *Ibid.*

52. *Ibid.*, p. 178.

53. *Ibid.*, p. 180.

54. *An Essay on Liberation*, p. 24.

55. *One-Dimensional Man*, p. 239.

56. *An Essay on Liberation*, pp. 21-28.

57. Cf. Marcuse, "The Foundations of Historical Materialism," in *Studies in Critical Philosophy*.

58. Reasserting the integrity of Marcuse's philosophic enterprise is of some importance given the outrageous political attacks by Eliseo Vivas, *Contra Marcuse* and, to a somewhat lesser extent, by Alisdair MacIntyre, *Herbert Marcuse: An Exposition and a Polemic*.

59. Jean-Paul Sartre, *What is Literature?* p. 117.

60. Marcuse, "Repressive Tolerance," in Robert Paul Wolff, Barrington Moore, Jr., and Herbert Marcuse, *A Critique of Pure Tolerance*, p. 88.

61. *Ibid.*, p. 89.

62. *Schriften* 1, pp. 347-407.

63. Soren Kierkegaard, *Fear and Trembling and The Sickness unto Death*, p. 65.

64. *Ibid.*, p. 41.

65. *One-Dimensional Man*, *passim*.

66. Ellul, *The Technological Society*, p. 404.

67. Hegel, *On Art*, p. 100; also note the section entitled "the law of the heart" in *The Phenomenology of Mind*, trans. J.B. Baillie, pp. 390ff.

68. Freud might consider this type of negativism "the derivative of expulsion (which) belongs to the instinct of destruction. The passion for universal negation, the 'negativism' displayed . . . is probably due to be regarded as a sign of the defusion of the instincts due to the withdrawal of the libidinal components." Cf. Sigmund Freud, "Negation," in *General Psychological Theory*, p. 216.

69. "Art and Revolution," p. 179.

70. *Counterrevolution and Revolt*, p. 102.

71. Ernst Fischer, *The Necessity of Art: A Marxist Approach*, p. 15.

72. Cf. Stephen Eric Bonner, "Expressionism and Marxism: Towards an Aesthetic of Emancipation," in *Passion and Rebellion: The Expressionist Heritage*.

73. Cf. Engels' defense of Balzac on precisely this point in his letter to Margaret Harkness of early April, 1888: "Well, Balzac was politically a Legitimist; his work is a constant elegy on the irretrievable decay of good society; his sympathies are all with the class doomed to extinction. But, for all that, his satire is never keener, his irony never bitterer, than when he sets in motion the very men and women with whom he sympathizes the most deeply - the nobles." Marx and Engels, *Selected Correspondence* (Moscow, 1965), pp. 402-3.

74. Marcuse, *Soviet Marxism* (New York, 1961), p. 113.

75. For a fuller explication of the "purpose" of socialist realism, cf. Abram Tertz, *The Trial Begins On Socialist Realism.*

76. Cf. Jean-Paul Sartre, "Francois Mauriac and Freedom," in his *Literary Essays*, pp. 7ff.

77. Bronner, "Expressionism and Marxism," pp. 437ff.

78. Georg Lukacs, *Goethe and His Age*, p. 105.

79. Jean-Paul Sartre, *The Words*, p. 1.

80. Leon Trotsky, *Literature and Revolution*, p. 138.

81. Jean-Paul Sartre, "The Artist and His Conscience," in *Situations*, p. 145.

82. Bertolt Brecht, "Volkstümlichkeit und Realismus," in *Gesammelte Werke*, vol. 19, p. 330-31.

83. Aside from the fact that the idealist tradition played a fundamental role in the development of Marxian theory, it is also interesting to note that Engels was a leading member of the Schiller *Verein* in Manchester.

84. Cf. Stephen Eric Bronner, "Reconstructing the Experiment: Politics, Ideology, and the American New Left," *Social Text*, no. 8 (Winter 1983-4), pp. 127-42.

85. *An Essay on Liberation*, p. 32.

86. *Eros and Civilization*, p. 106.

87. *Ibid.*, p. 110.

88. Geza Roheim, *Magic and Schizophrenia*, p. 4.

89. *Eros and Civilization*, pp. 106ff.

90. Roheim, *Magic and Schizophrenia*, p. 111.

91. Sigmund Freud, *Civilization and its Discontents*, trans. and ed. James Strachey (New York, 1961), pp. 62-3.

92. Cf. Henry Patcher, "The Idea of Progress in Marxism," in *Socialism in History: Political Essays of Henry Patcher*, ed. Stephen Eric Bronner.

93. It might be noted that the famous introduction to the *Grundrisse* breaks off precisely at the point where the question of aesthetic transcendence should begin.

94. *Eros and Civilization*, pp. 144ff.

95. Karl Marx and Frederick Engels, *Selected Works*, vol. 1, p. 121.

96. "The End of Utopia," p. 78.

97. See the superb essay "Technology and Science as Ideology," in Jürgen Habermas, *Toward a Rational Society*, pp. 81ff.

98. Marcuse, *The Aesthetic Dimension* (Boston, 1978).

99. Trotsky, *Literature and Revolution,* p. 256.

PART IV

□□□□□□□□□□

THE PSYCHOLOGICAL DIMENSION

Initially, it may seem odd to isolate a "psychological" dimension within Marcuse's critical theory. After all, the only "psychologist" Marcuse discussed in any detail was Freud, hardly a figure of endearment either to most academic psychologists or orthodox Marxists. Yet like his onetime Frankfurt contemporary Erich Fromm, Marcuse stressed from the essays of the 1930s on the crucial importance for radical social theory to understand the dialectics of history at least in part as the dynamics of transhistorical instincts or drives (*Triebe*). The oft-repeated failures of workers and others to play the revolutionary parts Marx had assigned them, and of radical intellectuals to mobilize the masses for a socialism with a truly human face, could not, according to Marcuse, be understood solely within the rationalistic categories of historical materialism. An analysis of subjectivity and class consciousness - of *irrationality* at both the individual and collective levels - was vital if Marxists and other progressives were not to continue to repeat the theoretical and practical "mistakes" made in Europe and elsewhere during the first half of the twentieth century. And this meant that Marxian social theory had to come to terms with the least deficient theory of irrationality, Freudian psychoanalysis.

Marcuse's efforts in his articles of the 1930s and in *Eros and Civilization* to bring together at least theoretically Marxian social theory and Freudian metapsychology must be applauded as an astute attempt to circumvent the arid determinism of orthodox Marxism and the ahistorical reductionism of both conventional psychotherapy and experimental psychology. His formulations of such notions as surplus repression, the reality principle, repressive desublimation, and non-repressive sublimation are valuable contributions to critical social theory. Regrettably, almost all efforts to confabulate a "Marxist psychology" or "Freudian Marxism" since the work done by Marcuse, Fromm, and Wilhelm Reich in the 1920s and 1930s have not succeeded in contributing much to the discussion. In any event, as Edward Hyman argues in his chapter, the critical psychology of Herbert Marcuse, for all its shortcomings, underscores the continuing need to link an historical analysis of social movements and class structures to a depth-psychological understanding of human drives.

CHAPTER EIGHT

Eros And Freedom: The Critical Psychology Of Herbert Marcuse

Edward Hyman

One rational voice is dumb, Over a grave
The household of Impulse mourns one dearly loved
Sad is Eros, builder of cities,
And weeping anarchic Aphrodite.
W. H. Auden, 1939
"In Memory of Sigmund Freud"

Introduction

Humanity's potential for liberation is a theme that has been systematically deleted over the last decade from the vocabulary of social discourse. Moreover, critical social and political issues have been increasingly displaced from the agenda of Western culture. Most participants in the social movements of the late sixties and early seventies, as well as their opponents and armchair spectators, would almost certainly have reacted with arrogant disbelief had they then been forewarned that this would be the intellectual and political "reality" of the 1980s in Western society.

Even the marginal social changes instituted or initiated during that period have been eliminated, diminished, or set on back burners. Black male and adolescent unemployment today is greater than during the tumultuous civil rights period. Women in the United States are reassessing estimates of their social victories in light of the failure to adopt even the minimal constitutional guarantees proposed in the Equal Rights Amendment, and of the increase in gender-identified differentials in mean income and unemployment. Recent U.S. involvements in Grenada, Nicaragua, and El Salvador call into question the endurance of any important lessons Americans may have gleened from their Southeast Asian adventures. Religious fundamentalism, political reaction, increasingly nihilistic social deviance, decreased real income, ominously high unemployment, repressive anti-sexuality, an anachronistic image of family life, and the self-images of powerlessness and defeat held even by the most marginal social movements and fragmented forms of political opposition appear as dominant themes of the eighties. The unity underlying these diverse phenomena can be articulated as their regressive reversion to an ideological and imaginary past and their dependence on and contribution to the daily replication of life established on the foundations of denigrated and alienated labor, hierarchical social and political order, trivialized leisure, and the commodification of everyday life.

It is in this context, without having to probe more deeply into the very fabric of contemporary Western industrial civilization, that the question of human liberation must be concretely posed. The potential for humanity to attain freedom and liberty, to cast aside the shackles of commodity relations, wage labor, social and political hierarchies, to dismiss concomitant surplus repression and purely repressive sublimation, and to establish humanity's victory over alienated labor and repressive authority, are at the core of Marcuse's psychological project.

Herbert Marcuse's provocative exploration of Freud's predominantly pessimistic metapsychological considerations of the purported antagonism between presumably "innate" human drives and organized civil social life is the point of departure for the current argument. In this chapter I will first outline the differences between Freud and Marcuse's metapsychologies, and will review critically Marcuse's concepts of surplus repression, the performance principle, and Marcuse and Freud's assertion of a dual drive theory. Next, I will consider some deficiencies in Marcuse's analysis of psychoanalytic metapsychology, identify the psychologisms in Marcuse's attempt to place psychology within the realm of critical social theory, and will analyze the disparity between Marcuse's psychological theory and his earlier more materially and historically oriented contributions to social theory. Finally, I will distinguish between Marcuse's formulation of the concept of sublimation and other ways of identifying and undermining the barriers to a critical psychology that could potentially contribute to liberatory social practice.

Sexuality: Asocial or Social?

The crucial issue in addressing Marcuse's psychological contributions must necessarily be the adequacy of Freud's metapsychology, and psychoanalytic theory in general, for adequately explaining social behavior, particularly that of the movement toward a liberatory society. In critically reviewing the specific reformulations of Freud's psychoanalytic theory proposed by Marcuse and the principles initially outlined by Freud himself, fundamental consideration must be focused on the material and historical context of social reality, the relationship of social theories to both the subjective and objective expressions of this reality, and the possible contributions of psychoanalysis to the practical project of a critical social theory: the elimination of the antagonism between generalized social will and individual desire established in the social practice of developing a liberatory society.

The origin of civilization from Freud's perspective is linked to the renunciation of strong drives.[1] Culture involves a frustration of strong drives by suppression, repression, and other psychological mechanisms.[2] For Freud, an intrinsic antagonism exists between individual liberty and the satisfaction of primary drives on the one hand, and the development of civilization on the other. Both drive satisfaction and the urge for freedom are restricted in civilization. For Freud, however, the construction of individual freedom and constraint of drive satisfaction within civilization must be contrasted with the unrestricted forces of nature that govern most of the activities of humans in pre-civilized societies. In these primitive situations, Freud argues, humans were so thoroughly subordinate to the fluctuations of nature, that they were little able to defend or enjoy either their individual liberty or their unconstrained drives.[3]

Within civilization, the juridical system catalyzes a sacrifice of drives by presumably allowing all but those incapable of entering the civilized community to benefit from the rule of law and the conquest of brute force.[4] In this context, notes Freud, the urge for human freedom is sometimes directed at social injustice, but also may arise from remnants of the pre-civilized personality that society has failed to subjugate.[5] The desire for freedom may prove favorable to civilization's further development when directed toward injustice, but may be hostile to society if derived from drives untamed by civilization. For Freud, then, a major focus of humanity's struggle is whether an expedient accommodation can be established between the claims of the individual and the cultural demands of society.

In Freud's view, the very fate of humanity is related to whether an accommodation can be established in some particular manifestation of society, or whether this conflict between individual and cultural demands is both intrinsic and inevitable.[6] In asserting "the antithesis between civilization and sexuality,"[7] Freud suggests that Eros is directed by civilized society when the aim-inhibited libido of sexuality is summoned by society to strengthen social bonds within civilization.[8]

From these arguments, Marcuse concludes that Freud had understood culture as a derivative of a transfer of libido to activities that accrue to the good of civilization.[9] Marcuse observes[10] that alienated labor and the reproductive unit of the classical nuclear family join with the established rule of law and order in constraining drive satisfaction to advance and maintain the progress of industrial society. Additional progress, however, has brought with it additional unfreedom.[11] The bourgeois notion of progress as a more or less uninterrupted ascent toward greater freedom from necessity has been increasingly debunked in the ashes of two world wars, concentration camps, genocide, the prevailing threat of thermonuclear warfare, and more fundamentally by the increasing, sustained, and nearly omnipresent social immiseration of everyday life. As one peers beyond spectacular events to the daily reproduction of human social relations, the contradictory nature of "progress" in the bourgeois epoch is revealed in Marcuse's subsequent psychological treatises only when his later views are linked theoretically and practically to his earlier materialist and historical works.

In the period prior to World War II, for instance, Marcuse observed that, "The labor process, in which the laborer's organs atrophy and are coarsened, guarantees that the sensuousness of the lower strata does not develop beyond the technically necessary minimum. What is allowed beyond this as immediate enjoyment is circumscribed by the penal code."[12] Marcuse's own sensuous grasp of the very fabric of capitalist social relations and social reproduction is obscured by subsequent psychologisms, and is nowhere as poignant. Critical social-theoretical observations, firmly rooted materially and historically, are lamentably absent from his subsequent psychologistic appropriation of psychoanalysis. Though he accurately points to the ideology of progress in describing the debasement of the proletariat, this clarity falls short of its target by the time Marcuse authored *Eros and Civilization*.

More recent illustrations of deficiencies in the bourgeois ideology of progress include decreased real income and increased infant mortality within even the major metropoles of the advanced industrial societies. Though social repressiveness is increasingly unnecessary, as the technological potential for abolishing scarcity becomes more real, domination and repression abound. Freud believed this repressiveness may be inherent in civilization,[13] a thesis Marcuse rejects.[14]

Marcuse argues that many of Freud's assumptions about social life are derived from the observation of current and past societies about which Freud generalizes ahistorically and incorrectly.[15] Marcuse engineers within Freudian theory the search for a key to how civilization need not be identified with repression. Though this undertaking was partially impaired by Marcuse's tenuous equation of social and psychological repression, and embodied other aspects requiring amendation, qualification, reservation or substantial reformulation, decades later his seminal contributions still merit serious debate.

Marcuse posed the question, for instance, of the degree to which the reality and pleasure principles are so irreconcilably opposed that a repressive transformation of the structure of human drives becomes necessary. Freud argues that the antagonism between freedom and repression, productivity and destruction, domination and progress may be basic to civilization. Marcuse interprets them as historically specific manifestations of a particular mode of human organization, a mode of organization that is at once both dominant and mutable in a non-repressive society, rendering Marcuse's concept of historically necessary repression analogous to Gabel's thesis of historically necessary reification.[16] Marcuse refutes Freud's consistent denial of the historical possibility of non-repressive society, and argues that in the achievements of repressive society are rooted the very preconditions of non-repressive society.[17]

According to Marcuse, progressive alienation itself increases the potential of freedom; the more objectified and therefore distanced necessary labor becomes for the individual, the less it involves him or her in the realm of necessity. In pleading his case, Marcuse claims to extract from Freud's metapsychology its inherent "radical" sociality, which has been obscured and tabooed by official mainstream and revisionist psychoanalysis, and by Freud's own deterministic pessimism.

The Inherent Sociality of Freud's Metapsychology

Unfettered in seeking their natural goals, argues Freud, human drives would preclude enduring human sociality, association, and the preservation of the human race. Even the universal human propensity for unity and formation that constitutes Eros, if released from control, would prove as lethal as the death drive itself. The aims of the drives are inhibited and deflected by the external reality of the sociohistorical world, as the reality principle increasingly determines the pleasure principle. Transitory, immediate or destructive pleasure is replaced by postponed, partial but socially useful gratification. In so doing, the substance as well the form and temporality of pleasure are transformed.

Ego development accompanies the ascendancy of the reality principle, which also harkens the advent of rationality and reflectivity. The mental apparatus of the conscious, thinking subject, with the sole exception of phantasy, according to Marcuse, is subordinated to the reality principle. Motor discharge is directed to the "appropriate alteration of reality."[18] Human desire and the means for its gratification, as well as the ability to alter reality consciously, are profoundly enhanced. Both this desire and the means for altering reality to attain its gratification are socially organized, repressing and altering the aim of original drive needs. This traumatic assertion of the reality principle over the pleasure principle occurs both phylogenetically and ontogenetically, socially and psychologically, in social and individual development, respectively.

In both the generic and individual instances, submission to the requirements of the reality principle is required. The mastery and suppression of the pleasure principle by the demands of civilization do not obliterate its goals or uproot its unconscious dynamism. As an unconscious force, the pleasure principle influences the reality principle that has superseded it. It is this "return of the repressed" that constitutes the tabooed subterranean history of civilization. Imposed not by nature, but by humanity, this subjugation of the drives is an historical phenomenon whereby external repression has been accompanied by a socialized self-repression in which repressed individuals have learned to introject both their masters and their masters' dictates.[19] In this sense, Marcuse identifies Freud's individual psychology as one that is thoroughly and inherently social.

To this extent, Marcuse has outlined the intricate relationship between social and individual behavior in an epoch in which the social production of individual perception, motivation, and behavior has become the rule rather than the exception. This premise certainly requires endorsement without reservation. Marcuse has created a social abstraction, however, in failing to detail adequately, as he had previously done with such eloquence, the concrete mode of material and historical reproduction in the bourgeois epoch.   In falling short of defining the precise process of social production by which particular social realities are developed in this epoch of the domination of multinational capital, Marcuse has created a social abstraction.   He has imposed on individual psychology its inherently social element, but has failed to define its specific material and historical social content.   This sociality remains a skeleton, awaiting both the skin of superstructure and the guts of infrastructure.

Guilt, Progress, and Sublimation

"In forfeiting happiness through the heightened sense of guilt," asserts Freud, civilization extracts its price.[20]   Guilt is constantly on the rise as civilization progresses.   Freud bases these claims on insights gleaned from psychoanalytic experiences, specifically the struggle of patients with guilt during the Oedipal stage, and from profound instances of contemporary social conflict, particularly the First World War.   It is the eternal struggle between Eros and the death drive that is at the heart of the superego's hyperseverity according to Freud.   Subordinating the death drive in the Oedipal conflict, the severe archetypal father represents Eros in establishing primitive social relations leading to the development of identification, exogamy, sublimation and aim-inhibited affection.   Eros manifests itself initially in the guise of synthetic projects that propel life-forms into ever-greater unities, with the archetypal father image magnified and reproduced in all types of social authority. Aggressive impulses and their objects are multipled as prohibitions and inhibitions flourish.

In contrast to the mechanistic and hydraulic Freudian analysis of the genesis of guilt, Marcuse focuses on the neglected question of the growing irrationality of guilt.   For Freud, however, guilt cannot be irrational if its rationality is that of civilization, for in Freud's crypto-sociology, the mere propagation of civilization has become its own justification.   The destruction of civilization is for Freud the most abject act conceivable; any institution that precludes its demise, regardless of the institution's social "costs," is inherently rational.   Defenses against destructiveness and aggression must be fortified to secure civilization.   But these defenses must also nourish Eros in its struggle to bind the death drive, which in the current epoch has become an increasingly futile battle due to increased routinization and domination.   Freud cites the suppression of the drives as the fundamental hallmark of civilized society.   Culture demands continuous desexualization, sublimation, and pain.[21]

Marcuse, however, observes that work need not remain either desexualized or unpleasant.   Cultural inhibitions act on derivatives of the death drive as well as on Eros.   Citing the social utility of some work, Marcuse argues that it is work in the service of Eros, with artistic work as its best example, that embodies libido.   Marcuse errs, however, in misappropriating the notion of sublimation, and asserting that the notion must be altered extensively to describe libidinal work.   This flawed concept of sublimation will be disussed in greater detail later in this chapter.

Freud, Scarcity, and Repression

Freud traces the development of repression to the instinctual nature of the individual. This biological (yet simultaneously special) theory of repression is at the heart of Freud's metapsychology.[22] Repression from within the socialized individual accompanies repression that is external; the struggle against freedom reproduces itself in the human psyche as self-repression. It is this self-repression ultimately that sustains the dominant order, and its institutions, and the social repression which in turn facilitates the process of self-repression. The most vivid contemporary expression of this phenomenon is identification with the oppressor. Freud argues that the repressive drive modifications necessary for identification with the oppressor under the reality principle were enhanced and enforced by the ethics of scarcity.

Freud thus attributes an economic motive to the social edict that limits sexual activities to the production of the work necessary for maintaining and enhancing society. Marcuse considers this an obsolete rationalization for social repression that is unnecessarily introduced as a cornerstone of Freud's theory. Marcuse suggests that Freud uncompromisingly insists on identifying the most advanced values and achievements of society as repressive, with unfreedom and constraint as the price that must be paid for civilization and culture. For Marcuse, Freud's metapsychology is a continuous attempt to reveal and scrutinize the relationship between civilization and barbarism, progress and pain, liberation and misery. Marcuse uncritically and erroneously accepts Freud's assertion that these relationships involved the association of Eros and the death drive.

At the earliest stages of its development, Freud's drive theory is dynamic and constructed around the theme of the opposition between libidinal and self-preservative instincts.[23] Following this period, Freud's original dualistic drive theory is altered for a short period to a unitary theory of the libido.[24] In its latest stage, the dualistic construction of the drives is reintroduced, this time as an antagonism between death and life drives.[25] Eros, according to this last insight, follows Fechner's principle of constant equilibrium, i.e. the libido relieves the mental apparatus from excitation by keeping the amount of excitation in it constant (cf. the Nirvana principle). Under the influence of Fechner's theory of constant equilibrium, which can be linked to the first and second laws of thermodynamics, Freud's Eros ultimately falls into the service of the death drive.[26] The viability of each and every of these formulations remains a current issue for psychoanalysis.

Freedom and Necessity

The co-existence of freedom and necessity is a social paradox - the tabooed and ambivalent human yearning that Freud reveals. The liberty that exists for the conscious mind and the world it has created is a derivative and compromised freedom that has been established only at the cost of a more comprehensive gratification of needs through genuine happiness.

To the extent that happiness is supposed to be the total satisfaction of drive needs, freedom in civilization necessarily involves the repressive modification of happiness. Sublimation as the modifier of happiness expresses the basic antagonism between civilized freedom and happiness. Tabooed from consciousness, the reconciliation of freedom and happiness thrives only in the unconscious, which retains memories of past incidents in the individual's development in which complete gratification has been attained, and it promotes the desire for the regeneration of paradise based on achievements of civilization. The retrieval of memory and the repressed affect associated with it are the focal point of psychoanalytic technique, and are at the heart of the metapsychology of freedom.

It is memory that preserves the promises and potentialities eschewed and prohibited by the mature socialized individual. These memories of fulfillment in the individual's distant past are not forgotten in their entirety. Prohibited images and impulses of childhood begin through memory to tell the truth that reason denies, only to have this function constrained by the reality principle. The censored images and impulses of childhood are not completely forgotten, though they are rejected by the instrumental rationality of the civilized social individual. Memory reveals their all-but-forgotten secrets, as phantasy assumes its content. But as humans relive portions of this unity of the past, they also re-enact archetypal traumas of human phylogenetic development. In the return of the repressed, individuals relive these traumatic experiences in the history of the human genus.[27] The ontogeny of the repressed individual is thereby intertwined with the phylogeny of the human species.

Freud, Naturalism, and Biologism

In the corporealization of the psyche, conscious condemnation is transformed into an unconscious repressive process. Social authority is internalized unconsciously as self-reproach. Past values become part of the drive structure of the present, culminating in a superego that enforces the demands of the past as well as those of the current reality. For humans, Marcuse asserts, the confrontation of the reality principle with the external world is a specific act of existence in historical time. Freud's formulation of the reality principle obliterates these historical contingencies by disguising them as natural or biological necessities, thereby precluding consideration of concrete socio-historical realities.

Freud's formulation is rooted in the ideology of naturalism, in which historically discrete acts are reductionistically attributed a universal, atemporal and quasi-natural character. Marcuse astutely observes this phenomenon.[28] He points out, on the contrary, that all historical manifestations of the reality principle have been shown by the repressive social organization of the drives. In this sense a dialectic of biological and historical forces emerges. An example of the historical expression of human drives is portrayed by Foucault, who depicts the body either as an object of pleasure or as one of specific historical incarceration.[29]

One cannot question the validity of Freud's observation that the historical development of civilization has included both progress and organized domination. One can only call into question the implicit ahistoricity of Freud's assumption that the repressive organization of the drives is derived of necessity from the inherent irreconcilable antagonism between the pleasure principle and the reality principle. It is this formulation of his reality principle for which Marcuse takes Freud to task.

Freud describes the phylogenetic organization of domination as a transfer of authority from the patriarchal primal horde to the more sophisticated internal despotism of the fraternal clan.[30] Reviewing the history of civilization solely as that of organized despotism and without considering historical facticity, Freud claims this development is natural and biological, rather than concretely historical. For Marcuse, however, this ahistorical formulation contains the very historical element it shuns. It is that element which Marcuse sets out to reformulate. In so doing, he eschews the mechanistic appendage of "social factors" to Freud's theory by the neo-Freudian revisionists.

This social content, argues Marcuse, is already in psychoanalytic theory, awaiting only to be revealed. To rectify Freud's biologism, Marcuse offers two conceptual extrapolations from psychoanalytic theory: the performance principle and surplus repression. With these metapsychological addenda, one can better sift through the dialectic of the biological and socio-historical within the drives by elaborating their socio-historical components, thus beginning to historicize Freud's ahistorical formulations.

Scarcity, Surplus Repression, and the Reality Principle

Freud has defined repression in terms of those modifications of the drive structure that are necessary to keep humanity from destroying itself entirely. Marcuse introduces the notion of surplus repression, which he differentiates from the more basic Freudian notion of repression, by delineating surplus repression as the biologically unnecessary restriction imposed by social (i.e. class) domination. Particular historical embodiments of a specific reality principle introduce constraints on the drives that are excessive to the controls required to sustain and advance human civilization. These excessive controls particular to the agencies and institutions of domination of a particular society are dubbed surplus repression by Marcuse. The reality principle that prevails in contemporary society, that which maintains the surplus repression of our collective and individual realities, has been called the performance principle by Marcuse. In contributing this concept, Marcuse disavows the biological formulation of the reality principle and suggests the existence of different historical forms of a generalized reality principle, though he falls short of identifying the etiology of the specific reality principle that currently prevails under the domination of capital.

In his concept of the performance principle, Marcuse eschews Freud's biological formulation of the reality principle (and repression). The introduction of the performance principle suggests that there may be different historical expressions of a generalized reality principle. It goes without saying, according to Marcuse, that some historically specific expressions of the reality principle would impose limitations on the performance principle in the form of reduced surplus repression.

Scarcity underlies the reality principle both for Freud and Marcuse. To satisfy human needs, the painful process of work must be undertaken. As the basic human drives seek only pleasure and reject pain, the pleasure principle is incompatible with the reality (of painful work). Accordingly, the drives undergo repressive constraint and modification. The distinct modes of scarcity that prevailed at different points in the history of civilization have neither been distributed collectively nor organized to respond to individual needs. The distribution of scarcity has been imposed both on individuals and society, first violently and then more rationally through the manipulation of power. Despite the utility of this form of rationality for the progress of civilization, scarcity remains the rationality of domination. The gradual elimination of scarcity by organized society engendered surplus repression resulting in the perpetuation of the *status quo* originated by scarcity. But such repression has now been rendered obsolete by the relative affluence and productive capacity in the period of "mature" capitalism. Surplus repression and the elimination of scarcity are never overcome, and for this reason, some degree of social repression is always necessary. In bourgeois society, Marcuse argues, the gradual overcoming of material scarcity results from the rise of another kind of scarcity: the scarcity of freedom.

Domination, Authority, and the Subordination of Eros

In defining the influence of domination on the historical development of the human psyche, Marcuse rejects simplistic anarchism and distinguishes carefully between domination and the rational exercise of authority, which he understands to be confined to acts of conscious agents and limited to those functions necessary for the advancement of society as a whole. Domination, in contrast, is exercised to establish and maintain the privilege of a particular group or individual. The various historical forms of the reality principle reflect specific modes of domination within specific periods of civilization, with different reality principles at different stages of civilization. The specific historical institutions of an epoch and the specific interests of domination in that period introduce surplus repression, which pertains only to a specific reality principle. This surplus repression is appended to the phylogenetic constraints on the drives.

Throughout the history of civilization, basic and surplus repression have acted in concert. The basic repression, which constrains partial impulses and directs the drives, permits the mediation of nature and the increase of gratification, the establishment of a fully human pleasure principle involved in the phallocentric and mature definition of pleasure. Mastery of the drives can be adopted in opposition to, as well as in favor of, human gratification. Partial impulses and zones have been nearly desexualized to conform to the needs of historically specific human social organizations. The phenomenological experience of time is transferred from spontaneous impulsivity to automatic self-regulation through mechanisms of social control. Organized domination stifles spontaneous relationships and their animal-like immediacy, thereby imposing social isolation. The imposition of social isolation is a necessary precondition for the establishment of a repressive social order.

A completely unrepressed development would threaten the desexualization of the human organism that is needed for productive labor and for the individual as an instrument of the labor process. The hierarchical organization of scarcity and labor has added its own constraints on the drives to those imposed by scarcity. Fear of a rebellion among the oppressed beckons an even greater constraint. Repression becomes oppression. The surplus repression of the drives has become the oppressive instrument for the domination of labor. The development of the death drive, argues Marcuse, is comprehensible only in terms of the repressive organization of sexuality that underlies the development of the life drive as modified by the reality principle.

Of all the drives, it is Eros that is modified most profoundly. The socially prescribed result is the subordination of the partial sexual impulses to the primacy of the genitals, and the mastery of primary (and, for Marcuse, secondary) narcissism, or the diversion of one's libido from cathexis on the self to cathexis on a heterosexual object. In varying degrees, these partial elements are subordinate to the requirements of procreation. This organization results in the qualitative and quantitative restriction of sexuality. The unity of the partial drives transforms sexuality from an autonomous principle governing the entire organism into a specialized temporary function with only instrumental value - procreation.

Marcuse then detects contradictory depictions of sexuality by Freud, who simultaneously describes its asociality, and then also depicts love relationships as the very essence of the group mind. Marcuse believes he has discovered an inner unreconciled tension in Freud's theory, contrasting the purported asociality of Freud's Eros to his equally forceful depiction of its biological predisposition to form ever greater unities. A free Eros, Marcuse continues, repels only the hyper-repressive civilized relationships organized in opposition to the pleasure principle. This same free Eros could sustain and nourish enduring civilized relationships under the reign of the pleasure principle. For Freud, culture lends a heavy hand to the inhibition of libido. Culture's antagonism toward sexuality is rooted in a fear of its aggressivity, which threatens to destroy civilization. A destructive dialectic emerges, however, regardless of these constraints on the drives. Constraints on Eros also debilitate the life drive and ally with the very destructive forces against which they were first mobilized.

Genitality and Repressive Unification

The "normal" organization of sexuality in the present epoch has fundamentally incorporated the substance of the performance principle and its social dictates. Unification and centralization of partial sexual impulses into a single heterosexual libidinal object, and the imposition of genital supremacy, are its two most salient features. In both cases, repression is the mode of unification, culminating in a socially dictated concentration of libido in one part of the body that allows the remainder of the body to become utilized by the labor process. A spatial transformation of libido accompanies its temporal transformation. Without these restrictions, sexuality originally accepted neither spatial nor temporal constraints on either the subject or the object. This original polymorphous sexuality has become fettered by the ethic of procreation and is now characterized as "perverse." The establishment of genital primacy and the "perversity" of polymorphous sexuality are basic constituents of the process of sublimation. Such "perversions" rebel against this subjugation of sexuality to the service of procreation and paternal domination.

Perversions cannot tolerate the domination of the pleasure principle by the reality principle.[31] In eschewing the reality principle and favoring the pleasure principle, perversions demonstrate for Marcuse a keen association with phantasy, a mental process also purportedly liberated from the control of reality-testing. In the imagination of the artist, phantasy links perversions with the images of freedom and gratification. It is sexuality *qua* sexuality for which perversions strive, and in so doing challenge the very foundation of the reality principle. Perversions permit libidinal relations that threaten the transformation of the body into the instrument of work, and the reproduction of humanity. The normally precarious fusion of Eros and the death drive is unravelled, revealing the erotic element of the death drive and the fatal component of Eros.

The perversions, Marcuse suggests, define the potential identification of Eros with the death drive, and perhaps even the subordination of the former to the latter. The libido's task of debilitating the destructive force of the death drive is defeated as society shifts from the pleasure principle to the Nirvana principle. Civilization has harkened the alliance of Eros and the death drive in its abundant sublimation and monogamous procreative organization, and has prohibited the partial but spontaneous expression of Eros. Illustrative of this is the increased tenacity with which the Right to Life Movement, the Moral Majority, and virtually every politician, endorse the classical nuclear family, despite clear demographic evidence heralding its decline.

The Dual Drive Theory and Social Progress

Finally, Marcuse suggests that, despite the absence of any social organization of the death drive, it is the transformation and use of the death drive by society that underlies the entire progress of civilization. The influence of the death drive in forming the superego provides for the supremacy of the reality principle over the pleasure principle, turns primary destructiveness away from the ego, and promotes the technological development and civilized morality necessary for the advancement of industrial society. Despite its social utility, the death drive also remains a constant fetter to civilization. The death drive promotes the cause of destruction in the logic underlying the final surrender of spontaneous time, unreified existence, and non-alienated humanity. It is this same logic that prompts neutron warheads, organized boredom, and global hostility. In the present period, ruling classes dominate by exhausting options for promoting the gratification of humanity's real needs, by commodifying social relations, and by creating increasing numbers of institutions dedicated to serving their domination. It is, Marcuse concludes, the establishment of these very institutions of domination that is currently eroding the basis of civilization in the advanced industrial period. To this he counterposes a speculative and utopian protrayal of the union of Eros and labor.[32]

Although the thrust of Marcuse's thesis is compelling, one must scrutinize the means through which he attains his ends. First and foremost is the issue of Freud's dual drive theory. Marcuse never questions the dualistic drive theory offered in Freud's later period. Rather than challenging Freud's metapsychological assumptions, Marcuse extrapolates from them an intricate ensemble of refinements to explain the historical development of society, the precarious situation of contemporary civilization, and the metatheoretical preconditions for utopian thought. These same trends can be interpreted very differently, leading to contrastingly different metapsychological conclusions. Wilhelm Reich, for instance, suggested that destructiveness and perversion can be understood as repressed libido, as inhibitions of sexuality. In this sense, they neither attest to the existence of a primary destructive or death drive, nor qualify perversions as an heroic outburst of unrestrained sexuality. Reich asserts that there is but one primary drive, Eros, from which the secondary force of destructiveness emerges only as a reaction. Reich argues that it is inhibition of sexuality that lends power to aggression when he returns to the earlier emphasis on the energic elements of the metapsychology and defends the primacy of sexuality, which Marcuse laments is lost at the hands of the neo-Freudian revisionists.[33] This is very different from Marcuse's suggestion that the power of aggressive and destructive drives have subdued Eros.

Though the very topic of inquiry in *Eros and Civilization* suggests the primacy of Eros, Marcuse resists stating this explicitly. Marcuse's failure to engage in a careful investigation of this hypotheses weakens the strength of his argument. His failure to consider this or alternative hypotheses about the role and nature of the drives becomes particularly apparent when one recognizes even in mainstream psychoanalysis considerable critical deliberation over the metapsychology and dual drive theory.[34] Subsequent critiques by even such heterodox analysts as Schafer only reinforce the significance of this deletion.[35] While this debate in mainstream psychoanalysis may well be part of the desexualization of psychoanalysis that Marcuse identified as one of the major theoretical shortcomings of the neo-Freudians, it is a serious question that must be addressed at length. Marcuse's failure to probe more deeply into these basic elements of the metapsychology establishes the point of departure for current explorations into the metapsychology of liberation.

Though Reich's perspective on the union of psychoanalytic and historical materialist theories suffers from both biologistic and economistic determinism, Marcuse's perspective is flawed by a voluntaristic humanism that nevertheless fails to come to grips with the deficiencies of Freud's dual drive theory, hardly a secure foundation on which to construct a radical psychology of emancipation. It is this failure to define specifically the relationship between materialist and historical social theories and the psychological contributions of the psychoanalytic tradition that are only recently beginning to be addressed (e.g. in Richard Lichtman's intriguing *The Production of Desire*).[36]

Metapsychology and History

Despite the truncated and uncritical treatment of the dual drive theory, and despite the deletion of social class, labor power, hierarchical social and political order, and other key historical and materialist considerations, Marcuse's crucial theoretical contributions - surplus repression and the performance principle - are formidable initial steps toward fulfilling one of Marcuse's most fundamental metapsychological goals: historicizing psychoanalysis. By asserting historically specific reality principles, though admittedly *in abstracto*, Marcuse deletes from the psychology of liberation an inherent biologism and naturalistic ideology that often fetters the psychoanalytic metapsychology. These ideological elements, with their accompanying dimensions of dehistoricization and reification, when introduced in the discussion of mental life, mystify the question of domination and liberation.

Marcuse's acceptance of a certain degree of repression, or basic repression, as a constituent of organized social life modifies his assertion of a non-repressive social organization. The complete absence of reification, presumably characteristic of aphasia, counterfactually would indicate the necessity of some degree of reification in social life. But beyond this socially necessary degree of reification, our epoch is characterized by excessive reification. The same can be said for repression. Without basic repression, civilization can neither form nor preserve itself.

With prevailing repression, encompassing both the necessary basic repression and the surplus repression useful only for domination, society is vitally imperiled. The nuclear arms race is merely the most vivid expression of this ultimate repression, which is expressed less poignantly but more constantly (and perhaps even more pathologically) in virtually every aspect of daily life in this epoch of the domination of all social relations by capital. Certainly, this ultimate repression could not exist without its regular and omnipresent replication. These materialist and historical observations, abundant in Marcuse's earlier writings, are lamentably absent in his discussion of basic and surplus repression.

Marcuse has accordingly shifted the discussion of the psychological basis of liberation away from the notion of a Kantian-like antinomy between repression and non-repression, and has established a concrete basis on which historical considerations of necessary and superfluous repression can be addressed. In a period when rampant impoverishment is more frequently contrasted with the obvious technological potential for wealth, when social problems are addressed chiefly through the construction of new prisons and the development of increasingly retributive concepts of justice, and when the potential for libidinal and social liberation is contrasted to increasingly social immiseration on a global scale, the addition of the topic of repression to the social agenda is a major contribution. That Marcuse has identified one of the crucial problems of our age is beyond dispute. That he has not resolved it thoroughly reflects more than anything else the failure of humanity to forge an emancipatory social practice.

Marcuse's avoidance of ahistorical considerations of reality and existence, and of simplistic formulations of repression goes a long way in removing reificatory elements from the theoretical and practical explorations of liberation. The impact of this contribution can be understood in terms of practice, however, when one considers the sizeable influence of Marcuse's theoretical contributions on the European and American movements of opposition during the late 1960s and early 1970s. Had Marcuse's later works been less ahistorical, he might have provided a deeper insight into shortcomings in the praxis of these movements.

The apparent failure of the movements of the late sixties and early seventies to impart on the eighties a stronger legacy of emancipation is due in a large part to the deletion from theory and practice of the notions of the commodification of social relations, the devaluation of social life, the existence of social and political hierarchies, and the nature of labor power. This deletion is characteristic of Marcuse's later writings, particularly his psychological ones, and despite their contributions toward a psychology of emancipation, makes them generally devoid of the practical and theoretical precision that characterized his earlier critical work. Had that precision been mantained in his psychological writings, perhaps the movements he influenced so profoundly might have moved further in the direction of the liberation sought so fervently by participants in these movements and by Marcuse himself, since he had astutely recognized the necessity of challenging the psychological barriers to freedom.

Sublimation, Eros, and Sexuality

A marked shortcoming of Marcuse's discussion of Freud's metapsychology is his inconsistent formulation of the notion of sublimation. Freud had understood sublimation to be an unconscious process in which the aim and object of Eros are modified, deflected or inhibited, and usually redirected toward an asexual or nonsexual aim. Acknowledging that most of cultural life is the product of sublimation, Marcuse expresses reservations about the desexualization it introduces. Suggesting the importance of a distinction between modifications of Eros and sexuality, Marcuse argues that sublimation is the fate theoretically attributed to sexuality by Freud. The specific mode of sublimation is spelled out by the requirements of a specific society in the service of a particular reality principle. Sublimation transports the repressiveness of the reality principle into acts that have utility for society. Marcuse also points to Freud's discussion of affectionate social relations that are unsublimated though not thoroughly sexual (e.g. friendship).

Freud does not clearly distinguish between Eros and sexuality. His use of the term Eros simply denotes in a classical platonic sense an expansion of the concept of sexuality. This expanded concept of sexuality, in its turn, modifies the notion of sublimation. As such, modifications of Eros and modifications of sexuality cannot be considered identical or even equivalent. For Marcuse, sublimation of sexuality refers basically to a repressive redirection of drives. Sublimation of Eros, however, does not entail the repressive redirection of drives and offers the possibility of nonrepressive sublimation. In the sublimation of Eros, one can speak of sublimation cum gratification.[37]

To understand better the distinction between sublimation of sexuality and sublimation of Eros, Marcuse's differentiation between Eros and sexuality is instructive. He views sexuality as a subset of Eros. Where Eros is a force that governs the entire organism and is only derivatively put into the service of reproduction and localized as genital sexuality, sexuality is merely a partial drive.[38] The oppositional elements previously critical of society which had earlier been incorporated into sublimated activities such as art have today increasingly surrendered their capacity for negation. Ideologically, this has involved the transformation of higher culture into popular culture, and materially it has been expressed as apparently greater personal satisfaction.[39] These tendencies have fostered a "sweeping desublimation," replacing mediated by immediate satisfaction, and promoting social cohesion and (until most recently) general contentment.[40]

The deviation, freedom, and 'refusal' inherent in the sublimation of drives and objectives are much weaker, if still present, in repressive modes of desublimation. This "liberalization" of sexuality in socially constructive forms is a repressive desublimation in the sphere of sexuality that joins with the desublimation of higher culture. These desublimations function as artifacts of the social controls of technological reality, extending liberty while simultaneously intensifying domination.[41] The increasingly immediate satisfaction of genital sexuality, in the context of the pervasive desublimation of Eros and the resulting frustrations of this drive, only underscores the essential distinction between sexuality as a partial drive impulse and Eros, which is a primary drive governing all the functions of the organism. This distinction can be demonstrated most clearly in Marcuse's notions of sublimation, repressive desublimation, and self-sublimation.

Freud had suggested that both sublimated and unsublimated relations are the foundations of community.[42] Marcuse perceives in this formulation the origins of a theory of civilization wherein culture is derived from and preserves free libidinal relations. Marcuse suggests the existence of a genital libidinal trend toward the creation of cultural phenomena not predicated on external repressive modification. This tendency is one away from centralization and genital supremacy, and toward the eroticization of the entire organism. Marcuse interprets these tendencies as indicators of a non-repressive sublimation, in which drives are not aim-inhibited, but are satisfied through erotic libidinal activities that are not fused within genital sexuality.

This self-sublimation is a process in which Eros can rediscover itself in sophisticated civilized relations without the repressive organization imposed on the drives. Marcuse recognizes the historical specificity of self-sublimation, suggesting that self-sublimation requires historical progress that transcends social institutions under the thumb of the reality principle. Self-sublimation would induce a modification of the drives, in which sexuality for pleasure would replace sexuality for procreation. Marcuse considers this a regression that would restore the primary structure of sexuality and challenge genital primacy. The organism itself would become thoroughly erotic, and the goal of human drives would no longer be that of genital union. In this expanded sense, the field and object of Eros become the life of the organism.

Sublimation: Repressive and Non-Repressive

Marcuse suggests that an expanded notion of Eros demands a similarly modified process of sublimation, since Freud's concept of sublimation described only modification of sexuality under a repressive reality principle. However, non-repressive sublimation can only stand in opposition to and subvert the very thread of society in which the culture of repressive sublimation prevails; it can only intellectually negate the accepted productivity and performance. But this, too, must be a social project, Marcuse reminds us, for libido can be self-sublimated only as a social project (such as that of the Surrealists).

For the isolated individual, in the absence of emancipatory social projects, attempts at self-sublimation often become quagmired in pathological narcissism. Only the social reactivation of the now narcissistically cathected ego is culture-building. In a society in which socially beneficial work fulfilled individual needs, in a world of non-alienated labor, Marcuse believes more human subjects would be able to sustain the reactivation of both polymorphous and narcissistic sexuality.[43] Rather than threatening society, these reconstituted forms would actually induce culture-building phenomena, such as deriving pleasure from doing socially necessary work. In such a society, the tendency to seek impulse gratification chiefly from one's own body will be redirected toward seeking gratification from ever greater and enduring libidinal relations. This expansion of the impulses actually increases and intensifies gratification of the drives. Agape becomes Eros.

Non-repressive sublimation, Marcuse believes, vitalizes Freud's observation that the goal of Eros is to "form living substance into ever greater unities, so that life may be prolonged and brought to higher development."[44] The project of maintaining the entire body as the subject-object of pleasure calls for the continuous refinement of the organism, the intensification of its senses, the growth of its sensuousness. Amelioration of the environment, abolition of alienated labor, the cure of disease and the relief of pain, and the provision of luxury to all are activities that involve work but derive directly from the pleasure principle. This is the work that evolves humanity to greater unities when relieved from the performance principle; it is the erotic tendency toward work. Marcuse concludes that "the problem of work, of socially useful activity without (repressive) sublimation can now be restated."[45]   In a society governed by the performance principle, libidinal work is rare.   In a society such as that imagined by Fourier, labor is transformed into pleasure, and non-repressive sublimation becomes the foundation of freedom.[46]

The Dialectic of Sublimation

There are three facets of this scenerio that are theoretically troubling. First, Marcuse discusses sublimation in only the most abstract historical terms, and nowhere points to the origins of this state of affairs. Lost is the poignancy of his earlier formulations, where for instance he describes so eloquently the social functions of sexuality and pleasure: "When value, the standard of the equity of exchange, is created only by abstract labor, then pleasure may not be a value . . . .   Nowhere does the connection between devaluation of enjoyment and its social justification manifest itself as clearly as in the interpretation of sexual pleasure."[47]   "Only," Marcuse continues, "when sexual relations are placed under the express purpose of the production of new labor power for the process of social domination of nature is their enjoyment worthy of a human being and sanctioned. . . . The function of labor within this society determines its attitude with respect to enjoyment."[48]   The lucidity of this critical insight into the materialist and historical contriction of drive expressions is nowhere in Marcuse's later psychological contributions.

Second, Marcuse's subsequent discussion of repression and sexuality fails to match the keen insights into the social production of drives expressed so coherently in his earlier treatises.   For example, in his initial discussion of the drives, Marcuse explains that the "class situation, especially the situation of the individual in the labor process, is active in them, for this situation has formed the (bodily and spiritual) organs and capacities of men and the horizon of their demands.   Since these appear as wants only in their stunted form, with all their repressions, renunciations, adaptations, and rationalizations, they can normally be satisfied within the given social framework."[49]   The social production of the drives, inextricably intertwining the hitherto separate categories of the social and the biological, is manifested throughout these early contributions, and sports a lucidity and assertiveness nearly absent in Marcuse's subsequent and more psychologistic discussion of sexuality and repression.

Third, one wonders if the lack of clarity that Marcuse attributes to Freud in his definition of Eros is not replicated in Marcuse's own definition of sublimation. Though Marcuse historicizes sublimation, he also appears to have stripped from it some of the complexity of its classical psychoanalytic definition.   Marcuse links his notion of sublimation too intimately with repression, and in so doing renders them virtually synonymous.

Schoolman interestingly suggests that a thoroughly non-repressive and unalienated activity would involve sublimation of both Eros and aggressive impulses of the death drive.[50] Schoolman begins to tap both the repressive and non-repressive qualities of sublimation, thereby indicating its dialectical nature. Though painting a more careful and substantial critique of Marcuse's notion of sublimation than most,[51] Schoolman misses the boat in failing to identify the fundamental riddle of Marcuse's formulation of sublimation: the question of social practice.

The primary question, if one accepts Marcuse's portrait of a completely repressive quality of sublimation under the rule of the performance principle, is how do we explain Marcuse's own contributions? Certainly they are sublimated Eros; they are clearly not sublimated destructiveness, whether considered empirically or theoretically. Are we to understand his *oeuvre* as a manifestation of repressive sublimation? Perhaps in part, but this, too, is clearly neither their thrust nor their substance. How is it, then, that non-repressive sublimation can exist under the rule of the reality principle?

Marcuse correctly introduces the theme of historicity by suggesting that the emergence of self-sublimation, or non-repressive subliminal effects, can be understood as not being atemporally possible, but must emerge when the specific historical preconditions are met. Marcuse believes those preconditions are the establishment of a new reality principle that supersedes the performance principle. In this psychologistic confusion of reality and performance principles, however, the foundation of material and historical realities under which these psychologisms, to whatever extent they are valid, must be subsumed, is completely lost.

These realities, expressed in social practice, are astutely observed by Marcuse himself in the earlier period, when he notes that "the content of the materialist notion is historical and oriented toward practice."[52] Marcuse's increasingly abstract psychologistic ideology is rooted theoretically in his de-emphasis of class structure, hierarchical society, commodification, the domination of capitalist social relations, and the significance of labor power. It is consequently expressed in the social practice of movements that only peripherally, if at all, touched upon these elements theoretically and practically necessary for the establishment of human liberation. This tendency contrasts vividly with his earlier elucidation of these matters, such as his exclamation that "Relationships function only in their reified form, mediated through the class distribution of the material output of the contractual partner"[53]; or in his observation that "essence is the totality of the social process as it is organized in a particular historical epoch . . . [and in the current epoch it is] the antagonism of the capitalist production process."[54] Similarly, he had astutely observed that, "Where the prevailing social relationship is the relation of men to one another as owners of commodities and where the value of every commodity is determined by the abstract labor time applied to it, enjoyment has no value in itself."[55] This lucidity is mystified in his subsequent quagmire of psychologisms. Confused with an integration of psychology and critical social theory is the unfortunately thorough subordination of the latter to the former in a manner that detracts from both, and precludes their dialectical unity.

It is a profound contribution of Marcuse that he began, however provisionally, to historicize the reality principle by establishing the existence of a particular reality principle in every historical period. It is a shortcoming of his theoretical work that he has failed to describe the progressive elements of the performance principle as adequately as he has their regressive elements. In psychologizing, through the abstract principle of a new reality principle lacking the necessarily specific sensuous definition of the social process through which it can be developed, Marcuse has forfeited again the awareness of the critical role of conscious social practice in the transformation of social reality.

But Marcuse had not always lacked this awareness. "The concept of what could be," Marcuse reminds us, "of inherent possibilities, acquires a precise meaning . . . . This definition of essence already implies the whole theory of history that deduces the totality of the conditions of life from the mode of social organization . . . . In making this demand of the essence of man, theory points away from the bad current state of humanity to a mankind that disposes of goods available to it in such a way that they are distributed in accordance with the true needs of the community. Here men would themselves take on the planning and shaping of the social process of life and not leave it to the arbitrariness of competition and the blind necessity of reified economic relations . . . . Instead of life being placed in the service of labor, labor would become a means of life."[56] This formulation of a metatheory of practice for creating the preconditions of human liberation is infinitely more precise, however abstract its formulation, than Marcuse's later psychologisms, which are nearly thoroughly devoid of a specific social context. As such they comprise not merely a deficient social theory, but represent a psychologistic ideology, rather than a more valid individual and social psychology of human emancipation.

True, Marcuse does suggest that particular difficulties in the superego formation of particular individuals and nonconformists may explain the existence of forces in opposition to the existing society. Explaining the existence of a few dissenters, however, is very different from linking a psychological explanation to a notion of the development of a non-alienated, self-fulfilling social endeavor encompassing the vast majority of humanity. In failing to understand the emergence of tabooed topics outside the realm of art, Marcuse has failed to grasp the essence of sublimation, even in a period in which repression abounds. Despite his strong support for feminism, class struggle, and erotic liberation in general, Marcuse never integrates these abstractions into a concrete theory of contemporary sublimation.

Sublimation and Repression: A Differential Diagnosis

Contrary to Marcuse's formulation, sublimation is certainly not to be equated with repression. Fenichel, for instance, distinguishes between successful and pathological ego defenses.[57] The successful ego defenses, which terminate the warding-off of various impulses, are understood by him to be sublimation. They are to be contrasted with unsuccessful or pathological ego defenses, which repeat or perpetuate the warding-off process, precluding the eruption of the warded-off impulses. The original impulse disappears when its energy is diverted to the cathexis of its substitute object in sublimation. Though they are desexualizations, sublimations are not de-eroticizations. They require a continuous stream of libido. From this perspective, sublimation may readily be distinguished from repression.

The very non-repressive quality of the sublimation of Eros is what allows the products of non-repressive sublimation to formulate the intellectual basis for the continuing transformation of psychological and social life, which must be both affective and intellectual in its manifestations of the drives. Neither a non-repressive intellect nor a non-repressive affective orientation to emancipatory social relations will appear miraculously overnight. No doubt the road to liberation is not one of even and steady progress. Nor, however, does the transformation from a repressive society to a non-repressive society occur *deus ex machina*. Though Marcuse has produced a compelling argument for the possibility of a transformation to a non-repressive society, the formulation of his concept of sublimation has blocked his insights into the establishment of the pre-conditions for an emancipated society.

Only in the potentially emancipatory kernels of sublimation in virtually every individual are the fragmentary origins of a non-repressive culture to be found in the contemporary context of heightened, automated, and mass-mediated repression. Much as the technological preconditions for the non-repressive organization of human society are already with us, so the rudiments of psychosocial transformation that will provide the point of departure for the conscious transformation of society are already within the repressive psychological organization of the individual.

The contradictory elements that are antagonistic to the prevailing culture and to the prevailing reality principle are, in their embryonic form, within that culture of the performance principle. Marcuse has introduced historicity in identifying the diversity of reality principles over various historical periods, but he has failed to grasp completely the dialectic of transformation within the current process of sublimation. The firm and strong hand of the prevailing reality principle does not rule out its inner tension and opposition even within those areas of organized desexualization. This abstract and limited critique of desexualization is rooted in Marcuse's failure to locate this desexualization within a broader critique of everyday life in bourgeois society. Marcuse's later work is a step back from his earlier critical considerations of wage labor and labor power, hierarchical social and political order, commodity production, and other material and historical underpinnings of a more viable critical theory of human emancipation.

That sublimation can be desexualized and yet embody the origins of non-repressive sublimation is a question from which Marcuse retreats. Although Marcuse was certainly more predisposed to political praxis than were his Frankfurt School colleagues after 1919, this predisposition tended to be articulated theoretically rather than practically, a necessary consequence of his failure to confront the focus of social production in the class nature of bourgeois society, the commodification of daily life, the denigration and alienation of labor, the trivialization of leisure, and the organization of humanity in social and political hierarchies.

Marcuse's failure to recognize himself and his self-activity in formulating his theory of sublimation only reflects the problem of concretely relating metatheory to sensuous social practice. This problem is not unique to Marcuse, but one that reveals a critical flaw in the thought of our epoch. Even where contradictions exist, humanity's theoretical appropriation of them is of yet sufficiently unsophisticated for the formation of a social movement adequate for the supersession of capital's domination of social production, and the total transformation of daily life. Herbert Marcuse has underscored for humanity the necessity of this project and has contributed substantially to the case for its potentiality. By critically assessing the shortcomings of Marcuse's formulations of the potential for human liberation, humanity may move a step closer to the fulfillment of that potential.

NOTES

1. Sigmund Freud, *Civilization and its Discontents* (New York, 1961), p. 44.

2. *Ibid.*

3. *Ibid.*, p. 42.

4. *Ibid.*

5. *Ibid.*, p. 43.

6. *Ibid.*

7. *Ibid.*, p. 55.

8. *Ibid.*, p. 56.

9. Herbert Marcuse, *Five Lectures* (Boston, 1970), *passim*, and *Eros and Civilization* (Boston, 1955), *passim*.

10. *Eros and Civilization, passim.*

11. *Ibid.*

12. Marcuse, *Negations* (Boston, 1968), p. 185.

13. *Civilization and its Discontents*, p. 43.

14. *Eros and Civilization, passim.*

15. *Ibid., passim.*

16. J. Gabel, *False Consciousness*, "La reification, essai d'une psychopathologie de la pensée dialectique," *Esprit*, (October 1951).

17. *Ibid., passim.*

18. Freud, *Collected Papers*, vol. 5 (London, 1950), p. 18.

19. *Eros and Civilization*, pp. 15ff.

20. *Civilization and its Discontents*, pp. 123ff.

21. *Eros and Civilization, passim.*

22. Freud, *New Introductory Lectures, passim.*

23. Freud, "'Civilized' Sexual Morality and Modern Nervous Illness," *Standard Edition*, vol. 9, pp. 179ff.

24. Freud, *Beyond the Pleasure Principle* (New York, 1961), pp. 28ff.

25. Freud, *Outline of Psycho-Analysis* (New York, 1949), pp. 19ff.

26. *Beyond the Pleasure Principle.*
27. Freud, *Totem and Taboo* (New York, 1912), *passim.*
28. *Eros and Civilization, passim.*
29. Michel Foucault, *History of Sexuality, passim.*
30. *Totem and Taboo, passim.*
31. Although societal prohibitions against homosexuality have declined generally in recent years, and have also been deleted from the nosology of mental disorders, nonetheless, homosexuality (like polymorphous perversity) is still considered by most psychoanalysts as a deviation from the norm of healthy heterosexual object choice. Curiously, no such stigma is attached to the ever more common phenomenon of asexuality, which itself is clearly a deviation from heterosexual norms and similarly a detriment to psycho-sexual health. Cf. Nancy Scheper-Hughes, *Saints, Scholars and Schizophrenics*, in which the phenomenon of celibacy's increasing epidemology is documented; as well as Charles Webel's review of Scheper-Hughes' book in *American Anthropologist* 84 (1982), pp. 496-498.
32. F. Armand and R. Maublanc, *Fourier: Textes Choisis.*
33. Wilhelm Reich, *Character Analysis.*
34. For example, cf. M. Gill, "Metapsychology is Not Psychology," *Psychological Issues* (1976), 9 (4, Mono 36), pp. 71-105; M. Gill and P. Holzman, *Psychology Versus Metapsychology*; H. Hartman, *Ego Psychology and the Problem of Adaptation*; H. Hartmann, E. Kris, and R. Lowenstein, "Comments on the Formulation of Psychic Structure," *Psychoanalytic Study of the Child* 2 (1946), pp. 11-38; H. Hartmann, E. Kris, and R. Lowenstein, "Papers on Psychoanalytic Psychology," *Psychological Issues* 4, no. 2 (1964), pp. 1-20; R. Holt and E. Peterfreund, eds., *Psychoanalysis and Contemporary Science*; R. Holt, "The Past and the Future of Ego Psychology," *Psychoanalytic Quarterly* 44, no.4 (1975), pp. 550-576; R. Holt, "Drive or Wish," *Psychological Issues* (1976), 9, (4, Mono 36), pp. 159-197; G. Klein, "The Ego in Psychoanalysis," *Psychoanalytic Review* 56, no. 4 (1969-1970), pp. 511-525; H. Kohut, *Restoration of the Self*; H. Kohut, *The Analysis of the Self*; and H. Kohut, *Essays on Ego Psychology.*
35. R. Schafer, *A New Language for Psychoanalysis, passim.*
36. Richard Lichtman, *The Production of Desire.*
37. *Eros and Civilization, passim.*
38. *Five Lectures*, p. 34.
39. Marcuse, *One-Dimensional Man* (Boston, 1968), p. 72.
40. *Ibid.*
41. *Five Lectures*, p. 40.
42. Freud, *Group Psychology and the Analysis of the Ego* (New York, 1959), *passim.*
43. *Eros and Civilization*, pp. 185ff.
44. Freud, *Collected Papers*, vol. 5 (London, 1950), p. 135.
45. *Eros and Civilization*, p. 195.
46. F. Armand and R. Maublanc, *Fourier: Textes Choisis, passim.*
47. *Negations*, pp. 185-86.
48. *Ibid.*, p. 187.

49. *Ibid.*

50. M. Schoolman, *The Imaginary Witness, passim.*

51. For example, cf. B. Brown, *Marx, Freud, and the Critique of Everyday Life*; S. Buck-Mors, *Origin of the Negative Dialectic*; G. Friedman, *The Political Psychology of the Frankfurt School*; D. Held, *Introduction to Critical Theory*; R. Jacoby, *Social Amnesia*; J. Mitchell, *Psychoanalysis and Feminism*; G. Rose, *The Melancholy Science*; and P. Slater, *Origins and Significance of the Frankfurt School.*

52. *Negations*, p. 76.

53. *Ibid.,* p. 164.

54. *Ibid.,* p. 70.

55. *Ibid.,* p. 185.

56. *Ibid.,* pp. 72-73.

57. O. Fenichel, *The Psychoanalytic Theory of Neurosis*, pp. 142ff.

Without the constant support and critical editorial acumen of my friend and colleague, Charles Webel, this essay would never have come to fruition. I am also indebted for their aid to Gerard A. Aglioni, Adam Cornford, Michael Lerner, Richard Lichtman, Nevitt Sanford, and Joseph Weiss. As one might anticipate, the errors are those of the author.

PART V

□□□□□□□□□

THE POLITICAL
DIMENSION

Until 1968, Marcuse was largely unknown to the public outside the universities and even within the academic world familiarity with his work was not widespread. This state of affairs was due at least in part to Marcuse's Marxist commitment, which was an oddity, to say the least, in the American academy of the fifties and sixties.

It was in the political turmoil of the late sixties that the political dimension of Marcuse's thought suddenly catapulted him to a kind of prominence he had never sought nor imagined possible for someone like himself. Marcuse, the author of an obscure and difficult philosophical critique of advanced industrial society, was billed in *Le Monde* as the "maitre a penser des etudiants en revolte." His name appeared regularly in the American media as a symbol of revolutionary intransigence. Following this attention from the media, denunciation of Marcuse's "anarchism," "revolutionary elitism," and "irrationalism" became standard fare in certain academic circles.

What did Marcuse really have to say about politics? This is not such an easy question to answer. Consider, for example, the controversy that surrounds Marcuse's relationship to Marxism and to democracy. Accused of being a Marxist, and gladly accepting the title, Marcuse was also denounced by certain Marxists as an idealist and anarchist who followed the fashions of bourgeois sociology instead of the method of Marx. Similarly, Marcuse defended the ideal of general social emancipation and supported movements for human rights for blacks and women, and yet some of his followers and critics were able to find support in his writings for attacks on freedom of speech and democracy.

Was Marcuse a Marxist? Did he believe in democracy? The chapters by Kellner and Lichtman which follow attempt to answer these questions. Kellner analyzes Marcuse's response to the "crisis of Marxism." In his view, Marcuse's many departures from traditional Marxist orthodoxy are legitimate attempts to update Marxist theory and to adapt it to a new historical situation. Lichtman offers a critique of one of Marcuse's most controversial and politically influential essays. In "Repressive Tolerance" Marcuse argued that under certain circumstances tolerance should not be extended to reactionary institutions and ideas. Lichtman's discussion identifies the contradictions and tensions which this idea introduces into Marcuse's commitment to general emancipation.

CHAPTER NINE

Herbert Marcuse's Reconstruction Of Marxism

Douglas Kellner

Although Herbert Marcuse's writings are frequently described as "anti-Marxist" or as "pre-Marxian," I believe that his writings should be instead interpreted as a series of responses to what has been described as "the crisis of Marxism."[1] It has been argued that sociohistorical changes since the death of Marx and inherent deficiencies of the Marxian theory render it obsolete and irrelevant to contemporary historical and political developments. One orthodox Marxian response to this alleged crisis is to ignore the critiques and to claim that there is no crisis of Marxism at all, that Marxism is alive and well, and still provides the most adequate theory and method to analyze historical and social structures and dynamics. Another response - of which Marcuse is an ideal type - is to claim that Marxian categories are inherently historical and dialectical and thus demand revision and development as new historical conditions and situations emerge. From this point of view, revision is the very life of the Marxian dialectic and the theory itself demands development, revision, and even abandonment of obsolete or inadequate features as conditions emerge which put tenets of the original Marxian theory in question.

Against claims that Marcuse's critiques or revisions of Marxism constitute an abandonment of the Marxian project, I shall argue that Marcuse continually attempted to reconstruct the Marxian theory in response to historical developments that classical Marxian theory could not account for due to various deficiencies in orthodox Marxism, or new historical conditions that classical Marxism did not envisage. In this reading, Marcuse's writings provide a set of valuable contributions to Marxian theory that would enable it to take account of historical and social developments since Marx's death, and add dimensions to the Marxian theory neglected by most classical Marxists. Consequently, I believe that Marcuse's attempts to reconstruct the Marxian theory should be seen as a life-long effort to improve and update the Marxian theory, rather than as an attempt to transcend or to abandon Marxism.

Previous studies of Marcuse have failed to grasp the complexity and depth of his thought because they have failed to properly interpret Marcuse's complex relation to Marxism. I shall attempt to correct previous misinterpretations of Marcuse's thought and to offer perspectives on Marcuse that both clarify its relation to Marxism and that capture the uniqueness and originality of Marcuse's specific type of Marxism. In the spirit of historical materialist hermeneutic, I shall also indicate what historical events led Marcuse to Marxism, how some historical events and conditions strengthened his belief in the Marxian theory, and how other events and situations led him to reconstruct Marxism.

Marcuse's Road to Marx

Marcuse's works span a historical epoch that at times seemed to confirm the Marxian theory of history, society, and critique of capitalism, and which at other times seemed to radically question Marxism. Talk of "the crisis of Marxism" began during Marcuse's youth when the Socialist International - pledged to internationalism and to not participating in imperialist wars - failed to prevent the eruption of World War I.[2] Most socialist parties supported their nation's war policies and socialist militants were forced to fight their comrades from other countries rather than the class enemy which Marxism proclaimed was their true exploiter and target of class struggle.

Marcuse's first "political" experiences were the devastation of Europe in World War I, and the aftermath of revolution and counterrevolution during the tumultuous Weimar period. Although the failure of the Second International deflated a generation of socialists' hopes that socialism could help eliminate nationalism and war, for someone like Marcuse, previously uninvolved politically, the Marxian theory of imperialism provided a coherent account of how European capitalist countries were led inevitably to war by relentless economic and political competition. The eruption of the October Revolution of 1917, followed by a series of revolutionary upheavals in Germany, Italy, and Central Europe after the war, seemed to confirm the Marxian theory of history and its prognosis that the crises of capitalism would lead to socialist revolution.

During 1917, Marcuse joined the German Social Democratic Party (SPD) in protest against the war.[3] In 1918, however, Marcuse was attracted by the more radical positions of Rosa Luxemburg and Karl Liebkneckt. After their murders, with the possibility of SPD complicity,

Marcuse quit the Social Democratic party, and never officially joined any political party thereafter.   It would have been quite unusual for a young intellectual of Marcuse's class to join the more working class oriented communist party which formed in 1919.   But it is not surprising that a young intellectual, such as Marcuse, profoundly shaken by his historical experiences, would turn to Marxism.   Indeed, Marcuse told me that it was his experiences in World War I that led him to study Marxism and he said that he first read Marx while stationed in Berlin during the war.   After the war, he deepened his study of Marxism while in Berlin and Freiburg, and his first published essays were deeply influenced by the Marxian theory.[4]

Throughout his life, Marcuse was convinced that the Marxian theory provided the most adequate conceptual framework and method to study history and society.   More specifically, he believed that the Marxian dialectic, which explained social change as the result of conflicting social forces and historical transformation as a result of revolutionary upheavals, was superior to the evolutionary theories of history.   His experiences confirmed that Marxian theory provided a more accurate account of historical development. In his theory and his politics Marcuse was a "revolutionist" and not a gradualist, reformist, or evolutionist.   Indeed, Marcuse thought that revolution was an integral part of the historical process and wrote in his first published essay: "Organic historical development and revolution are not simply a contradiction; rather, revolution appears as the necessary form of historical movement. Further, revolution alone can transform the *existence* of the historical human being (*Dasein*)."[5]

But Marxism not only provided a coherent account of Marcuse's own historical experience, it also offered solutions to the sociocultural problems experienced by Marcuse's generation.   Obviously, Marcuse and others were deeply alienated from bourgeois society by the catastrophes of World War I and were attracted to Marxism's compelling account of what was wrong with bourgeois civilization.   Moreover, Marxism conceived of bourgeois society as but a historical stage in humanity's inevitable trek to a better, higher form of society - socialism.   The Russian revolution and its effects in Europe inflamed young radical's hopes that a new society *was* emerging from the ruins of bourgeois civilization.   These hopes, of course, would be tested by the experiences of Stalinism and the Bolshevization of European communist movements, fascism, and the seemingly endless ability of capitalism to survive despite unending crises.

Marcuse's doctoral dissertation, in fact, *Der deutsche Kunstlerroman*, focused on the problem of the alienation of the individual (artist) from society and the yearning to produce a new world which would synthesize the higher realm of culture with everyday life so that beauty, freedom, community, and love could be realized in everyday life.[6]   Marcuse received his doctorate in 1922 at the age of 24 and then returned to Berlin where he briefly attempted an unsuccessful business career.   Bourgeois society failed to satisfy his yearning for an unalienated existence and he returned to Freiburg in 1928 to study philosophy with Martin Heidegger. Heidegger's magnum opus *Sein und Zeit* focused on the distinction between authentic and inauthentic existence and used concepts of alienation to criticize existing society. Heidegger's ontological problematic ultimately proved too abstract for Marcuse who also saw the *individual* project of seeking an authentic existence as too limiting for the sort of social transformation that he envisaged.[7]

Marcuse also perceived during this period that Marxism did not have an adequate concept of the individual and lacked a sufficient philosophical and cultural dimension. The "crisis of Marxism" that Marcuse experienced during the 1920s was in part a theoretical crisis, for Marxism had failed to keep up with the most advanced currents of modern philosophy and culture. Most Marxist theorists of the time - with the exception of people like Korsch, Lukacs, and Gramsci - were primarily interested in politics and economics: consequently the philosophical dimension of Marxism tended to be neglected. In fact, the sort of philosophical materialism, economic reductionism, and historical determinism enshrined in certain forms of orthodox Marxism, which were institutionalized in both the Social Democratic and Communist movements, were anathema to intellectuals like Marcuse. Consequently, he and his more philosophically oriented contemporaries - Korsch, Lukacs, Bloch, Horkheimer, Fromm, and later Adorno, Benjamin, Sartre, etc. - attempted to strengthen the Marxian philosophy by developing its basic concepts and bringing in theoretical material that would enrich the theory.

This operation, I would argue, defines Marcuse's entire theoretical project. Historical situations would occur which would put in question aspects of the Marxian theory; Marcuse would then reconstruct Marxism to take account of these historical developments. If Marxism was conceptually insufficient to deal with fundamental problems of the day, Marcuse would turn to other theoretical currents which he would then synthesize with Marxism. Rather than seeing this as an illegitimate revisionism, Marcuse believed that this exercise was integral to Marxian dialectics, writing at various times that Marxism, "as a historical and dialectical theory," demands periodic re-examination, development and updating of its categories.[8]

Marcuse's first synthesis of Marxism and contemporary philosophy consisted in an attempt to combine Marxism and Heidegger into what he called a "concrete philosophy."[9] The attempt was not particularly successful but anticipated later efforts to develop "phenomenological" or "existential" Marxisms.[10] Marcuse evidently believed that phenomenology, with its injunction to go to "the things themselves," to put aside outmoded theories and concepts, and to describe afresh the data of experience, would compensate for the tendency of Marxism to degenerate into a scholastic theory. He believed that the phenomenological injunction to "bracket" metaphysical questions would enable radical theorists to put aside what he considered abstract and sterile philosophical debates over whether "idea" or "matter" was primary. And he thought that Heidegger's emphasis on the problems of the individual provided an "existential" and "personal" dimension lacking in Marxism.

In fact, emphasis on the individual was not really foreign to Marxism, especially the early Marx. Marcuse was one of the first European theorists to study Marx's and Engel's recently published *German Ideology*, a text full of references to the individual and individual needs, potentialities, desires, etc.[11]   Although Marx himself defined socialism as a social organization that would fully develop individual potentialities and fulfill individual needs, most Marxian political parties and official theorists did not really emphasize these aspects of the Marxian theory which were and would remain of crucial importance to Marcuse - and later to Sartre and a generation of French Marxists, and to the New Left which was deeply individualist in both political style and theoretic discourse.

But Marcuse also believed for a time that Heidegger's philosophy provided a philosophical foundation for Marxism. Marcuse seemed to believe that Marxism required a theory of ontological structures of human being and history in order to provide norms and a standpoint from which capitalist society could be adequately criticized.[12]   He was especially impressed at this time with Heidegger's theory of historicity and ontology of human existence that seemed to provide an account of the underlying sociohistorical structures of all societies and an account of the fundamental traits of human existence - a theory that also provided a distinction between authentic and inauthentic existence.   Although from the beginning Marcuse was critical of Heidegger's philosophy - and provides what to this day is one of the best interpretations and critiques of *Sein und Zeit* - he is insufficiently critical of Heidegger's ontology in his early writings.   In fact, Marxian historicism and Heidegger's notion of historicity are rather fundamentally opposed.   Marxism holds that all society's produce their own characteristic institutions, values, ways of life, etc., and   analyzes specific social formations   within given historical conditions.   Heidegger's ontology is more universal and metaphysical, and   generalizes   away   from   historical   conditions   to   universal-transcendental   conditions.   Thus   there   are   obvious   obstacles   to synthesizing Heidegger and Marx which Marcuse did not seem sufficiently aware of in his early essays, though later he tended to identify with the more concrete and historically specific methodological focus of Marxism.

Marcuse's first essays attempt to undercut the dichotomy between historicism and universalism and provide frequently convoluted and ultimately unsuccessful attempts to merge Marx and Heidegger.   The other focus of his writings from 1928-1933 is an attempt to study Hegel and to make clear the Hegelian roots of Marxism.   In taking this approach to Marxism, Marcuse was aligning himself with the theoretical endeavors of Lukacs and Korsch, who in the early 1920s argued, against positivistic Marxism,   that   precisely   the   Hegelian   dialectical   method   is   the distinguishing characteristic of Marxism by contrast with all forms of bourgeois thought.   Lukacs and Korsch, partly due to political pressures, abandoned this enterprise which was continued with great philosophical rigor   by   Marcuse.[13]   Many   of   his   essays   from   1930-1933   provide illuminating interpretations of Hegelian dialectics and his doctoral dissertation, written under Heidegger's supervision, provides a scholarly study of Hegel's ontology.[14]

The fruits of Marcuse's rigorous study of Marx and Hegel are evident in *Reason   and   Revolution*,   which   examines   in   detail   the   origins   and development of Hegel's social theory, the Hegelian roots of Marxism, and the similarities between Hegel and Marx. But this important book - one of Marcuse's best - was also marked by his experiences of and exile from fascism, and his work with the Institute for Social Research in the United States.

Marcuse, Fascism, and Stalinism

One of the reasons why Marcuse turned away from Heidegger was obviously Heidegger's support of the National Socialist party. When Hitler came to power in 1933, Marcuse, a Jew and Marxist radical, decided to go into exile, emigrating first to Geneva, and then to the United States in 1934. In 1933, Marcuse secured employment with the Institute of Social Research, which moved its headquarters from Frankfurt to Columbia University in New York during this period.[15] The experience of the triumph of fascism was obviously a key event for Marcuse's generation, and is often conceived as one of the stages in "the crisis of Marxism." The triumph of such a regressive social movement, which plunged the entire world into war, erected concentration camps, and claimed millions of lives, challenged the Marxian theory of history that predicted a socialist solution to such crises of capitalism. Moreover, Marxism tended to share the historical optimism and amelioristic theory of history typical of 19th century Europeans.[16]

Fascism, however, designated historical *regression* on a massive, world-wide scale. Moreover, it, temporarily at least, seemed to mark a definite triumph over socialist and communist political movements who supplied the first victims for concentration camps. In other ways, however, Marxism provided a coherent account of the rise of fascism as a solution to capitalism in crisis threatened by historical forces tending to overthrow it. Marcuse, in fact, seemed to subscribe to the orthodox Marxian theory that fascism is basically capitalism in crisis.[17]

But Marcuse and his colleagues provided a richer account of fascism than did most orthodox Marxists. He and his co-workers at the Institute for Social Research wanted to discern how fascist culture and ideology contributed to the triumph of fascism in order to see what sociopsychological factors predisposed individuals to submit to irrational authority.[18] Again, orthodox Marxism had provided few concrete studies of contemporary bourgeois ideologies, and lacked altogether a sociopsychological dimension. At this point, Erich Fromm and other Institute colleagues proposed a synthesis of Marx and Freud, and attempted to use Freudian categories to develop a theory that would account for the authoritarian personality and irrational submission.[19]

Although Marcuse would later develop his own synthesis of Marx and Freud, in the 1930s Marcuse focused on carrying out critiques of the ideological and institutional features of bourgeois culture that contributed to the rise of fascism. Marcuse's essay "The Struggle Against Liberalism in the Totalitarian View of the State" was one of the first comprehensive Marxian critiques of fascist ideology and provided a compelling account of the continuities between classical liberalism and fascism as well.[20]

Marcuse characterized liberalism as "the social and economic theory of European industrial capitalism in the period when the actual economic bearer of capitalism was the individual capitalist, the private enterpreneur."[21]   The pillar of liberalism was "free ownership and control of private property, and the politically and legally guaranteed security of these rights." Although both liberalism and fascism successively defended the capitalist mode of production, Marcuse argues that their basic differences are produced by the transition from competitive capitalism, based on the enterprise of the individual entrepreneur, to monopoly capitalism, which concentrates economic power in the hands of a small corporate-political elite.   Fascism provided an ideology which legitimated the concentration of power, and thus served the interests of dominant economic and political elites in the transition to monopoly capitalism.   Consequently, in Marcuse's view, fascism contributed to the stabilization of capitalism, and only attacked those aspects of liberalism and capitalism that were already rendered obsolete by the requirements of monopoly capitalism.

Marcuse also made an excellent study of the idea of authority that traced the concepts of freedom and authority through the Reformation, Kant, Hegel, the European counterrevolution, and Marx, to recent totalitarian theories of authority.[22] In "Freedom and Authority," Marcuse is concerned to show the dichotomy in the bourgeois concept of freedom which split the individual into two spheres: an inner realm of freedom (autonomy) and an external realm of submission and bondage (authority). The inner freedom of Protestantism and Kant, Hegel's deification of the State, and the irrational and traditionalistic doctrine of authority of the counterrevolution (Burke, de Maistre, F.J. Stahl) all contribute, Marcuse argues, to preparing the way for the totalitarian theory of authority.   In addition, Marcuse and his colleagues showed how the family produced authoritarian personalities who readily submit to irrational authority, and Marcuse contributed a study of "Authority and Family in German Sociology to 1933."[23]   These studies provided analyses of institutions and ideologies that Marxists had previously failed to examine in any detail and exemplify the sort of creative contributions to Marxism carried out by Marcuse and his colleagues in the 1930s.

Finally, Marcuse's work during the epoch of fascism culminated in his first book in English, *Reason and Revolution*.[24]   Here Marcuse attempted to vindicate the tradition of critical social theory that, since the 19th century, had criticized all forms of irrational authority. He opposed critical social theory to what he called "positivism," which he defined as uncritical submission to the powers that be, to "facts" of experience, and to "common sense." Such a posture, Marcuse argues, predisposes individuals to submit to existing authority and power.   Opposed to uncritical submission is a dialectical logic of negation, critique, and opposition.   Indeed, dialectics for Marcuse was always a logic of negation linked to revolutionary theory and practice.   Dialectics conceives of sociohistorical processes as proceeding through a clash of opposites in which higher potentialities struggle against more restrictive institutions, behavior, values, etc. Historical progress takes place, in this view, through negating or overcoming lower stages of development. Dialectical analysis thus involves analyzing conflicting forces or tendencies, discerning higher potentialities, and seeing how the higher potentials can be freed from limitations and restrictions. Thus dialectics for Marcuse is a "negative" and critical method: "Its function is to break down the self-assurance and self-contentment of common sense, to undermine the sinister confidence in the power and language of facts, to demonstrate that unfreedom is so much at the core of things that the development of their internal contradictions leads necessarily to qualitative change: the explosion and catastrophe of the established state of affairs."[25]

In addition, in *Reason and Revolution*, Marcuse attempted to argue that Hegel was not really a precursor or ideologue of the totalitarian state and was in fact closer to Marx with his critical rationalism and revolutionary dialectics. Here Marcuse at once attempts to defend Hegel against the charges that he was a proto-fascist thinker, and to explicate the Hegelian roots of Marxism and the continuity between Marx and Hegel which he believed was the key to genuine Marxism. The result is a somewhat uncritical posture toward Hegel, compensated in part by illuminating analyses of how Hegel anticipated some of Marx's central ideals and discussions of substantive similarities in their theories and method.

The experience of fascism thus did not seem to shake Marcuse's commitment to Marxism.[26] Although he worked with US intelligence agencies like the OSS, and then the State Department, he saw this as part of his struggle against fascism and not as a turn to reformism.[27] He told me that he was never particularly attracted to Roosevelt's liberalism and continued to be committed to Marxism. But the era of fascism was also the era of Stalinism, making it extremely difficult for a radical intellectual like Marcuse to commit himself to the communist movement. Marcuse told me that from the late 1920s he was disturbed by the Bolshevizing of the German and European communist parties and that he never felt able to join a communist party, though in Weimar Germany he said that he usually voted communist "as a protest."[28] During the 1930s, Marcuse thus chose to work on developing the Marxian theory and did not really involve himself in either socialist or communist party politics. And after the war he chose to remain in the United States. He continued to work in the State Department until around 1950, due in part to his wife Sophie's illness from cancer (she died in 1951), and in part because he had not been able to secure an adequate academic position.

Marcuse returned to academia in the early 1950s, taking temporary positions at Columbia and Harvard until he secured a full-time position at Brandeis in 1956. His work at Columbia and Harvard was in their Russian Departments and in 1955 he published the result of his studies of Soviet ideology and society in his book *Soviet Marxism*.[29] This book purports to be an "objective" study that desists both from Cold War anti-communism and pro-Soviet apologetics. The book was attacked by American liberals and conservatives alike, and some Marxists, as being too uncritical of Stalinism, while Stalinists claimed that the book was an attack on the Soviet Union.[30] In a 1961 Preface to the Vintage edition, Marcuse cited this reception as evidence that he indeed achieved a high level of objectivity, but I believe that the text also reveals his own increasingly complex, and ambiguous, relation to Marxism.

Marcuse, Marxism, and Advanced Capitalism

During the 1950s and 1960s Marcuse undertook what was probably the most radical critique and reconstruction of classical Marxism. Contemporary accounts of him during the 1930s and 1940s always stress that he impressed people as a rather orthodox Marxist, and in fact he identified himself as a Marxist up until his death.[31] Nonetheless, he questioned certain central tenets of the Marxian theory, such as the theory of capitalist crisis and the revolutionary role of the proletariat, and presented a version of Marxism substantively different from classical Marxism. Seen from this perspective, his work *One-Dimensional Man* articulates the crisis of Marxism in an era which seemed to refute the Marxian theory of history and socialist revolution. But although Marcuse challenges some of the basic postulates of Marx's theory, he also uses other Marxian categories and its methods of analysis and social critique.

The characteristic themes of Marcuse's post-World War II writings build on the Frankfurt School's analyses of the role of technology and technological rationality, administration and bureaucracy, the capitalist state, mass media and consumerism, which in their view produced both a decline in the revolutionary potential of the working class and a decline of individuality, freedom, and democracy. Although their writings certainly articulate historical pessimism still, their work makes many original contributions to the Marxian theory and, for the most part (especially so in the case of Marcuse) develops critical theory within the framework of Marxism. To substantiate this claim in Marcuse's case, I shall next look at his development of a theory of advanced capitalist society, and shall argue that despite reexamination and questioning of some central Marxian positions, nonetheless, his work remains within a Marxian framework and makes many valuable contributes to developing a neo-Marxian theory of the contemporary era.

In a 1954 epilogue to the second edition of *Reason and Revolution*, Marcuse's questioning of orthodox Marxism is evident. He points to increased tendencies toward totalitarian social control in contemporary industrial societies and indicates that both Hegel's hope that reason would shape and control reality, and Marx's hope that reason would be embodied in a revolutionary class and rational society seemed to have come to naught.[32] The proletariat was not the "absolute negation of capitalist society presupposed by Marx" (p. 435), and the contradictions of capitalism had not proved as explosive as Marx had forecast:

> When Marx envisaged the transition to socialism from the advanced industrial countries, he did so because not only the maturity of the productive forces, but also the irrationality of their use, the maturity of the internal contradictions of capitalism and of the will to their abolition were essential to his idea of socialism. But precisely in the advanced industrial countries, since about the turn of the

century, the internal contradictions became subject to increasingly efficient organization, and the negative force of the proletariat was increasingly whittled down. Not only a small 'labor aristocracy' but the larger part of the laboring classes were made into a positive part of the established society (p. 436).

Marcuse argued that technological progress made possible both raising the standard of living and administering and satisfying individual needs so as to increase the power of society over the individual:

> [T]he tremendous rise in the productivity of labor within the framework of the prevailing social institutions made mass production inevitable - but also mass manipulation. The result was that the standard of living rose with the concentration of economic power to monopolistic proportions. Concurrently, technological progress fundamentally changed the balance of social power. The scope and effectiveness of the instruments of destruction controlled by the government made the classical forms of the social struggle old-fashioned and romantic. The barricade lost its revolutionary value just as the strike lost its revolutionary content. The economic and cultural co-ordination of the laboring classes was accompanied and supplemented by the obsolescence of their traditional weapons (p. 438).

"Organized capitalism" was therefore both able to stabilize itself, to manage its contradictions and conflicts, and to integrate the working class within the system so that a once revolutionary force became "affirmative."[33] Marcuse claimed that the term "organized capitalism" took on new historical content, first, in the European war economies during the First World War, when the state took over, or managed, various sectors of the economy, and then during the stage of what his colleague Friedrich Pollock called "state capitalism" when Keynesian steering strategies were used to manage the economy and New Deal reform policies were used to manage social conflict. Pollock's studies of economic planning in the state and the automatization of industry outlined new ways of utilizing technologies as instruments of domination and capitalist stabilization, providing the socio-economic foundation for critical theory's concept of the "administered society."[34] Marcuse concluded that organized capitalism seemed to have stabilized the classical contradictions of capitalism so as to avert major crises and conflicts which were presupposed as necessary conditions for socialist revolution in Marx's theory. Instead, Marcuse saw that the unparalleled affluence and apparatus of planning and management in advanced capitalism had produced new forms of social control and a "society without opposition" that closed off possibilities of radical social change.[35]

In such a historical situation, neo-Marxian theories had to both conceptualize the changing historical conditions and to develop new strategies of social change based on new historical tendencies and possibilities. Against those who claim that Marcuse abandons Marxism, I would argue that the method and framework in which Marcuse undertakes his investigations of advanced industrial society uses Marx's critique of capitalism and method to describe a more advanced form of a social order which still contains many of the features that Marx ascribed to capitalism. In the Introduction to *One-Dimensional Man* Marcuse writes that in the capitalist world the bourgeoisie and the proletariat "are still the basic classes. However, the capitalist development has altered the structure and function of these two classes in such a way that they no longer appear to be agents of historical transformation."[36] In my view, Marcuse provides a theory of advanced capitalism in *One-Dimensional Man* that conceptualizes changes in the class structure and the socioeconomic foundation in advanced capitalist societies which require a reformulation of the Marxian theory of the proletariat as the revolutionary class and which requires new concepts and analyses to describe historical conditions which had changed since Marx's day. Accordingly, Marcuse provides new theories of the consumer society, the media and mass culture, the nature and social functions of science and technology, the integrative effects of liberalized sexuality, the ideological nature of language, social research, and philosophy in contemporary American society, and the power of the society to absorb opposition and develop new forms of social control.[37]

Unlike most orthodox Marxists, Marcuse drew on critical US social scientists, theorists, and even critical journalists like Vance Packard and Fred Cook to develop his theory of advanced capitalist societies. *One-Dimensional Man* angered both orthodox Marxists who could not assent to such thorough-going critiques of orthodox Marxism and such radical rethinking of the Marxian theory of capitalism and social change, and academics who could not accept such comprehensive critiques of advanced capitalism. The book was, however, well received by the New Left and a generation dissatisfied with the current social system and the orthodoxies of both the dominant Marxist and academic theories. For the New Left, *One-Dimensional Man* provided an articulation of what young radicals felt was wrong with the existing society, and the book's dialectic of liberation and domination provided a context for radical politics which struggled against domination and for liberation. Moreover, *One-Dimensional Man* showed that the problems confronting the emerging radical movement were not simply the Vietnam war, racism or inequality, but the system itself, and that solving a wide range of social problems required fundamental social restructuring. In this way, *One-Dimensional Man* played an important role in the political education of a generation of radicals - including many contributors to this book.[38]

To understand and evaluate adequately both the achievements and shortcomings of *One-Dimensional Man*, one must consider the historical context in which the book was written and the poverty of radical social theory during that period. When *One-Dimensional Man* appeared in 1964, there had been few attempts within Marxism to develop a theory of advanced capitalism that seriously questioned Marxian orthodoxy, and both Marxism and "bourgeois" social sciences were in the grip of positivistic empiricism and ideological orthodoxies. During the 1950s, conformist social theory proclaiming the "end of ideology" was in vogue, and there were few radical critiques that matched Marcuse's. However, social opposition and revolt was also at a low ebb, due to the combined forces of Cold War repression in the McCarthy era and unprecedented affluence after World War II.[39] Succeeding events would put in question the theory of capitalist stabilization developed in *One-Dimensional Man* but it seems in retrospect to provide a fairly accurate view of its historical epoch.

The orthodox Marxist strategy of critique tended either to quote classical Marxian doctrine against Marcuse, or to present social facts and tendencies which put in question Marcuse's theses.[40] Against Marcuse's theory of an affluent society which "delivers the goods" and minimizes class differences, it was argued that Marcuse's analysis in *One-Dimensional Man* focuses too exclusively on the post-war boom in the USA and underestimates the deep contradictions and explosive disequilibrium in advanced capitalism.[41] Critics contended that although the reconstruction period after World War II created highly advantageous conditions for the expansion of American and world capitalism, this period of capitalist expansion and stability is coming to an end, and that advanced capitalism is entering a period of crisis and intensified class conflict.[42] It was alleged that Marcuse shared the Keynesian illusion that capital had finally found a strategy and practice to manage capitalism's crisis tendencies and business cycles, whereas, in fact, it was argued that during the 1970s and 1980s the global crisis of capitalism put in question theories of capitalist stabilization.[43]

There is no doubt that in *One-Dimensional Man* Marcuse exaggerated the stability of capitalism and failed to analyze adequately its crisis-tendencies and contradictions. Consequently, his theory of "one-dimensional society" cannot account either for the eruption of social revolt on a global scale in the 1960s, or for the global crisis of capitalism in the 1970s and 1980s. It seems that Marcuse failed to perceive the extent to which his theory articulated a stage of historical development that was soon coming to a close and that would give way to a new era marked by a world crisis of capitalism and by social revolt and revolutionary struggles both within and without advanced capitalist societies. By failing to show how the "one-dimensional" tendencies were a function of specific historical conditions, and by failing to specify counter-tendencies in more detail, Marcuse blurred the distinction between temporary containment of crisis-tendencies, revolt and struggles in contrast to permanent transcendence of negativity in a new social order characterized by the generalization of technological rationality and the integration of culture, politics, and society into one monolithic system.

Yet it is also true that Marcuse *does* indicate that he is analyzing trends of social development to which there are countertrends (see *One-Dimensional Man*, pp. xv-xvii). In the Introduction, he writes that his study "will vacillate throughout between two contradictory hypotheses: (1) that advanced industrial society is capable of containing qualitative change for the foreseeable future; (2) that forces and tendencies exist which may break this containment and explode the society" (xv). Near the end of *One-Dimensional Man* he writes: "The unification of opposites in the medium of technological rationality must be, *in all its reality* an illusory unification, which eliminates neither the contradiction between the growing productivity and its repressive use, nor the vital need for solving the contradictions" (256).

Thus Marcuse does recognize that both social conflicts and tendencies toward change continue to exist and that radical social transformation may eventually be possible. Although the focus of his analysis is on the containment of the contradictions of capitalism, he describes it in the passage just cited as a "forced unity," or "illusory unification" rather than as an elimination of all contradictions and conflicts. In my view, to interpret properly both *One-Dimensional Man* and Marcuse's project as a whole, *One-Dimensional Man* should be read in relation to *Eros and Civilization* as well as to the works that follow, such as *An Essay on Liberation* and *Counterrevolution and Revolt*. It is precisely the vision of "what could be" articulated in *Eros and Civilization, An Essay on Liberation*, and Marcuse's other, more utopian writings, that creates the bleakness of "what is" in *One-Dimensional Man*.

In fact, in his writings after *One-Dimensional Man*, Marcuse focuses more on social contradictions, struggles, and disintegrating factors in advanced capitalism, and thus comes closer to the orthodox Marxian stress on capitalist crisis tendencies and seams of weakness that make possible social intervention. There is also more traditional Marxian emphasis on forces of social revolt and transformation.

During this period, although Marcuse himself was often sharply attacked by orthodox Marxists, he continued to identify himself as a Marxist and to defend Marxism against its critics. In a revealing passage in "The Obsolescence of Marxism?" he writes:

> The title of my paper is not supposed to suggest that Marx's analysis of the capitalist system is outdated; on the contrary I think that the most fundamental notions of this analysis have been validated, and they can be summarized in the following propositions. 1) In capitalism the social relationships among men are governed by the exchange value rather than use value of the goods and services they produce, that is to say their position is governed by their marketability. (2) In this exchange society, the satisfaction of human needs occurs only as a by-product of profitable production. (3) In the progress of capitalism, a twofold contradiction develops between (a) the growing productivity of labor and the ever-growing social wealth on the one side, and their repressive and destructive use on the other; and (b) between the social character of the means of production (no longer individual but collective instruments of labor) and their private ownership and control. (4) Capitalism can solve this contradiction only temporarily through increasing waste, luxury and destruction of productive forces. The competitive drive for armament production profit leads to a vast concentration of economic power, aggressive expansion abroad, conflicts with other imperialist powers and finally to a recurrent cycle of war and depression. (5) This cycle can be broken only if the laboring classes,

who bear the brunt of exploitation, seize the productive apparatus and bring it under the collective control of the producers themselves. I submit that all these propositions with the exception of the last one seem to be corroborated by the factual development. The last proposition refers to the advanced industrial countries where the transition to socialism was to take place, and precisely in these countries, the laboring classes are in no sense a prevolutionary potential.[44]

This situation led Marcuse to search for non-integrated forces of social transformation successively in marginal groups like blacks and intellectuals, students and movement activists, and Third World revolutionaries.[45] However, he didn't go as far as his critics maintain in supposedly writing off the working class as an agent of social change. In a 1968 interview, in fact, he stated: "In spite of everything that has been said, I still cannot imagine a revolution without the working class," and, in fact, repeatedly argued that he never saw students or hippies as "revolutionary forces" capable of carrying through a revolution without working class support.[46]

Marcuse saw his theory as an attempt to update the Marxian theory in relation to changes in contemporary society. In his view, "a re-examination and even reformulation of Marxian theory cannot simply mean adjusting this theory to new facts but must proceed as an internal development and critique of Marxian concepts;" consequently, Marxism "is obsolete precisely to the degree to which this obsolescence of some decisive concepts of Marx are anticipated in Marxian theory itself as alternatives and tendencies of the capitalist system."[47] Marcuse continued to identify his work as a development of the Marxian theory up until his death, while continually questioning those elements of the Marxian theory that he believed were obsolete or were not radical enough for contemporary prospects for social change. Throughout *One-Dimensional Man* and his later writings, Marcuse indicates his preference for socialism over capitalism, and constantly uses Marxian methods and theories to both critique existing societies and to project emancipatory, alternative societies.

But the absence of clearly articulated ideals of liberation and a non-repressive society in orthodox Marxism led him to study utopian socialists, as well as poets and philosophers who projected ideals of liberation and a non-repressive existence. Indeed, Marcuse injects a much-needed transfusion of imagination and creative thinking into Marxism, adding a cultural dimension lacking in many versions of Marxism and a philosophical-utopian dimension that dares to conceive of and posit radical alternatives. For example, he reconstructs the ideas of Schiller and Nietzsche as Marxian theories of cultural revolution and the "transvaluation of values."[48] His belief that classical Marxism lacked an adequate psychology and theory of sexuality led him to use Freud to develop a Marxian social psychology and theory of instinctual liberation. The lack of adequate theories of technology in contemporary Marxism led him to use theories of Max Weber and other contemporary critics of technology to analyze the role of technology and "technological rationality" in constituting contemporary society. Marcuse also perceived changed conditions of everyday life and leisure, and analyzed the roles of consumerism, mass culture and communications, and various forms of ideology in reproducing advanced capitalism. Neglect within Marxism of the problems of women led him to feminism and the development of what he called "socialist feminism."[49]

Marcuse was one of the few Marxist philosophers who attempted to unite philosophy and politics and to restore the utopian dimension of socialist thought. Most Marxists who aim at the union of theory and practice mold revolutionary theory into an instrument of practical politics. Marcuse, on the other hand, developed revolutionary theory as a theory of liberation and sought to resurrect the utopian moment in Marx that had been covered by the tradition of scientific Marxism and ignored by most orthodox Marxists.[50] In fact, part of the "crisis of Marxism" has been its lack of utopian thinking and underdeveloped perspectives on socialism and liberation. For most people today in the West, existing socialist societies fail to provide an attractive form of democratic and emancipatory socialism which could be used as a model for advanced industrial societies. Although Marcuse never projected any detailed blueprints for an alternative society, institutions, and way of life, he continually concerned himself with projecting more attractive and emancipatory values and ideals.

Conclusion

I have suggested in this chapter that Herbert Marcuse's responses to what has been called the "crisis of Marxism" is a key to his thought and writings. However, in conclusion, I want to propose that we view the "crisis of Marxism" not so much as a sign of the obsolescence of Marxian theory but rather as a typical situation for a social theory that faces anomalies or events which challenge its theories. The term "crisis" in Marxian discourse suggests cataclysmic collapse and, as Habermas suggests, a terminal illness that could bring death to its patient.[51] The concept of "crisis" within Marxian theory has its origins in theories of the "crisis of capitalism" which were generally linked to notions of the collapse of capitalism and triumph of socialism. The term "crisis" was then applied to Marxism itself by Sorel, Korsch, and others. In recent years, references to the "crisis of Marxism" have proliferated, and have been used to cover a variety of phenomena.

However, just as capitalism has survived many crises, so has Marxism. Moreover, just as various crises of capitalism have elicited new survival strategies which in certain ways have strengthened the capitalist system (i.e. imperialism, organized capitalism, state capitalism, multinational capitalism, etc.), so too "crises of Marxism" have periodically led to the development and improvement of Marxian theory. A "crisis" brings about a challenge to a social system or theory that may lead to its collapse or to its strengthening. Crises of Marxism are like the events that global sociohistorical theories continually undergo when events belie forecasts, or historical changes appear that force development or revision of the theory.   When theories like Marxism are put in question during a "crisis," debates ensue which frequently improve the theory.   Consequently, crises of Marxism do not necessarily refer to failures of Marxism that portend its collapse and irrelevance but rather point toward opportunities to grow, develop, and strengthen itself.

Seen in this context, Herbert Marcuse's work can be interpreted as a series of attempts to reconstruct Marxian theory in the light of historical changes and challenges that require revision and development.   Marcuse himself constantly argued that Marxian theory periodically demands revision and development since the categories are historical categories, which are necessarily open to change and transformation.   He believed that Marxism was not yet obsolescent, or passe, despite the vicissitudes of advanced capitalist development which put in question certain of its theories.   Rather than abandoning Marxism, Marcuse sought to update and transform it.   Thus Marcuse's work emerges as an attempt to reconstruct the Marxian theory during a historical epoch that seemed to put in question some of its central tenets and to confirm others.   I propose, therefore, reading Marcuse's work in terms of how it reconstructs Marxism in response to historical conditions rather than seeing him as anti-Marxist, or as abandoning Marxism.

NOTES

1.   Alasdair MacIntyre calls Marcuse a "pre-Marxist" thinker, while various Soviet critics, Maurice Cranston, and others call Marcuse "anti-Marxist" or "anarchist."   See Alasdair MacIntyre, *Herbert Marcuse: An Exposition and a Polemic* (New York: Viking, 1970); Robert Steigerwald, *Herbert Marcuses Dritter Weg* (Cologne: Pahl-Rugenstein, 1969); Maurice Cranston, "Herbert Marcuse," *Encounter* 32, 3 (1969), pp. 38-50.   In this article, I draw on the research in my book *Herbert Marcuse and the Crisis of Marxism* (London and Berkeley: Macmillian and University of California, 1984) which contains a much more detailed account of some of the ideas presented here.

2.   On the "crisis of Marxism," see the analysis by Karl Korsch in my book *Karl Korsch: Revolutionary Theory*, edited by Douglas Kellner (Austin: University of Texas Press, 1977), and the discussion in Alvin W. Gouldner, *The Two Marxisms* (New York: Seabury, 1980).   The failure of the Second International socialists to prevent World War I is sometimes seen as the beginning of the "crisis of Marxism."   See Korsch, *op. cit.*, and Carl Schorske, *German Social Democracy, 1905-1917* (Cambridge: Harvard University Press, 1955).

3.   Interview with Herbert Marcuse, Dec. 28, 1978, La Jolla, California, and *Five Lectures* (Boston: Beacon Press, 1970), pp. 102-103.

4.   See the articles collected in *Schriften* 1 (Frankfurt: Suhrkamp, 1979), pp. 347ff.

5.   Marcuse, "Beiträge," in *Schriften*, pp. 384-85.   In a review of a book on sociology by Hans Freyer, Marcuse identifies the actual movement of history with revolution, as if revolution were the very dynamic factor in

history itself. See "Zur Auseinandersetzung mit Hans Freyers 'Soziologie als Wirklichkeitswissenschaft,'" *Philosophische Hefte* 3, 1/2 (1931), pp. 89-90.

6. Marcuse, "Der deutsche Künstlerroman"; doctoral dissertation submitted to the University of Freiburg, 1922; reprinted in *Schriften*.

7. Martin Heidegger, *Being and Time*, and Marcuse, "Beiträge." On Heidegger's distinction between authentic and inauthentic existence, see my doctoral dissertation, "Heidegger's Concept of Authenticity," and my article "Authenticity and Heidegger's Challenge to Ethical Theory," in *Thinking About Being*, ed. Robert W. Shahar and J. N. Mohanty, pp. 159-76.

8. See, for example, Marcuse's interview with Bryan Magee in *Men of Ideas*, pp. 64ff, and the sources in note 48.

9. *Schriften*.

10. See Paul Piccone, "Phenomenological Marxism," *Telos* 9 (Fall 1971), pp. 3-31, and Mark Poster, *Existential Marxism in Postwar France*.

11. See Karl Marx and Friedrich Engels, *Collected Works*, vol. 5 (New York, 1976). See Marcuse's appropriation of ideas in the *German Ideology*, in "Beiträge."

12. See the passage in a review article on Mannheim where Marcuse writes: "In that unique transcendence of historical processes, contexts become visible which render problematic the taking of the historical stages as the final givens. Neither the current historical situation as facticity, nor the continuous historical development as a causal connection without gaps constitutes the full reality of historical processes; rather, these factical states of affairs constitute themselves in a reality whose fundamental structures lie at the foundation of all factical realizations in history. All historical situations are as factical realizations only historical transformations of such basic structures that will be realized in every order of life in various ways. The way of the realization of human living-with-one-another in capitalist society, for example, is a realization of the basic structures of human being-with-one-another in general - not in some formal-abstract sense, but as highly concrete basic structures: an order of life would be true when it fulfilled, false when it concealed or repressed them." "Zur Wahrheitsproblematik der soziologischen Methode," *Die Gesellschaft* 5 (1929); reprinted in Adorno, Horkheimer, and Marcuse, *Kritische Theorie der Gesellschaft* pp. 338-9.

13. See Karl Korsch, *Marxism and Philosophy*, and Georg Lukacs, *History and Class Consciousness*.

14. See *Schriften*, pp. 407-87, and *Hegels Ontologie und die Grundlegung einer Theorie der Geschichtlichkeit*.

15. On the Institute for Social Research, see Alfred Schmidt, *Zur Idee der Kritischen Theorie*; Martin Jay, *The Dialectical Imagination*, and Douglas Kellner, "The Frankfurt School Revisited," *New German Critique* 4 (Winter 1975), pp. 131-52.

16. For an analysis of how the triumph of fascism put in question the Marxian philosophy of history, see Douglas Kellner, ed., *Karl Korsch: Revolutionary Theory*. On fascist and Stalinist holocausts, see Ronald Aronson, *The Dialectics of Disaster*.

17. For the orthodox Marxian theory of fascism, see George Dimitrov who, at the Seventh World Congress of the Communist International, advanced the orthodox Communist line that "fascism is the open, terroristic dictatorship of the most reactionary, most chauvinistic, and most imperialist elements of finance capitalism. In *United Front.*

18. On the Institute theory of fascism, see Jay, *The Dialectical Imagination*; *Wirtschaft, Recht und Staat im Nationalsozialismus*, eds. Helmut Dubiel and Alfons Sollner; and the collective volume *Studien über Autoritat und Familie*, 2 vols.

19. See *Studien*, and Erich Fromm's 1930 articles translated in *The Crisis of Psychoanalysis*, especially pp. 109-67.

20. Marcuse, *Negations* (Boston, 1963), pp. 3-42.

21. *Negations*, p. 8ff.

22. Marcuse, "A Study on Authority," in *Studies in Critical Philosophy* (Boston, 1971), pp. 49-156.

23. Marcuse, "Autorität und Familie in der deutschen Soziologie bis 1933," in *Studien*, pp. 737-52.

24. Marcuse, *Reason and Revolution* (New York: Oxford University Press, 1941; reprinted by Humanities Press in 1954 with a new Epilogue, and by Beacon Press in 1960 with a new Preface).

25. *Reason and Revolution*, p. ix, *passim.*

26. Attesting to the depth of Marcuse's commitment to Marxism, Karl Korsch wrote his friend Paul Mattick in 1938: "Marcuse is a sort of orthodox Marxist who might even be still a Stalinist, and is bureaucratically authoritarian in matters of bourgeois philosophy and Marxism (which today have become one and the same). Theoretically, he has somewhat more character and solidity than the others, whose greater 'freedom' consists only in a greater fluctuation and uncertainty," quoted in Kellner, *Karl Korsch*, p. 284. Marcuse told me that he hesitated to criticize Stalinism and the Soviet Union openly until after the Czechoslovakia invasion of 1968 for fear of playing into the hands of anti-communists - although, in my view, his 1958 book *Soviet Marxism* contains sharp critiques of the Soviet political system and ideology.

27. Interview with Marcuse.

28. Interview with Marcuse.

29. Marcuse, *Soviet Marxism* (New York, 1961).

30. *Soviet Marxism.*

31. See note 26 for Korsch's appraisal of Marcuse's Marxism in the late 1930s. Arthur Mitzman told me that after one of Marcuse's seminars on social change at Columbia in the 1950s at the height of McCarthyism, when professors, among others, were being scrutinized by the FBI and the repressive state agencies for their political beliefs, he approached Marcuse after class and asked him directly if he was a Marxist. Marcuse coolly looked Mitzman in the eyes and answered, "Yes. And what is your question?" Interview with Arthur Mitzman, Austin, Texas, October 1980. In my last interview with Marcuse, he reaffirmed his life-long commitment to Marxism and mentioned how he was always annoyed when interpreters claimed that he had abandoned Marxism.

32. Marcuse, "Epilogue," *Reason and Revolution,* pp.   433ff.

(Subsequent page references in the text will appear in parentheses.)

33. The term "organized capitalism" derives from Rudolf Hilferding; see Marcuse's discussion in *Soviet Marxism*, pp. 18ff.

34. I believed that Pollock's studies of automation and state capitalism exerted a generally overlooked influence on Marcuse's theory of "advanced industrial society." See Frederick Pollock, *The Economic and Social Consequences of Automation*, which anticipates some of Marcuse's analysis in *One-Dimensional Man*.

35. Marcuse's theory of advanced industrial society in *One-Dimensional Man*, which sets forth this position, is the product of many years work. The genesis of his theory is found in "Some Social Implications of Modern Technology," *Studies in Philosophy and Social Science* 9, no. 3 (1941), pp. 414-39, and in several studies such as a review of John Nef's *War and Human Progress*, *American Historical Review* 57, no. 1 (October 1951), pp. 97-100; his Preface to Raya Dunayevskaya, *Marxism and Freedom*; and "De l'ontologie à la technologie," *Arguments*, 4, no. 18 (1960), pp. 54-9. These and other articles and reviews published before *One-Dimensional Man* are a valuable source for study of *One-Dimensional Man* for they often elucidate some of its presuppositions in more detail than in later work, and disclose the historical genesis of his theory of one-dimensional society as an articulation of historical conditions.

36. *One-Dimensional Man*, pp. xii-xiii.

37. On Marcuse's contribution to these themes, see my book *Herbert Marcuse and the Crisis of Marxism*, and my articles "Critical Theory, Commodities, and the Consumer Society," *Theory, Culture, and Society* 3 (1983), 66-84; "Critical Theory, Max Weber, and the Dialectics of Domination," in *The Weber-Marx Dialogue*, Robert J. Antonio and Ronald Glassman, eds.; and "Critical Theory, Mass Communications, and Popular Culture," *Telos* (forthcoming 1984).

38. On Marcuse and the New Left, see *Critical Interruptions*, ed. Paul Breines; and Jean-Michel Palmier, *Herbert Marcuse et la nouvelle gauche*.

39. On the historical context during which Marcuse conceived *One-Dimensional Man*, see Godfrey Hodgson, *America in Our Time*, and on the situation of radical thought in this context, which discusses the relation between Marcuse's work and other radical theorists, see Peter Clecak, *Radical Paradoxes*.

40. See, for example, Paul Mattick, *Critique of Marcuse*; and John Fry, *Marcuse - Dilemma and Liberation*.

41. Mattick; Fry; and David Horowitz's critique in *International Socialist Journal* 4 (Nov.-Dec. 1967).

42. *International Socialist Journal* 4 (Nov.-Dec. 1967).

43. *International Socialist Journal* 4 (Nov.-Dec. 1967). In the last decade, there has been an upsurge of interest in theories of capitalist crisis which have to some extent displaced Marcusean types of theories of capitalist hegemony from the center of radical social theory. In my view, theories of hegemony and crisis have to be balanced and set off against each other; Marcuse frequently erred by going too far in the direction of capitalist hegemony theories which failed to note weakness within

contemporary capitalism and points of intervention, whereas many capitalist crisis tendencies exaggerate the weaknesses of contemporary capitalism and fail to properly analyze its continuing strengths.

44.   Marcuse, "The Obsolescence of Marxism," in *Marx and the Western World*, ed. Nicholas Lobkowicz, p. 409-10.

45.   See Marcuse, *An Essay on Liberation* (Boston, 1969); *Five Lectures*; *Counterrevolution and Revolt* (Boston, 1972); and the many articles written by Marcuse during this period which tended to focus on the prospects for radical social change.

46.   Interview with Marcuse, *The New York Times* (October 27, 1968), p. 89.   Marcuse modified this position somewhat in the 1970s; see my discussion in *Herbert Marcuse*.

47.   "Obsolescence," p. 409.

48.   *Eros and Civilization* (Boston, 1955); *An Essay on Liberation*, and many articles.

49.   See *Counterrevolution and Revolt*, pp. 74ff; and "Marxism and Feminism," *Womens Studies* 2 no. 3 (1974), pp. 279-88.

50.   See Kellner, *Herbert Marcuse*.

51.   See Gouldner, *The Two Marxisms*; and Jürgen Habermas, *Legitimation Crisis*.

CHAPTER TEN

Repressive Tolerance

Richard Lichtman

Although Marcuse's brief essay "Repressive Tolerance" has been largely neglected, it remains a most powerful prism through which to view his conception of the transition from capitalism to socialism. The critical question of how a people constituted by false need, saturated with ideological consciousness and unaware even of the nature of its own unhappiness, is to make and sustain a revolution, is more forcefully (even blatantly) posed in this essay than in anything else Marcuse wrote. And the answer Marcuse offers, though deeply defective, has the merit for which Marcuse is correctly appreciated: of forcing us to deal with a profoundly disturbing question in terms which do not permit escape.

Of course, Marcuse's argument on behalf of repression for the sake of freedom was articulated in other works.[1] But in the remainder of his writings, with the exception of his late essay on Bahro, his redefinition of tolerance was usually presented as one side of a fateful dilemma: tolerance must be withdrawn from movements, practices, ideas and attitudes which favor oppression and aggression; and yet, a central authority claiming to break the pattern of false need is a threat to democratic self-determination. In "Repressive Tolerance," however, the argument on behalf of intolerance itself is presented in its purest form. "The objective of tolerance would call for intolerance toward prevailing policies, attitudes, opinions, and the extension of tolerance to policies, attitudes, and opinions which are outlawed or suppressed."[2]

There are many reasons to be surprised by this outcome in Marcuse's work, and his own playful, non-dogmatic, anti-authoritarian presence, as we knew him, is not the least of them. We have often assumed that since Marcuse was so passionately committed to the overthrow of totalitarianism in all its forms, it was inconceivable that he would have seriously entertained any such alternative, no matter how expedient. And yet, there is another aspect to the situation. For however much Marcuse may have insisted on the role of *self*-emancipation, the radically transcendent nature of this demand could only force him to a fateful choice. Given the severity of his indictment of the perversion of late capitalism he could either resign himself to the masked misery of this world, or call for a chiliastic break with its inexorably diminishing human semblance. Seen in this light, it is not surprising that as he witnessed the historical dialectic coagulate before his eyes, and the possible utopia of technological hope slide further into the potential terror of triangulated annihilation, the desire to cut history at its axis grew irresistible. Were these the only choices it would be difficult to decide otherwise. Better with Plato and Rousseau to force humanity to freedom, than tolerate its fearful descent into disintegration, no matter how apparently "free" this suicide might seem.

I

In making any assessment of Marcuse's argument it is important to note the total bankruptcy of liberal theories of the right to free speech. The fact that we generally favor free speech and regard an appropriate socialist society as constituted by the freest interchange of ideas among its members in no way redeems either the conditions of such purported freedom under "liberal" capitalism nor the validity of such liberal theory as has been proposed as a justification for actual and ideal conditions of freedom. Although it is impossible in these few pages to survey the history of liberal justifications for freedom of speech it is easy enough to state the fundamental contradiction which underlies and undermines all such positions: the capitalist structure of power is in flagrant contradiction with equality presupposed by liberal theories of toleration, autonomy and free expression. In fact, it is only in socialism that one can conceive of the free production, distribution, consumption, and exchange of ideas.

The doctrine of toleration was originally born in the period of turmoil following the breakdown of medieval absolutism. It was the conflict of rival factions for power that led the expediency of pluralism. A contemporary Quaker advocate acknowledges that

> toleration was largely due to political, economic and other practical considerations, more than to increased spiritual insights.[3]

And Laski is perfectly correct in noting that

> the history of toleration shows that it is the economic destruction wrought by civil war which creates the mental climate favorable to

toleration.   It comes because, at the bottom, persecution is a threat to property.[4]

Laski might well have drawn the logical conclusion from this observation; that when freedom of speech itself becomes a threat to property, its own security will be endangered.

It is, of course, in Mill's essay *On Liberty* that the liberal argument for freedom of speech was given its classic voice.   But the conflictual nature of the essay has rarely been noted: it has been interpreted either as a defense of individual liberty against the incursion of the state, or as a warning against the mediocrity and intolerance of a newly enfranchised mass citizenry.   Mill never recognized the essential relationship between the capitalist system on whose behalf the state was inclined to violate individual liberties and the mass banality of capitalist culture in which the citizenry was itself deformed; that the high ideals of individual self-realization and social diversity were rendered inoperative by the brutalization of everyday capitalist life.[5]

Mill's most famous claim, that the individual is wholly sovereign in regard to that part of himself which merely concerns himself, "his own body and mind,"[6] was certainly in the tradition of Locke's similar assertion on behalf of the individual viewed as private property: ". . . every man has property in his own person.   This nobody has any right to but himself."[7] It was also an impossible claim to defend.   For Mill was quickly forced to concede that no such line could be drawn and his original principle of inalienable rights to private personhood soon gave way to the utilitarian claim that it was on society's behalf that individuals should be permitted their diversity. But precisely what sort of diversity could British capitalist culture nourish among its citizenry, and how extensive were the limits of respect for opposition which this new mass populace might be expected to entertain? Simply put, how much confidence had Mill in the capacity of British mass democracy to encourage the desire for self-realization among its members?   To the credit of his honesty, Mill was forced to a pessimistic conclusion, although it is difficult to avoid the judgment that he wholly misconstrued its grounds.

Mill held a largely ideological view of the nature of government which he judged a threat to individual freedom on the assumption that it was the only institutional agent capable of exercising power over the individual. And yet, Mill himself also knew (as this example of his testimony before the House of Commons in 1850 bears out) that

> the advantages which the possession of large capital gives, which are very great, and which are growing greater and greater, inasmuch as it is the tendency of business more and more to be conducted on a large scale; these advantages are at present, not from any intention of the legislature, *but arising from things into which intention does not enter at all*, to a great degree a monopoly in the hands of the rich . . . .[8]

Had Mill but speculated on the connection between this rising economic power and the government functions necessary for its expanded accumulation, his argument in *On Liberty* might have proceeded very differently. He would at the least have had to consider the issue of liberty in the face of the growing predatory economic power of the wealthy and of its capacity to dominate and exploit those who suffered under it. And this consideration would have forced a re-assessment of Mill's crucial claim that individual liberty is warranted by the fact that the individual

> is the person *most interested in his own well-being*. The interest which any other person . . . can have in it, is trifling compared with that which he himself has . . . with respect to his own *feelings and circumstances*, the most ordinary man or woman has means of knowledge immeasurably surpassing those that can be possessed by anyone else.[9]

This passage makes a number of unsupported assertions: (1) that individuals know themselves best, (2) care *most* about their own well being, (3) and care most about their own *well-being*. Long before one engages the onslaught of *One-Dimensional Man* these claims are extremely dubious. We have no privileged awareness of our own feelings if this means anything more than the barest acquaintance, for if their source, consequence and value are included in the account, these become inseparable from "circumstances," whose knowledge depends on an understanding of the entire set of social-historical relationships in which they arise and function. This argument, in fact, is inseparable from Mill's previously discredited claim that individual and social spheres could be sharply demarcated, and that in regard to exclusive, private existence, the individual remains sovereign.

Furthermore, the claim that individuals are most concerned with their own well being is seriously flawed. First, because other powers are extremely interested in the destruction of the individual's well-being, and second, because Mill fails to distinguish an interest in one's self - however defined - from an interest in one's "well-being." To be motivated by an interest in one's gratification is wholly different from being moved to advance our "permanent interests as progressive beings." Mill was plagued by this difficulty in many of his writings, but in his argument for individual liberty the failure is wholly overwhelming. For if "self-interest" is defined in terms of qualitative hedonism, the argument may be plausible, but cannot provide what Mill needs - a justification for laissez-faire self-realization. On the other hand, if "well-being" is understood as moral perfection the argument loses all plausibility. The essence of Mill's situation lay in the fact that he was himself aware of this failure, though not its cause.

I will briefly cite evidence which could easily be reproduced at greater length:

> The primary and perennial sources of all social evils are ignorance and want of culture. These are not reached by the best contrived system of political checks, necessary as such checks are for other

purposes. There is also an unfortunate peculiarity attending these evils. Of all calamities, they are those of which the persons suffering from them are apt to be least aware. Of their bodily wants and ailments mankind are generally conscious; but the want of the mind, the want of being wiser and better, is in the far greater number of cases unfelt .... On what, then, have mankind depended, on what must they continue to be, dependent for the removal of their ignorance and of their defect of culture? Mainly, in the unremitting exertions of the more instructed and cultivated, whether in the position of the government or in a private station, to awaken in their minds a consciousness of this want and facilitate to them a means of supplying it.[10]

It might be claimed that this is a very early reflection in Mill's life. But forty years later he noted again:

Now, the proposition that the consumer is competent judge of the commodity, can be admitted only with numerous statements and exceptions . . . there . . . are . . . things, of the worth of which the demand of the market is by no means a test; things of which the utility does not consist in ministering to the inclinations, nor in serving the daily uses of life, and *the want of which is least felt where the need is its greatest*. This is particularly true of those things which are chiefly useful as tending to raise the character of human beings. The uncultivated cannot be competent judges of cultivation. Those who must need to be made wiser and better, usually desire it least, and, if they desired it, would be incapable of finding the way to it by their own lights.[11]

With these reflections Mill approaches a recognition of the existence of ideology, a pervasively structured false consciousness which falls between the want and need as a malicious shadow obscuring freedom. But he cannot proceed any further, and the tones of this passage, which bear a strong resemblance to themes prevalent in Marcuse, do not elaborate themselves more deeply throughout the course of Mill's argument. He is brought to the limit of his insight because he is pressed against a basic failure of liberal capitalism, a position he came to criticize, but could not finally reject. Having begun with the contention that individuals contribute most to the general happiness by being left alone, he was forced to the contrary position that they must be protected by an elite from the consequences of their moral ignorance and lassitude. Obviously, the argument for freedom of expression and inquiry are left without foundation.

What lurks in Mill's argument is an awareness that "choice" does not lead to self-realization, but to its denial. This recognition, however, vitiates the very core contention of Mill's credo, that

it is the privilege and proper condition of a human being arrived at the maturity of his faculties, to use and interpret experience in his own way.[12]   He who lets the world, or his own portion of it choose his plan of life for him, has no need of any of the faculty than ape-like imitation.[13]

However, Mill's tragic insight into the disparity of want and need negates his reliance on freedom as a means to self-perfection and throws the entire argument into disarray.   Nor is the issue of theoretical interest alone. For according to Mill men and women enjoyed considerable freedom in middle 19th century England, so that the choices they enacted, without fundamental interference, spoke empirically of their actual "self-determination."   In fact, the mass of

> present individuals are lost in the crowd . . . . Those whose opinions go by the name of public opinion, are not always the same sort of public . . . But they are always a mass, that is to say, collective mediocrity . . . I do not assert that anything better is compatible, as a general rule, with the present low state of the human mind. But that does not hinder the government of mediocrity from being a mediocre government.[14]

The "choices" made by this "collective mediocrity" reveal their *refusal of self-realization*, the crucial disconfirmation of Mill's deepest conviction:

> The spirit of improvement is not always a spirit of liberty, for it may aim at forcing improvements on an unwilling people . . . but the only unfailing and permanent source of improvement is liberty, since by there are so many *possible independent centers of improvement as there are individuals.*[15]

It is perfectly clear at   this point how vain and desperate a wish this last assertion expresses. A "collective mediocrity" reveals precisely the absence of "independent centres of improvement," and confirms exactly how deeply the denial of improvement has insinuated itself into the structure of public life and discourse.   It is little wonder then, that Mill was attracted to the same solution that persistently intrigued Marcuse:

> No government by a democracy of a numerous aristocracy . . . ever did or could rise above a mediocrity, except in so far as the sovereign.   Many have let themselves be guided . . . by the counsels of a more highly gifted and instructed one of few.[16]

Perhaps the elite will save the masses? But should they in historical circumstances be willing and competent to succeed in such a task, they certainly cannot fulfill the mission within the strictures of Mill's passion for individual self-determination.   Nor are they likely to win mass approval for their ideal standardship, for in regard to genius ". . . all, at heart, think they can do very well without it."[17] But worse still, when Mill later came to examine the proposition that the mass could in fact entrust their perfection to a superior elite he was forced to a severe and compelling conclusion:

> All privileged and powerful classes, as such, have used their power in the interest of their own selfishness, and indulged their self-importance in despising, and not in lovingly caring for, those who were in their estimation, degraded, by being under the necessity of working for their benefit.[18]

It is important to note Mill's explanation for the growing perversion of mass society before concluding our critique. It is his contention that "the circumstances which surround different classes and individuals, and shape their characters, are daily becoming more assimilated."[19] The different social ranks, previously inhabiting their own worlds, now read, hear, see, feel and act in similar ways. And this, because of the leveling influences in education, means of communication and "commerce and manufacture."[20] Mill has moved to adopt this fantasy because the alternative, which he did occasionally entertain, was not an alternative whose consequences he could embrace.

Mill knew quite well that the predominant character of the British educational system was its division of private and public education along rigid class lines. The forms of communication and manufacture only strengthened this portrait of class domination. The victorian "middle class" did not number more than 200,000 persons out of a population of 24 million, three quarters of whose population belonged to the "manual labor class." When Booth and Rowntree surveyed British life at the end of the 19th century, they noted that forty percent of the working class lived in what was then regarded as poverty, ". . . a miserable mass of whom two thirds would, at some time or other in their lives - generally in old age - become actual paupers."[21] But there are numerous passages in Mill's writings which testify to the same point:

> The generality of labourers in this and most countries has as little choice of occupation or freedom of locomotion, are practically as dependent on fixed rules and the will of others, as they could be on any system short of actual slavery.[22]

Mill's description hardly characterizes "assimilation" or "diffusing more widely the advantages of easy circumstances."[23] Mill confuses two radically different tendencies: 1) equalization, and 2) the growing integration of large areas of social life into the hegemony of capitalist social relations. So for all of his often heroic struggle Mill never related the "fatiguing and exhausting" work of the great majority of British subjects to their "mass mediocrity."

I cannot resist quoting a passage from Marx which puts the entire issue in proper perspective:

> To the continentals, originality or individuality are the features of the insular John Bull. By and large this image confuses the

Englishman of the past with the Englishman of today. The rapid growth of classes, the exceptionally advanced division of labor and so-called "public opinion" in the hands of the Brahamans of the press, have, on the contrary, produced a monotony of character in which Shakespeare, for example, would not recognize his countrymen. The differences do not belong to individuals, but to the "professions" and classes - apart from their professions, in every day life, one "respectable" Englishman is so like another that even Leibnitz would find it difficult to discover any differences, and *differential specifica* among them.[24]

Bourgeois individuality and diversity of action and opinion were the consumatory mask of growing capitalist centralization. If this were the case in Mill's time, how much more insidious is the influence today. It is left to such analyses as Marcuse's *One-Dimensional Man* to reveal the full weight of late capitalist hegemony. But a fundamental point which emerges from Mill's classic essay suggests that freedom and equality are indissolubly linked, and that it is only when a people is engaged, as equal members of a practicing commonwealth in a life of critical self-production, that they can be expected to employ their energies, sensitivities and interests to the realization of their nature.

Liberalism could not successfully resolve the problem of democracy. Its adherence to capitalist power maintained a system of exploitation which deformed and exhausted human labor and life at their productive source. It then mystified this domination through ideological adherence to liberal values in the schools, courts, media, bureaucratic structures and "popular" culture. It was little wonder that liberal optimism turned to despair and whether in Weber's "idealism" or the "behavioral" "political science" of American theory, the still "pristine" values of Rousseau or Mill were revealed as naive speculations.

But whereas, for classical liberalism, the fundamental political question concerned the right of others to interfere with the satisfaction of the needs of the individual, for Marcuse and critical theory the new insidious question concerned the manner in which the very satisfaction by individuals of their own needs interfered with and even destroyed the possibility of their human survival. Between Mill's question and Marcuse's lay a century of capitalist reproduction, expansion, ever increasing accumulation and sophistication of technological dominance, bureaucratic control and ideological hegemony. The threat to the individual no longer derived from some powerful and malicious "other," but from one's self, one's "second nature," the form of social exploitation reproduced within the individual and misconceived as individual freedom. It is unnecessary to review here the argument by which Marcuse establishes the contention that "Capitalism reproduces itself by transforming itself, and this transformation is mainly in the improvement of exploitation."[25] The fact that domination is compensated, de-sublimated and mystified by "previously unknown comforts" does not contradict the essential thesis, but merely underscores the severity of the situation - the minimal awareness among the people of its own deterioration. The new domination infects the nature of needs themselves, and with the universalization of false needs the difficulty is confronted in its most portentious form:

> Does labor cease to be debilitating if mental energy increasingly replaces physical energy in producing the goods and services which sustain a system that makes hell of large areas of the globe. An affirmative answer would justify any form of oppression which keeps the populace calm and content; while a negative answer would deprive the individual of being the judge of his own happiness.[26]

The more radically the doctrine of false needs is pressed, the more difficult it becomes for Marcuse to avoid the necessity of an elite that would substitute for the individual as "the judge of his own happiness . . . ." For while Marcuse understands Marx to have championed the proletariat precisely because it was free of the repressive needs of capitalism and was not dominated by those of the older society, today, he maintains that the "working class" no longer rebels against, or even comprehends that its needs are self-destructive, and that its first priority is the negation of its presently formed existence.[27]

Over and over Marcuse confronts the same doleful dilemma: a rupture with present self-destructive needs must precede the revolution which is to introduce a free society, but such a rupture can only be envisioned in and through a revolution in need; a revolution which would disclaim "destructive productivity" for a qualitatively different form of life.[28] The transformation of needs must both precede and follow a revolution which must itself precede and follow a transformation of needs. And it is merely a short step to the same vicious stasis manifesting itself on the political level: if current "toleration" is maintained, the status of dehumanizing "pseudo-democracy" is confirmed; but if "toleration" is destroyed, an "anti-democratic" elite is required and a free society itself becomes unthinkable. It will certainly disturb a number of Marcuse's admirers to realize that he has periodically raised the issue of a "transitional dictatorship" in a most serious way; but it is not a surprise which arises from the character of his theory.[29] And it is not an alternative he rejects a priori as violating fundamental principles of a socialist society, but rather a question of "whether the dictatorial means are adequate to *attain the end, namely, liberation.*[30] In the "Repressive Tolerance" the general question is given its most compressed reply.

Tolerance is defined as "an end in itself. The elimination of violence, and the reduction of suppression to the extent required for protecting man and animals from cruelty and aggression are preconditions for the creation of a human society."[31] Apparently, the precondition is identified with its end, another version of the transformative dilemma we have already encountered. But if genuine tolerance is defined as the elimination of suppression, Marcuse views today's form of tolerance as a necessary adjunct to the maintenance of suppression. For tolerance is extended precisely to those movements which impede the creation of a free, peaceful society. So, in an echo of Mill, Marcuse states that "This sort of tolerance strengthens the tyranny of the majority against which authentic liberals protested."[32]

If genuine tolerance means the elimination of violence, defined as force or the threat of force, and suppression, defined as domination of others through the alienation of character and consciousness, then it apparently requires a freely chosen society of equals. However, Marcuse maintains that today's suppressed capitalist populations are mystified by the affluent cohesion of the whole, so that which is evil appears to them as good. The traditional liberal challenge to this assertion is likely to demand a standard by which to judge this "apparent" evil, and the designation of some authority who can be entrusted to comprehend and apply it. The whole corpus of Marcuse's writing is an answer to the first part of the question and need not be recapitulated here. But in regard to the second point Marcuse is frank "The author is fully aware that, at present, no power, no authority, no government exists which would translate liberating tolerance into practice . . . ."[33] This does not lead him to reject the necessity of exploring a possibly utopian solution, and in this connection he seems to me correct. But it is important to keep several factors in mind: thus far Marcuse does not distinguish between thought and practice (the heart of the classical liberal position) identifying, "policies, attitudes (and) opinions"; and he draws a ubiquitous and radically novel picture of current suppression in which the evil previously opposed by social orders struggling for freedom has now been traced to the very self-destructive and mystified populations themselves.

In light of this last point Marcuse characteristically views even progressive movements as means of their own inversion. The exercise of political opposition "in a society of total administration" only testifies to the "existence of democratic liberties which, in reality, have changed their content and lost their effectiveness."[34] But of course the practice of such oppositional liberties remains a "precondition for the restoration of their original oppositional function."[35] In fact, the significance of tolerance, in regard to its effectiveness and value, depends upon the social context in which it is exercised; and the most vital aspect of that context is the extent to which the equality of the citizenry is prevalent. So we have to make a fundamental addition to the original definition of tolerance, which is now to be understood as an end in itself only when it is truly *universal*, a condition which Marcuse views as incompatible with violence and destruction.

This last requirement of universality is vital to the argument, for it forces us to recast the meaning of previously asserted "political liberties." Although Marcuse does not sufficiently articulate his own argument its logic appears to me to be clear; political rights (including both speech and practice) are dialectically progressive to the extent to which they contribute to the equalization of power, and politically regressive in so far as they encourage, sustain and mystify the nature of domination. This is to transfer the liberal requirement for freedom and equality in the marketplace of ideas to a demand for freedom and equal power in the "marketplace" itself. Once again, whether Marcuse fully intended this point or not, the argument seems to me persuasive. A successful theory of tolerance requires the elimination of domination, in all its forms.

From this perspective the difference between Marcuse's position and that of traditional liberalism is strikingly clear. For liberalism, the exercise of toleration, freedom of speech, political rights and the guarantee of dissent are the only legitimate means which may be used to effect a distribution of power. Speech precedes practice. For the counter-argument employed by Marcuse, however, speech is genuinely free only to the extent that it arises from an already established liberating practice among equals. Practice precedes speech. It is instructive at this point to note a passage from Lenin's comment on the elections to the Russian Constituent Assembly of 1917:

> The opportunist gentlemen, among them the followers of Kautsky, are "instructing" the people, in mockery of Marx's teaching, that the proletariat must first achieve a majority by means of universal suffrage, then on the basis of such a majority vote take over the government, and only then proceed to organize socialism on the foundation of this "progressive" (others say "pure") democracy but we speak from the vantage-ground of Marxist doctrine and the experience of the Russian Revolution: the proletariat must first overthrow the bourgeoisie and conquer for *itself* the power of state, then use this power - i.e. the dictatorship of the proletariat - as an instrument of its own class for the purpose of winning the sympathies of a majority of the toilers.[36]

What Lenin rightly insists upon is the predominant influence of the actual structure of power upon the function of political speech and persuasion. And Marcuse has often made his own version of this point. In *One-Dimensional Man*, he notes that he is often accused of overrating the power of the media to indoctrinate capitalist populations.

> The objection misses the point. The preconditioning does not start with the mass production of radio and television and with the centralization of their control - the people enter this stage as preconditioned receptacles of long standing.[37]

The problem of ideology does not thus diminish in importance. It merely moves to a more insidious ground, for "today the ideology is in the process of production itself."[38] The classical liberal view tends to regard the public as an impartial screen upon which conflicting views struggle, under conditions of rough equality, to etch themselves through sheer persuasion, upon popular consciousness. And Marcuse too insists that utmost impartiality, "equal treatment of competing and conflicting issues is indeed a basic requirement for decision-making in the democratic process."

> But in a democracy with totalitarian organization, objectivity may fulfill a very different function, namely, to foster a mental attitude which tends to obliterate the difference between true and false,

information and indoctrination, right and wrong.[39]

For, in fact, the decision has actually "been made" before the discussion commences. The people to whom the arguments are addressed are no *tabulae rasae*; they are indoctrinated by the conditions under which they live and think and which they do not transcend."[40]

There are several points to note here. First, the transcendental pessimism of Marcuse's absolute dictum, "which they do not transcend." It is this wholly condemnatory judgment that makes for later difficulty, as we shall see. But there is a second and more formidable objection which may be raised against Marcuse's position, namely the difficulty in establishing what it could possibly mean for a society to act as the neutral ground for genuine, impartial discourse. Now, although Marcuse tends to vitiate the strength of his own argument by occasionally accepting the possibility of impartiality, by conceding too much to liberalism, as it were,[41] the appropriate reply, as I understand it, must be the denial of the possibility of such a neutral ground for social discourse. All speech takes place in a particular social context, a structure of power, an organization of prohibitions, necessities and inducements which engage and nurture one actual human condition at the expense of other possibilities. Like Leibnitz's God, reality, as it asserts itself, relegates the myriad other merely possible worlds of being to the insubstantial status of unsuccessful competitors for existence; they may be entertained by mind, but that status will not drive the existing system from the field. Reality is always the exclusion of alternative possibilities; and social reality always deeply affects the nature, meaning and function of such speech as occurs within it, as Marcuse often correctly insists. So the question must be recast: which society makes possible the fullest emancipation of human capacities in action and thought? This is a question which Marcuse can and has addressed, if only in a general way.

We can sum up the argument at this stage by underscoring Marcuse's contention that tolerance must be understood in its historical context. Under present conditions of advanced capitalism its function is to promote passivity toward present exploitation and the continued viability of conditions and movements of destruction. Its "impartiality" protects the structure of domination. Conversely, Marcuse insists that such tolerance as enlarged freedom in the past was always intolerant toward the then given structure of repressive power.[42]

It is difficult to assess this contention for two reasons: first, and this is a crucial failure of the essay, "freedom" itself is never adequately defined. Second, since Marcuse does not distinguish clearly between speech and action, even within their historical context, he cannot distinguish properly between the mere *replacement* of one system of power by another, and a possible *enlargement* in the accompanying sphere of discourse. It is difficult to deny that the range of speech grew with the overthrow of medieval religiosity by the Enlightenment, but it is equally difficult to know how to rate the scope of practical freedom in these contrasting societies.

When the historical context is underscored the question of the historical subject is necessarily raised. Even Mill maintained that his argument was only intended to apply to "human beings in the maturity of their faculties." Human beings must be "capable of being improved by free and equal discussion." Marcuse is quick to seize the implication, which he defines as "the internal connection between liberty and truth."[43] He apparently takes Mill to mean that tolerance was to be granted to human beings only to the extent that they were capable of comprehending the truth. If liberty is to be defined as self-determination, then liberty is granted so that one shall "be able to determine what to do and what not to do." I assume here that Marcuse means that we must know which judgments about the good life are true to be able to determine what we should in fact do. And yet, the subject of this purported liberty is not the "contingent, private individual" as presently existent, but the individual "capable of being free with the others."[44]

Several crucial difficulties arise at this point from what seems to me the fatal, underlying defect of Marcuse's argument. First, it is important to note that Mill does not argue that the telos of liberty is truth. In fact he maintains, quite explicitly, that "we can never be sure that the opinion we are endeavoring to stifle is false opinion; and *if we were sure, stifling it would be an evil still*"[45] (emphasis added). He has several grounds for this contention, of which the most important are the following: 1) When truth is maintained without discussion and debate, it is "held as a dead dogma, not a living truth."[46] For if "the truth" is maintained without a grasp of its proper ground, it is no different from superstition. So, Mill insists, to know only one side of the case, is, in fact, not really to know at all; for knowledge requires an understanding of the ground of one's judgment, which is impossible when one cannot refute one's opponent. When the truth is enforced, it ceases to be truth for the mind on which it is imposed. 2) But beyond this largely negative argument is a vital positive consideration, which is, perhaps, the heart of Mill's contribution to the subject:

> The human faculties of perception, judgment, discriminative feeling, mental activity and even moral preference, are exercised only in making a choice. He who does anything because it is the custom, makes no choice.[47]

The telos, or end of liberty, then, for Mill, is not at all "truth," but self-realization as constituted by the self-determined exercise of choice. This is a vital difference between Mill's argument and that of Marcuse. For the latter, since liberty is justified by the truth to which it leads, its value and claim to protection will depend upon the results which it produces. So Marcuse's position becomes identical with the old Scholastic dogma that error has no right. In replacing his earlier contention that universal toleration was an end in itself with this new claim that there is "a sense in which truth is the end of liberty," Marcuse falls beneath the achievement of Mill's essay and opens himself to the charge of despotism or totalitarianism which was so widely and passionately brought against him. For he is clearly required to nominate some elite to break the hold of one-dimensional consciousness and lead the multitude from false-consciousness to emancipation.

Now, I may seem at this point to have contradicted myself by suddenly forgetting my own critique of Mill and evaluating his argument as superior to Marcuse's. But it is necessary to remember what was actually deficient in Mill's argument. And it was not the claim that human self-realization occurs under conditions of the freest possible exchange of views. Quite the contrary. It was Mill's failure to recognize the incompatibility of this ideal with the existing conditions of capitalism that rendered his position vacuous. I did not fault Mill for commending toleration and diversity, but for ignoring the extent to which they were actually disappearing. Marcuse, on the other hand, is forced to argue for a narrowing of discourse, for whatever the intention of the defenders of "truth," their procedure must be to eliminate falsehood as it presently flourishes amongst the populace. They may regard this drastic remedy as temporary, but there can be no doubt as to its character, for it is the main contention of Marcuse's essay: "intolerance toward prevailing policies, attitudes, opinions."

There is a second formidable difficulty. Remember that Marcuse seized upon Mill's claim that freedom was only suitable to those "capable of being improved by free and equal discussion" to argue that the subject of this freedom is not the "contingent, private individual" *as presently existent*, but the individual "capable of being free with . . . others." The first problem here is the meaning of "capable," for it can either signify a present power, unexercised but available for realization under some set of current conditions, or a power which exists under no set of presently conceivable circumstances. It is at this point that Marcuse's denial of transcendence weighs so heavily, for since he has previously insisted that the members of capitalist countries "are indoctrinated by the conditions under which they live and think and which they do not transcend," he cannot provide any meaning to the term "capable" which would relate it to present conditions.

The difficulty here can be sharpened even further by dwelling on the denial of freedom to the "contingent, private individual as . . . he actually is or happens to be."[48] The implication of this assertion is more globally stultifying than Marcuse himself recognized. For it clearly indicates that no revolutionary transformation can be carried out on behalf of present generations of oppressed individuals. For they (we) are the presently "contingent, private" individuals, and not those, who in Marcuse's brutally austere meaning, are *capable* of freedom. So the very need and possibility of revolution are eliminated. For if present humanity is not a fit subject for freedom it cannot claim the right to revolution. Conversely, if humanity is "capable of being free with others" it no longer requires a revolution. The vicious conjunction of continually self-demanding and self-negating revolutionary requirements reasserts itself once more. This revolution cannot begin without having been consummated, nor consummated without having already occurred. Marcuse is far closer to Hegel's "real will" and Lukacs' "imputed class consciousness" than he realizes. But whereas the former could adduce a metaphysical subject on his behalf the latter was forced to rely on a secular party to dissolve the coagulation of history.

Marcuse is forced to a similar conclusion. However his elite is defined, it is clearly required. This is another necessary consequence of the view which justifies freedom by truth. Mill not only accepted vigorous disagreement as compatible with self-realization; he viewed it as a necessary precondition. But "truth" as Marcuse seems to understand the term, admits of no such contestation. Certainly not under present circumstances when it is illusion that prevails, and none so calamitously as the illusion of diversity itself. Marcuse insists that as the future free society cannot be defined, neither can its truth. But it bears its potential truth, and now, as well as then, this truth must prevail. That is why Marcuse returns in his argument to insist that tolerance finally "cannot be indiscriminate and equal with respect to the contents of expression, neither in word nor in deed."[49]

Marcuse's replies to this objection are not satisfactory. He is at his strongest in deriding the notion that indiscriminate toleration of "sense and nonsense" will lead to the truth, or that since nobody can claim the truth, all views must be regarded as equally valid. Despite liberal arguments for fallibilism or relativism as grounds for toleration, the truth is that if we know that all views are equally mistaken or capable of error we must know in principle how to correct them; if we don't, it matters very little which of them prevails. In fact, "fallibility" was not Mill's actual argument; it was rather the "corrigibility" of beliefs, their capacity to be improved, that justified the free marketplace in his estimation.

But Marcuse cannot proceed beyond this critique of capitalist democracy. For once it is acknowledged that authentic democracy requires universal access to knowledge as the ground of rational choice, we are still left sightless as to the manner of advance. Because if the capacity to distinguish between the true and the false is so wholly obliterated as Marcuse maintains, we are devoid of a reasonable subject of the required revolution. Furthermore, if social being so wholly conditions thought, an autonomous mind, that is, a mind capable of entertaining opposing possibilities,[50] would have to live in opposing societies. Since this is impossible as a simultaneous condition, Marcuse adopts the nearest conceivable possibility and argues that as thought has been indoctrinated by society under conditions of current domination, so it will have to be given information "slanted in the opposite direction,"[51] a possibility which could only claim credibility in an opposing society. But then in this new society the old possibilities would apparently have disappeared and the fitful pendulum of contradiction would, to no ultimate avail, poise on the arch of still another historical reversal. Marcuse appears to struggle valiantly and vainly against his own argument: With all its limitations and distortions, democratic tolerance is under all circumstances more humane than an institutionalized intolerance which sacrifices the rights and liberties of the living generations for the sake of future generations.[52]

Does this protect us against totalitarian domination? I think not. First, because the present contention is unsubstantiated. Doesn't democratic intolerance sacrifice the liberties of both present and future generations? Perhaps the difference lies in considerations of violence? This would have to be argued.   Direct and indirect American support of imperialism presents an extraordinary weight of violent suffering against which any alternative system would have to be balanced.   But we are even less assured as Marcuse returns immediately to insist that when appropriately subversive majorities are blocked, "their reopening may require apparently undemocratic means."[53]

> They would include the withdrawal of toleration of speech and assembly from groups and movements which promote aggressive policies, armament, chauvinism, discrimination on the grounds of race and religion, or which oppose the extension of public services, social security, medical care, etc.   Moreover, the restoration of freedom of thought may necessitate new and rigid restrictions on teachings and practices in the educational institutions . . . .[54]

The fearful detail of this proposal indicates its confusion. For Marcuse acknowledges that such a transformation, "which would amount to an upheaval . . . would presuppose that which is still to be accomplished."[55] Given Marcuse's account of massive, one-dimensional false-consciousness, it could in fact only be brought about through violence, a possibility Marcuse does not ignore.   Of course, it is one thing to renounce violence in the face of greater violence, but quite another to renounce it a priori on moral principle.   And still Marcuse cannot decide.   For on the one hand

> Robespierre's distinction between the terror of liberty and the terror of despotism, and his moral glorification of the former belongs to the most convincingly condemned aberrations, even if the white terror was more bloody than the red.

And yet,

> In terms of historical function, there is a difference between revolutionary and reactionary violence, between violence practiced by the oppressed and by the oppressors.[56]

But however this difference is defined, whether in terms of the self-negating character of revolutionary terror, by its lesser extent, or in terms of those against whom it is carried out, none of this touches the main difficulty. For even if the right to revolutionary counter-violence were granted, the question remains as to what it could accomplish.   That it could end present violence might be argued.   But what could it introduce in its place?   I have previously maintained that the strength of Marcuse's critique of current repressive tolerance lay precisely in the demand for *equal* self-determination upon which it was based.   If potentially subversive democracies can only be liberated by undemocratic means, then an elite minority must impose itself upon the larger populace, enforcing and witholding "emancipatory" alternatives of which the majority is itself ignorant.   This is the clear implication of the essay, and of much else that

Marcuse wrote in the last decade of his life. But then, if it is true that "the function and value of tolerance depends on the equality prevalent in the society in which toleration is practiced"[57] and it is also true that present society is unequal and could only be transformed by a superior elite, it follows that "intolerance" cannot be employed as a means to further an appropriately tolerant society. Appeal to an elite is appeal to the negation of genuine tolerance itself. As Andrew Arato has noted in his reflections on Marcuse's endorsement of Bahro's appeals to forced equalizations, "the only possible road to this form of equality vitiates equality on the political level. The result can only be achieved with the strengthening of repressive, bureacratic institutions of execution and enforcement, and a bureaucracy is by definition not the equal in power to those it administers."[58] Moving the discussion to Marcuse's position on Bahro does change the context, but it does not alter the principle. Rather it clarifies its implications by pointing to the need which follows from the logic of Marcuse's argument for an elite to initiate the equalization of power. But its own relationship to the proposed transformation is the fatal defect in the position.

Who is qualified to lead this new movement, "to make all these distinctions, definitions, identifications for the society as a whole?" Everyone "who has learned to think rationally and autonomously . . . the democratic educational dictatorship of free men."[59] However, Marcuse notes that where "society has entered the phase of total domination, this would be a small number indeed."[60] This last recognition understandably draws all the accusations of practical impossibility which it deserves: How can any such minority make a revolution? If it were possible, wouldn't it be unnecessary; if necessary, impossible? Doesn't the argument itself justify those with present power in further curtailing such opposition as exists, etc?

But the greatest practical difficulty still remains. How, in principle, can an elite exercising violence (even were the success of this possibility imaginable) succeed in fostering the rational self-determination of a massively mystified, passively "comfortable self-destructive population. Marcuse himself has insisted:

> No matter how rationally one may justify revolutionary means in terms of the demonstrable chance of obtaining freedom and happiness for future generations, and thereby justify violating existing rights and liberties and life itself, there are forms of violence and suppression which no revolutionary situation can justify because they negate the very end for which the revolution is a means.[61]

It is extremely difficult to escape the conclusion that the only kind of revolution which an elite minority could carry on against a resistant majority would indeed negate "the very end for which the revolution is a means."

It might be thought that I am taking Marcuse too literally in these points. I think not. He himself asserts that "Liberating tolerance, then, would mean intolerance against movements of the Right, and toleration of movements of the Left."[62] In this country the remark implies "intolerance" of the majority. And the seriousness of Marcuse's intention is borne out by his rejection of the traditional distinction between speech and action for "clear and present danger seems no longer adequate to a stage where the whole society is in the situation of a theatre audience when somebody cries, fire."[63]

The example seems confused. It is not the crying of "fire" but the setting of fire we seem so dangerously exposed to. And Marcuse does not seem to me to help his argument when he invokes the often repeated claim that "the speeches of the fascist and Nazi leaders were the immediate prologue to the massacre."[64] It was not the privilege of speech that established the power of Nazi barbarism. The members and hirelings of the party were treated with impunity while they committed assault, arson, violence and murder against trade unions, radicals, Jews and opponents of all variety. A society which cannot restrain criminal action has already disintegrated beyond the point where its remedy lies in curtailing speech. Had they been punished for their acts, their speech alone would have been ineffective. Shorn of the power they exercised through intimidation and the destruction of opposition, their speech could not have ushered in the massacre at all. Since the present stage of our history indicates that it is precisely the forces of reaction who have the power to violate individual safeguards of thought and action, the very argument for such an option can only be employed to destroy movements for emancipation. So the argument is not only theoretically defective, but practically dangerous, if not suicidal. "The small and powerless minorities"[65] are likely to bear the painful consequences of this position while the actual elites of corporate, military and bureacratic power continue to dominate a mass population only too susceptible to appeals for the elimination of possible subversion.

What is valid in Marcuse's argument remains his insistence on the need to create "the mental space for denial and reflection." But the strategy for this creation must employ the basic commitment to the universality of tolerance which Marcuse earlier alluded to and then seemed to negate. The appeal to elites only breaks the power of equal emancipation and leaves the oppositional minority without a ground in justice. If we could impose equality, we would have to impose the consciousness of the need for equality and of the need for freedom and of the meaning of emancipation itself. But such imposition would of course destroy its own telos, for the mind cannot, as Mill rightly insisted, be forced to recognition. It can however be drawn toward its own recognition of the necessity of emancipation by such discourse as can articulate its latent needs and speak in the voice of its thwarted enterprise. So, finally, the issue turns on whether there is such an inhibited desire among the oppressed population, such a need for self-transformation as will respond in passion to the eliciting of its prefigured realization.

Obviously, Marcuse has often addressed this issue. In *An Essay on Liberation* for example, a central chapter is devoted to "Subverting Forces - in Transition," in which current movements in technology, particularly the replacement of physical by mental energy, the potentialities of automation for freeing "the play of the productive imagination," the technical transformation of nature, the weakening of repressive social forces through commodification, and other such changes are noted. However Marcuse notes quite clearly that the major impetus for dissatisfaction - the separation between the present destructive tendencies of an oppressive society and the ideal hopes unleashed by growing mastery over nature - remain confined to the limbo of potentiality. In fact, this fissure between actual exploitation and possible emancipation produces also a "diffused aggressiveness" which can be turned against a number of "defined enemies," as likely of the Left as of the Right. Marcuse refuses to predict the outcome of current tendencies. His statement in *One-Dimensional Man* seems to me to hold throughout his later work, however much the stress on it may vary from one particular expression to another.

> One-Dimensional Man will vacillate throughout two contradictory hypotheses: (1) that advanced industrial society is capable of containing qualitative change for the foreseeable future: (2) that forces and tendencies exist which may break this containment and explode the society.[66]

An analysis and evaluation of this crucial tension in Marcuse's work is clearly beyond the scope of the present essay.   I simply note in conclusion those areas toward which critical scrutiny need to be directed.   I certainly have no intention here of admonishing Marcuse for difficulties which remain unsolved along the entire spectrum of Left positions.
  1. Is there an adequate analysis of the movements, tendencies and underlying structures of capitalism? Marcuse often refers to the capitalist system and to significant changes which it is undergoing.   At times, however, as in *One-Dimensional Man*, his account is not significantly different from standard bourgeois explanations of the period. When his own account does become more novel and exploratory, it tends to become eclectic and fragmentary.   He can in the same essay refer at one moment to the "ever-increasing productivity of labor," and at another to capitalism producing "the objective conditions for its own abolition (structural unemployment, saturation of the market, inflation, inter-capitalist conflicts, competition with communism . . .)."[67]   It is of vital interest to know how these tendencies will develop or decline, but Marcuse leaves the situation in this contradictory state.
  2.   Closely related to this issue is the question of the revolutionary subject as Marcuse seeks it out in various strata and interest groups in the capitalist world. Students, intellectuals, women, hippies, members of third-world minorities or even majorities in other countries have all been suggested for the role.   One often has the sense that these categories have not been adequately related to changing capitalist structures, particularly the nature of class, and that they consequently remain too heterogeneous and contingent as revolutionary social subjects.   Marcuse sometimes seems to operate with a distinction between those who have not yet been incorporated into the capitalist system as against others who have already

passed beyond it.[68]   But the account is not sufficently clarified.   And in
regard to particular groups, such as women, it is not merely that political
tendencies run in various and conflicting directions, but that one needs to
understand whether the very revolutionary potential of the group is not
intimately tied to the form of its oppression under capitalism.[69]   At times,
in fact, Marcuse goes so far as to seek the revolutionary subject in "the
consciousness of individuals from all strata . . . who despite all differences
constitute a potential unity by virtue of their common interest"[70] - an
account which seems to deny any social analysis whatever.

3.   In a parallel move Marcuse has often sought out particular human
agencies - intellectual work, play, memory, imagination, erotic activity, as
human functions which have escaped the exploitation of commodified
labor.   He has attempted to discover some enclave of the spirit "a haven
in a heartless world" where we might discover a source of human
regeneration."[71]   But it is unlikely that any aspect of our nature can
defend itself against what Marcuse himself has on other occasions cogently
described as total intrusion of capitalist domination.   The path out of
capitalism, to cite Marcuse himself once again, must be through the
institutions of this society and not beyond them.

4.   If any such movement is conceivable, the power of false
consciousness becomes the fundamental issue.   There are two themes in
Marcuse's work which call for a much fuller discussion.

The first concerns the ability of capitalism to bind the unhappiness of its
members; or differently stated, to produce conditions of exploitation in
which unhappiness does not arise.   Over and over in his writings Marcuse
can refer to capitalism as producing "an ever-more-comfortable life,"
"freedom from want . . . becoming a real possibility," "the administered life
is the comfortable and even the 'good' life" and finally assert that "loss of
conscience due to the satisfactory liberties granted by an unfree society
makes for a *happy consciousness* which facilitates acceptance of the
misdeeds of this society."   And yet, typically, on the same page as the last
citation, Marcuse can also assert that "there is pervasive unhappiness, and
the happy consciousness is shaky enough - a thin surface over fear,
frustration and disgust."[72]   The difference between an unhappiness
immune even to its own self-consciousness, and a "pervasive unhappiness,
seems to me absolutely critical.   The first is without apparent remedy; the
second offers grounds for provocation, articulation and redirection.

The second major issue at this point concerns Marcuse's constant
insistence on an "instinctual" foundation for transcendence.   I have
criticized this unfortunate dependency on Freudian metapsychology
elsewhere[73] and merely return to make a final point.   To the extent to
which "an emancipatory instinctual structure"[74] is sought as the agency of
social transformation, we are, I believe, fated to languish without hope.
We have no instinct for emancipation, as the history of human oppression
indicates. If however Marcuse intends by the term "instinct" and by his
concept of "biological" or "organic need" for freedom a thoroughly
historical and socially constituted tendency, it would be far better to part
company with Freud and articulate a truly social theory of human desire.
What we require for our transformation does not already exist, buried

beneath our immediate surface in some prefashioned "archeological" agency. Those historically transcendent concepts[75] to which Marcuse sometimes refers are not existent movements but as yet unrealized values. It is perfectly true that articulation must appeal to some "hidden remnant" for its agency. But it is finally the capacity to *form*ulate a new vision which will direct whatever potentiality exists for freedom. The telos of freedom remains self-perfection in a community with equals, as Marcuse himself insisted at the most significant moments of his own exploration. Marcuse's work itself testifies to the capacity of human beings to create the novel conditions of their own transcendence.

NOTES

1. Herbert Marcuse, *One-Dimensional Man* (Boston, 1964), pp. xv, 1, 4-8, 11, 29, 40-41, 76. *Five Lectures* (Boston, 1970), pp. 79-80. *An Essay on Liberation* (Boston, 1969), pp. 4, 13, 14, 17-18, 49, 64, 68-70. "Ethics and Revolution," in *Ethics and Society*, ed. Richard T. de George. "Protosocialism and Late Capitalism: Toward a Theoretical Synthesis Based on Bahro's Analysis," in *Rudolf Bahro: Critical Responses*, ed. Ulf Wolter.
2. Marcuse, "Repressive Tolerance," in Robert Paul Wolff, Barrington Moore, Jr., and Herbert Marcuse, *A Critique of Pure Tolerance*, p. 81.
3. Richard K. Ullman, *Tolerance and Intolerance*, p. 2.
4. Harold J. Lasky, *The Rise of European Liberalism*, p. 61.
5. See Richard Lichtman, "The Facade of Equality in Liberal Democratic Theory," *Inquiry* 12 (1969), pp. 170-208.
6. John Stuart Mill, "On Liberty," in *The Philosophy of John Stuart Mill*, ed. Marshall Cohen (New York, 1961), p. 197.
7. John Locke, *Second Treatise on Government*, #27.
8. John Stuart Mill, Testimony in *Report from the Select Committee on Investments for the Savings of the Middle and Working Classes*, pp. 79-80.
9. "On Liberty," p. 273.
10. John Stuart Mill, *Dissertations and Discussions*, p. 28.
11. John Stuart Mill, *Principles of Political Economy*, p. 953.
12. "On Liberty," p. 251.
13. *Ibid.*, p. 252.
14. *Ibid.*, p. 261.
15. *Ibid.*, p. 266.
16. *Ibid.*, p. 261.
17. *Ibid.*, p. 260.
18. *Principles of Political Economy*, p. 754.
19. "On Liberty," p. 269.
20. *Ibid.*, p. 270.
21. E. J. Hobsbawm, *Industry and Empire*, vol. 2, 1750 to the Present Day, p. 134.
22. *Principles of Political Economy*, p. 210.
23. "On Liberty," p. 270.
24. Cited in Eduard Urbanek, "Rules, Masks and Characters," in *Marxism and Sociology*, ed. Peter Berger, p. 199.

25. *An Essay on Liberation*, p. 13.

26. *Ibid.*, pp. 13-14.

27. *Five Lectures*, p. 70.

28. *An Essay on Liberation*, pp. 18-19, *Five Lectures*, p. 80.

29. "Ethics and Revolution," pp. 137ff., *Essay on Liberation*, pp. 64ff., p.70.

30. "Ethics and Revolution," p. 138.

31. "Repressive Tolerance," p. 82.

32. *Ibid.*

33. *Ibid.*, p. 81.

34. *Ibid.*, p. 84.

35. *Ibid.*

36. Cited in Oliver Henry Radkey, *The Election of the Russian Constituent Assembly of 1917*, p. 7.

37. *One-Dimensional Man*, p. 8.

38. *Ibid.*, pp. 11, 29. Also, see Richard Lichtman, "Marx's Theory of Ideology," *Socialist Revolution* 23 (1975), pp. 45-76.

39. "Repressive Tolerance," p. 97.

40. *Ibid.*, p. 98.

41. *Ibid.*, pp. 97ff. (but also p. 99), pp. 112-113.

42. *Ibid.*, p. 85.

43. *Ibid.*, pp. 86, 90.

44. *Ibid.*, p. 87.

45. "On Liberty," p. 205.

46. *Ibid.*, p. 225.

47. *Ibid.*, p. 252.

48. "Repressive Tolerance," p. 86.

49. *Ibid.*, p. 88.

50. As Marcuse seems to recognize on page 90.

51. *Ibid.*, p. 99.

52. *Ibid.*

53. *Ibid.*, p. 100.

54. *Ibid.*

55. *Ibid.*, p. 101.

56. *Ibid.*, p. 103; see also *Five Lectures*, p. 89.

57. *Ibid.*, p. 84.

58. Andrew Arato in his review of *Rudolf Bahro: Critical Responses*, *Telos*, no. 48 (Summer 1981), pp. 153-67, 163.

59. "Repressive Tolerance," p. 106.

60. *Ibid.*

61. "Ethics and Revolution," p. 141.

62. "Repressive Tolerance," p. 109.

63. *Ibid.*

64. *Ibid.*

65. *Ibid.*, p. 110.

66. *One-Dimensional Man*, p. xv.

67. "Protosocialism and Late Capitalism," pp. 27, 41.

68. *Five Lectures*, p. 75.

69. See Joan B. Landes, "Marcuse's Feminist Dimension," *Telos*, no.

41 (Fall 1979), pp. 158-65.

70. "Protosocialism and Late Capitalism," p. 39.
71. As in *Eros and Civilization*, for example.
72. *One-Dimensional Man*, pp. 1, 5-8, 23, and particularly 76.
73. Richard Lichtman, *The Production of Desire*.
74. "Protosocialism and Late Capitalism," p. 45.
75. This seems to me the intent of the passage on page 96 of *Five Lectures*.

PART VI

□□□□□□□□□□

THE TECHNOLOGICAL DIMENSION

The critique of technology plays a central role in Marcuse's later work. Technology contains both the possibility of liberation through an end to the struggle for existence, and the threat of ever more effective repression of the individual. "One-Dimensional" society is above all a technological society, integrated through the achievements of technology and through a new kind of legitimating ideology arising on the basis of technical forms of thought. This society effectively suppresses the consciousness of opposition in the vast majority of the population, including the working class.

This Marcusean critique of technology poses foundational problems for Marxism discussed by Offe in the first chapter of this section. The critical theory of society has always rejected the idea of a transcendental foundation and instead based itself on actual historical interests. These interests may be latent for a time, but in the end it is their empirical manifestation which demonstrates that the critique is not merely arbitrary or idealistic. Marcuse's concept of "one-dimensionality" converges, Offe charges, with the "technocracy thesis" of writers who believe history has ended finally in a perfectly integrated technological universe. On these terms the latency of opposition is no longer temporary but derives in principle from the structure of society. Offe concludes that Marcuse's formulation of critical theory undermines its own basis.

Feenberg's chapter is an attempt to distinguish and reconstruct the various strands of Marcuse's later critique of technology. Feenberg shows that Marcuse has in fact two separate critiques of technology, one Marxist and the other "ontological," which coexist in his works and complement each other. His chapter concludes with a discussion of Marcuse's hypothesis that a socialist society would eventually create a "new technology" corresponding to emancipatory demands.

CHAPTER ELEVEN

Technology
And One-Dimensionality:
A Version of the Technocracy Thesis?

Claus Offe

Translated by Anne-Marie Feenberg

I

Marcuse's object of study is industrial society, a type of society that is distinguished from all others by the level of technical rationalization it has achieved. The dominant structural elements of industrial societies have become the scientific organization of production and service technology and rational administrative practice based on the application of impersonal rules by a hierarchy of cooperating experts. The "spirit of capitalism," which first revolutionized production through methodical calculation in the sphere of means, has spread throughout all spheres of social life. In its modern form, it also includes manipulated leisure consumption, petrified party machines, alienated labor and the gigantic military machinery of annihilation.

Marcuse's analysis of the "one-dimensionality" of industrial society amounts to the diagnosis that definite qualitative changes have arisen out of this *process of diffusion* of technical rationality. To be sure, the practice of an industrial society which commands both men and things indiscriminately is historically derived from the process of the exploitation of capital and from the dominant interests sustaining it in the mature phase of capitalist development. However, in the present phase of the universal technicization of life, it is no longer possible to recognize clearly the *capitalist* origins and conditions of this process of rationalization in each of its manifestations.

In the perspective of Max Weber's concept of capitalism, Marcuse refers to the continuity between the instrumental rationality of mature capitalism and the structural principle of modern "technological society": "Reason, as seen by Max Weber, is revealed as technical reason: the production and transformation of materials (both things and people) by a methodical and scientific apparatus set up with productivity as its goal; its rationality organizes and controls things and people, the factory and civil service bureaucracy, work and leisure."[1] The constant accumulation of abstract functional procedures seems to have led to a social situation in which technology is no longer clearly subordinated to a particular interest in the realization of capital; economic exploitation tends gradually to dissolve in abstract totalitarian control. Marcuse suggests an interpretation of the social process of rationalization according to which bureaucracy and technology have been released from the control of particular interests and have themselves become institutions of domination. No longer a purely "neutral" potential for power, abstract rationality expands into the total structure of society; the dominant technological system no longer possesses the transparency it once derived from its definite orientation towards the interests of certain social classes or groups.

Marcuse has three, mutually independent systematic arguments for this diagnosis:

1. Scientific rationality as such has become the organizational principle of domination. Inhuman administrative and manipulative intentions infect the system not just in the concrete goals for which technology is *employed* but even prior to that in the very origins of the *production* of technology at the level of basic scientific research. "Science has become in itself technological . . . . To the degree to which this operationalism becomes the center of the scientific enterprise, rationality assumes the form of methodical construction, of organization and handling of matter as the mere stuff of control, as instrumentality which lends itself to all purposes and ends . . . . Scientific rationality results in a specific societal organization precisely because it projects mere form . . . which can be bent to practically all ends. Formalization and functionalization are, *prior* to all application, the "pure form" of a concrete societal practice . . . . It is my purpose to demonstrate the *internal* instrumentalist character of this scientific rationality by virtue of which it is *a priori* technology and the *a priori* of a *specific* technology - namely, technology as form of social control and domination."[2]

Marcuse's critique of technical rationality is not so much based on its relation to the capitalist system of appropriation as on a direct critique of the scientific formalism which underlies technology. As formal rationality it is neutral in contrast to the immediate relation to the objects of outer nature determined by needs or aesthetic considerations. The indifference with which the sciences' instrumentalist procedures screen from us the practical significance of natural objects, shows them to be disinterested in the pacification of the struggle for existence, and incapable of understanding their objects as the raw material of needs. This indifference makes scientific rationality per se into an instance of repression.[3] Just as formal-rational capital accounting included in its calculations the possibility of a threat to the physical existence of free - and hence destitute - proletarians, the generalized rationality of formal science reckons with the destruction of life.[4]

The insight that technique itself has become domination obliges revolutionary thought to take upon itself the project of a "new technology." Marcuse does not attempt to avoid this consequence: since "technological society's" structure of domination has become "system neutral," the mere transformation of political and economic institutions is insufficient. "A qualitative change also must include a change in the technical base," if the pacification of existence is to take place.[5] The details of this program, however, remain so unclear that it is not easy to see how Marcuse can escape the reproach of obscurantism he rejects in advance.[6] It remains to be seen whether a change in the "direction of technical progress"[7] would suffice to concretize the concept of a revolutionary technology; for the pursuit of new research *goals* would still remain closely bound by the strict rules of the empirical conception of nature, and therefore also by the repressive character of formal rationality.

In another version of this argument,[8] Marcuse anticipates the emergence of the "technology of liberation" from the revolutionary consciousness of the technical intelligentsia. Yet again, the emergence of the new technology is seen as the result of an objective process in which the progress of automation eases the burden of fatigue and suffering in work and brings about the *convergence* of work and play, technique and art, in a new construction of social labor.[9] In any case the birth of a new technology seems to be conceived only on the other side of a threshold characterized by the pacification of existence, the transformation of consciousness and the clarification of non-alienated needs. However, it is precisely technological society as a structure of domination which, according to Marcuse, blocks movement towards this threshold.

2. This is explained in the second argument which Marcuse advances for the emergence of autonomous technological rationality as a form of domination *sui generis*. Rational control over nature and bureaucratic control over the work process, either through integration or through effective repression of deviance, form the basis of the "happy consciousness" of a society that is practically unopposed. Regimentation of needs and eradication of progressive thought take place on three levels: the economic, the political and the cultural level. The progress of the productive forces and the concrete technical and organizational conditions of work have brought about a situation in which "the working class no longer represents the class possessing the negation of existing needs."[10] Its revolutionary impulse disintegrates under the conditions of greater consumption opportunities and industrial production discipline.[11] The immediate consequences for the functioning of the political system are taken up and reinforced by the social techniques of manipulation and the consciousness industry. The very *experience* of need and want, even more

its articulation at the level of political practice, is thus stifled. Finally, the domain of culture is also industrialized; esthetic expressions are robbed of their critical function and circulate as mediators of affirmative contents of consciousness.

These lines of analysis bring critical thought to a point where there is no longer any hope of finding a social group or institutional sector that could be the starting point for the progressive unfolding of contradictions. However, when it is no longer possible to identify the social-structural locus of the contradictions that nevertheless continue objectively to exist, when critique, hope and need for change are no longer represented socially, then the critical theory of industrial society is forced to safeguard the objectivity of its pronouncements on a *psychological* and *anthropological* level. The *system of needs*, the essential starting point of Marcuse's critical theory, as of every other, shifts its sources from political economy to psychoanalysis.

This change in perspective is the logical consequence of a critique which sees its object not as a late capitalist but as an industrial or "technological" society. In terms of this new definition, the front of the struggle no longer lies in the conflicts between social classes but between reified rationality and latent human need. However, this position not only ignores old problems but also raises new questions. Can one conceive of historical progress arising from the dynamic of twisted and suppressed instinctual energy as that progress was supposed to arise from the consciousness of the revolutionary class? And what mechanism will substitute for the practical learning process of crisis and class struggle postulated by the classical theory of the Left to set in motion the self-emancipation of a "happy consciousness" that is now so self-satisfied?

Marcuse identifies a dilemma that he himself cannot overcome: "How can administered individuals, who have made their mutilation into their own freedom and gratification, reproducing it on an expanded scale, free themselves *from themselves* as from their masters?"[12] "Today we are faced with the problem that the transformation is objectively necessary, but that the need for it is not even present among the strata that were classically defined for the transformation. First, the mechanisms which suppress this need must be destroyed, but that in turn presupposes a need for their destruction. This is a dialectic from which I have found no escape."[13]

3. It would also be misleading to understand today's socialist societies as examples of a liberation "from without." The system of domination in industrial societies, characterized by a perfected rationality that has silenced the sort of self-transcendence which could emerge from a practical critique, is also proof against such contradictions as could surface in the developed socialist societies of Eastern Europe. Indeed, Marcuse's concept of industrial society includes the hypothesis of an at least latent convergence between the systems in the East and West. During the Stalinist period, the Soviet industrialization process was able to block and suppress the emergence of new forms of freedom and spontaneity by employing a bureaucracy and production discipline based on Western forms of rationality in production and administration. To be sure, this

occurred in the context of a different institutional framework although with parallel results. As far as the fulfillment of human needs and the "pacification of existence," is concerned, a technically based, structurally similar system of repression appears in the West and the East.[14]

The two systems are converging not only because of their common technological substratum: also involved are the mutual interactions of peaceful coexistence, i.e. non-military, political and economic competition. The rules of participation in this competition make it impossible for the Soviet variant of industrial society to free the accumulated social wealth for utilization in a "realm of freedom." In spite of all his reservations against a formal convergence theory, Marcuse occasionally goes so far as to affirm that "there is today a collaboration between the Soviet Union and the USA that goes beyond temporary *realpolitik*, which seems to conform with the absolutely non-Marxist thesis according to which there is a community of interests uniting the rich countries against the poorer countries and which encompasses both capitalist and socialist society despite all their differences."[15] It is precisely the relatively advanced stage of industrial development of the socialist states of Eastern Europe which makes it improbable that they would be able to serve the developed capitalist countries as agents of contradiction: internally, they reproduce the same structures of repression and externally, "they are today linked with capitalism, for better or for worse, in a world system."[16]

What remains as a possible theory is a Third World strategy which would provide the non-industrialized countries not only with liberation from imperialist relations of dependency, but beyond that with an indigenous model for the process of industrialization which would avoid the repressive rationality of both the Western and Soviet type of development. Marcuse announces this proposal in a series of questions[17] without ever showing its realization to be likely. His analysis seems to say that if they are to be found anywhere, the starting points for a "post-technical" culture and society are precisely in those Third World countries that have been spared the process of industrialization, where new technology, a new anthropology, and a revolutionary "without" might be able to coincide. In the best of cases, these countries would be supported by a strategy of refusal on the part of socially marginal groups in the metropols. This vague perspective appears to be only a narrow crack in industrialism's system of domination, constituted as such through repressive rationality.

II

Marcuse's technological determinism, expressed in the three arguments outlined above, has become the starting point of the objections of Marxist critics to *One-Dimensional Man*.[18] Traditional classical Marxism is indeed confronted with an analytical model in Marcuse's theses which, I believe, shows an astounding and disquieting affinity with the conservative institutional analyses of authors such as Hans Freyer, Helmut Schelsky and Arnold Gehlen. To be sure, there can be no doubt about the opposed practical intentions by which Herbert Marcuse distinguishes himself from this group. The consensus at the analytical level is, however, sufficiently striking to raise the question of the relation between sociological analysis and practical intention in Marcuse's work itself.

First of all, here is some evidence for the idea that a profound conformity of views underlies Marcuse's analysis and the conservative "technocracy thesis." The latter is primarily concerned with the role of *science and technology* in the social system of industrialism.

1. Like Marcuse, Hans Freyer constructs a "theory of the contemporary era" on the hypothesis of the existence of a technological universe that can reach into both the inner and outer nature of man.[19] Science has become technical in its substance; the basis of modern natural and social scientific operationalism is the prior technical construction of the processes to be researched. "We only know what we can make" is the catchword recited in unison by Freyer, Gehlen and Schelsky to deal with this situation.[20]

2. Scientific-technical administration and production processes become the *dominant* element of the industrial social system in so far as their perfection and superior rationality invalidate every project that aims to transcend the system, indeed ultimately every political will. "We assert that the construction of a scientific-technical civilization institutes a new foundation of social relations in terms of which the relations of domination lose their old personal connection to the power of persons over persons. In this civilization the place of political norms and laws is taken by the laws of things, which cannot be thought of as political decisions or understood in terms of normative opinions and ideology. Thus the idea of democracy essentially loses its classical substance."[21] Whether the abdication of the practical will to change is understood as a relatively nonconflictual process, as in Schelsky, or as an objective act of violent, repressive regimentation, as in Marcuse, what is common to both positions is the diagnosis that the structure of domination in industrial society can no longer be described in the framework of a theory of class or elite, but only in terms of technological and administrative rationality.

3. Even the terminology with which these authors describe the alienated system of technologized work and domination coincides in its very nuances with that of Marcuse. Examples are the antitheses of "consumer behavior" and "autonomous self-activity," "functionalization" and the "autonomous subject of a way of life" (Freyer). To be sure, an explanation of this rhetoric in the works of Freyer, Gehlen and Schelsky would very soon reveal a normative afterthought in favor of an affirmative insertion into existing institutions (Gehlen), or correspondingly a private retreat from them (Shelsky). (A certain formal coincidence is even present in the origin of such recommendations in an anthropological biologism.) It is questionable how far Marcuse's categories of "project" and "refusal" can be distinguished in practice from this program. Quite a few marginal zones of the existing system of institutions can claim to represent "the subjective existence of man" (Schelsky), so long as the possibility of transcending the system is not concretized in a historical dimension.

4. The thesis of *post-histoire* (Gehlen)[22] enables the conservative variants of the critique of the "technological universe" to do without an initial examination of the historical dimension. The disappearance of

history in the industrial system along with the loss of future prospects grounds the dismissal of promising global alternatives in favor of technological advances and practical proposals. What remains is the opportunity to work out and complete what is given, under the assumption of its stability in principle.

World-wide systems of information, trade and weapons have joined all societies together into the world society, but at the same time they have ended world history.[23] A peculiar similarity with Marcuse's thought appears here: he too presents the thesis of "the end of history,"[24] and with the end of history he also posits "the end of utopia," its still unattainable vanishing point. Marcuse gives this thesis a technological basis, in terms of productive forces: "all the material and intellectual forces are present which must be called upon for the realisation of a free society. The fact that they are not used is wholly attributable to the total mobilisation of the existing society against its own possibilities of freedom."[25] Accordingly, the misapplied technology could become the basis of a free society if only it experienced the shock of a conscious need. This shock would be without a historical dimension; it would be a need that would shine forth like lightning, not a step in the continuum of historical progress. It would be a decision announcing vital biological, erotic and aesthetic claims and realizing them *uno actu.*

III

Our attempt to sum up the most important arguments of Marcuse's critique of the technological universe has purposely omitted a discussion of empirical arguments. Yet a series of controversial empirical criteria would have to be defined to answer such questions as: whether the potential of the empirical analytical sciences has actually shrunk to the one-dimensionality of mere classificatory knowledge; whether the manipulation of needs has really made all strata and classes integral parts of the political and economic status quo to the same extent; whether the sort of political antagonisms which promote progress show clear and obvious signs of being silenced by the spread of a framework of technological structures; and whether the potential of the available technological knowledge can seriously be considered adequate to make possible a human existence that is pacified in the strict sense and that can thus realize utopian ideas in the reality of social life. We can disregard such arguments, however, as long as we concern ourselves primarily with the strategic structure of Marcuse's critique of industrial society.

Every critical theory analyzes the existing social system from the point of view of a possible transformation of its basic structure. But it must conceive of the possibility of transformation under what might be called prerevolutionary conditions - and this in a situation where the need for change has not yet manifested itself. In this precarious situation, critical theory can only remain consistent when it succeeds in interpreting the latent character of the need for change as *temporary* and *transcendable* in practice. In other words, critical theory must include an account of its own possibility. Independently of the requirement of cogency which its empirical and sociological affirmations must meet, it is imperative for critical theory *somehow* to demonstrate that its train of thought condenses a historical process that can be initiated in practice or can be anticipated theoretically. It is this demonstration which relativizes the privilege of its knowledge.

In the tradition of classical Marxism the proletariat takes on the function of the self-foundation of theory: it can be shown that in the historical process, the proletariat both constitutes capital and negates it as a relation of production. This movement articulates the Marxist theory and the articulated theory supports and guides the theoretically conceived process. A critical theory which transcends the system authenticates its own truth by representing the concrete subjects of concrete historical situations. Therefore it must be *historical* theory, locating its historical projections on a continuum that includes history up to the present and the empirical intentions active in it.

With the "one-dimensionality" thesis, Marcuse now abandons this traditional model of critical theory. He believes he can show that the latency of the need for change is somehow not temporary, but is produced and reproduced by the system of the technological universe itself. In such a situation the model of critique and enlightenment through the interpretation of *concrete* interests and processes can no longer claim a role in the construction of the theory. The very fact of historical continuity implied in this model would pervert the critical theory into an immanent one; for this continuity would have to be based in social instances and processes which could themselves be suspected of belonging to the network of manipulation of the technological universe.

In working with the "one-dimensionality" thesis, critical theory faces a dilemma: it must either limit the hypothesis of comprehensive manipulation, conceding structural gaps in the system of repressive rationality; or it is compelled to abandon any explanation for its own possibility as thought. If the system is really totally closed to change, the vision of a liberated society becomes a mysterious privilege for whoever conceives it, insofar as he cannot trace it back to the structural conflicts and interests to which he owes it. The appeal to anthropological and biological constants also remains abstract to the extent that it is impossible to identify the spheres and institutions of the structure of industrial societies through which these constants could be articulated and realized as *social interests*; for biological needs can never immediately transform a system of institutions, but can only act via the detour of translation into changed intentions. The repression Marcuse describes has no more direct consciousness-raising effect than does plain poverty - however short the historical distance may be to the possibility of a "liberated society."

Marcuse believes that he can construct his critical theory without reference to foreseeable, manifest historical conflicts and motives because, on the one hand, manipulation is universal and on the other hand, the realization of a pacified existence is so close that only a collective decision is needed to bring it about. Since no social force capable of destroying it can be identified, the extremely fine line which separates repressive reality from promised liberation remains impossible to cross; on the other side, the smallest shock would in principle suffice to overcome it at one blow, under the assumption that the satisfaction of human needs is objectively within sight. The reality of a pacified existence is both near and far.[26]

Marcuse underestimates the historical role of practical intentions on both sides of this paradox. The historical threshold is remote because the notion of one-dimensionality is so thoroughgoing that it completely integrates practical intentions. On the other hand, the proximity of change follows from the purely technological analysis of industrial society: the network of mystifications is volatile since it is in no way anchored in the practical will of the people.

Marcuse dispenses with the notion of an *interest* that would ground the stability of the industrial system, and that could only be challenged by a practically elaborated counter-interest. As a result, he reaches the point of destroying the problematic of the possibility of a fundamental transformation of the system. By contrast, it would be possible to trace the technological universe itself back to an underlying conflict of interests. However difficult the social and structural localization of the latter might be today, nothing is gained by denying it but the loss of the historical dimension on which critical theory depends.

If it does not want to collapse into an already disintegrating immanence, critical theory, for the sake of its own internal consistency must reconstruct both the stability and the historical weakness of the industrial system of domination out of the dynamic of concrete, *socially interpreted interests*. It must not set up an immediate opposition between the external *manifestations* of interests, i.e. the technological universe, and its historically changing *substratum*, i.e. the anthropology of needs. To be sure, contemporary history is not the history of the traditional class struggle; but the contemporary form of class struggle, the analysis of which cannot be dismissed in favor of anthropological categories, continues to be the condition of history.

NOTES

1. Herbert Marcuse, "Industrialiserung und Kapitalismus im Werk Max Webers," in *Kultur und Gesellschaft ll* (Frankfurt/Main, 1965), pp. 110-111.
2. Herbert Marcuse, *One-Dimensional Man* (Boston, 1964), pp. 157-160.
3. Cf. *One-Dimensional Man*, pp. 216-217.
4. Cf. Marcuse, "Industrialiserung und Kapitalismus im Werk Max Webers," in *Kultur und Gesellschaft ll*, p. 116.
5. *One-Dimensional Man*, p. 23.
6. *Ibid.*, p. 166.
7. *Ibid.*, p. 222.
8. Herbert Marcuse, *Das Ende der Utopie* (Berlin, 1967), pp. 105-106.
9. *Ibid.*, p. 19.
10. *Ibid.*, p. 22.
11. Cf. *One-Dimensional Man*, p. 23.
12. *One-Dimensional Man*, p. 250-251; italics are mine.

13. Marcuse, *Das Ende der Utopie*, p. 61.

14. Herbert Marcuse, *Die Gesellschaftslehre des sowjetischen Marxismus,* Neuwied and Berlin, 1964), p. 87ff.; *One-Dimensional Man*, p. 55.

15. *Das Ende der Utopie*, p. 67.

16. *Ibid.*, p. 56.

17. *One-Dimensional Man*, p. 45ff.

18. Cf. for instance H. H. Holz, "Der Irrtum der 'Grossen Weigerung,'" in *Blätter für deutsche und internationale Politik* 1, (1968); P. Sedgwick, "Natural Science and Human Theory," in *The Socialist Register* 1966 (London, 1966), pp. 163-192; H. Wessel, "Die kritische Theorie bleibt negativ," in *Forum*, nos. 2-5 (1968).

19. Cf. H. Freyer, *Theorie des gegenwartigen Zeitalters.*

20. Cf. H. Freyer, *Über das Dominantwerden technischer Kategorien in der Lebenswelt der industriellen Gesellschaft*; A. Gehlen, *Die Seele im technischen Zeitalter*; and H. Schelsky, *Der Mensch in der wissenschaftlichen Zivilisation.*

21. H. Schelsky, *Der Mensch in der wissenschaftlichen Zivilisation*, pp. 21-22.

22. Cf. A. Gehlen, "*Über kulturelle Kristallisation*," in *Studien zur Anthropologie und Soziologie.*

23. Cf. *Ibid.*

24. *Das Ende der Utopie*, p. 11ff.

25. *Ibid.*, p. 14.

26. Cf. for this P. Sedgwick, "Natural Science and Human Theory," p. 169: "One's principal objection to Marcuse cannot then rest on his pessimism, but on his thoroughgoing mechanism: his hope and despair are equally based on some assumption of a constant, predeterminate technological threshold that can in itself function either to exclude or to impel the action of the class."

CHAPTER TWELVE

The Bias Of Technology

Andrew Feenberg

Neutrality and Bias: An Ambiguous Critique

Herbert Marcuse's *One-Dimensional Man* appeared in 1964, at a time when both Marxism and liberalism were unanimous in their praise for the new technological society coming into being. The appearance of Marcuse's sharp critique of technology was a surprise. It is now easy enough to attach Marcuse's ideas to a tradition of Marxist technology criticism, but at the time that current ran underground and was invisible to all but a few aficionados of 20th century intellectual history. Such soon-to-become classics as Lukacs' *History and Class Consciousness* and Adorno and Horkheimer's *Dialectic of Enlightenment* were untranslated and out of print, scarcely mentioned in the few works that noticed their existence at all.

The immediate impact of Marcuse's book was atmospheric rather than academic. It contributed to a rapidly growing climate of resistance to the technocratic dystopia feared by the newly emerging cultural and political opposition of the 1960s. Marcuse's name became a symbol of these oppositional currents and, in response, his ideas were attacked as anti-technological and anti-scientific. This was the real scandal of *One-Dimensional Man*, which outraged readers on the right and the left even more by its critique of progress than by its social and political radicalism.

In this chapter, I propose to re-examine Marcuse's critique of technology from a distance, so to speak, outside the context of its time and the debates it sparked, strictly in terms of its theoretical contribution. I will show that Marcuse's critique of technology, while radical indeed, does not imply an irrationalist hostility to science and reason as is often supposed. The demonstration will require not only a break with the accepted image of Marcuse, but also with the peculiar rhetorical strategy of his later works. His style is itself a conscious provocation, a refusal of the accepted canons of academic discourse. The effectiveness of this strategy can be measured by Marcuse's remarkable impact. However, there is a cost: the constant compression of ideas into dramatic formulations emphasizes the dialectical connections, but often obscures the meaning of the concepts so connected.

Here is a passage from *One-Dimensional Man* which can serve as an example of the difficulties of Marcuse's style, while introducing the main themes of the discussion to follow.

> Technology serves to institute new, more effective, and more pleasant forms of social control and social cohesion . . . . In the face of the totalitarian features of this society, the traditional notion of the "neutrality" of technology can no longer be maintained. Technology as such cannot be isolated from the use to which it is put; the technological society is a system of domination which operates already in the concept and construction of techniques . . . . As a technological universe, advanced industrial society is a *political* universe, the latest stage in the realization of a specific historical *project* - namely, the experience, transformation, and organization of nature as the mere stuff of domination. As the project unfolds, it shapes the entire universe of discourse and action, intellectual and material culture. In the medium of technology, culture, politics, and the economy merge into an omnipresent system which swallows up or repulses all alternatives. The productivity and growth potential of this system stabilize the society and contain technical progress within the framework of domination. Technological rationality has become political rationality.[1]

Marcuse's basic claim is that there is an essential connection between modern technology and the domination of man by man in the existing industrial societies. He asserts this claim by employing two familiar concepts - domination and technology - in a strange and unfamiliar combination: technology *is* domination and vice versa. By "technology" Marcuse means just what we would expect: machines, industry. His concept of domination refers to the suppression of the individual by society, both in the external form of exploitative hierarchy and coercive power, and the internal or "introjected" form of conformism and authoritarianism. (Despite the claims of his critics, Marcuse never extended his critique of domination to a rejection of all authority in society and moral conscience in the individual.) Thus Marcuse's argument holds that today the machine is not merely *used* for the purpose of suppressing individuality but that it is the basis for new types of suppression it alone makes possible and which it is in some sense destined to carry out.

Marcuse's dialectical style works on the ambiguities of certain terms in a way which is both illuminating and confusing. When he writes, for example, that science is "political," or that technology is "ideological," he makes the strong point that science and technology cannot be understood outside their connection with the historical universe in which they function. Yet in making his point in this way, Marcuse blurs the essential difference between science and technology, on the one hand, and politics and ideology, on the other. He might be taken to mean that, as ideology, science and technology are nothing more than the rationalization of the interests of a particular class. But then opposition to that class would include opposition to "its" science and technology. This view is undoubtedly irrationalist, and bears a certain ominous resemblance to romantic critiques of technology which call for a return to religious values or a simpler, pre-technological way of life.

Yet this is not at all Marcuse's intent. Despite his sharp criticism of "technological rationality," he still maintains the old Marxist faith in the ultimate liberating potential of technology. Technology still represents for Marcuse the hypothetical possibility of overcoming scarcity and the conflict to which it gives rise, but capitalism "represses" this technical potential for emancipation by casting society in the form of an ever renewed struggle for existence.

To avoid an irrationalist misrepresentation of his position, Marcuse is obliged to offer correctives to his strong critical claims, asserting the neutrality, validity and instrumental effectiveness of science and technology despite their "ideological" character. Thus he asserts with equal assurance that "technology has become the great vehicle of *reification*," and that "science and technology are the great vehicles of liberation."[2] He writes:

> If the completion of the technological project involves a break with the prevailing technological rationality, the break in turn depends on the continued existence of the technical base itself. For it is this base which has rendered possible the satisfaction of needs and the reduction of toil - it remains the very base of all forms of human freedom. The qualitative change lies in the reconstruction of this base - that is, in its development with a view of different ends . . . . The new ends, as technical ends, would then operate in the project and construction of the machinery, and not only in its utilization.[3]

The mutually cancelling formulae do actually add up to a theory, but one that is buried in the interplay of the inadequate concepts used to present it. The meaning of Marcuse's theory is clouded by the lack of explicit distinctions; he insists, rather, on making distinctions implicit in the use and context of his concepts. But his rhetorical strategy is clear enough: from a variant of the Marxist position he extracts results that one would expect from the irrationalist critique. He wants to both have his conceptual cake and eat it too, making the strongest possible critique of technology without paying the "luddist" price.

The conceptual chaos that results from this procedure has confused Marcuse's critics and even the most sympathetic have drawn back from his more radical formulations. Their reluctance gains authority from Marcuse's own attempts to rectify his aim by waffling occasionally on his strongest claims. Thus, at one point he states that a computer or a cyclotron can equally serve capitalism and socialism, apparently oblivious to the fact that, if this is taken as a general example, it seems to invalidate his own argument that "technology as such cannot be isolated from the use to which it is put . . ." Habermas, among others, has taken this concession to mean that Marcuse really believed in the political neutrality of technology all along.[4] Another critic, Joachim Bergmann, has pointed out that without a distinction between the purely neutral technical resources of advanced societies and their actual realization in particular ideologically biased technologies, there can no be critique of "repressed potential" such as Marcuse wishes to elaborate.[5] How indeed would one measure this potential if it were not with respect to purely technical powers, abstracted from specific social embodiments in particular technologies and therefore also from whatever political or ideological function these technologies may serve?

Worse yet, in his considerations on the new emancipatory technology, Marcuse seems to waver back and forth between the utopian idea of a technology that liberates nature in responding to human aesthetic needs, and the "realistic" affirmation that basic needs will continue to be served by the very "technological rationality" he condemns so sharply for its connection to domination.[6] But the core of Marcuse's argument holds that in a liberated society technology as a whole would contribute to freedom precisely through serving basic needs in a new way. This would mean a new direction for progress, not the addition of a thin veneer of "humanized" technology on the surface of a world engineered in all its essential features to the destruction of man and nature.

It is puzzling that Marcuse did not arrive at a clearer formulation of his theory in response to his critics. It seems unlikely that terminological failings and rhetorical temptations suffice as an explanation for his problems. I will argue that many of the difficulties in Marcuse's position stem from the fact that it has two independent but converging sources. The first of these sources is the classical Marxist theory of the alienation of "free labor" in capitalist society. This strand of the theory leads directly to the promise of a disalienated industrial society in a socialist future, a future for which, Marcuse readily admits, there is still no precedent.

However, there is another strand to Marcuse's argument which holds that technical reason is a priori adapted to the maintenance of social domination, not just under capitalism and in response to the class interests of capital, but essentially, *in itself*. This position seems closer in spirit to critics of technology such as Martin Heidegger or Jacques Ellul who are frequently described as romantics. It is this "romantic" or better still "ontological" strand of the theory which leads to Marcuse's rejection of "the traditional notion of the 'neutrality' of technology," and his belief that technical reason cannot be adapted to the requirements of a free society without fundamental transformation.

Rather than resolving the tension between these two sources of his views, Marcuse seems to have used each as a corrective for the excesses of the other. Where Marxism tends toward technological optimism, Marcuse drew on his more radical critique of technical reason to sharpen the issues. Where that radical critique tends to slide into a metaphysical despair, Marcuse drew back from the comfort of the abyss with a Marxian emphasis on the concrete social causes of distress and misery.

I am not convinced that Marcuse reconciled these positions successfully, but his attempt is extremely interesting and invites us to further reflection on the issues he raised. Can we, through the further elaboration of Marcuse's own concepts, bring these two approaches to the critique of technology together? This is the difficult question of the internal consistency of a radical critique of technology such as Marcuse's. I will address it in the remainder of this chapter.

The Neutrality of Technology

Perhaps the best way to gain a deeper insight into Marcuse's position is to focus on his assertion that "the traditional notion of the 'neutrality' of technology can no longer be maintained." Here is a claim that runs through his whole critique of technology. Yet in reality, Marcuse's rejection of the neutrality thesis is by no means so categorical as it seems. What is the traditional notion of the neutrality of technology, and with what new conception does Marcuse propose to replace it?

The neutrality of technology consists first of all in its indifference, as pure instrumentality, to the variety of ends it can be made to serve. In this sense of the term, the neutrality of technology is merely a special case of the neutrality of instrumental means, which, in themselves, stand essentially under the norm of efficiency but are only contingently related to the substantive values they may be made to serve in concrete applications. This conception of neutrality is familiar and self-evident.

There is a second sense in which technology is said to be "neutral." Not only is technology claimed to be indifferent with respect to ends, but it also appears to be indifferent with respect to culture, at least among the modern nations, and especially with respect to the political distinction between capitalist and socialist society. A hammer is a hammer, a steam turbine is a steam turbine, and such tools are useful in any social context, assuming the existence of a suitable technical infrastructure to support their employment. In this respect, technology appears to be quite different from legal or religious institutions, which cannot be readily transferred to new social contexts because they are so deeply embedded in the institutional structure of the society of their origin. The transfer of technology, on the contrary, seems to be inhibited only by its cost.

The sociopolitical neutrality of technology is usually attributed to its "rational" character and is related to the universality of the truth embodied in the technology, a truth which can be formulated in verifiable causal propositions. Insofar as such propositions are true, they are not socially and politically relative but, like scientific ideas, maintain their cognitive status in every conceivable social context. Hence, what works in one society can be expected to work equally well in another.

The rational universality of technology also makes it possible to apply the same standards of measurement to technologies employed in different settings. Thus the progress of technology is routinely said to increase the productivity of labor and social wealth in comparisons not only between different countries but also between different eras and different types of societies.

In opposition to these widely accepted views of the neutrality of technology, Marcuse asserts that technology is fundamentally biased toward domination. His alternative position can be formulated as follows in three "theses," each of which summarizes an aspect of his argument.

1. Technology as a means is not politically innocent because, even as it serves generic ends such as increasing the productivity of labor, its specific design and application in the existing industrial societies forms the basis for a way of life that involves the domination of man by man. In this sense, the means (technology) are not truly "value free" but can be said to include within their very structure the end of preserving the status quo.

2. Technology as a total system, a cultural formation, takes the place traditionally occupied by ideology in legitimating the existing society. It thereby forecloses opposition to the wrongs of the society, obstructs progress in its humanization, and sustains the continuity of domination inherited from the past history of class society.

3. Scientific-technical rationality is a priori adapted to the maintenance of social domination.

These theses contradict the conventional view of the neutrality of technology described above. Marcuse insists on linking means and ends, denies that technology is indifferent with respect to the alternative of capitalism or socialism, and challenges the apparent value-freedom of technological rationality. And yet, as we have seen, Marcuse's insistence on the possibility of a transition to socialism based on the "reconstruction" of existing technology implies some sort of notion of the neutrality of technology, albeit a different one from the "traditional notion" he rejects.

But what kind of neutrality would be compatible with Marcuse's claim that technology in advanced industrial societies is designed to serve the end of domination? What peculiar kind of neutrality can describe scientific-technical reason if it is a priori biased toward domination? Is this not a contradiction in terms? Or is it possible that neutrality and bias can coexist together?

I will argue that neutrality and bias can and do in fact coexist and that Marcuse's theory rests on the possibility of their coexistence. It may be helpful here at the outset to make the reasons for this position clear. I will attempt to do so at first in terms that are not internal to Marcuse's highly speculative discussion of the same topic in his critique of formal rationality. I hope that by beginning in this way I will be able to make the general line of Marcuse's approach more plausible by clearly distinguishing between the type of bias that Marcuse attributes to formally neutral systems such as science and technology and the more familiar type of bias that characterizes ideologies, prejudices and discriminatory arrangements of all sorts.

Substantive and Formal Bias

Marcuse's position on technology implies that bias is not the opposite of neutrality, and that bias in fact cuts across the distinction between ideological and neutral elements of social systems.   To my knowledge, the first recorded statment of this position is in Plato's *Gorgias* where Callicles rejects the laws on the grounds that their neutrality, which takes the form of equal treatment of the strong and weak, responds to special interests of the weak.   He argues,

> I can quite imagine that the manufacturers of laws and conventions are the weak, the majority, in fact.   It is for themselves and their own advantage that they make their laws and distribute their praises and their censures.   It is to frighten men who are stronger and able to enforce superiority that they keep declaring . . . that injustice consists in seeking to get the better of one's neighbor.   They are quite content, I suppose, to be on equal terms with others since they are themselves inferior.[7]

It is curious that Marcuse's attempt to revive the critique of neutrality should follow Callicles in attributing bias to law - although in this case it is not legislation but science that is in question - and yet arrive at the opposite conclusion so far as the beneficiary of the bias is concerned, connecting scientific law to the interest in domination of the strong.   This reversal is undoubtedly related to changes in the concept and function of reason in advanced societies as compared with classical antiquity.

Callicles' critique of law shows clearly that there are not one but two quite different types of bias that we normally distinguish in criticizing unfair actions and institutions.   In the first place, there is the bias that results from applying different standards to individuals where they ought properly to be judged by the same standard.   Racist discrimination is in this category.   Second, there is a more subtle form of bias which consists in applying the same standard to individuals but under conditions that favor some unfairly at the expense of others.

This second form of bias is present in a great many different contexts, and it is often difficult to identify.   It characterizes conditions in which "formal" equality contradicts biased social "content," such as where equality before the law is systematically frustrated by the unequal ability to pay for legal representation, or where equal educational opportunity is denied not by discriminatory exclusions but by teaching a class or ethnically biased cultural heritage that is difficult for the unfavored groups to learn.   This type of bias is also present wherever procedures based on equal treatment for all are introduced or suspended according to instrumental considerations at times or places favoring the interests of one group at the expense of others.   This is the case, for example, in certain countries where military leaders respect the results of elections only when the candidates of which they approve win office.   For reasons that should become clear in a later section of this chapter, I will borrow a distinction from Max Weber's theory of rationality, and call the first type "substantive" bias and the second "formal" bias.

The epistemological implications of these two types of bias are very different, representing two different types of methodological error. Substantive bias, based on the application of unequal standards, is most often associated with prejudice, with explicit norms that discriminate between people of different classes, races, sexes or nationalities. However, since it is difficult to justify unfair treatment on the basis of mere personal preferences, such norms are generally represented as factual judgments arbitrarily attributing abilities or merits, disabilities or demerits to the more or less favored groups. The epistemological critique of such bias proceeds by showing up these pseudo-factual judgments as "rationalizations," or, where they are highly elaborated, as "ideologies."

Formal bias implies no necessary feeling of prejudice, nor is it associated with factual errors based on rationalization of feelings. On the contrary, the facts, honestly reported, generally support claims of fairness aimed at justifying this type of bias, so long as their selection carefully excludes embarassing contextual considerations. Outside the larger context, fair treatment seems to be rendered through an equal application of the same standards to all. But in that context, it becomes clear that the apparent fairness of the system, taken in isolation, hides the systematic unfairness of the results of its application.

Criticism of formal bias therefore requires redefining the relevant domain of considerations that need to be taken into account in judging the action or institution in question. It is not the particular factual claims advanced in favor of the discriminatory activity that are challenged, but the horizon under which those facts are defined as the totality of relevant considerations. The enlargement of the cognitive horizon in such cases involves passing from arbitrarily isolated elements to a larger system which embraces them all and grants them their functional significance. Thus to show discrimination in the case of a culturally biased test, it is necessary to demonstrate that the discriminatory outcome is functionally related to the goals of the dominant social groups.

Criticism of this type is compatible with various epistemological stances, among which is the Hegelian-Marxist approach of Marcuse. This form of critique implies an epistemology based on essential relations in a functionally structured whole. Its proponents sometimes refer to the Hegelian distinction of "abstract" and "concrete" to explain their approach. For Hegel, the "abstract" is not the conceptually universal but the part isolated from the whole to which it properly belongs. "Concrete" is the network of relations binding the parts to the whole.

In Marxist terminology, a methodology is "reified" if it insists on working with such "abstract" elements, refusing systematically to enlarge its horizons of explanation to the dimensions of the "concrete" wholes through which the parts take on their meaning and significance. A society is likewise "reified" if its structure systematically obscures the inner connections between its various sectors and institutions, protecting them from critical scrutiny by the uninformed observer. On these terms, advanced industrial societies exhibit a typical reification through which the formal bias of their institutions is occluded. "One-Dimensional" thought is complicit in this bias in so far as it refuses the critical-theoretic gesture of enlarging the contexts of explanation to encompass the concrete whole.

Technique and Technology

A considerable advance in understanding Marcuse's position on technology can be made from the standpoint of the distinction between substantive and formal bias. Typically, critics of technology like Marcuse find themselves accused of irrationalism because they are believed to be attributing what I have called substantive bias to technology. This would amount to saying that technology, like religious beliefs or social customs, has validity only in so far as it is part of the shared myths of the society to which it belongs. The scientific-technical principles underlying technologies would have to be treated on the same terms as magical rituals or political doctrines. The logical order of the scientific-technical disciplines would be as empty of intrinsic meaning as the rules of chess or bridge. This position is clearly incompatible with the Marxist one, to which Marcuse subscribes, according to which the science and technology developed under capitalism form the basis for an advance to socialism, subject to the necessary "reconstruction," to be sure.

In fact, Marcuse attributes formal rather than substantive bias to science and technology. If it is difficult to see this implication of Marcuse's theory, part of the reason lies in his lack of a clear terminology in which to express the moment of truth in the idea of the neutrality of technical reason.

The distinction required by Marcuse's theory can be made by abstracting the level of application of objective knowledge of nature embodied in technologies from their concrete social realization. As a matter of convenience, it makes sense to reserve the term "technique" for specific technical elements, such as the lever or the electric circuit, which are in themselves neutral with respect to concrete social ends. These elements are like the vocabulary of a language; they can be strung together to form a variety of "sentences" with different meanings and intentions. "Technologies," defined as developed ensembles of technical elements, are greater than the sum of their parts. They meet social criteria of purpose in the very selection and arrangement of the intrinsically neutral elements from which they are built. These social purposes can be understood as "embodied" in the technology and not simply as an extrinsic use to which a neutral tool might be put. Thus the study of any specific technology ought to be able to trace the impress of a mesh of social determinations which preconstruct in some sense a whole domain of social activity aimed at quite definite social goals.

On the basis of this distinction, it is possible to construct an approach with the critical results Marcuse seeks to achieve, that is, to show that social values penetrate technologies despite the fact that technologies embody an objective knowledge of nature with a quite different epistemological status from such socially relative phenomena as customs, political institutions or religious beliefs. In the case of technologies, values can be shown to operate in the choice of technical elements and the resulting "fit" of the formally rational technological subsystems and society at large. The bias originates not in the formal system itself but in its concrete realization in a real world of times, places, historical inheritances, in sum, a world of concrete contingencies.

This explains why "reconstruction" of technology is a possible and necessary feature of the transition to socialism. The social environment of the transitional society is in flux and the old "fit," which favored certain groups at the expense of others, no longer works. A new way must be found of organizing the formally neutral materials from which technologies are built up, appropriate to the new society growing up around them.

The traditional notion of the neutrality of technology discussed earlier represents the reified approach to formal neutrality. It succeeds in demonstrating the value-freedom of technology precisely to the extent that it abstracts from all contextual considerations. Marcuse's method consists in recovering these lost contexts through which finally it is possible to develop a historically concrete understanding of technology. But it is also important to note that in this as in other instances of formal bias, the decontextualized elements from which the biased system is built up *are* in fact neutral in their abstract form. The illusion of technological neutrality arises from the attempt to understand socially concrete technologies on the model of the abstract technical principles they embody in a unique and value-laden combination.

The first two theses on technology which I have attributed to Marcuse flow directly from these considerations. They reflect the social consequences of the systemic involvement of technologies in a society based on class rule. These theses summarize the Marxian "moment" in Marcuse's critique of technology. They will be treated in the next section of this chapter. The third thesis has a different status. It attributes intrinsic bias to the formally neutral materials, the very scientific-technical rationality, from which technologies are built up. This is the other strand in the Marcusian critique, the "ontological" moment. This strand of the argument aims to uncover what might be called the ontological preconditions for the possibility of formal bias. Why, in fact, are formally biased systems so commonplace in modern societies? Can it be an accident that formally neutral concepts and procedures lend themselves so readily to applications we consider misuses or abuses? Marcuse's response will be treated in a third section of this chapter.

The Marxian Moment: Technology and Class Power

Marcuse interprets Marx's theory of alienation as a critique of capitalist technology. Despite the widely held view that Marx was a latent technocrat, this interpretation of his position finds considerable support in early sections of *Capital* and the *Grundrisse*. In these texts, Marx attempts to understand how capitalism has fused the drive to increase economic productivity, and the equally important drive to maintain capitalist power on the workplace.

To the extent that workers are divorced from the means of production, the control of their labor falls to the capitalist owners of enterprise, who must devise technological and managerial solutions to the problems of labor discipline. Thus Marx writes that

> the control exercised by the capitalist is not only a special function due to the nature of the social labour-process, and peculiar to that process, but it is, at the same time, a function of the exploitation of a social labour-process, and is consequently rooted in the unavoidable antagonism between the exploiter and the living and labouring raw material he exploits.[8]

Technological choices, like all other aspects of production, are determined by the fact that the pursuit of efficiency involves the imposition of effective control, not only over nature, but also over human beings at work. Technological progress is subtly influenced by this requirement. It proceeds under the aegis of two goals, a purely technical and a socially specific goal, one serving generic human interests and the other serving class interests.

These considerations explain how the very same Marx who foresaw the liberation of humanity in a technologically advanced socialist society could also be the author of sharply critical diatribes against the division of labor and the use of machinery under capitalism. He wrote of science, for example, that it "is the most powerful weapon for repressing strikes, those periodical revolts of the working class against the autocracy of capital."[9] And in another passage, Marx claims that "it would be possible to write quite a history of inventions, made since 1830, for the sole purpose of supplying capital with weapons against the revolts of the working class."[10]

Arguing in part on this basis, Marcuse writes that "the machine is *not neutral*; technical reason is the social reason ruling a given society and can be changed in its very structure."[11] What is new in Marcuse's formulation is the passage from a critique of *technology* to a critique of *technical reason*. This is certainly not in Marx, although it is possible, as Lukacs demonstrated, to develop such a critique out of Marx's theory of economic fetishism and his attempts at explaining the way in which capitalist economic science masks exploitative relations in the economy. In his essay on Max Weber and in *One-Dimensional Man*, Marcuse attempts to derive his critique of technical reason directly from the Marxian theory of the dual criteria of progress under capitalism. A consistent interpretation of one major strand of Marcuse's argument can be drawn from this source. This interpretation holds that technical reason has been distorted by the same forces that have distorted technological development. I will present such an interpretation very briefly below.

In his essay on Weber, Marcuse shows how Weber's explanation of the general concept of formal economic rationality implicitly presupposes "the separation of the workers from the means of production ... (as) a *technical* necessity requiring the individual and private direction and control of the means of production . . . . The highly *material*, historical fact of the private-capitalist enterprise thus becomes . . . a *formal* structural element of capitalism and of *rational* economic activity itself."[12]   Thus the terms in which Weber comprehends the social world introject the given forms of domination as a priori bases of conceptualization.   Marcuse considers Weber's analysis to be significant in revealing by its example the generally ideological character of formal social concepts under capitalism.   The definitions of social objects, the criteria of means/ends rationality, concepts of efficiency, progress and so on all exhibit this a priori bias toward domination.

This explains why capitalist technical concepts are operational in themselves and do not require constant reference to an explicit sociological analysis to be employed.   The concept of "efficiency," for example, implicitly includes domination of the labor force without reference to the problems of capitalist labor discipline because such domination is already implied in the very notion of means/ends rationality in this society.   What Marcuse calls the "technological rationality" of this society is indelibly marked by the presupposition that domination is the necessary condition for effective control. The trace of this presupposition can be found in economic thought, managerial methods and the design criteria of technology itself.

One-Dimensional Man takes this argument still further by showing the ideological function of such capitalist-distorted forms of technical rationality in advanced society.   Marcuse argues that today technological rationality is no longer simply biased in its operational employment, but has become a legitimating mechanism for the perpetuation of domination. This thesis carries us well beyond the Marxian position.   In Marx's theory, capitalism is still subject to criticism on the grounds of technical inefficiency.   Since alienation has become an obstacle to the growth and development of the productive forces, the normative goal of creating a more humane society is in conformity with the purely technical goal of increasing economic productivity.   The critique of capitalism can thus proceed simultaneously on technical and normative grounds.

Marcuse believes this original Marxian position has been invalidated by the progress of contemporary capitalism.   Technical considerations no longer demonstrate the inadequacy of the capitalist organization of production.   Technological rationality can no longer serve, as it still did for Marx, as the basis of a critique of the prevailing relations of production, but becomes, in fact, the legitimating discourse of the society. Habermas summarizes this aspect of Marcuse's theory:

> At the stage of their scientific-technical development, then, the forces of production appear to enter a new constellation with the relations of production.   Now they no longer function as the basis of a critique of prevailing legitimations in the interest of political enlightenment, but become instead the basis of legitimation.   *This* is what Marcuse conceives of as world-historically new.[13]

Under these conditions, technological rationality tends more and more to support the system as the (apparently) only efficient way of operating a technological society. The problem is no longer the inability of capitalism to make effective use of the technologies it has developed, but rather the catastrophic human consequences of the effective use of these very technologies.

Not only is technical progress distorted by the requirements of capitalist control, but the "universe of discourse," public and eventually even private speech and thought, limit themselves to the posing and resolving of technical problems within the double constraints of the simultaneous interest in technical advance and domination that characterizes capitalist rationality. "When technics becomes the universal form of material production, it circumscribes an entire culture; it projects a historical totality - a 'world.'"[14] The universalization of technical modes of thought changes the cultural conditions presupposed by the Marxian theory of emancipatory struggle. There is no place for critical consciousness in this world: it is "one-dimensional." The normative critique is thus forced to appear explicitly and independently; it can no longer hide behind the Marxian demand for a liberation of the productive forces to full development.

This explains why Marcuse, unlike Marx, not only attacks the dominant social interests that preside over technological choices, but also criticizes technical modes of thought and criteria of progress. His critique is directed at "technological rationality," a self-propelling system of domination through technology, increasingly out of control of its human masters. He writes that "Today, domination perpetuates and extends itself not only through technology, but *as* technology, and the latter provides the great legitimation of the expanding political power, which absorbs all spheres of culture."[15]

Socialism and Reason

How deep is the challenge to rationality posed by this "Marxian moment" in Marcuse's theory? As summarized above, the theory in fact has no irrationalist implications. Yet it is often difficult to isolate this strand in Marcuse's argument from the other far more radical ontological critique of technology, and the terminological shortcomings of Marcuse's argument exaggerate the difficulty unnecessarily.

The significance of this strand of Marcuse's argument becomes clearer when it is viewed in its political context. Despite the political discouragement implied by his conclusion, Marcuse's theory quickly inspired widespread critical discussion in advanced societies. Some of this criticism was irrationalist in the proper sense of the term - Marcuse was himself criticized as "soft" on technology by Roszak and others he influenced. But Marcuse's influence flowed also into other intellectual currents that pressed for a critical rationalism, independent of political power and its so-called "experts," and able to assess the social world historically and philosophically in opposition to the dominant overemphasis on quantitative methods and social engineering. The outcome of this tendency included such characteristic and essentially positive phenomena of the 1960s as a growing rejection of the technocratic pretensions of both capitalist and communist elites, movements for self-criticism among professionals, and the interest in "appropriate technology," and environmental reform.

All these developments have in common an implicit reference to a level of technical rationality purified of exploitative features by a historically informed critique.   The doctor critical of current medical practice or the teacher involved in the radicalization of his or her discipline does not generally aim to destroy the technical underpinnings of his or her own work, but to identify the ways in which bourgeois society has penetrated and distorted these underpinnings.   A new "paradigm" is required, not an alternative to reason.   Marcuse's theory opens the way to just such a critical search for new paradigms by identifying the point at which technical reason becomes historical, that is to say, *class* reason through introjecting the specific requirements of capitalist control at its basis.

From this standpoint, we are returned to something very much like Marx's own views on the transition to socialism, insofar as they can be inferred from his scattered remarks on the subject.   Marx rejected utopian thinking in favor of the idea of a dynamic process of social change which would start out with the capitalist inheritance and gradually transform it under the conditions of a new class power.   While Marx did not apply this schema explicitly to technology, it can be inferred from his harsh critique of the capitalist factory that he envisaged radical changes in its design and employment under socialism, long before the transition to the highly automated system projected in some of his more speculative writings.   The reshaping of inherited technology can be understood as a process of bootstrapping.   The technology would not be thrown out, nor would it simply be put to new uses in a different social context, but rather it would be employed to produce new technological means, fully adapted to the requirements of a socialist society.

It is important to distinguish clearly between this developmental approach, and the notion that the technology developed under capitalism is neutral with respect to social systems, that the same means can be used for different ends.   Marx's position suggests the further relationship: not what different *ends* may be directly served by a given technology, but what new technological *means* it may produce, in a technically and culturally feasible sequence leading from one type of industrial society, oriented toward certain definite values, to a quite different type of society oriented toward other values.   Marcuse makes this alternative clear in writing that, "what is at stake is the redefinition of values in *technical terms*, as elements in the technological process.   The new ends, as technical ends, would then operate in the project and in the construction of the machinery, and not only in its utilization."[16]

The Marxian moment in Marcuse's critique of technical rationality reaches its extreme limit at this point.   The historically institutionalized forms of technical reason, whether they be technologies or professional specializations or social sciences, fall before a critique which reveals their inhumanity in revealing their limitations *qua* technical reason.   But reason itself emerges unscathed, in fact purified by the fire of criticism, its ultimate neutrality confirmed by the critical glance that strips it bare of sociological accretions. This is the paradox of the Marxian moment, that it can only achieve a historically concrete critique of reason's bias toward domination by gesturing toward an abstract ideal of truly neutral technical reason, undistorted by power and ideology.

Is this enough? Can criticism stop short at this point, essentially the point where Marx stopped, without risking a collapse into renewed positivity, naive rationalism, perhaps even technocracy? This is truly the parting of the ways. A version of critical theory can be elaborated starting out from the Marxian moment in Marcuse's critique of rationality. Such a version of critical theory has the immense advantage, in terms of gaining wide acceptance and producing conviction, of requiring no metaphysical concepts, and can be elaborated against a background of common assumptions about the nature of reality. But Marcuse did not accept this position. He insisted stubbornly and to the last on pushing the critique far beyond this point, attacking the metaphysical roots of the problems, braving the scorn of empiricist and neo-Kantian alike by proposing a speculative theory of reason more deeply critical than the one sketched above, more surely protected against affirmative regressions.

Here is where the second strand in Marcuse's critique of technology comes in. This "ontological" critique is based on the refusal to separate technology and technical reason per se from the social and cultural framework within which they operate. The technical reason on the basis of which modern technology has been developed may in itself be "neutral" in some sense, but it is an abstraction insofar as it is considered outside the entire context of involvements in which it emerged as theory and to which it returns as practice. Technical reason is not just an epistemological category but also a civilizational one. The complex formed by modern society and technology is no more neutral than medieval cathedrals or Egyptian pyramids, but embodies the specific values of a particular civilization, Western civilization, the civilization of "Reason." The task of the philosopher, from this standpoint, is to articulate and judge these values embodied in technology and in the course of doing so to uncover the bias of reason itself.

The Ontological Moment: The Radical Critique of Technology

The preceding discussion has shown that Marcuse's theory of technological bias implies the neutrality of technique. We are now ready to consider his demonstration of the complementary point that the neutrality of technique implies in its turn a kind of bias. This is Marcuse's most controversial thesis on technology, according to which there is an intrinsic a priori connection between scientific-technical rationality and domination. According to this thesis, "science, *by virtue of its own method* and concepts, has projected and promoted a universe in which the domination of nature has remained linked to the domination of man."[17]

This proposition is in some sense shocking, and the consensus of

Marcuse's critics has been entirely negative as far as it is concerned. Such generally sympathetic critics as Habermas and William Leiss dismiss it as a vestige of romantic nature philosophy.[18] Not only is this position extremely unpopular, it is far more difficult to understand than the themes treated above. It stems from a different tradition, less widely known and followed in the United States than even the Marxism which inspires Marcuse's other ideas on technology. This tradition begins with Hegel's critique of the "understanding," and, more specifically, of scientific quantification and lawfulness. It continues in Nietzsche's genealogy of the "will to truth," and his attempt to demonstrate the power drive behind rationality. Finally, Marcuse himself is strongly influenced by the development of these themes in the work of contemporaries, primarily, Husserl, Heidegger, Lukacs, Adorno and Horkheimer.

With the possible exception of Hegel, all these thinkers reject the representation of scientific objectivity as detached and disinterested knowledge. They are all engaged in demystifying what Nietzsche calls the "last idol," the ideal of "truth" conceived as the absolute vision of a subject which, as knower, situates itself beyond the world. It is important to note that the emphasis of this critique is not on human fallibility, and the critique is not necessarily associated with scepticism. Rather, it is the traditional conception of truth itself which is in question because that conception is based on the theological assumption that truth is the sort of knowledge achieved by a disembodied, decontextualized and "perfect" subject.

According to this traditional theological notion of truth, finite subjects are not "perfect" in this same way, and can therefore achieve knowledge only by abstracting themselves from their facticity as embodied, senuous, feeling beings. To Nietzsche and his successors it is quite arbitrary to propose a purely ideal and imaginary perfection as a standard and to measure real subjects by it. To rid the concept of truth of this theological assumption, it must be subjected to one or another type of radical reconstruction in accord with the ontological requirements of a conception of the universe in which even the hypothesis of an infinite subject of knowledge is dismissed as meaningless.

These requirements include the necessary involvement of the (finite) subject of knowledge in the world which it knows. But this is equivalent to saying that the subject of knowledge must be conceived first and foremost as an acting being, therefore as a being engaged with reality for essentially interested reasons. From this point of view, the customary pretensions to objectivity and detachment associated with scientific-technical knowledge appears as an ideology covering undisclosed existential involvements.

The interests masked by scientific objectivity have been variously interpreted. At the very least, the "philosophers of finitude" under discussion here see destiny at work in the relation of modern science to technology. They invariably reject the commonplace view that science "works" because "knowledge is power," that scientific theories are susceptible to technological application for the simple reason that they are true. Clearly, some kinds of knowledge yield power over nature, but this must be due to an a priori orientation toward power characteristic of the most basic methods and concepts associated with those ways of knowing. Thus it is not knowledge which is power but rather power which is a form of knowledge. On these terms, formal classification under laws, cause-effect reasoning, and especially quantification have been identified as epistemological expressions of the interest in instrumental control underlying the pursuit of scientific knowledge.

This is one aspect of Marcuse's position, argued at great length with the aid of citations from Husserl, Heidegger, Adorno, and Horkheimer. However, from Marcuse's standpoint merely pointing out the internal link between science and instrumental control is insufficiently critical. This view does not really threaten the customary idea of scientific objectivity, nor does it *essentially* connect science and technology to the progress of domination.

Habermas has shown, for example, that the theory of science as instrumental reason can be worked out to its logical conclusion in complete abstraction from all political content. It proves possible to relate science to a general interest in instrumental control without actually toppling the "idol" of objectivity because, as Kant already demonstrated long ago, the generically human can be treated "as if" it were true for all practical purposes. Indeed, if science represents generically human interests, it is "detached" and "neutral" with respect to all particular interests, that is to say, all really historically existing interests such as we know them. What more can one ask in the way of disinterestedness?

Marcuse goes far beyond this initial step toward a demonstration that the instrumentalist character of science binds it essentially to the practice of domination. Now this is quite a different proposition. On these terms science is truly "political," as Marcuse argues, and its pretension to occupying a neutral post above the struggles of history is shattered. But these considerations seem to imply a fundamental inconsistency between Marcuse's various critiques of technology. For, if reason is *essentially* tied to domination, then it is difficult to see how any amount of "reconstruction" of its technological products can transform them into suitable "vehicles of liberation."

Two puzzling features of Marcuse's theory are aimed at overcoming this apparent inconsistency, and reconciling the ontological and the Marxian moments of his critique. The first of these consists in the *historical* treatment of reason as an *ontological* category. Marcuse's critique of rationality is unusual in that he rejects the idea of an ahistorical category "reason," essentially burdened by transhistorical values such as the will to power. But if the nature of reason changes in history, then so, in a sense, does its object, being. For Marcuse, such basic categories as essence and existence, fact and value have a historical meaning and are not fixed once and for all by an ontology that would transcend and underlie history.

On these terms, reason (and its technological products) can be analyzed in its contemporary form as the product of forces that lie at the crossroads of ontology and history. In support of this position, Marcuse follows the lead of Horkheimer and Adorno in relating the historically specific forms of technology and reason to the emergence of class society. The technical reason of modern capitalist societies is thus doubly determined by class power, once in the specific forms criticized in the previous section, and a second time in the vaster context of the overriding history of class society as a whole. The critique corresponding to this larger form of class determination is aimed not at distortions introduced into a fundamentally neutral technical reason, but rather at identifying the intrinsic bias in technical reason itself insofar as it emerges from the conditions and requirements of class society in general. This way of developing the critique holds open the possibility of historical change in the ontologically essential determinations of technology and reason in a classless society of the future.

This historical treatment of reason is connected to another still more paradoxical feature of Marcuse's theory. Where the irrationalist critique of reason attempts to undermine the claims of science to neutrality and objectivity by showing them to be an ideological veil for hidden interests, Marcuse argues that it is the very neutrality and objectivity of science that supplies the link between its instrumental and its repressive dimensions. He writes, for example, that "it is precisely its neutral character which relates objectivity to a specific historical Subject - namely, to the consciousness that prevails in the society by which and for which this neutrality is established."[19]

As we have seen, the Marxian moment in Marcuse's critique leads to recognition of the neutrality of a hypothetical technical reason purified of class distortions. The ontological moment in Marcuse's critique is designed to foreclose any possibility of uncritical acceptance of this idealized model of a purified technical reason. Technical reason is indeed neutral at some level, Marcuse will argue, but its very neutrality subserves it to domination and so ties it to the history of class society. In what follows I will attempt to explain the articulation of these two critiques in more detail.

The Problem of Rationality

The best place to begin this discussion is with the attempts of Marx, Weber and Lukacs to explain the function of rationality in capitalist society. Marx demonstrated that the power of the capitalist class is reproduced through the formally equivalent exchange of wages for labor power. This demonstration opened the way to the study of the formal bias of apparently neutral social subsystems, and raised one of the fundamental questions that gave rise to the science of sociology - the question of the social significance of rationality. As a chapter in the history of attempts to answer this question, Marcuse's theory is unusual in drawing on the philosophical critique of science and technology discussed above.

Weber plays a pivotal role in the evolution leading from Marx to Marcuse. His theory of rationalization continued and enlarged Marx's approach to formal neutrality. For the purpose of this theory, Weber introduced the terms "substantive" and "formal" rationality, adapted above to the discussion of the forms of bias, to describe two different types of social thought and action.[20] Rationality is "substantive" to the extent that it responds to norms embodying a higher purpose such as feeding a population, winning a war or maintaining the social hierarchy. The "formal" rationality of capitalism primarily characterizes those economic arrangements which optimize calculability and control and which aim directly at efficiency in production and distribution rather than at the fulfillment of "substantive" needs. Formally rational systems lie under technical norms that have to do with efficiency in the organization of means rather than the achievement of specific ends.

In Weber, the term "rationalization" refers to the generalization of formal rationality in capitalist society, often at the expense of traditional substantively rational modes of action, with paradoxical consequences for the distribution of social power. While the application of Weber's concept of substantive rationality is unclear and subject to controversy, it seems reasonable to consider precapitalist societies as substantively rational to the extent that reason enters into their organization at all. These societies exhibit a specific type of rationality that supports the power of the dominant social groups. Nowhere does one find any claim to cognitive neutrality in the forms of rationality that maintain such systems. On the contrary, their bias is explicit and rests on a hierarchy of functions presumed to be consecrated by God. Thus in these cases there is perfect consistency between the forms of rationality, penetrated as they are by substantive ends, and the discriminatory social outcomes.

This is not the case in capitalism, where the neutral forms of rationality support discriminatory outcomes despite (or because of!) their neutrality. Weber is quite aware that the outcome of rationalization is favorable to the ambitions and claims of certain social groups, capitalists and the bureaucracy, which tend to rise to the top of any rationalized society. Yet the formally rational systems of accounting, control, production and exchange which produce this effect are in themselves value-free. The inconsistency between this neutrality of the means and the discriminatory outcomes characterizes capitalist society as a whole.

Like Marx's theory, Weber's leads to the recognition of the discrimination resulting from the normal operation of formally rational systems such as markets, administrations, the law, and professionalization. And like Marx's theory, Weber's is subversive of melioristic attempts to soften the hard edges of a formally rationalized society. Attempts to overcome the bias introduced by formal rationalization generally proceed through new types of substantively rational systems, such as affirmative action quotas, compensatory educational programs, or provisions for aid to the poor in the exercise of their rights. But such substantively rational systems are subject to criticism on grounds of formal irrationality. These were, in fact, the terms on which Marx himself criticized proposals for redistribution of wealth under capitalism. The current crisis of the welfare state seems to confirm that if socialism is conceived merely as a substantively rational corrective to formal rationality, the result will be the dismal one foreseen by Weber - generalized inefficiency leading to the imposition of new types of control from above.

The first, and to my knowledge still the major, attempt to achieve a really penetrating theoretical explanation for the bias of rationality under capitalism is contained in Lukacs' early Marxist work, *History and Class Consciousness*. Lukacs introduced the term "reification" to describe the processes Weber had summed up under the category of "rationalization." The difference in emphasis this change in terminology connotes is significant, for Weber still tends to see the impact of rationalization on social power as externally related to rationalization itself, whereas Lukacs conceptualizes these contextual considerations as internal to the process of reification. Lukacs brings to light the congruence of modes of thought and action that rest on the fragmentation of society, formalistic thinking, and the autonomization of production units under the control of private owners.[21]

This approach opens the way to a theory of socialism as more and other than a mere corrective to the injustices of capitalism. However Lukacs himself failed to pursue the discussion to its logical conclusion and did not develop such a theory. Nor did he criticize scientific-technical thought per se, but rather he confined his attack to the social sciences and the institutions of capitalism. Thus while Lukacs' theory does explain why formal rationalization supports the specific inequalities that characterize capitalism, this theory does not explain the curious "accident" that formal rationality of the scientific-technical type became available at a certain point in history as the cultural form of a system of class domination. Marcuse goes beyond Lukacs in this regard, and attempts to account for the growing political role of science and technology in advanced capitalism in terms of the essential bias of scientific-technical rationality. He aims at nothing less than a general theory of the link between formalism and class domination throughout history, and on that basis he tries to sketch the main outlines of a new society, including the forms of its scientific and technical practice.

The Critique of Formal Neutrality

Like Lukacs before him, Marcuse considers the universality of bias in the rationalization process to be a *problem* and not simply an accident of world-historical scope. He writes:

> Scientific-technical rationality and manipulation are welded together into new forms of social control. Can one rest content with the assumption that this unscientific outcome is the result of a specific societal *application* of science? I think that the general direction in which it came to be applied was inherent in pure science even where no practical purposes were intended, and that the point can be identified where theoretical Reason turns into social practice.[22]

We can rephrase the problem he poses by asking, What the significance is of the general availability of formal systems for applications that are biased to favor domination? Is there something about their very neutrality which opens them to such applications? What happened "originally" in the initial construction of the formal mode of abstraction that rendered it pliable in this particular way?

To follow Marcuse's argument to this point is difficult because we do not normally think of formally neutral systems as essentially implicated in their applications. Rather, the involvement of formal systems in strategies of domination appears to proceed from the subject who makes a repressive use of these systems just as he might pick up a rock and use it as a weapon. It would be comical to suggest that the rock is "biased" a priori toward such uses, that its hardness is the essential precondition by which it lends itself to violence. Marcuse's very question reverses our normal assumption that biased applications are a "distortion" or "misapplication" of formally neutral systems. But Marcuse is seeking precisely to connect formal neutrality and domination as moments in a dialectical totality. This is perhaps admissable to the extent that, unlike rocks, formal systems are human inventions created in a specific social context.

Marcuse's treatment of this problem depends on his dialectical ontology which, in turn, is based on the distinction between "substantive" and "logico-mathematical" or "formal" universals. He attempts to show why formal universals are available for repressive application, and then takes the argument one step further, to demonstrate that this availability is not accidental but proceeds from the very essence of this mode of abstraction. The outcome of this demonstration is a general theory of the possibility of the phenomena I describe with the term "formal bias," understood not as a contingent aspect of formal systems, but as an intrinsic dimension of those systems themselves.

The construction of substantive universals involves a kind of idealization, a reduction of contingency which makes possible the conceptualization of the "essence" of what actually exists. In the case of social universals such as freedom or justice, this essence does not refer directly to its given instanciations, but rather expresses their historical potentialities, beyond the confining facts of life in any existing society. For Marcuse, these potentialities are not merely ideal but are immanent to the things themselves, where they appear as internal contradictions in reality. Thus substantive universals transcend the split between "ought" and "is," and as such provide the basis of a critical consciousness which, in the course of history, learns to struggle for its realization through social action.

Marcuse's theory of substantive universals is rooted in a unique form of conceptual realism. Particulars are not independently real for Marcuse, but their essential connections to other things are perceptible only through concepts. These concepts,

> are identical with and yet different from the real objects of immediate experience. "Identical" in as much as the concept denotes the same thing; "different" in as much as the concept is the result of a reflection which has understood the thing in the context (and in the light) of other things which did not appear in the immediate experience and which "explain" the thing (mediation) . . . By the same token, all cognitive concepts have a transitive meaning:

they go beyond descriptive reference to particular facts.   And if the facts are those of society, the cognitive concepts also go beyond any particular context of facts - into processes and conditions on which the respective society rests, and which enter into all particular facts, making, sustaining, and destroying the society.   By virtue of their reference to this historical totality, cognitive concepts transcend all operational context, but their transcendence is empirical because it renders the facts recognizable as that which they really are.[23]

According to Marcuse, the dialectical concept of potentiality reflects consciousness of a demand for freedom which is present implicitly in philosophy from the very beginning.   To be sure, throughout most of history, the overwhelming realities of scarcity and domination block and distort philosophical thought.   As a result, the potentialities it identifies appear as an unhistorical, metaphysical dimension beyond the given. Philosophy suffers the same fate as the imagination and artistic creation. In all these domains the demand for a better reality is blunted through marginalization of the dangerous visions in which the truth attempts to shine forth.   Simultaneously, the merely given reality appears to be completely disconnected from its metaphysical or artistic truth, and therefore subject to another, purely formal kind of abstraction.   In Hegelian terms, the given is delivered over to "immediate facticity." Formal thinking originates in the split between essence and existence which results from the conditions of life in class society.

Formal thinking is a specific negation of dialectics, its active suppression in favor of another ontology.   This type of thinking starts out from the a priori acceptance of what is and abstracts from the given not toward its potentialities   but   rather   toward   its   form.   Formal   abstraction systematically evacuates the "content" of its objects, classifying or quantifying them in terms of the function they can be made to serve in a system of instrumental controls.   Thus instead of transcending the given toward its essential potentialities, which this type of universality cannot conceptualize in any case once it has abstracted from all concrete contents and   the   dialectical   contradictions   they   contain,   formalism exposes its objects to manipulation, transforms them into means.

The essence of formal thinking is the refusal of precisely that mode of conceptual and practical mediation in which the potentialities of being are revealed.   Mediation appears as mere fantasy, the potentialities of the given as objects of derealized evaluation or imagination.   The suppression of dialectical mediation is reflected in the sharp split formal thinking sets up between reason and imagination, fact and value, reality and art.   Now the "content" dialectics had identified as pointing toward suppressed potentialities is redefined as mere "value," subjective and arbitrary, with no ontological roots at all.   Being is strictly defined as the object of instrumental manipulations.   In recent times, formalistic positivism finally does away with even the metaphysically marginalized expressions of the tension in reality between what is and what might be.

Here is the core of Marcuse's argument.   Formal universals are "value-free" in the sense that they do not prescribe the ends of the objects they construct conceptually as means. However, they are value-laden in another deeper sense. The very conception of value from which formal universals are "free" is itself a product of the abstractive process in which formalism suppresses the dialectical concept of potentiality. Thus formalism is not in fact "neutral" with respect to the alternative of actual and potential in its objects. Rather, it is clearly biased toward the actual, what is already fully realized and present to hand.

Methodologically, this bias appears in the refusal (or rather, the inability) to integrate history and social contexts as the scene of development. Formal abstraction restricts its range to the artificially isolated, individual, given object as it immediately appears. It accepts this given being as truth and in so doing comes under the horizon of the existing society and its modes of practice. Thus the horizon of the manipulations it opens is the uncritically accepted horizon of domination under which its objects lie. These objects can be used, but not transformed, adapted to the dominant social purposes, but not transcended toward the realization of higher potentialities in the context of a possible, better society.

This is the reason why formal bias is an intrinsic possibility of formal systems. Formal abstraction cuts the essential connections between objects and their contexts in terms of which dialectics uncover their potentialities. In so doing, it ignores an important dimension of the truth of reality, that which concerns the inner tensions in its objects that point toward possibilities of progressive development. Instead, the objects are conceptualized as fixed and frozen, unchanging in themselves but available for manipulation from without. It is this way of constructing its objects that comes back to haunt formal thinking in the biased application of its products. Formal bias arises as soon as the abstracted objects it constructs are reintegrated to a real world of historical contingencies. At that point, the essential relation between the abstraction and the residue of material content from which it was abstracted is revealed as a predestination to domination. Then it becomes clear that "formalization and functionalization are, *prior* to all application, the 'pure form' of a concrete societal practice."[24]

> The hypothetical system of forms and functions becomes dependent on another system - a pre-established universe of ends, in which and *for* which it develops. What appeared extraneous, foreign to the theoretical project, shows forth as part of its very structure (method and concepts); pure objectivity reveals itself as object *for* a *subjectivity* which provides the Telos, the ends. In the construction of the technological reality, there is no such thing as a purely rational scientific order; the process of technological rationality is a political process.[25]

So long as formal abstractions co-exist with the "second dimension" of substantive universals, culture is divided to reflect the real contradictions of class society. It is possible, on the terms of such a divided culture, to formulate transcending potentialities of the society. Under these conditions, social criticism can become mass consciousness and lead to revolutionary change in the interest of realizing the emancipatory potential of the given level of technical civilization. Marxism was elaborated under just such conditions.

However, in advanced industrial societies, Marcuse argues, the second dimension is increasingly replaced by concepts drawn from the apparatus of technological rationality. As every aspect of social life comes to be articulated exclusively through technical concepts, "transcending" thought and action becomes correspondingly more difficult to conceive. The identification of social crises and injustices no longer points toward the need for fundamental social change, but instead indicates technical problems that must be resolved under the norm of efficiency. The modes of action and organization of the given society, which presuppose domination, operate as invariant, a priori concepts in the "solutions" offered, and so technological rationality takes on a distinctly conservative political cast.

The link between this form of instrumentalism and domination becomes apparent in the paradox of advanced societies, increasingly effective in controlling not only nature but also man himself. Every advance in the power of formalistic thought and action is an advance in the suppression of men. Minimally, this suppression takes the form of repressing the potentialities for peace and freedom made possible by technical progress itself. At its extreme point of absurdity, pure formalism may someday become material in the destruction of the earth through the untrammelled exercise of technical power in nuclear war.

Science, Technology, and Socialism: Science and Liberation

On what condition can the advance of human intelligence and control of nature issue not in the instrumentalization and domination of man but in human liberation? In answering this question, Marcuse's thought becomes frankly speculative and utopian. He argues that reason can only serve humane purposes through the recovery of a dialectical conception of reality, in which being is recognized as fraught with potentialities for liberation. This he believes to be possible on the basis of the Marxist historical reformulation of the concept of being and the immense technical power of advanced societies. The split between metaphysical and technical goals is no longer rational, but can finally be overcome. Marcuse foresees the day when his third thesis would be rendered historically obsolete by the emergence of a new science and technology.

The exploration of these themes is really the subject of another essay on Marcuse's theory of liberation. However, the discussion of Marcuse's critique of technology would not be complete without an examination of some of its positive implications. This examination will show that Marcuse's approach is rich in speculative anticipations of the new society, but also marred by tensions and problems that result, I believe, from the lack of a conceptual framework such as one introduced above for the analysis of the forms of bias and the relation of technique and technology. It is in fact here in Marcuse's theory of liberation that the limitations of his rhetorical strategy, based on playing off his two critiques of technology against each other, finally pose serious problems for the coherence of his position.

The worst of these problems arise in his speculations on the new science. Marcuse's critique of formal rationality helps to understand the role of scientific-technical knowledge in the elaboration of formally biased systems of all sorts, including technology. However, it is unclear from Marcuse's discussion how this can be changed. Did Marcuse wish to suggest the abolition of formal thinking in a free society? If not, in what would this new science consist?

Marcuse has far more trouble offering a plausible answer to this question than to similar ones concerning technology. There is a good reason for this. The socialist reconstruction of social systems and institutions, technologies and forms of organization can proceed through the recombination of formally neutral elements. But what raw material is available for the reconstruction of those elements themselves? How can the process of formal abstraction be transformed as Marcuse proposes without being negated as such? And yet Marcuse explicitly rejects the regression to a "qualitative physics."[26]

Instead he argues for the necessity of science "becoming political," incorporating human values into its very structure. And he claims that "in constituting themselves *methodically* as political enterprise, science and technology would *pass beyond* the stage at which they were, because of their neutrality, *subjected* to politics and against their intent functioning as political instrumentalities."[27] For example, he suggests that science would overcome the split between value and fact, essence and existence, in "quantifying" values, and he proposes that the ability of science to calculate such things as necessary food supplies shows this to be possible.[28] The significance of this example escapes me, for such quantification might serve besiegers starving out a city just as well as humanitarians fending off world hunger. Still more confusing is the suggestion that a new science could determine values for a socialist society, for surely Marcuse would have rejected the technocratic implications of such a proposal.[29] I do not believe this to be a plausible path toward a solution, at least not in Marcuse's very rough and programmatic formulations. In the domain of science, affirmative action in favor of values simply will not work.

These suggestions are characterized by the failure to distinguish between countering formal bias at the basic a priori level where it is present in pure scientific and technical knowledge, and countering such bias at the level of concrete social realizations such as technologies or institutions. Marcuse's suggestions for a radical reform of science and technique are modeled directly on effective strategies for dealing with formal bias as it appears in those latter realizations. He appears to believe that the way to remove the a priori bias of formal abstraction per se is to change the abstractive process to reincorporate the material content the exclusion of which is defining for it. Perhaps for lack of a terminology in which to state this problem, Marcuse seems unaware of it and never proposes an argument for the analogy he insists on making.

Marcuse's failure to clarify these issues adequately has consequences that are politically dangerous, for it suggests an analogy between the very active role of political power in institutional and technological change and its role in scientific change. We have seen that according to Marcuse's ontological critique of scientific-technical reason the neutral technical elements used in the reconstruction of society are themselves biased a priori toward domination, and it is this intrinsic bias which forms the background to their effective combination in technologies that serve to perpetuate the specific forms of domination prevailing in each historical epoch. Socialism would thus be working in some sense against the grain of its materials so long as a new cognitive dispensation had not occurred. Does this mean that political intervention into the development of scientific-technical rationality is necessary, by analogy with the role of politics in technological change? It would be possible to conclude as much from the structure of Marcuse's theory. And yet nowhere does he suggest that the necessary transformation of scientific-technical rationality is a political task. Rather, it is a scientific-technical task with political implications. The distinction is critical.

This clarification of Marcuse's position should help to distinguish it from the quite different position of the "Proletcult" group to which it bears an embarrassing resemblance. Shortly after the Russian Revolution, the Proletcult argued that all culture is intrinsically ideological - substantively biased in my terms - including such supposedly neutral elements as language, technology and science. The revolution would not be complete until a new "proletarian" culture had been created and substituted for the reactionary inheritance of the past.[30]

The assimilation of science to the superstructures as an ideological expression of bourgeois society seemed to resolve an inconsistency in the traditional Marxist treatment of the problem. Following Engels, most Marxists attributed the genesis of modern science to the uniquely favorable conditions of early bourgeois society, while insisting that this specific historical background in no way diminished the universality of the achievements of modern science. Proletcult treated science as Marxism had always treated law, art and other superstructures, eliminating the embarrassing residue of transhistorical scientific truth from the system.

Although both Lenin and Stalin opposed this view in theory, Lysenko was able to introduce political criteria into the actual institutional structure of Russian science. The catastrophic failure of this experiment in "proletarian" science continues to inspire a widespread and justified fear that the failure to distinguish between science and ideology threatens freedom of thought.

Marcuse was, of course, aware of this history, and his discussion of science in *One-Dimensional Man* is marked by an implicit worry that he will be misread as supporting political controls over science, if not its outright abolition. Yet without an explicit concept of formal bias, he has trouble differentiating his position from that of the Proletcult. Still, his intent to do so is clear enough. The most telling evidence for this is his refusal to attack the truth claims of modern science. He writes, for example, that "contemporary science is of immensely greater objective validity than its predecessors." And he argues that under socialism, scientific "hypotheses, without losing their rational character, would develop in an essentially different experimental context (that of a pacified world); consequently, science would arrive at essentially different concepts of nature and establish essentially different facts."[31] Thus not political power but scientists' own changing categories and perceptions in a radically new social environment would eventually inspire new types of questions and new theories, generated spontaneously in the course of research by scientists themselves. Presumably a similar change would occur at the level of pure technical knowledge.

The claim that such an evolution could ultimately eliminate the formal bias of scientific-technical rationality is probably not decidable in advance of the actual discoveries that would accomplish this immense revolution in the nature of reason. Philosophical study can at best hope to hold open the possibility that scientific development may proceed toward a new methodology embracing the contradictory character of reality. With respect to this possibility, Marcuse's speculations on the new science may be seen as imaginative symbols, but not as concrete proposals. The task of elaborating such proposals remains to be accomplished. It may be that new developments in science are already available to facilitate that task. There have been a number of attempts to argue this, for example by Prigogine and his collaborators. However, to examine their claims would take us far afield.

Toward a New Technology

Marcuse's ideas on the new technology are no less speculative than his ideas on science. However, they are far more interesting and suggestive. Under socialism, he argues, instrumental action would no longer be autonomized under the horizon of the given stage in the history of domination, but would come to incorporate elements of imagination, value and artistic consciousness working toward a higher stage of historical freedom. Formal thinking and modern technology would be reconciled with the suppressed dialectical mode of thought and the historical practice of realizing potentialities it guides. This reconciliation would mark the end of the history of class society and its associated subject. It would involve the emergence of a new subject with differently ordered faculties and correspondingly new forms of practice, unlike those of societies based on the domination of man by man.

It is evident that Marcuse's argument had to lead to a sort of eschatology of Reason. If it is class society that gives rise to the split in the concept of reason that divides the dialectical understanding of essence from the formalistic achievement of control, then the end of class society will see the end of this split. The theory leads rigorously to the conclusion that the derealized dimensions of metaphysics, art and the imagination, in which essence has been confined, must now be rejoined with real life through a completely new kind of scientific and technical practice. The two worlds must become one through a final reconciliation of essence and existence, real and ideal.

Technique would then tend to become art and art would tend to form reality: the opposition between imagination and reason, higher and lower faculties, poetic and scientific thought, would be invalidated. Emergence of a new Reality Principle: under which a new sensibility and a desublimated scientific intelligence would combine in the creation of an *aesthetic ethos*.[32]

What would be the content of this new form of technical practice? Obviously, it would have to continue to provide the food, shelter, medical care, and other amenities of civilized life. These goods are not relative to a particular type of society but relate to universal requirements of human nature. But according to Marcuse there are other human needs that are equally vital but which have been suppressed under the conditions of scarcity and class domination prevailing in the existing technological societies. These needs are loosely defined as "aesthetic," relating to beauty: the harmony of freedom and order exemplified by great works of art, the transcendence of struggle and striving in images of peace and fulfillment.

Marcuse argues that these aesthetic needs are not merely subjective, a function of changing taste, or merely spiritual, confined to the "higher" sphere of contemplation and feeling. Rather, the realm of the aesthetic is rooted in the order of nature itself and expresses tendencies in nature which come to consciousness in and through man. Marcuse suggests the "outrageous" concept of a "liberation of nature" to describe these tendencies, not in the sense of a natural teleology, but rather in the sense "that there are forces in nature which have been distorted and suppressed - forces which could support and enhance the liberation of man."[33]

In a free society, the realization of these tendencies would operate not alongside or over and above ordinary technical practice, as in the marginalized world of artistic production today, but in the very practice of transforming nature to make it serve human needs.

It remains to consider whether a beginning could be made toward creating such a new form of technical practice by applying the existing scientific-technical rationality. Although Marcuse himself does not seem to be aware of it, this is in reality the question of the consistency of his two critiques of technology.

According to Marcuse, socialism is only possible on the basis of the transformation of the technology inherited from capitalism. If the technical base is conserved rather than transformed, a "fateful continuity" will link the new society with the old, and insure the reproduction of the forms of repression and alienation the revolution was supposed to overcome. However, it will be recalled that scientific-technical rationality develops according to its own internal motives, under the influence of the social environment to be sure, but not on a schedule set by political events such as revolutions and policy changes. Thus there is no reason to assume that the revolution will be accompanied by simultaneous changes in the nature of rationality. And this means that the revolution can only succeed if it is able to employ the existing scientific-technical rationality *transitionally* while awaiting a new cognitive dispensation it cannot force by political means. How then would such transitional employment be distinguished from the sort of "fateful continuity" that would doom the revolution to failure?

Perhaps Marcuse does not pose this question because he fails to make explicit the different temporalities implied by his treatment of technology as subject to political control in contrast to science which is only loosely influenced by the environment. Unfortunately, the incompleteness of his theory on this point makes it appear either incoherent or unnecessarily utopian: Marcuse seems to call for a simultaneous and "total" revolution in so many spheres that no humanly possible social change could possibly satisfy him. His concept of the "great refusal" has been interpreted to support such a view although in fact it is the choice between lesser evils Marcuse rejects and not the achievement of positive but partial goods.

Although Marcuse does not solve this problem satisfactorily, his theory contains the means to construct a solution which avoids the excesses of both utopian technophobia and uncritical acceptance of given technology as a fate. Recall that the essential flaw in scientific-technical rationality, by which it is bound to biased application, lies in its reified decontextualization of the objects it constructs. Thus it should be possible to at least advance toward a new technology by multiplying the contexts and technical systems that interact in any given application to take into account more and more of the essential features of the object. ' The initial steps in this direction are obvious and concern the integration of ecological, medical, aesthetic, and work-democratic considerations into the existing technologies to begin the movement toward a better society.' Thus just as technical practice now incorporates the requirements of domination in its basic structure, in a free society it would instead incorporate the requirements of peace and freedom.

The Radical Critique of Bourgeois Culture

Marcuse's theory of socialism draws together the Marxist aim of a disalienation of industrial society, the modern avant garde's struggle for a radical desublimation of art, and the contemporary environmental critique of productivist industrialism. At the core of his positive theory is a reevaluation of the aesthetic, as the source of new needs and a new practice of freedom. He believes his theory of the aesthetic can be rooted in Marx's work, and he refers to Marx's *Economic and Philosophic Manuscripts* as the evidence for this surprising notion. He writes:

> Aesthetics of liberation, beauty as a "form" of freedom: it looks as if Marx has shied away from this anthropomorphist, idealistic conception. Or is this apparently idealistic notion rather the *enlargement of the materialistic base?* For "man is directly a *natural being*; he is a corporeal, living, real, sensuous, objective being" who has "real, sensuous objects" as the objects of his life . . . . This is . . . the extension of Historical Materialism to a dimension which is to play a vital role in the liberation of man.[34]

The connection to Marx suggested by Marcuse is not entirely persuasive, and yet there is a larger context to Marcuse's projections which encompasses Marx as well. This context is the mood of revulsion at bourgeois culture that runs through the whole history of the European intelligensia and artistic avant gardes from the mid nineteenth century until quite recently.

It is Marcuse's relationship to this traditional radical critique of bourgeois culture which determines his positive attitude toward the future despite his abandonment of orthodox Marxist determinism. Yet even this revised form of historical hope seems eccentric in the contemporary theoretical context. In recent years, non-communist left theory has paid more and more attention to the procedural defense of socialism in terms of its potential for enlarging democratic dialogue. This approach no doubt represents a reasonable reaction to charges of totalitarianism increasingly addressed to Marxism. Yet at the same time, one wonders if the procedural emphasis is not a function of the success of the system in "delivering the goods," as Marcuse would say. To provide a substantive theory today of the "content" of freedom poses especially difficult problems since it is not immediately obvious what needs require satisfaction beyond the horizon of the advanced societies.

As a Hegelian and a Marxist, Marcuse refused to address the formal question of freedom in isolation from the content or purpose for which men and women might struggle to achieve it. If this content could no longer be found in the necessities of life, then it had to be sought elsewhere - for example in the aesthetic - if socialist theory were ever to connect with real history again. Marcuse's response to this challenge is astonishingly radical and imaginative. It flows from his critique of technological rationality as a cultural system, a way of life, a general form of social practice and corresponding needs.

Marcuse's rejection of this culture must be understood on the analogy of the rejection of bourgeois society and its culture by earlier critics. Like them Marcuse attempts to project a different way of life from that of the existing societies, one which fulfills dimensions of the human personality that are systematically suppressed today. It is this extremely radical cultural break with the existing societies that thrusts Marcuse headlong into imaginative speculations drawn from the whole history of modern artistic and political critique.

It is strange that such a radical theory, based on such sources, should be so obviously out of tune with the mood of the left today, only a few years after Marcuse's death, and yet this is the case. If Marcuse already seems to come from another era, this may be due less to the implausibility of his speculative projections than to the increasing resignation of intellectuals in the West, less and less able to imagine a truly radical break with the present.

I want to take this opportunity to thank Gerald Doppelt for his criticism of an earlier draft of this chapter. Comments by Robert Pippin, Douglas Kellner, and Anne-Marie Feenberg were also useful to me in improving the chapter, and I thank them for their help.

NOTES

1. Herbert Marcuse, *One-Dimensional Man* (Boston, 1964), pp. xv-xvi.
2. *One-Dimensional Man*, p. 168; Marcuse, *An Essay on Liberation* (Boston, 1969), p. 12.
3. *One-Dimensional Man* p. 231-32; cf. pp. 221-22.
4. Habermas, "Technology and Science as 'Ideology,'" in *Toward a Rational Society*, pp. 88-90.
5. Joachim Bergmann, "Technologische Rationalität und spätkapitalistische Ökonomie," in Jürgen Habermas, ed., *Antworten auf Herbert Marcuse*, pp. 99-100.
6. *One-Dimensional Man*, p. 251.
7. Plato, *Gorgias*, p. 51.
8. Karl Marx, *Capital* New York, 1906 reprint), vol. 1, p. 363.
9. *Ibid.,* vol. 1, p.
10. *Ibid.,* vol. 1, pp. 475-76.
11. Marcuse, "Industrialization and Capitalism in the Work of Max Weber," in *Negations* (Boston, 1968), p. 225.
12. *Ibid.,* p. 212. Cf. *One-Dimensional Man* p. 144-45.
13. Habermas, "Technology and Science as 'Ideology,'" p. 84.
14. *One-Dimensional Man*, p. 154.
15. *Ibid.,* p. 158.
16. *Ibid.,* p. 232. For more on this subject, see Andrew Feenberg, "Transition or Convergence: Communism and the Paradox of Development," in Frederick Fleron, ed., *Technology and Communist Culture.*
17. *One-Dimensional Man*, p. 166.
18. Habermas, "Technology and Science as 'Ideology,'" pp. 85-86; William Leiss, *The Domination of Nature*, pp. 211-12.
19. *One-Dimensional Man*, p. 156; cf. pp. 138, 147, 158, 168; and in Marcuse's essay on Max Weber in *Negations*, p. 215.
20. For a useful discussion of relevant issues in Weber, see, Donald McIntosh, "Max Weber as a Critical Theorist," *Theory and Society* (January 1983).
21. For more on this subject, see Andrew Feenberg, *Lukacs, Marx and the Sources of Critical Theory*, chapter 3.
22. *One-Dimensional Man*, p. 146.
23. *Ibid.,* pp. 105-106.
24. *Ibid.,* p. 157.
25. *Ibid.,* p. 168.
26. *Ibid.,* p. 166.
27. *Ibid.,* pp. 233-34.
28. *Ibid.,* p. 232.
29. *Ibid.,* p. 233.
30. For an interesting analysis of the cultural problems raised by this group, see Carmen Claudin-Urondo, *Lénin et la révolution culturelle,* pp. 47-60.
31. *One-Dimensional Man*, pp. 166-67.
32. Marcuse, *An Essay on Liberation*, p. 24. For a more detailed

account of these new forms of social practice, see Andrew Feenberg, *Lukacs, Marx and the Sources of Critical Theory*, chapter 8.

33. Marcuse, *Counterrevolution and Revolt* (Boston, 1972), p. 66.

34. *Ibid.*, pp. 67-68.

BIBLIOGRAPHY

Abrams, M. H. *Natural Supernaturalism*. New York: Norton, 1973.
Adorno, Theodor. *Über Walter Benjamin*. Frankfurt: 1970.
_____. *Zur Metakritik der Erkenntnistheorie*. Stuttgart: 1956.
Allison, David B., ed. *The New Nietzsche: Contemporary Styles in Interpretation*. With introduction by editor. New York: Dell Pub. Co., 1977.
Apel, Karl Otto. "Sprechaktstheorie und transzendentale Sprachprogramatik - Zur Frage ethischer Normen." In *Sprachprogramatik und Philosophie*. Frankfurt: 1976.
Arato, Andrew. Review of *Rudolf Bahro: Critical Responses*. In *Telos* no. 48 (Summer 1981).
Arendt, Hannah, ed. *Illuminations*. Translated by Harry Zohn. New York: Harcourt, Brace and World, 1968.
Armand, F., and **R. Maublanc.** *Fourier: Textes Choisis*. Paris: Editions Sociales Internationales, 1937.
Aronson, Ronald. *The Dialectic of Disaster*. London: New Left Books, 1983.
Axelos, Kostas. *Einführung in ein kunftiges Denken: Über Marx und Heidegger*. Tübingen: 1966.
Beck, Maximilian, ed. *Philosophische Hefte*, no. 1 (Berlin, July 1928).
Benjamin, Walter. "Eduard Fuchs: Collector and Historian." In *New German Critique* 5 (Spring 1975). Reprinted in Arendt, ed., *Illuminations*.
_____. "Theses on the Philosophy of History." In Arendt, ed., *Illuminations*.
Bergmann, Joachim. "Technologische Rationalität und spätkapitalistische Ökonomie." In *Antworten auf Herbert Marcuse*, edited by Jürgen Habermas. Frankfurt: Suhrkamp, 1968.

257

Bernstein, Richard. "Herbert Marcuse: An Immanent Critique." In *Social Theory and Practice* 1, no. 4 (Fall 1971).

_____. *Praxis and Action.* Philadelphia: 1971.

Blondel, Eric. "Nietzsche: Life as Metaphor." In *The New Nietzsche: Contemporary Styles in Interpretation.* Edited, with introduction by David B. Allison. New York: Dell Pub. Co., 1977.

Brecht, Bertolt. "Volkstumlichkeit und Realismus." In *Gesammelte Werke.* 20 volumes. Frankfurt am Main: Suhrkamp, 1967.

Breines, Paul, ed. *Critical Interruptions.* New York: Herder and Herder, 1970.

Breton, André. *What is Surrealism?* Translated by David Gascoyne. London: 1936.

Bronner, Stephen Eric. "Expressionism and Marxism: Towards an Aesthetic of Emancipation." In *Passion and Rebellion: The Expressionist Heritage.* Edited by Stephen Eric Bronner and Douglas Kellner. South Hadley, Mass.: Bergin & Garvey, 1983.

_____. "Reconstructing the Experiment: Politics, Ideology and the American New Left." In *Social Text* 8 (Winter 1983-84).

Brown, B. *Marx, Freud and the Critique of Everyday Life.* Boston: Monthly Review Press, 1973.

Buck-Morss, S. *The Origin of the Negative Dialectic.* New York: Free Press, 1977.

Bulthaup, Peter, ed. *Materialien zu Benjamins Thesen "Über den Begriff der Geschichte."* Frankfurt: 1975.

Claudin-Orondo, Carmen. *Lénin et la révolution culturelle.* The Hague: Mouton, 1975.

Clecak, Peter. *Radical Paradoxes.* New York: Harper and Row, 1973.

Coleridge. *Biographia Literaria.* Edited by J. Shawcross. Oxford: The Clarendon Press, 1965.

Cranston, Maurice. "Herbert Marcuse." *Encounter* 32, no. 3 (1969).

Dawson, Carl. *Victorian Noon; English Literature in 1850.* Baltimore: Johns Hopkins University Press, 1979.

Dilthey, Wilhelm. *Aufbau der geschichtlichen Welt in den Geisteswissenschaften.*

_____. *Gesammelte Schriften.* vol. 7 3d. ed. Stuttgart/Gottingen: 1960.

Dilthey, Wilhelm, and **Paul Yorck von Wartenburg.** *Briefwechsel zwischen Wilhelm Dilthey und dem Grafen Paul Yorck von Wartenburg, 1877-1897.* Edited by Sigrid von der Schulenberg. Halle a.d.s.: Max Niemeyer, 1923.

Dimitrov, George. In *United Front.* San Francisco: Proletarian Publishers, 1975.

Dubiel, Helmut, and **Alfons Sollner,** eds. *Wirtschaft, Recht und Staat im Nationalsozialismus.* Frankfurt: Europäische Verlangsanstalt, 1981. *Studien über Autorität und Familie.* 2 volumes. Paris: Felix Alcan, 1936.

Ebbinhaus. *Über das Gedachtnis.* Leipzig: 1885.

Ellul, Jacques. *The Technological Society.* Translated by John

Wilkinson. New York: 1964.

Engels, Frederick. "Die Kommunisten und Herr Heinzen." In *Deutschen-Brusseler-Zeitung. 1847.*

_____. Letter to Margaret Harkness. In Marx and Engels. *Selected Correspondence.* Moscow: 1965.

_____. *Ludwig Feuerbach and the End of Classical German Philosophy.* In Karl Marx and Frederick Engels, *Selected Works.* 3 volumes. Moscow: 1969.

Ermath, Michael. *Wilhelm Dilthey: The Critique of Historical Reason.* Chicago: University of Chicago Press, 1978.

Feenberg, Andrew. "Transition or Convergence: Communism and the Paradox of Development." In *Technology and Communist Culture.* Edited by Frederick Fleron. New York: Praeger, 1977.

_____. *Lukacs, Marx and the Sources of Critical Theory.* Totowa, New Jersey: Rowman and Littlefield, 1981.

Fenichel O. *The Psychoanalytic Theory of Neurosis.* New York: Norton, 1945.

Fischer, Ernst. *The Necessity of Art: A Marxist Approach.* Translated by Anna Bostock. London: 1959.

Foucault, Michel. *History of Sexuality.* New York: Random House, 1978.

Freud, Sigmund. *Beyond the Pleasure Principle.* New York: Norton, 1920.

_____. *Civilization and Its Discontents.* Translated and Edited by James Strachey. New York: Norton, 1961.

_____. *Collected Papers.* vol. 3. London: Hogarth Press, 1950.

_____. *The Ego and the Id.* Translated by Joan Riviere. New York: 1960.

_____. *Group Psychology and the Analysis of the Ego.* New York: Norton, 1959; 1922.

_____. "Negation." In *General Psychological Theory.* Edited by Philip Rieff. New York: 1963.

_____. *New Introductory Lectures.* New York: Norton, 1965; 1932.

_____. "Repression." In *General Psychological Theory.*

_____. *The Standard Edition of the Complete Psychological Works of Sigmund Freud.* Translated by James Strachey and Anna Freud. vol. 3. London: 1962.

_____. "The Theme of the Three Caskets." In *Character and Culture.*

_____. "Two Principles in Mental Functioning." In *General Psychological Theory.*

_____. *Totem and Taboo.* New York: Vintage, 1912.

Freyer, H. *Theorie des gegenwartigen Zeitalters.* Stuttgart: 1956.

_____. *Über das Dominantwerden technischer Kategorien in der Lebenswelt der industrieller Gesellschaft.* Mainz: Mainzer Akademie der Wissenschaften und der Literatur, 1960.

Friedman, G. *The Political Psychology of the Frankfurt School.* Ithaca: Cornell University Press, 1981.

Fromm, Erich. *The Crisis of Psychoanalysis.* New York: Holt, Rinehart and Winston, 1970.

Fry, John. *Marcuse - Dilemma and Liberation.* New York: Humanities Press, 1974.

Furlong, E. J. *A Study of Memory.* London: 1951.

Gabel, J. *False Consciousness.* New York: Harper and Row, 1975.

_____. "La Reification, essai d'une psychopathologie de la pensée dialectique." *Esprit*, October, 1951.

Gadamer, H. G. *Truth and Method.* New York: Seabury, 1975.

Gagnebin, Jeanne M. *Zur Geschichtsphilosophie Walter Benjamins. Die Unabgeschlossenheit des Sinnes.* Erlangen: Palm und Enke, 1978.

Gehlen, A. *Die Seele im technischen Zeitalter.* Hamburg: 1957.

_____. "Über kulturelle Kristallisation." In *Studien zur Anthropologie und Soziologie.* Neuwied und Berlin: 1963.

de George, Richard T., ed., *Ethics and Society.* New York: Anchor Books, 1966.

Gill, M. "Metapsychology is not Psychology." *Psychological Issues,* 9 (4, Mono 36), 1967.

Gill, M., and P. Holzman. *Psychology Versus Metapsychology.* New York: International Universities Press, 1976.

Gould, Carol. *Marx's Social Ontology.* Cambridge: M.I.T. Press, 1978.

Gouldner, Alvin W. *The Two Marxisms.* New York: Seabury, 1980.

Habermas, Jürgen. "Consciousness-Raising or Redemptive Criticism - The Contemporaneity of Walter Benjamin." In *New German Critique* 17 (Spring 1979).

_____. *Karl Löwiths stoischer Rückzug vom historischen Bewusstsein.*

_____. *Legitimation Crisis.* Boston: Beacon Press, 1975.

_____. "Technology and Science as Ideology: For Herbert Marcuse on his 70th Birthday." In Jürgen Habermas, *Toward a Rational Society.* Translated by Jeremy Shapiro. Boston: 1970.

_____. *Theorie und Praxis.* Neuwied/Berlin: 1963.

_____. "Toward a Reconstruction of Historical Materialism." In *Communication and the Evolution of Society.* Translated by Thomas McCarthy. Boston: Beacon Press, 1979.

Hartmann, H. *Ego Psychology and the Problem of Adaptation.* New York: International Universities Press, 1958.

Hartmann, H., E. Kris, and **R. Lowenstein.** "Comments on the Formation of Psychic Structure." *Psychoanalytic Study of the Child.* 2 (1946): 11-38.

_____. "Papers on Psychoanalytic Psychology." *Psychological Issues,* 4 (2), 1964.

Hegel, G. W. F. *On Art, Religion, and Philosophy.* Edited by J. Glenn Gray. New York: 1970.

_____. *Phenomenology of Spirit.* Translated by A. V. Miller. Oxford: Oxford University Press, 1977.

_____. *The Phenomenology of Mind.* Translated by J. B. Baille. New York: 1967.

Heidegger, Martin. *Being and Time.* Translated by John Macquarrie and Edward Robinson. New York: Harper and Row, 1962.

_____. *Sein und Zeit.* 9th edition. Tübingen: 1960.

Held, D. *Introduction to Critical Theory*. Berkeley: University of California Press, 1980.

Hobsbawm, E. J. *Industry and Empire*. vol. 2, 1750 to the Present Day. New York: Random House, 1968.

Hodgson, Godffrey. *America in Our Time*. New York: Random House: 1976.

Holt, R. "Drive or Wish." In *Psychological Issues*, 1976, 9, (4, Mono 36).

_____. *Freud's Mechanistic and Humanistic Images of Man*. In Holt, R. and Peterfreund, eds., *Psychoanalysis and Contemporary Science*. New York: Macmillan, 1972.

_____. "The Past and Future of Ego Psychology." In *Psychoanalytic Quarterly*, 1975, 44, (4), 550-576.

Holz, H. H. "Der Irrtum der 'Grossen Weigerung'." In *Blätter für deutsche und internationale Politik*, 1, (1968).

Horkheimer, Max. "Thoughts on Religion." In *Critical Theory; Selected Essays*. Translated by Matthew J. O'Connell and others. New York: Seabury Press, 1972.

_____. "Traditional and Critical Theory." In *Critical Theory*. New York: Seabury Press, 1972.

Horkheimer, Max, and **Theodor Adorno.** *Dialectic of Enlightenment*. Translated by John Cumming. New York: 1972.

_____. *Dialektik der Aufklärung*. Amsterdam: 1947. English translation by John Cumming. New York: 1972.

Jacoby, Russel. *Social Amnesia: a Critique of Conformist Psychology from Adler to Laing*. Boston: Beacon Press, 1975.

Jameson, Fredric. *Marxism and Form: Twentieth-Century Theories of Literature*. Princeton: Princeton University Press, 1971.

Jay, Martin. *The Dialectical Imagination*. Boston: Little, Brown, 1973.

_____. "The Extraterritorial Life of Siegfried Kracauer." In *Salmagundi* 31-32 (Fall 1975 - Winter 1976).

Katz, Barry. *Herbert Marcuse and the Art of Liberation*. London: 1982.

Kellner, Douglas. "Authenticity and Heidegger's Challenge to Ethical Theory." In *Thinking about Being*. Edited by Robert W. Shahar and J. W. Mohanty. Norman: University of Oklahoma Press, 1984.

_____. "Critical Theory, Commodities, and the Consumer Society. In *Theory, Culture, and Society* n.3 (1983):66-84.

_____. "Critical Theory, Mass Communications, and Popular Culture." In *Telos*. (Forthcoming.)

_____. "Critical Theory, Max Weber, and the Dialectics of Domination." In Antonio, Robert J., and Ronald Glassman, eds. *The Weber-Marx Dialogue*. Lawrence: University of Kansas Press, 1985.

_____. "The Frankfurt School Revisited." In *New German Critique* 4 (Winter 1975):131-152.

_____. *Heidegger's Concept of Authenticity*. Ph.D. dissertation. Columbia University, 1973.

_____. *Herbert Marcuse and the Crisis of Marxism*. London and

Berkeley: Macmillan and University of California, 1984.

_____. ed. *Karl Korsch: Revolutionary Theory.* University of Texas Press, 1977.

Kierkegaard, Søren. *Fear and Trembling and The Sickness unto Death.* Translated by Walter Lowrie. Princeton: 1969.

Klein, G. "Ego in Psychoanalysis." In *Psychoanalytic Review* 56, no. 4 (1969-70):511-25.

Klossowsky, Pierre. "Nietzsche's Experience of the Eternal Return." In Allison, ed., *The New Nietzsche: Contemporary Styles of Interpretation.*

Kohut, H. *The Analysis of the Self.* New York: International Universities Press, 1971.

_____. *Essays on Ego Psychology.* New York: International Universities Press, 1964.

_____. *Restoration of the Self.* New York: International Universities Press, 1977.

Korsch, Karl. *Marxism and Philosophy.* London: New Left Books, 1970.

Kosik. *Dialektik des Konkreten.*

Landes, Joan B. "Marcuse's Feminist Dimension." *Telos* 41 (Fall 1979).

Landmann, Michael. "Talking With Ernst Bloch: Korcula, 1968." *Telos* 25 (Fall 1975).

Langbaum, Robert. *Mysteries of Identity: A Theme in Modern Literature.* New York: Oxford University Press, 1977.

Laski, Harold J. *The Rise of European Liberalism.* London: George Allen and Unwin Ltd., 1958.

Lauth, Reinhard. *Die absolute Ungeschichtlichkeit der Wahrheit.* Stuttgart: 1966.

Leiss, William. *The Domination of Nature.* New York: Braziller, 1972.

Lenhardt, Christian. "Anamnestic Solidarity: The Proletariat and its *Manes.*" *Telos* 25 (Fall 1975).

Lenin, V. I. *Zwei Arbeiten zur Gewerkschaftsfrage.* Berlin: 1957.

_____. "Zwei Taktiken der Sozialdemokratie in der demokratischen Revolution." In *Ausgewählte Werke in zwei Bänden.* vol. 1. Berlin: 1955.

von Leyden, W. *Remembering: A Philosophical Problem.* New York: Philosophical Library, 1961.

Lichtman, Richard. "Marx's Theory of Ideology." *Socialist Revolution* 23 (1975).

_____. "The Facade of Equality in Liberal Democratic Theory." *Inquiry* 12 (1969).

_____. *The Production of Desire.* New York: The Free Press, 1982.

Lingis, Alphonso. "The Will to Power." In Allison, ed., *The New Nietzsche: Contemporary Styles of Interpretation.*

Locke, John. *Second Treatise on Government.*

Löwith, Karl. *Heidegger, Denker in dürftiger Zeit.* 2d. ed. Gottingen: 1960

Lukacs, George. *Die Seele und die Formen.* Neuwied: 1971.

_____. *Goethe and His Age.* Translated by Robert Anchor. New

York: 1969.
_____. *History and Class Consciousness*. Cambridge: M.I.T. Press, 1971.
_____. *Lenin*. Vienna: 1924.
_____. *The Theory of the Novel*. Translated by Anna Bostock. Cambridge, Mass.: M.I.T. Press, 1971.
MacIntyre, Alisdair. *Herbert Marcuse: An Exposition and a Polemic.* New York: Viking, 1970.
Magee, Bryan. Interview with Herbert Marcuse. In *Men and Ideas.* London: BBC Publications, 1978.
Malcolm, Norman. *Memory and Mind.* Ithaca and London: Cornell University Press, 1977.
Marcuse, Herbert. *The Aesthetic Dimension: Toward a Critique of Marxist Aesthetics.* Boston: Beacon Press, 1978.
_____. "The Affirmative Character of Culture." In *Negations.*
_____. "Art and Revolution." In *Partisan Review.* (Spring 1972).
_____. "Autorität und Familie in der deutschen Soziologie bis 1933." In *Studium*: 737-752.
_____. "Beiträge zu einer Phänomenologie des Historischen Materialismus." In *Philosophische Hefte.* 1 (July 1928); in *Hegels Ontologie.* Frankfurt am Main: 1932; in *Schriften* 1. Frankfurt: Suhrkamp, 1979.
_____. "The Concept of Essence." In *Negations.*
_____. *Counterrevolution and Revolt.* Boston: Beacon Press, 1972.
_____. *Das Ende der Utopie.* Berlin: 1967.
_____. "De l'ontologie à la technologie." In *Arguments* 4, no. 18 (1960):54-59.
_____. *Der deutsche Künstlerroman.* Ph.D. dissertation submitted to the University of Freiburg, 1922. Reprinted in *Schriften.*
_____. *Die Gesellschaftslehre des sowjetischen Marxismus.* Neuwied and Berlin: 1964.
_____. "The End of Utopia." In *Five Lectures.*
_____. *Eros and Civilization; A Philosophical Inquiry into Freud.* Boston: Beacon Press, 1955, 1966; New York: Vintage, 1962, 1966.
_____. *An Essay on Liberation.* Boston: Beacon Press, 1969.
_____. *Five Lectures: Psychoanalysis, Politics, and Utopia.* Translated by Jeremy Shapiro and Shierry M. Weber. Boston: Beacon Press 1969, 1970.
_____. "The Foundations of Historical Materialism." In *Studies in Critical Philosophy.* Translated by Joris de Bres. Boston: Beacon Press, 1972, 1973.
_____. *Hegels Ontologie und die Grundlegung einer Theorie der Geschichtlichkeit.* Leipzig and Frankfurt am Main: 1932.
_____. *Hegels Ontologie und die Theorie der Geschichtlichkeit.* Frankfurt: Klostermann, 1968.
_____. "Industrialiserung und Kapitalismus im Werk Max Webers." In *Kultur und Gesellschaft 2.* Frankfurt am Main: 1965.
_____. "Industrialization and Capitalism in the Work of Max Weber." In *Negations.* Boston: Beacon Press, 1968.

____. Interview with *The New York Times* (October 27, 1968):89.

____. *Kultur und Gesellschaft 2.* Frankfurt am Main: 1965.

____. "Marxism and Feminism." In *Women's Studies* 2, no. 3 (1974):279-288.

____. *Negations.* Translated by Jeremy Shapiro. Boston: Beacon Press, 1963.

____. "Neue Quellen zur Grundlegung des Historischen Materialismus." In *Die Gesellschaft.* vol. 9, part 2, 1932. Reprinted in *Philosophie und Revolution.*

____. "On the Problem of the Dialectic." Translated by Morton Schoolman and Duncan Smith. *Telos* 27 (Spring 1976).

____. "The Obsolescence of Marxism." In *Marx and the Western World.* Edited by Nicholas Lobkowicz. Notre Dame: Notre Dame University Press, 1967.

____. "The Obsolescence of the Freudian Concept of Man." In *Five Lectures.*

____. *One-Dimensional Man: Studies in the Ideology of Advanced Industrial Society.* Boston: Beacon Press: 1964.

____. *Philosophie und Revolution*, vol. 1. Berlin: 1967.

____. "Philosophy and Critical Theory." In *Negations.* Translated by Jeremy Shapiro. Harmondsworth: Penguin, 1968; Boston: Beacon Press, 1968.

____. Preface to Raya Dunayevskaya. *Marxism and Freedom.* New York: Bookman, 1957.

____. "Progress and Freud's Theory of Instincts." In *Five Lectures.* Translated by Jeremy J. Shapiro and Shierry M. Weber. Boston: 1969.

____. "Protosocialism and Late Capitalism: Toward a Theoretical Synthesis Based on Bahro's Analysis." In *Rudolf Bahro: Critical Responses.* Edited by Ulf Wolter. New York: 1980.

____. *Reason and Revolution: Hegel and the Rise of Social Theory.* New York: Oxford University Press, 1941. 2nd ed., New York: Humanities Press, 1954, with a new Epilogue; London, 1955; Boston: Beacon Press, 1960, with a new Preface; 1969.

____. "Repressive Tolerance." In *A Critique of Pure Tolerance.* Edited by Robert Paul Wolff, Barrington Moore, Jr., and Herbert Marcuse. Boston: 1969.

____. Review of John Nef's *War and Human Progress.* In *American Historical Review* 57, no. 1 (October 1951):97-100.

____. *Schriften* 1. Frankfurt: Suhrkamp, 1978.

____. "Some Social Implications of Modern Technology." In *Studies Philosophy and Social Science* 9, no. 3 (1941):414-439.

____. *Soviet Marxism: A Critical Analysis.* New York: Columbia University Press, 1958; New York: Vintage, 1961.

____. "Über die philosophischen Grundlagen des wirtschafts-wissenschaftlichen Arbeitsbegriffs." In *Kultur und Gesellschaft.*

____. "Über konkrete Philosophie." In Herbert Marcuse, *Philosophie und Revolution.* Bk. 1. Berlin: 1967.

____. "Zur Auseinandersetzung mit Hans Freyers 'Soziologie als Wirklichkeitswissenschaft.'" In *Philosophische Hefte* 3, 1/2 (1931).

_____. "Zur Wahrheitsproblematique der soziologischen Methode." In *Die Gesellschaft* 6 (1929). Reprinted in Adorno, Horkheimer, Marcuse. *Kritische Theorie der Gesellschaft.*

Marcuse, Herbert, Jürgen Habermas, Heinz Lubascz, and Telman Spengler. "Theory and Politics: A Discussion with Herbert Marcuse, Jürgen Habermas, Heinz Lubascz, and Telman Spengler." In *Telos* 38 (Winter 1978-79).

Marx, Karl. *Capital.* vol. 1. New York: Modern Library, 1906 reprint.

_____. *Das Kapital.* vol. 1. Berlin: 1955.

_____. *Die deutsche Ideologie.* Berlin: 1953.

_____. *Selected Writings.* Edited by David McLellan. Oxford: Oxford University Press, 1977.

_____. *Zur Kritik der politischen Ökonomie.* Berlin: 1951.

Marx, Karl, and Friedrich Engels. *Collected Works.* vol. 5. New York: International Publishers, 1976.

_____. *Selected Works.* vol. 1. Moscow: 1969.

_____. *Werke.* vol. 4. Berlin: 1964.

Mattick, Paul. *Critique of Marcuse.* New York: Seabury, 1973.

McIntosh, Donald. "Max Weber as a Critical Theorist." In *Theory and Society* (January 1983).

Mill, John Stuart. *Dissertations and Discussions.* London: John W. Parker and Son, 1859.

_____. "On Liberty." In *The Philosophy of John Stuart Mill,* edited by Marshall Cohen. New York: Modern Library, 1961.

_____. *Principles of Political Economy.* London: John W. Parker and Son, 1857.

_____. Testimony in *Report from the Select Committee on Investments for the Savings of the Middle and Working Classes.* London: House of Commons, 1850.

Mitchell, J. *Psychoanalysis and Feminism.* New York: Pantheon, 1974.

Mitzman, Arthur. Interview with Herbert Marcuse. Austin, Texas, October 1980.

Nietzsche, F. *The Genealogy of Morals.* Translated by Walter Kaufmann. New York: Vintage Books, 1967.

O'Neill, John. "Critique and Remembrance." In *On Critical Theory,* edited by John O'Neill. New York: Seabury Press, 1976.

Olafson, Frederick. "Heidegger's Politics: Interview with Herbert Marcuse." *Graduate Faculty Philosophy Journal* 6 (Winter 1977).

Palmier, Jean-Michel. *Herbert Marcuse et la nouvelle gauche.* Paris: Belfond, 1973.

Patcher, Henry. "The Idea of Progress in Marxism." In *Socialism in History: Political Essays of Henry Patcher.* Edited by Stephen Eric Bronner. New York: 1984.

Piccone, Paul. "Phenomenological Marxism." *Telos* 9 (Fall 1971).

Piccone, Paul, and Alexander Delfini. "Herbert Marcuse's Heideggerean Marxism." *Telos* 6 (Fall 1970).

Pippin, Robert B. "Hegel's Phenomenological Criticism." In *Man and*

World 8 (1975).

Plato. *Gorgias.* New York: Bobbs-Merrill, 1952.

Pogrebin Brown, Alison. *Marcuse: The Path of His Thought.* (Forthcoming.)

Pollock, Frederick. *The Economic and Social Consequences of Automation.* Oxford: Blackwell, 1957.

Poster, Mark. *Existential Marxism in Postwar France.* Princeton: Princeton University Press, 1975.

Radkey, Oliver Henry. *The Election of the Russian Constituent Assembly of 1917.* Cambridge: Harvard University Press, 1950.

Reich, W. *Character Analysis.* New York: Noonday, 1949.

Reiche, Reimut. *Sexuality and Class Struggle.* Translated by Susan Bennett. New York: 1971.

Ricoeur, Paul. *Freud and Philosophy; An Essay on Interpretation.* Translated by Danis Savage. New Haven : Yale University Press, 1970.

Robinson, Paul A. *The Freudian Left.* New York: 1969.

Roheim, Geza. *Magic and Schizophrenia.* Bloomington: 1970.

Rose, G. *The Melancholy Science.* New York: Columbia University Press, 1978.

Sartre, Jean-Paul. "Francois Mauriac and Freedom." In *Literary Essays.* New York: 1957.

_____. *Materialismus und Revolution.* Stuttgart: 1950.

_____. "The Artist and His Conscience." In *Situations.* Translated by Benita Eisler. Conn.: 1965.

_____. *The Words.* Translated by Bernard Frechtman. Conn.: 1964.

_____. *What is Literature?* Translated by Bernard Frechtman. New York: 1965.

Schachtel. "Memory and Childhood Amnesia." *A Study of Interpersonal Relations.* Edited by Patrick Mullahy. New York: Science House, 1950.

_____. *Metamorphosis: On the Development of Affect, Perception, Attention and Memory.* New York: Basic Books, 1959.

Schelsky, H. *Der Mensch in der wissenschaftlichen Zivilisation.* Koln/Opladen: 1961.

Scheper-Hughes, H. *Saints, Scholars and Schizophrenics.* Berkeley: University of California Press, 1978.

Schiller, Friedrich. *On the Aesthetic Education of Man.* New York: 1965.

Schmidt, Alfred. "Existential Ontologie und Historischer Materialismus bei Herbert Marcuse." In *Antworten Auf Marcuse.* Frankfurt: 1968.

_____. *History and Structure.* Translated by Jeffrey Hart. Cambridge: M.I.T. Press, 1981.

_____. *Zur Idee der Kritschen Theorie.* Munchen: Hanser, 1974.

Schmidt, F. "Über Geschichte und Geschichtsbeschreibung in der materialistischen Dialectic." In *Folgen einer Theorie: Essays über das 'Kapital' von Karl Marx.* Frankfurt am Main: 1967.

Schmidt, Friederich W. "Hegel in der kritischen Theorie der

'Frankfurter Schuler.'" In *Aktualität und Folgen der Philosophie Hegels,* herausgegeben v. Oskar Negt. Frankfurt am Main: Suhrkamp, 1971.

Schoolman, Morton. *The Imaginary Witness.* New York: Free Press, 1980.

Schorske, Carl. *German Social Democracy, 1905-1917.* Cambridge: Harvard University Press, 1955.

Sedgwick, P. "Natural Science and Human Theory." In *The Socialist Register 1966.* London: 1966.

Shafer, R. *A New Language for Psychoanalysis.* New Haven: Yale University Press, 1976.

Shroyer, Trent. *The Critique of Domination: The Origins and Development of Critical Theory.* New York: Braziller, 1973.

Slater, P. *Origins and Significance of the Frankfurt School.* Boston: Routledge and Kegan Paul, 1977.

Smith, Brian. *Memory.* London and New York: 1966.

Sontheimer, Kurt. "Der Antihistorismus des gegenwartigen Zeitalters," *Neue Rundschau,* no. 75, vol. 4.

Steigerwald, Robert. *Herbert Marcuses Dritter Weg.* Cologne: Pahl-Rugenstein, 1969.

Tertz, Abram. *The Trial Begins / On Socialist Realism.* New York: 1960.

Theunissen, Michael. "Die Verwirklichung der Vernunft: Zur Theorie-Praxis Diskussion in Anschluss an Hegel." In *Philosophie Rundschau.* Tübingen: Mohr, 1970.

_____. *Gesellschaft und Geschichte: Zur Kritik der Kritischen Theorie.* Berlin: de Gruyter, 1969.

Trotsky, Leon. *Literature and Revolution.* Translated by Rose Strunsky. Ann Arbor: 1971.

Ullman, Richard K. *Tolerance and the Intolerable.* London: George Allen and Unwin Ltd., 1961.

Urbanek, Eduard. "Rules, Masks and Characters." In *Marxism and Sociology,* edited by Peter Berger. New York: Appleton, Century Crofts, 1969.

Vivas, Eliseo. *Contra Marcuse.* New York: 1971.

Weber, Shierry M. "Individuation as Praxis." In *Critical Interruptions.* Edited by Paul Breines. New York: 1970.

Wessel, H. "Die kritische Theorie bleibt negativ." In *Forum,* no. 2, 3, 4, 5 (1968).

Wohlfahrt, Irving. "Walter Benjamin's Image of Interpretation." In *German Critique* 17 (Spring 1979).

Wolff, Robert Paul, Barrington Moore, Jr., and **Herbert Marcuse.** *A Critique of Pure Tolerance.* Boston: Beacon Press, 1969.

Wolter, Ulf, ed., *Rudolf Bahro: Critical Responses.* New York: M. E. Sharpe, Inc., 1980.

Wyschograd, Michael. "Memory in the History of Philosophy." In *Phenomenology of Memory,* edited by Erwin W. Strauss and Richard M. Griffith. Pittsburgh: 1970.

Yates, Frances A. *The Art of Memory.* Chicago: University of Chicago Press, 1966.

CONTRIBUTORS

Professor Richard Bernstein
Department of Philosophy
Haverford College
Haverford, Pennsylvania 19041

Professor Stephen Bronner
Department of Political Science
Rutgers University
New Brunswick, New Jersey 08903

Professor Andrew Feenberg
Department of Philosophy
San Diego State University
San Diego, California 92115

Professor Dr. Jürgen Habermas
Johann-Wolfgang-Goethe Universität
Dante Strasse 4-6
Frankfurt am Main
Federal Republic of Germany

Professor Edward J. Hyman
Scientific Director
Center for Social Research
Berkeley, California 94720

Professor Martin Jay
Department of History
University of California, Berkeley
Berkeley, California 94720

Professor Douglas Kellner
Department of Philosophy
University of Texas at Austin
Austin, Texas 78712

Professor Richard Lichtman
Wright Institute
Berkeley, California 94704

Professor Dr. Claus Offe
Universität Bielefeld
Postfach 8640
4800 Bielefeld 1
Federal Republic of Germany

Professor Frederick Olafson
Department of Philosophy
University of California, San Diego
La Jolla, California 92093

Professor Robert Pippin
Department of Philosophy
University of California, San Diego
La Jolla, California 92093

Professor Dr. Alfred Schmidt
Johann-Wolfgang-Goethe Universität
Dante Strasse 4-6
Frankfurt am Main
Federal Republic of Germany

Professor Charles Webel
Department of Philosophy
California State University at Chico
Chico, California 95926

INDEX

Marcuse, Herbert, *continued*
of death in Heidegger, 101; on
phenomenology as "method of
action," 58; psychological dimension of his critical theory, 142;
reflections on Heidegger's
thought, 96; his road to Marx,
170-74; synthesis of dialectical
and phenomenological method,
59; on technology question in
Heidegger, 98; and theme of
recognition, 25; with Heidegger
at Freiburg, 95
Marx, Karl, 54, 135
Marxism: and contemporary historical development, 169, 171;
crisis of, 172, 183; Hegelian
roots of, 173-74; historical
dimension of, 58; Marcuse's critique and reconstruction of, 2,
62-63, 172, 177, 182
Marxist fundamental situation, 51
Memory: and aesthetics, 24; concept of, 29-30, 150; concept of
in philosophical tradition, 30;
emancipatory potential of, in
Lukacs, 32-33; Frankfurt School
view of, 40; individual and collective, 39; ontological and epistemological implications of, 30-31;
psychology of, 35-36; role of in
The Aesthetic Dimension, 35; role
of in *Being and Time*, 30; and the
romantic tradition, 34
Mill, John Stuart, 191-94, 201-2
Moral justifications, nature of, 11
Motility, 77-78

Naturalism, ideology of, 150
Nature, and history, 59-60
Needs: historical nature of, 87;
satisfaction of, 196; trans-
formation of, and universaliz-
ation of, 197; and wants, 217-18
Negation, 3
Negative art, 112
Negative culture, 123-24
Negativity: abstract, 14; concept of,
82; in Hegel, 13, 15; as hidden

power in social reality, 16; pervasive theme in Marcuse, 13; and
positivity, 14; and the proletariat, 16; two-dimensionality of,
14
New heroes, 116
New Left, The: as movement, 26;
response to *One-Dimensional Man*,
179-80
New man, 120
New science, 120, 249-52
New sensibility, 120-21
New technology, 251-53

"Obsolescence of Marxism," The,
181-82
One-Dimensional Man: ambiguity of,
20-21; discussion of, 179-80,
196, 199; and historicity, 87;
impact of, 225-27; and technical
rationality, 236
One-dimensionality, analysis of,
215-16, 222-23
Ontology: and historicity, 70;
Marcuse's notion of, 70; in
philosophical tradition, 70
"Organized capitalism," 178

Pacification, of existence, 134
Past, notion of, 134
Performance principle, 86, 151
Perversions, 154
Phantasy: expression in art, 20;
function of, 19
"Phenomenology of Historical Mate-
rialism," 59-60. *See also*
Nature; Economy
Phenomenology of Spirit, 81
Philosophy, and truth, 17
Pleasure principle, 151
Potentialities, 15, 79
Potentiality: concept of, 246-47;
in Hegel and Marx, 24; in
Marcuse, 24
Power, impotence of, 27
Practical rationality, 23
Progress: bourgeois ideology of,
46; historical, 175-76; idea of,
34-37; technical consequences